2002

THE ZONDERVAN

PASTOR'S
ANNUAL

An Idea and Resource Book

T. T. Crabtree

D1212293

ZONDERVAN™

GRAND RAPIDS, MICHIGAN 49530

ZONDERVAN™

THE ZONDERVAN 2002 PASTOR'S ANNUAL
Copyright © 1981, 2001 by Zondervan

Requests for information should be addressed to:

Zondervan, *Grand Rapids, Michigan 49530*

Much of the contents of this book was previously published in *Pastor's Annual 1982.*

ISBN: 0-310-23739-4

Printed in the United States of America

01 02 03 04 05 06 /❖ DC/ 10 9 8 7 6 5 4 3 2 1

18.99

BS

2-14-2002 HEH

MISCELLANEOUS HELPS

Messages on the Lord's Supper

Messages for Children and Young People

Funeral Meditations

Weddings

Sentence Sermonettes

Indexes

ACKNOWLEDGMENTS

All Scripture quotations, unless otherwise noted are taken from the *King James Version*. Additional translations used are the following:

The Amplified Bible, copyright © 1965 by Zondervan Publishing House.

The American Standard Version, copyright © 1901 by Thomas Nelson and Sons.

The Bible: An American Translation by Smith and Goodspeed. Copyright © 1931 by the University of Chicago Press.

The *Holy Bible, New International Version®*. NIV®. Copyright © 1973, 1978, 1984 by International Bible Society.

The Living Bible. Copyright © 1971 by Tyndale House Publishers, Wheaton, Illinois.

The New American Standard Bible. Copyright © by the Lockman Foundation 1960, 1962, 1963, 1968, 1971, 1972, 1973, 1975, 1977.

The New English Bible: New Testament, copyright © 1961 by The Delegates of the Oxford University Press and The Syndics of the Cambridge University Press.

The New Revised Standard Version of the Bible, copyright 1989 by the Division of Christian Education of the National Council of the Churches of Christ in the USA.

The New Testament in Modern English by J. B. Phillips, copyright © 1958, 1959, 1960 by J. B. Phillips.

The New Testament in Today's English Version. Copyright © 1966 by the American Bible Society.

Revised Standard Version, copyright © 1946, 1952, 1956, 1971, and 1973 by the Division of Christian Education of the National Council of the Churches of Christ in the United States of America.

PREFACE

Favorable comments from ministers who serve in many different types of churches suggest that the *Pastor's Annual* provides valuable assistance to many busy pastors as they seek to improve the quality, freshness, and variety of their pulpit ministry. To be of service to fellow pastors in their continuing quest to obey our Lord's command to Peter, "Feed my sheep," is a calling to which I respond with gratitude.

I pray that this issue of the *Pastor's Annual* will be blessed by our Lord in helping each pastor to plan and produce a preaching program that will better meet the spiritual needs of his or her congregation.

This issue contains series of sermons by several contributing authors who have been effective contemporary preachers and successful pastors. Each author is listed with his sermons by date in the section titled "Contributing Authors." I accept responsibility for those sermons not listed there.

This issue of the *Pastor's Annual* is dedicated to the Lord with a prayer that he will bless these efforts to let the Holy Spirit lead us in preparing a planned preaching program for the year.

CONTRIBUTING AUTHORS

Harold T. Bryson . . . . .Wed	August 28	
	September 4, 11, 18, 25	
PM	October 6, 13, 20, 27	
Robert G. Campell . . . . .PM	April 7, 14, 21, 28	
	May 5, 12, 19, 26	
	December 1, 8, 15, 22	
James E. Carter . . . . .Wed	October 2, 9, 16, 23, 30	
	November 6, 13, 20, 27	
	December 4, 11, 18, 25	
Bennie Cole Crabtree	Sentence Sermonettes	
T. T. Crabtree	All messages except	
	those indicated otherwise	
David R. Grant . . . . .Wed	January 2, 9, 16, 23, 30	
	February 6, 13, 20, 27	
	March 6, 13, 20, 27	
	April 3, 10, 17, 24	
	May 1, 8, 15, 22, 29	
	June 5, 12, 19, 26	
	July 3, 10, 17, 24, 31	
	August 7, 14, 21	
PM	November 3, 10, 17, 24	
James F. Heaton . . . . .PM	August 4, 11, 18, 25	
	September 1, 8, 15, 22, 29	
W. T. Holland . . . . .PM	January 6, 13, 20, 27	
	February 3, 10, 17, 24	
	March 3, 10, 17, 24, 31	
David L. Jenkins . . . . .PM	June 2, 9, 16, 23, 30	
	July 7, 14, 21, 28	
Howard S. Kolb . . . . .AM	November 24	
	December 1	
PM	December 29	
Jerold R. McBride . . . . .AM	October 6, 13, 20, 27	
	November 3	
Charles R. Wade . . . . .AM	January 27	
	February 3, 10, 17, 24	
	March 3, 10, 17, 24, 31	
Fred M. Wood . . . . .AM	July 14, 21, 28	
	August 4, 11, 18, 25	
	September 1	

JANUARY

■ Sunday Mornings

Without a proper response to the Holy Spirit, our lives will be unproductive and our service will be feeble. The suggested theme for the first three messages of the year is "Recognizing and Responding to the Indwelling Spirit."

On the last Sunday of the month, begin a series from John's gospel entitled "Responding to the Living Word."

■ Sunday Evenings

The Old Testament prophets were primarily forthtellers rather than foretellers. They communicated the message of God to the needs of the day. The suggested theme is "Listen to the Major Messages of the Minor Prophets."

■ Wednesday Evenings

The suggested theme is "Studies in Paul's Letter to the Corinthians."

WEDNESDAY EVENING, JANUARY 2

Title: In All Things Enriched by Him

Text: "That in every thing ye are enriched by him, in all utterance, and in all knowledge" (**1 Cor. 1:5**).

Scripture Reading: 1 Corinthians 1:1–9

Introduction

The story is told of a tax collector who went to a poor minister in order to determine the amount of tax the minister owed. The minister replied to the tax collector that he was a rich man. He said he was the possessor of a Savior who earned for him everlasting life and who had prepared a place for him in the eternal city. He also said he had a virtuous wife and that the Bible said her price was far above rubies. He added to these possessions healthy and obedient children and a merry heart. When the minister had told of his wealth, the official said, "You are a rich man, but, fortunately for you, your property is not taxable."

I. The source of these riches is found in Jesus Christ.

The passage says, "in him."

A. *God wants the best for his children.* God's knowledge is such that it covers all of one's life and all lives that each one touches. His power and presence are such that when his conditions are met whatever happens will ultimately always be the very best.

B. *God's promises are riches for all.* Philippians 4:19 says, "My God shall supply all your need according to his riches in glory by Christ Jesus."

A pastor was having a difficult time in the church where he was serving. Because of certain circumstances, he could expect no forthcoming raise in salary. At just about that time, an automobile dealer came to the pastor and said, "I want to furnish you with a car at my company's expense." The car far exceeded the raise the church would have given him.

II. The promise of these riches is that a person is enriched in everything.

A. *Christ makes a difference in every facet of life.* He makes a difference in what one wants. Paul said, "Not that I speak in respect of want: for I have learned, in whatsoever state I am, therewith to be content. I know both how to be abased, and I know how to abound: everywhere and in all things I am instructed both to be full and to be hungry, both to abound and to suffer need" (Phil. 4:11–12). Christ also makes a difference in what one does with what one has.

B. *This enrichment is "in all utterance, and in all knowledge."* "All utterance" is the outward expression and "all knowledge" is the inward. These apply to such areas as husband-wife relations, parent-child relations, and relations with friends and acquaintances. They also apply to one's physical welfare, such as blessings and privileges of health and the sufferings and sorrows of illness. Enrichment can also apply to one's economic life, which would include earnings and expenditures. Most of all, enrichment applies to one's spiritual life.

III. To have this enrichment, certain conditions must be met.

A. *One must surrender all aspects of one's life to the Lord Jesus.*

B. *One must have an abiding faith in Jesus and his promises as set forth in God's Word.*

C. *One must be obedient to God's will after first determining what it is.*

Conclusion

For you and me to appreciate the riches of Christ in our lives, we must focus our attention on him and his promises and not on ourselves.

SUNDAY MORNING, JANUARY 6

Title: Another Comforter

Text: "And I will pray the Father, and he shall give you another Comforter, that he may abide with you for ever" **(John 14:16).**

Scripture Reading: John 14:15–18

Hymns: "Holy, Holy, Holy," Heber
          "Have Faith in God," McKinney
          "Holy Ghost, with Light Divine," Reed

Offertory Prayer: Holy Father, we thank you for all of your blessings upon us during the past year. We thank you for the privilege of being alive in this new year of 2002. Help us as we bring our financial gifts that we might do so with loving and grateful hearts, eager to share with those in need. Help us to give our total being in order that our heart might be your royal throne. In Jesus' name. Amen.

Introduction

It is always exciting when a new year arrives before us as a page upon which we will write the history of our life. Let us pray for each other that it might be a good year for our Lord's work, for ourselves personally, and for our families.

When we face the future seriously, we often feel anxious. Particularly is this true if the future looks fearful and if we are plagued with a feeling of our helplessness and insignificance. The disciples of our Lord were horrified at the thought of facing the future without the comfort of his continuing companionship. Our Lord sought to allay their fears and to challenge them to faithfulness with a promise of another Comforter.

Toward the end of his earthly ministry, our Lord concentrated on his twelve apostles. He spent much time with them in seclusion because of his desire to avoid his enemies. At the same time, he wanted to strengthen these men for the task that was before them. He gave them some exceedingly great and precious promises (see John 14:1, 11–14), including the promise that he would give them "another Comforter," a promise they were incapable of understanding at the time. Furthermore, he said, "I will not leave you comfortless: I will come to you" (John 14:18). And in John 14:28 he said, "Ye have heard how I said unto you, I go away, and come again unto you. If ye loved me, ye would rejoice, because I said, I go unto the Father: for my Father is greater than I." In order that we might better understand the significance of these promises for the present, let us look at what discipleship meant to these disciples.

I. The call to discipleship is:

A. *A call to trust in Jesus Christ.*
B. *A call to a profound learning experience.*
C. *A call to leave lesser things.*
D. *A call that involved the excitement of true fulfillment.*
E. *A call to partnership and friendship with Jesus Christ.*
F. *A call to serious self-discipline.*
G. *A call to high rewards.*

II. Jesus invited his disciples to draw close to him.

A. *To Philip he said, "Follow me" (John 1:43).*
B. *To Philip and Nathaniel, Jesus said, "Come and see" (John 1:46).*
C. *To James, John, Peter, and Andrew, Jesus said, "Come ye after me, and I will make you to become fishers of men" (Mark 1:17; see also Matt. 4:19 and Luke 5:10).*
D. *Jesus chose the Twelve "that they should be with him" (Mark 3:14; see also Luke 6:13).* As these men followed Jesus, they experienced a transforming friendship. They visited together in crowded cities. They sailed and fished together on the Sea of Galilee. They prayed together in the mountains and deserts. They worshiped together in the temple. They watched Jesus and listened to him.

   1. They saw in Jesus Christ what it meant to make a complete surrender to the absolute claims of God over one's life.
   2. They saw what it meant to completely forsake sin.
   3. They saw the perfection of love in all attitudes, all ambitions, and all relationships.
   4. They saw a supreme example of one who was willing to deny himself for the sake of others.
   5. They witnessed one who demonstrated a unique aloofness from attachment to material things.
   6. They saw and experienced one who lived totally for eternity.

Eleven of these apostles became so committed to Jesus Christ that they could not even consider their future existence without his companionship. For him to depart was totally unacceptable and unthinkable to them. It was in that context that Jesus continued to tell them that he must go back to the Father. He sought to comfort them with a promise of "another Comforter" (John 14:16) who would be their counselor and helper.

III. Jesus promises another comforter.

A. *Note the word that Jesus used in making this promise.* In the original language of the New Testament, two different words can be translated by our English word *another.* The context determines which of these Greek words is used. *Allos* is used when "another of like kind" is referred to, while *heteros* is used when "another of a different kind" is referred to. When Jesus spoke of the Comforter who would come, he used *allos*. Jesus was saying, "I am going to ask the Father, and he will give you another counselor, another comforter, another helper of exactly the same kind as I am." The word translated "comforter" literally means "one called to walk by the side of." This had been Jesus' relationship with his disciples for three years.

B. *"To be with you forever."* Jesus' bodily presence with his disciples had been very brief, and now it was necessary that he depart. This was devastating to them. He promised that the Comforter would be with them always, forever.

C. *"For he dwells with you."* Christ as Immanuel is God "with us." Jesus promises the Holy Spirit who will dwell "within us." The Holy Spirit is a far greater blessing that Jesus' earthly presence, for he can be within each one of his disciples.

Conclusion

As we face the new year, we need to accept by faith the presence of this Comforter who came on the Day of Pentecost to dwell in the church. He came on the day of your conversion experience to dwell in your heart (1 Cor. 3:16). We should with joy recognize the Holy Spirit's indwelling presence and find the strength we need for living effectively in this year 2002 (Eph. 6:10).

With eagerness we should listen for the Holy Spirit's voice as he speaks to our innermost being as we study the Scriptures, as we pray, and as we see a needy world (Heb. 3:7–8). With love for our Lord and his people, let each of us decide to cooperate with this divine Comforter and Counselor as we walk through the days of this new year.

If you have come to this first Sunday in the year 2002 without knowing Jesus Christ as Savior, this would be a wonderful time to respond as the Holy Spirit leads you. Invite Jesus Christ to come and live in your heart as Savior, Lord, Teacher, and Friend.

SUNDAY EVENING, JANUARY 6

Title: What Manner of Man Is the Prophet?

Text: "Now the word of Jehovah came unto me, saying, Before I formed thee in the belly I knew thee, and before thou camest forth out of the womb I sanctified thee; I have appointed thee a prophet unto the nations" **(Jer. 1:4–5 ASV).**

Scripture Reading: Jeremiah 1:4–10

Introduction

In the long struggle of the Hebrews to be a people pleasing to God, the prophets, for the most part, appeared in times of crisis as models of what God wanted his people to be. As God's spokesmen for many centuries, they sounded warnings and gave direction to their nation.

In our English Bible we have sixteen books that record the words and deeds of the "writing prophets." Other great prophets in Israel were "nonwriting prophets"—they did not write prophetic books. The greatest of these were Moses, Samuel, Elijah, and Elisha. Upon the sole basis of length, the books bearing the names of the writing prophets are classified as "major" and "minor," with Isaiah, Jeremiah, Ezekiel, and Daniel called "Major Prophets" and the other twelve "Minor Prophets." The term *minor* in regard to these twelve books is unfortunate, for there is nothing minor about them. The twelve together cover the whole range of prophecy and illustrate its development from the eighth to the fourth century B.C.

For the following twelve Sunday evenings we will consider this Book of the Twelve, as the Hebrew Bible designates these twelve prophecies, in the order in which they appear in our English Bible. In introducing this series let us ponder this question: "What manner of man is a prophet? Let us consider this from two points of view.

I. First, consider what a prophet is not.

A. *A prophet is not a microphone through which God speaks, bypassing the prophet's mind, will, emotions, character, and convictions.* Inspiration is not merely mechanical. Revelation does not take place in a vacuum, ignoring the context of history in which the prophet lives and serves.

B. *A prophet is not a superhuman being.* He does not have near supernatural powers. The prophet is unique but still human. Moses, Samuel, Elijah, Elisha, Jonah, Jeremiah, and Ezekiel were indeed human beings with certain faults and frailties despite their unquestioned greatness. James says of the one considered by most Hebrews in Jesus' day to be the greatest of the prophets: "Elijah was a man of like passions with us" (5:17 ASV). Thank God for that word.

C. *A prophet is not a windbag.* As Moffatt translates it, Jeremiah said of certain pretenders among his contemporaries: "The prophets are but windbags" (Jer. 5:13 MOFFATT). There are many varieties of windbags.

  1. For some, the emptiness of their prophecy does not come from the betrayal of their faith; instead, it comes from their failure to have any faith worth proclaiming.

  2. Often men who might have been prophets, or even who had been prophets, become windbags just through the process of taking on administrative responsibilities. This is one of the perils of an ecclesiastical hierarchy. Forced to talk unceasingly and feeling the necessity of "judicious" utterance on all occasions, they fall back on wind. Wind is easier and safer than ideas.

3. Sometimes, on a far lower scale, morally, false prophets become mere echoes of their employer's ideas and desires. This is the bottom rung on the ladder. Isaiah charges that the people of his day did not desire true prophets, but windbags. They requested: "Prophesy not unto us right things, speak unto us smooth things, prophesy deceits" (Isa. 30:10 ASV). Let every minister ask himself or herself, "Am I God's prophet, or am I a windbag?"

D. *A prophet is not a wolf in sheep's clothing.* Jesus warns us against those masquerading as prophets, part of God's flock, when inwardly they are "ferocious wolves" (Matt. 7:15 NIV), enemies within the Christian community. When so many pretenders are predicting peace and prosperity, offering cheerful words, adding strength to self-reliance, and bolstering human pride, the true prophet may be called upon to predict disaster, agony, pestilence, and destruction. Thus, a prophet's life is often uncomfortable.

II. Second, consider what a prophet is.

A. *A prophet is one whom God has called and commissioned.* God tells Jeremiah: "I knew you,...I set you apart; I appointed you as a prophet to the nations" (1:5 NIV). In recounting his call, Amos says in substance: "The Lord took me, told me, and sent me" (see Amos 7:15). We do not have a record of the call of all the prophets, but of those we do have, no two are the same. A prophet is a distinct individual endowed with a mission and empowered with a word not his own. His divine commission is his authority.

B. *A prophet is a preacher.* He is not primarily a foreteller, but a forthteller. Although sometimes used of God to foretell impending catastrophes or to promise future blessings and reward, this is only one part of his work. The prophet is God's spokesman. He is a preacher whose purpose is not self-gratification or self-expression, but communication. His message burns like fire. It assaults the mind and sears the spirit. "Prophecy is the voice that God has lent to the silent agony, a voice to the plundered poor, to the profaned riches of the world. It is a form of living, a crossing point of God and man. God is raging in the prophet's words" (Abraham J. Heschel, *The Prophets* [New York: Harper & Row, 1962], 50).

    The prophet's message differs sharply from the tellers of oracles of the pagan gods. The pagan god who would let enemies destroy his shrine or conquer those who worship him would commit suicide. Incredibly, Israel's prophets proclaim that the enemy may be God's instrument in history. For example, the God of Israel refers to the archenemies of his people as "the Assyrian, the rod of mine anger" (Isa. 10:5 NIV); Nebuchadnezzar, "the king of Babylon, my servant" (Jer. 25:9); and the Chaldeans, "that bitter and hasty nation" whom he would "raise up" (Hab. 1:6). Instead of cursing the enemy, the prophets condemn their own nation.

C. *A prophet is a mediator.* He is not only a censurer and accuser, but also a
    defender and consoler. In the presence of God, he takes the part of the
    people. Moses pleads with God: "Oh, what a great sin these people have
    committed!…But now, please forgive their sins—but if not, then blot me
    out of the book you have written" (Exod. 32:31–32 NIV). In response to
    the vision of locusts, Amos says to God: "Sovereign LORD, forgive! How
    can Jacob survive? He is so small!" (Amos 7:2 NIV). But in the presence of
    the people he takes the part of God. From this point of view it is the main
    vocation of a prophet "to declare unto Jacob his transgression, and to
    Israel his sin" (Mic. 3:8), to let the people know "that it is an evil thing
    and bitter" to forsake the Lord (Jer. 2:19), and to call upon them to
    return.

D. *A prophet is often the object of scorn and reproach.* To be a prophet means to
    challenge and to defy the defenders of the status quo, the "powers that
    be," and to cast out fear. The prophet is a lonely man. He alienates the
    wicked as well as the good, the judges and the false prophets, the priests
    and the princes, the cynics as well as the believers. He may count on hear-
    ing the echo of the words hurled at Hosea: "A prophet is a crazy fool, a
    man inspired is a man insane" (Hos. 9:7 MOFFATT). Jesus heard this. They
    said, "He is beside himself" (Mark 3:21). Paul heard it. "Paul, thou art
    mad" (Acts 26:24 ASV), cried a typical man of the world. Let God's
    prophets take courage, for the epithet "fools for Christ's sake" (1 Cor.
    4:10) is a badge of honor.

E. *A prophet is the conscience of his nation.* His life is not futile. Though the
    people may remain deaf to the prophet's admonitions; they cannot
    ignore his existence, nor can they forget his words. The prophet's duty
    is to speak God's word to the people, whether they hear or refuse to
    hear.

    Zedekiah, Judah's last king, had not treated the great prophet Jere-
    miah with the kindness and respect he deserved. Yet God's message
    through his prophet had lodged in his heart to challenge his conscience.
    When the city was surrounded, the fighting men discouraged and
    exhausted, and the food almost gone, Zedekiah sent for Jeremiah
    secretly to ask, "Is there any word from the LORD?" (Jer. 37:17). Centuries
    later, when God himself walked the earth in the person of his Son, God's
    own people said of him, "This is Jeremiah." This prophet's mark on a
    nation's conscience had survived the centuries.

Conclusion

No series of sermons could be more relevant or more fascinating than
one on the Hebrew prophets. As people thought in the eighth through the
fourth centuries B.C., so they think now. Indeed, yesterday's prophets are for
today's world.

WEDNESDAY EVENING, JANUARY 9

Title: God Is Faithful

Text: "God is faithful, by whom ye were called unto the fellowship of his Son Jesus Christ our Lord **(1 Cor. 1:9).**

Scripture Reading: 1 Corinthians 1:1–9

Introduction

> *Great is thy faithfulness, O God my Father,*
> *There is no shadow of turning with thee;*
> *Thou changest not, thy compassions, they fail not;*
> *As thou hast been thou forever wilt be.*
>
> *Great is thy faithfulness! Great is thy faithfulness!*
> *Morning by morning new mercies I see;*
> *All I have needed thy hand hath provided;*
> *Great is thy faithfulness, Lord, unto me!*

> —Thomas O. Chisholm

I. Faithfulness is found in the Eternal One.

A. *Other Bible passages confirm God's faithfulness.* "Jesus Christ is the same yesterday and today and forever" (Heb. 13:8 NIV). "If we confess our sins, he is faithful and just and will forgive us our sins" (1 John 1:9 NIV).

B. *Consider some areas of God's faithfulness.*

1. God is faithful in his plan and purpose for all humankind. His plan is for all humans to be free moral beings. Humans have freedom to choose whether they will have fellowship with the Lord. God does not invade that plan. He is faithful, however, to have fellowship with humans. This was his purpose in creation and redemption. He is also faithful in his plans for people's lives.

2. God is faithful in his promises and power. "Let us hold unswervingly to the hope we profess, for he who promised is faithful" (Heb. 10:23 NIV). The Lord is faithful in answering prayer as he promised (Mark 11:24). He is faithful to supply needs (Phil. 4:19). He is faithful in sending a Comforter (John 14:18). He is faithful in his promises of redemption, reward, and judgment.

3. God is faithful in his presence and patience. He is with his servants in Christian work (Matt. 28:20), in the valley of despair (Ps. 23:4), at any time (Prov. 18:24). No one can flee from his presence (Ps. 139:7).

II. Because of God's faithfulness, people should trust him more and more.

A. *Each person should trust Jesus Christ for salvation.* Lay aside all excuses, human rationalization, and the like, and see him as completely trustworthy for the eternal soul.

B. *Each person should trust him with his or her life.* People, within their own ability, are not able to make the most of their lives, but Jesus Christ has all knowledge, power, and love to do the best for us.

C. *Each person needs to obey God's wishes and orders so he can prove his faithfulness.*

Conclusion

There is no part of your life that you cannot trust God with, for he is faithful in every respect to each person.

SUNDAY MORNING, JANUARY 13

Title: The Continuing Presence of the Holy Spirit

Text: "I will pray the Father, and he will give you another Counselor, to be with you for ever" **(John 14:16 RSV).**

Scripture Reading: John 14:15–18

Hymns: "Great Is Thy Faithfulness," Chisholm
    "Abide with Me," Lyte
    "Never Alone," Anonymous

Offertory Prayer: Holy Father, we thank you for the gift of this day in which we have the privilege of rejoicing in you and responding to your purposes for our lives. We come in humility to worship you as the giver of every good and perfect gift. We thank you for life itself. We thank you for this opportunity to worship with your family. We thank you for the joy of being a coworker with others and with you in bringing your kingdom into the lives of men, women, and children. Bless these gifts to that end. We pray in Jesus' name. Amen.

Introduction

It is possible to experience painful loneliness in the midst of a crowd. To feel separated by distance or by death from someone who is very precious is one of life's most painful experiences.

As our Lord approached the end of his ministry, his disciples were horrified at the thought of their loneliness and helplessness if he should be taken from them. They sought to persuade him to avoid danger and the possibility of imprisonment or death. We can sympathize with their anxiety.

From our perspective as those who live on this side of Calvary, the first Easter, and the Day of Pentecost, we can understand better what they found impossible to understand. Jesus sought to encourage them and to equip them for future ministry by his teachings and by his promise of another Comforter, another Counselor, another Helper. This one, in contrast to Jesus' brief ministry of three short years, would come to abide with them as a continuing presence never to depart. They came to understand this only after Pentecost. Jesus told them that the Father would give to them another Counselor of exactly the same kind as he was, but who would be different in that he would "be with you for ever" (John 14:16 RSV). Jesus the Savior, the visible manifestation of the invisible God, was limited during his earthly ministry to being at one place at one time. For this reason, he said to them, "It is expedient for you that I go away" (John 16:7). The Revised Standard Version translates this statement, "It is to your advantage that I go away, for if I go not away, the Counselor will not come to you; but if I go, I will send him to you." The New International Version translates it, "It is for your good that I am going away."

I. The Holy Spirit is God's good gift to each believer.

In the Old Testament the Holy Spirit did not indwell all believers as he does on this side of Pentecost. Rather, he would come upon chosen individuals for a limited period of time to equip them and to empower them for some unique task. There is a marked difference in the manner in which the Spirit came upon individuals before Pentecost and the manner in which he comes to indwell each believer following Pentecost (see John 7:39).

A. *The gift of the Holy Spirit comes by God's grace.* We do not earn the privilege of having the Holy Spirit abide within us.

B. *The gift of the Holy Spirit comes to us through faith (Gal. 3:2).* By faith we receive Christ, and by faith we receive the gift of the Holy Spirit.

II. The Holy Spirit is the continuing presence of the resurrected Christ within each believer.

Jesus said to his disciples, "I will not leave you desolate; I will come to you" (John 14:18 RSV). In this specific passage our Lord is not referring to his glorious return at the end of the age. He is referring to his return in the Holy Spirit on the Day of Pentecost following his ascension to the Father.

As our Lord gave the Great Commission to his disciples regarding their evangelistic task in the world, he said, "Lo, I am with you always, to the close of the age" (Matt. 28:20 RSV). We experience the presence of the living, triumphant Lord in and through the ministry of the Holy Spirit, who has come to abide within the heart of each believer.

Paul wrote to the Galatians, "I have been crucified with Christ and I no longer live, but Christ lives in me. The life I live in the body, I live by faith in the Son of God, who loved me and gave himself for me" (Gal. 2:20 NIV). Paul experienced the presence of the living Christ through the abiding Spirit who had come to dwell within him and within the heart of every believer.

III. The Holy Spirit abides within us to teach us God's truth.

He is the Spirit of truth who came to teach us all of the things that God wants us to understand (John 14:17, 26). His mission is to guide us into all of the truth of God (John 16:13). Since God is a spirit, those who worship him must worship him in spirit and in truth.

The Holy Spirit uses the Scriptures to teach us God's truth, the church to help us understand the truth, and other believers to lead us into the truth. The Holy Spirit works in our mind, emotions, and will.

IV. The Holy Spirit creates conflict with the lower nature of each believer.

The Holy Spirit creates a civil war between himself and the lower nature of each believer (Gal. 5:17). He fills us with a holy discontent until we let the living Christ reign supreme within our hearts.

A. *The Holy Spirit comes to fill us and to give us victory over evil (Eph. 5:18; 6:10).*
B. *The Holy Spirit produces within us the fruit of the Spirit (Gal. 5:22–23).*

Conclusion

God has given us the gift of the Holy Spirit as the abiding presence of Jesus Christ. Let each of us recognize and rejoice in this precious gift of the Holy Spirit. Let us respond to the tender words, gentle impulses, and loving leadings of the Holy Spirit. Let us trust the Holy Spirit to guide us and enable us to do all that God wants us to do.

If you have not yet received Jesus as Savior, the Holy Spirit is prompting you to open the door of your life for the entrance of him who can forgive your sins and give you the gift of eternal life. Open the door today.

SUNDAY EVENING, JANUARY 13

Title: Hosea—Time to Seek the Lord

Text: "Sow for yourselves righteousness, reap the fruit of unfailing love, and break up your unplowed ground; for it is time to seek the LORD, until he comes and showers righteousness on you" **(Hos. 10:12 NIV).**

Scripture Reading: Hosea 10:12–11:9; 14:1–4

Introduction

Hosea has been called "the prophet of the broken heart." His experience demonstrates that love yields the sweetest joy on earth and also the most profound sorrow. The framework of the book is that of a shattered romance, a tale of unfaithfulness to the marital vow. That this prophecy is the very Word of God is evidenced by the fact that this sordid story has little appeal at the secular level but runs much deeper.

Against the backdrop of his own personal woe, his shattered home and betrayed love, Hosea received a vivid revelation of the very heart of God. He was able to see that God too was a sufferer, a victim of unfaithfulness. Israel was the unfaithful wife, and God was the wronged husband, the victim of his beloved's infidelity as she deserted him to go off after false gods. So great was Hosea's love, so gracious was his forgiving heart, that he searched and found Gomer, long since deserted by her paramours, and took her back into his own home. After that experience he winsomely preached God's love for Israel and tenderly pleaded, "O Israel, return unto the LORD thy God" (14:1). Hosea anticipated and prefigured the one who "came unto his own, and they that were his own received him not" (John 1:11 ASV), the one who was "a man of sorrows, and acquainted with grief" (Isa. 53:3).

The prophecy of Hosea falls naturally, but unequally, into two parts. Part 1 is God's Word through Hosea's marriage: revelation through heartache (1:1–3:5). Recorded here are details about Hosea's marriage and children (1:2–9); the account of the restoration of Israel and Judah (1:10–11); the lesson that Gomer's unfaithfulness to Hosea is symbolic of Israel's unfaithfulness to God (2:1–23); and the moral that Hosea's love for Gomer illustrates God's love for Israel (3:1–5). Part 2 is God's Word through Hosea's messages: revelation through proclamation (4:1–14:9); a historical retrospect and Israel's current crisis (9:10–12:14); and the ways of life and death (13:1–14:9).

Hosea wrote during turbulent times, the last years of the reign of Jeroboam II; the Indian summer of Israel's history was fast passing into the winter of her discontent. After Jeroboam came a period of anarchy, assassinations, and confusion. In quick succession Zechariah, Shallum, Pekahiah, Pekah, and Hoshea came to the throne, and all but the last came by slaying his predecessor. Confusion in the nation reflected the confusion in Hosea's own home. Sin was everywhere. "There is nought but swearing and breaking faith, and killing, and stealing, and committing adultery; they break out, and blood toucheth blood" (Hos. 4:2 ASV).

That is the fertile field of ripened fruit from which our text is taken. "For it is time to seek the LORD" (10:12). These words are no random saying out of touch with the main line of the book's thinking. This was the heart of God's appeal to Israel; and it is God's appeal to us. If the seedtime is far spent, the farmer sows his grain with more diligence. Seeking the Lord is the privilege of every day, but there are special seasons when by his providence and grace it is time to seek him in a peculiar and urgent manner. How potent is this text against the dark background of Hosea's day! How pertinent today! Time to seek the Lord? Indeed it is!

I. For whom is it time to seek the Lord?

It is time to seek the Lord:

A. *In the councils of the world where the representatives of nations meet.* Only God can transform the United Nations organization from its international weakness into a potent factor for peace. But until now he has been left outside. His name is not in the charter nor mentioned in its deliberations.

B. *In the parliaments and congresses where the fate of the people hangs in the balance.* What responsibility these lawmakers have! Do we pray for them?

C. *In the high councils of our own government.* Nothing is more shocking than the news of corruption and double-dealing coming out of Washington, unless it is the failure of people in general to be shocked by it. A book on the Civil War, *Reveille in Washington,* published several years ago, made the point convincingly that had our government in Washington not been so corrupt at the time, the South would have been overwhelmed in six months. What if we should become involved in a war today?

D. *In our own communities.* A pastor said he felt good about his own rapidly growing Sunday school. Then he totaled the attendance of all the Sunday schools in town and subtracted the number from the total population of his city to discover how many were not in anybody's Sunday school. It was a sobering discovery.

E. *In our churches.* The indifference, the lack of enlistment, the few who are being won outside the families of our own members, the failure to train leaders—all this is appalling. Our failure to train leaders a generation ago is being reaped in a lack of leaders now.

F. *In our own hearts.* Our hearts are cold. Our minds are divided. Our hands are idle. Dutifully, though not joyfully, we haul these respectable carcasses of ours to the church and plunk them down in our chosen places in a sparsely-filled auditorium like some huge walk-in refrigerator—and what happens? Nothing!

Friends, it is time to seek the Lord.

II. Why is it time to seek the Lord?

Why should we be urgent? Why should the Christian's witness "be urgent in season, out of season" (2 Tim. 4:2 ASV)? Why should the unsaved person "give the more earnest heed to the things which we have heard, lest at any time we should let them slip" (Heb. 2:1 KJV)?

This is the time to seek the Lord because:

A. *The time for sowing is passing, the harvest time is coming.* And what shall the harvest be? It all depends on whether we seek the Lord or not. Here is our exact image: "Sow to yourselves in righteousness, reap in mercy; break up your fallow ground: for it is time to seek the LORD, till he come and rain righteousness upon you" (Hos. 10:12). We are already beginning to see the harvest of secular education. We are already seeing the harvest of the influence of pornographic movies, "shoot 'em up" TV programs, lewd comic books, and licentious magazines. It is time to seek the Lord and to keep on seeking until he comes and rains righteousness upon us.

B. *The time when we may seek the Lord will end.* The owner of a fig tree had sought fruit for three years but to no avail. His patience ended, he said to the vinedresser, "Cut it down! Why should it use up the soil?" (Luke

13:7 NIV). And why didn't they cut it down? Because of the vinedresser's plea: "Sir, leave it alone for one more year, and I'll dig around it and fertilize it. If it bears fruit next year, fine! If not, then cut it down" (Luke 13:8–9 NIV). The day of grace for the fruitless tree was a year. The point is that every period of grace has an end. The time when one may seek the Lord will end.

C. *The results are immediate and eternal.* Those who accept Christ as Savior are not going to receive eternal life out yonder some day; they have already received it. For the Christian, eternal life has already begun.

Conclusion

Does someone ask: "How can I be sure? How may I know?"

A. *This is the plain and urgent word of the Scriptures.* "Behold, now is the acceptable time; behold now is the day of salvation" (2 Cor. 6:2 ASV).

B. *This is the confirmation of our own observation.* Who does not know someone who delayed too long to seek the Lord?

C. *This is the inward testimony of our own conscience.* Is not your own heart repeating the words of the psalmist: "And now, LORD, what wait I for? my hope is in thee"? (Ps. 39:7).

WEDNESDAY EVENING, JANUARY 16

Title: Unity in Christ

Text: "Now I beseech you, brethren, by the name of our Lord Jesus Christ, that ye all speak the same thing, and that there be no divisions among you; but that ye be perfectly joined together in the same mind and in the same judgment" **(1 Cor. 1:10).**

Scripture Reading: 1 Corinthians 1:10–17

Introduction

A young student pastor was involved in some phase of church business when two distinct factions within the little church began making cutting remarks toward each other. The following Sunday the young pastor used as his text, "Let there be no divisions among you." This is an admonition that is fitting for many congregations all over the world. The text emphasizes both the positive and negative.

I. The negative, or unpleasant, is the first consideration.

A. *The first word in the sentence, "now," indicates a transition from thanksgiving to reproof.*

In the earlier part of this chapter in 1 Corinthians, Paul had talked about the grace all Christians experience. He also talked about the riches each Christian has in Christ Jesus. He talked still further about God's dependability. He then turned to the matter of rebuke and, on through 1 Corinthians 3:23, discussed this theme.

B. *Paul gives severe condemnation for having division.*

   The origin of division in the church at Corinth was intellectual conceit and disagreement over leadership. Paul did not accept any excuse for division but severely condemned it. The dangers that result from a break within the fellowship of a congregation are multiple and costly.

II. The application of the idea of divisions is the second consideration.

A. *The origin of modern-day contention is basically the same as in the day of Paul's writings.* Most contentions are over personalities. They are also caused by intellectual conceit or by a lack of consecration and humility.

B. *The evils connected with divisions in modern-day churches are legion.* Division makes a church weak. The energy that should be expended for the cause of Christ is used for internal fighting. Division makes for such a scandal that God is dishonored, the world stands in contempt, and Satan is the victor. Non-Christians see the contention and are turned off.

III. The opposite of division is unity.

A. *Paul made the appeal that the people "be perfectly joined together."* This is an appeal for oneness in disposition and voice. Paul was not making an appeal to ecclesiastical union, conformity in worship, or even theological unity, but to oneness in love, fellowship, attitude, and purpose.

B. *The appeal is made "by the name of our Lord Jesus Christ."* This is a title referring to both the person and the office of the Savior. His person is divinely and perfectly blended. His office is Redeemer. He is the sole head of the church.

C. *The appeal is made that the unity be "in the same mind and in the same judgment."* The appeal is made in meekness—"I beseech you"—and in love—"brethren." Unity, then, is realized when members of a congregation turn their thoughts to Christ rather than to individual feelings.

Conclusion

One of the greatest of all needs today is for individuals within the church to adhere to this admonition—namely, not to be divided but to be one in Christ in the church.

SUNDAY MORNING, JANUARY 20

Title: Your Helplessness without the Help of the Holy Spirit

Text: "Then he said to me, 'This is the word of the LORD to Zerubbabel: Not by might, nor by power, but by my Spirit, says the LORD of hosts'" (**Zech. 4:6 RSV**).

Scripture Reading: Zechariah 4:1–10

Hymns: "All Creatures of Our God and King," Francis of Assisi
              "I Need Thee Every Hour," Hawks
              "Breathe on Me," Hatch

Offertory Prayer: Loving Father, from your generous hand comes the gift of life and all of the necessities of life. From your loving heart comes the gift of eternal life and all of the blessings associated with it. We come believing today that from you comes the power to get wealth. Thank you for the privilege of receiving an income. Today we come bringing tithes and offerings to express our desire to cooperate with you in bringing your kingdom into the hearts and lives of people around this entire planet. Accept these gifts and bless them to your glory. In Jesus' name we pray. Amen.

Introduction

The words of our text were designed to encourage the heart of Zerubbabel, providing he would think God's thoughts and walk in God's ways. The text could throw one who seeks to accomplish heaven's work with one's own abilities and strength alone into the depths of despair.

A great missionary to China and later to Korea said, "You cannot do God's work without God's power." This truth is affirmed in the words of the text, "Not by might, nor by power, but by my Spirit, says the LORD of hosts."

Have you been trying to do God's work without God's power? Have you been trying to develop a Christian personality without the help of the Holy Spirit? Have you been seeking to teach a Bible class without a conscious dependence on the Holy Spirit for God's enabling power? Have you been seeking to speak to those who do not know Jesus as Savior without a sincere dependence on the power of the Holy Spirit to make your efforts effective?

Much of the weakness and the failure of God's people today can be traced directly to the fact that we are helpless without the help of the Holy Spirit.

I. Without the Holy Spirit's help you are helpless and the future is hopeless.

A. *Zerubbabel could not accomplish his purpose by the might and strength of military action.*
B. *No human power could enable the prophet to accomplish his divine mission.* We experience great failure and our lives are unfruitful if we attempt to do the work of God without the help of the Holy Spirit.

II. Without the Holy Spirit's help everything divine is impossible.

Human effort alone cannot produce divine effects in our lives or the lives of others.

A. *The Holy Spirit effects the birth from above in the hearts of believers.*

B. *The Holy Spirit bears testimony to new believers, following their conversion, regarding their membership in God's family (Rom. 8:16–17).* Without this divine testimony they have no assurance and no joy of salvation.

C. *The Holy Spirit takes up residence in believers' bodies at the moment of conversion (1 Cor. 3:16; 6:19–20).* The Holy Spirit then works in their hearts and minds and wills.

D. *The Holy Spirit comes into believers' hearts in order to bring about a renewal or transformation of their minds (see Phil. 2:13; Rom. 12:2).*

E. *The Holy Spirit dwells within each believer, seeking to reproduce the character of the Christ (Gal. 5:22–23).* The Holy Spirit wants to present each of us as an exhibit of what Christ can do in one who will trust him.

F. *The Holy Spirit energizes believers for service and makes them strong for the struggle against evil (Eph. 6:10).*

G. *The Holy Spirit calls believers into the harvest fields for witnessing opportunities (Acts 13:1–3).*

H. *The Holy Spirit seeks to teach us the truth of God as it is revealed in and taught by Jesus Christ (John 14:26; 16:13–14).*

These truths prove that the Father God does not intend that we labor in human strength alone. It is not his will that we experience the despair of failure. He has provided the help of the Holy Spirit that we might not be helpless.

III. How can the believer experience the help of the Holy Spirit?

Why do we not see more evidence of the work of the Holy Spirit?

A. *Believers must believe that they have already received the Holy Spirit and respond with trust to his indwelling presence (1 Cor. 6:19–20).*

B. *We should ask for the fullness of the power of the Holy Spirit in our lives (Luke 11:13).*

C. *Obedience to the known will of God is one of the essentials for the fullness of the power of the Spirit in one's life (Acts 5:32).*

Conclusion

You are helpless without the help of the Holy Spirit. You cannot convert a soul to Christ without the Holy Spirit's help. You cannot develop a Christian personality or character without the Holy Spirit's help. You cannot understand the real truth of the Bible without the illuminating work of the Holy Spirit. You cannot pray effectively without the assistance of the Holy Spirit.

Today the Holy Spirit exalts Jesus Christ as the adequate, loving, powerful Savior who is eager to come into your life. Today the Holy Spirit calls you to total trust and loving obedience to Jesus Christ. Today the Holy Spirit wants to begin God's good work in you, and you can trust him to continue it until the Lord returns or until he calls you home.

SUNDAY EVENING, JANUARY 20

Title: Joel—Redeeming the Lost Years

Text: "I will restore to you the years the locust hath eaten, the cankerworm, and the caterpillar, and the palmerworm, my great army which I sent among you" **(Joel 2:25).**

Scripture Reading: Joel 2:18–27

Introduction

In most lives there are periods, which, as far as productive labor, happiness in our hearts, or worth to the kingdom of God are concerned, are lost years. Joel speaks of such a gap in the life of his nation as "the years the locust hath eaten."

Joel's message was called forth by a national calamity. A devastating plague of locusts had stripped the land bare of food for man and beast. This was followed by famine, poverty, and misery. Such a time called for some sure word from the Lord, and Joel was God's spokesman. Joel has been aptly called "the prophet of consolation."

This prophecy of three chapters, having only seventy-three verses, is made up of two distinct divisions: the first (1:1–2:27) calls the nation to repentance and prayer; the second (2:28–3:21) records God's promise to hear the cry of his people, remove the cause of their suffering, and restore prosperity and enrich them spiritually.

The words of our text, "I will restore to you the years the locust hath eaten" (2:25), form a summary statement, looking back to the national calamity and forward to the time of revival and restoration. Joel sounds a relevant note. To Israel, God promises years of plenty to redeem the lean years. To us, God promises to redeem the years we have lost if we will repent of our sins and return to him.

I. Note the cause of lost years.

A. *Years are lost because of fear and indecision.* They are lost to God, lost to his church, and lost to oneself. An adult woman, the mother of teenage children, came down the aisle all alone before a great Sunday morning congregation to confess Christ and ask for baptism. Her husband, not a Christian, admired her courageous act and said, "I could never have the courage to do that before all those people." He could, but to date, he hasn't.

B. *Years are lost because of complacency.* Three people attended the funeral of an eighty-four-year-old man who had no surviving relatives. He had lived in his town thirty-five years but had never joined any local congregation. When asked, three days before his death, why not, he replied, "I meant to; I just put it off."

C. *Years are lost because of self-centeredness.* Some people live for themselves and unto themselves. For them life is a circle that grows smaller and smaller. This violates one of life's fundamental laws. Paul expressed it this way: "For none of us liveth to himself, and no man dieth to himself" (Rom. 14:7).

D. *Years are lost because people do not discern between the important and the unimportant in their lives.* One of Methodism's greatest preachers had been, as a young man, the owner of a bottling plant in a small Arkansas city. A kindly pastor had helped him to understand his divine call. He would say, "When you die and enter heaven, someone will ask, 'What did you do on earth?' And you will have to answer, 'I made red soda pop.'" There is nothing disgraceful about making red soda pop, but this young man was called to be a minister of Jesus Christ.

E. *Years are lost because people are spiritually immature (see Jesus' allegory of children playing in the marketplace in Luke 7:31–32).* Jesus showed the folly of playing at religion. For example, consider a person who, because of some trifle of no consequence, holds a grudge against a pastor or church member and deliberately pouts for ten years, staying away from the church and all its services. Those are lost years.

F. *But most tragic of all, years are lost because of sin.* Dr. E. Stanley Jones tells of a medical missionary who ran away with his secretary and deserted his wife and children. When Dr. Jones urged him to return to God and to his family, he replied, "I am called to organize another religion—less rigid, more liberal, more of the love of God." What a pathetic defense of indefensible conduct! Years later, as this former missionary lay dying, he told Jones, "I'm an old prodigal that never returned" (E. Stanley Jones, *Conversion* [New York: Abingdon, 1959], 205). In the end he repented, but the locusts of sin had eaten up the years of his life.

II. Note the cost of lost years.

The locusts, God's "great army" sent among the Israelites because of their sins, brought Israel to famine and ruin. To us, on every level, in every relationship, the lost years are costly.

A. *Costly to the lives of individuals.*

1. Because of fear and indecision, some people lose their immortal souls and go down to a devil's hell.
2. Because of neglect, some people miss the blessings of the fellowship of God's people.
3. Because of the self-centeredness, some people miss the joy of large horizons, and their world shrinks until it hems them in.
4. Because of spiritual immaturity, some people's lives are soured, misdirected, and permanently off-center. An unforgiving spirit renders a person unable to receive forgiveness.

B. *Costly to the churches.* The business of a church is too important for anyone to indulge personal grievances. Christ calls us to be spiritual adults (Eph. 4:15). In the second year of a certain minister's pastorate, a woman member became offended, dropped out of the church, and let it be known that as long as that minister was the pastor, she would not set foot inside the door. After a fruitful pastorate of twelve years, this minister went on to another church. The first Sunday after his departure the woman returned. She told those at the church that she forgave them for not "taking a stand" and leaving the way she did. But she made the mistake of saying to one faithful member, "Oh, it is so good to be back in *my* church." This faithful soul replied, "I'm glad you feel that way. A number of us have worked hard to keep it alive the ten years you have been gone."

C. *Costly to the cause of righteousness.* With so many who are indifferent, it is a marvel of grace that the average church can accomplish what it does. The gospel has been preached for two thousand years, but this is still a lost world. Why so? There is too much mud on the wheels of his chariot, his church.

III. Last of all, note the cure for lost years.

Lost years can be redeemed. This is the promise of God: "I will restore to you the years the locust hath eaten." How are we to make up for the lost years?

A. *For some of us this means recasting our lives around a new center.* Only God can do this as we respond through an act of utter faith. In 2 Corinthians Paul describes the conversion experience: "He died for all, that they that live should no longer live unto themselves, but unto him who for their sakes died and rose again" (5:15 ASV). For a person to live for himself and unto himself is for life to revolve around the wrong center. Christ is the only true center for a life.

B. *For others, this means returning to God in sincere repentance that they may be restored.* If we truly repent, God will restore us, and we will be led by his Spirit to adopt a new approach to life's problems.

C. *But for still others, this means redoubling their efforts for God.* A good man made what was for him a very large pledge toward the budget of his church. His daughter protested, "Daddy, that is far more than a tithe for you." "Yes, Sue," he replied. "I know it is, but if God will let me live, maybe I can make up some of the tithe I owe him for the years before I started tithing."

Conclusion

The consoling truth is this: It is God who restores us if we do return unto him with all our hearts.

WEDNESDAY EVENING, JANUARY 23

Title: The Preaching of the Cross

Text: "For the preaching of the cross is to them that perish foolishness; but unto us which are saved it is the power of God" **(1 Cor. 1:18).**

Scripture Reading: 1 Corinthians 1:18–24

Introduction

People hold many varying attitudes about preaching. To some, preaching is being loud. To others, it is eloquence. To still others, it is being illustrative. Some believe it is a type of teaching. Some think the preacher ought to use notes, and others think he or she should not. Paul believed that good preaching is the preaching of the cross.

I. First, think of the meaning of the term *preaching.*

A. *The word is found three times in the first chapter of 1 Corinthians.* In verse 17 the word means to evangelize. It means to cast the net. The technical meaning is to proclaim glad tidings. In verse 18 the word is implied in the Greek language, but is well used in the English. Here the emphasis is on the content, not the method. The content is the *cross.* In verse 21 it is used in the form of heralding or proclaiming.

B. *The primary function of preaching is to bear a witness.* "Go ye into all the world, and preach the gospel to every creature" (Mark 16:15).

C. *Preaching is the essential function of the Christian minister.*

II. Second, think about the preaching of the cross.

A. *This cross is the cross on which Jesus died.* The death of Jesus is God's sacrifice for sin and his power for salvation. Christians should not be ashamed of this gospel. Paul said, "I am not ashamed of the gospel of Christ: for it is the power of God unto salvation to every one that believeth" (Rom. 1:16).

B. *The preaching of the cross is proclaiming a message.* It is not the discussion of a philosophy. The gospel is a person—namely, Jesus—on whom to rely, and not a system of truth to be understood. It is the whole message of redemption.

C. *The preaching of the cross causes a great division: to those who believe, it is God's power unto their salvation; to those who are perishing, it is foolishness.*

III. Third, consider who is to preach the cross and who is to believe it.

A. *All who have experienced God's saving power should tell the good news.* It is every Christian's duty. Also, it is every Christian's privilege and every Christian's commission.

B. *All who want to be saved must believe it.* Acts 4:12 declares, "Salvation is found in no one else, for there is no other name under heaven given to men by which we must be saved" (NIV).

Conclusion

This text has a twofold message. The first message is for all believers to tell the story of the death of Jesus. The second message is for all lost people to believe it.

SUNDAY MORNING, JANUARY 27

Title: The Incarnate God

Text: "And the Word became flesh and dwelt among us, full of grace and truth; we have beheld his glory, glory as of the only Son from the Father" (**John 1:14** RSV).

Scripture Reading: John 1:1–14

Hymns: "Come, Thou Almighty King," Anonymous
"Joy to the World!" Watts
"Tell the Good News," Bartlett
"Send Me, O Lord, Send Me," Coggins

Offertory Prayer: Eternal Lord, we are called to give our offerings unto you. But we give in response to what you have already given. We do not give to pressure you to give more to us. You have already given your Son Jesus to save us, your Holy Spirit to comfort and strengthen us, your church to teach and encourage us, your holy Word to guide and correct us. We have been greatly blessed. Please accept these gifts as expressions of our gratitude to you. In Jesus' name. Amen.

Introduction

A young boy was excited. His parents had carefully told him how God was sending a little brother or sister to their family for them to love and care for. The great day had arrived. His parents were bringing a little sister home to live with them. When the baby had been safely settled in her crib, the brother stood close by and whispered, "Quick, little sister, tell me, before you forget, what does God look like?"

Who can answer that question? John's gospel is an attempt to put into words what God is like, but its success in showing God to us is not in the words of the book, but in the Word made flesh, Jesus Christ of Nazareth. Jesus said, "He who has seen me has seen the Father" (John 14:9 RSV). So let us see if we can really be put in touch with God through Jesus Christ.

After a lifetime of preaching, a minister said that the five most important words in all of the Bible are: "And the Word became flesh." Without this happening there would be no life of Jesus, no Sermon on the Mount, no atoning death, no victory in resurrection. Without the incarnation we would have no way to know God as he wishes to be known.

I. The meaning of the incarnation.

Incarnation is the word we use to communicate the truth that God became flesh and dwelt among us. *Carnal* is an English word for flesh, as in "carnal desires." *Carnivorous* means a flesh-eating animal. *Incarnation* means the "infleshment." God took on human flesh and revealed himself to us; he was incarnated among us (see Phil. 2:6–11).

This truth points to the greatest mystery of the Christian faith—Jesus, fully human and fully divine—held up for us to see, to attempt to comprehend, and finally to bow our knee before in worship.

We know with John Calvin that if Jesus is not God, he could not have saved us, and if he is not man, he could not have reached us. The incarnate God has come to us in the flesh, not simply in spirit, which we could not see or touch, but in a body of flesh (see 1 John 1:1).

Matthew and Luke tell us that God became flesh through the willing obedience of the Virgin Mary. They tell us of Mary's faith, of Joseph's fears, of the angels' songs, and of the shepherds' worship. Through the Christmas story, the great and powerful truth rings out: "In the beginning was the Word, and the Word was with God, and the Word was God. And the Word became flesh and dwelt among us" (John 1:1, 14 RSV).

The truth is this: It is not simply a little baby innocently snuggled to his mother's breast in view here: it is the Lord God incarnate who calls us to believe and follow and who warns us of the consequences of unbelief. "He who believes in him is not condemned; he who does not believe is condemned already, because he has not believed in the name of the only Son of God" (John 3:18 RSV).

II. The purpose of the incarnation.

The reason for the incarnation is to bring life to all. This truth is suggested by John 1:4: "In him was life and the life was the light of men" (RSV). Notice also in John 10:10 where Jesus clearly says, "I came that they may have life, and have it abundantly" (RSV). The writer of the gospel gives his purpose for writing the book and points directly to the purpose of the incarnation when he says he has written these things "that you may believe that Jesus is the Christ, the Son of God, and that believing you may have life in his name" (John 20:31 RSV).

God's purpose was to bring eternal life to us through the life of the Son, who is the Light of the World. Through him the light shines into every dark nook and cranny of our loneliness, brokenness, and emptiness. Eternal life has two dimensions—length and depth. Eternal life with God is forever—that is the length of it. Eternal life with God is in the present moment, abundant, meaningful, filled with courage and joy—that is the depth of it. Jesus, the incarnate God, has come with the purpose of delivering you from the darkness of death into the light of life. And it is not just existence, not simply breathing, not merely getting by; it is life that is full now, in the world, fulfilled together, in the joy of all that heaven promises to be.

III. The church and the incarnation.

The task of the church is previewed in the incarnation. Since God sent the Son into the world to minister to us and redeem us, then is that not our best clue as to what the church is to be doing? Jesus said it himself: "As the Father has sent me, even so send I you" (John 20:21 RSV).

Jesus did not remain aloof from our need; he entered into the desperate situation of our community, of our lives. Whenever missionaries go on behalf of a church to preach the gospel and minister to human and spiritual needs, they are following in the tracks of our Lord Jesus, who came on a mission to redeem our world. Every time a church goes out to care for men and women, boys and girls who are sick or hungry, lonely or frightened, left out and ignored, lost without Christ, we go as a continuation of the ministry of Jesus. He is the God who traveled from the security of heaven's glory to the risk and threat of human existence in order to touch us at our hurting places.

When the church shares the good news that people do not have to die, but they can live, the message comes straight from the open tomb where the incarnate God left death defeated and the grave clothes behind him.

Every time the church bows in worship, it knows that the transcendent God has come to earth, refusing to remain aloof that he might by his presence bring us to a sense of intimacy with him. It is Jesus who taught us to call God "Father" and know his love for us as his children.

In W. H. Auden's *For the Time Being, a Christmas Oratorio,* Simeon, as he held the baby Jesus in his arms for blessing, sang, "Because of his visitation, we may no longer desire God as if he were lacking. Our redemption is no longer a question of pursuit, but of surrender to him who is always and everywhere present. Therefore, at every moment we pray that following him we may depart from our anxiety into his peace" ([New York: Random House, 1945], 454).

Conclusion

God has come to us in Jesus. We can never be the same again. He invites you to believe and to move from darkness to light, from dying to life, from aimless wandering to meaning and purpose. The journey may be long, but it begins with one decision and one step. Believe and live!

SUNDAY EVENING, JANUARY 27

Title: Amos—The Prophet of Tekoa

Text: "The LORD will roar from Zion, and utter his voice from Jerusalem" **(Amos 1:2)**. "But let justice roll down as waters, and righteousness as a mighty stream" **(Amos 5:24 ASV)**.

Scripture Reading: Amos 1:1–2; 5:14–24

Introduction

Amos was a disturbing man. This first of the writing prophets does not steal upon us like an author lecturing at a literary tea. He bursts upon us like an earthquake. The mention of a literal earthquake in Amos 1:1 is symbolically prophetic of the national cataclysm that befell Israel in 722 B.C. In Amos the notes that dominate are judgment and righteousness.

I. Note the prophet Amos.

The times demanded a man of extraordinary commitment and qualifications. Amos was that man.

A. *He had a simple occupation.* Amos was a herdsman and a "dresser of sycamore-trees" (1:1; 7:14 ASV). His flock was made up of a breed of small, short-limbed sheep noted for their choice wool. The sycamore produced a fig-like fruit, important in the diet of poor people. Selling his wool and his figs would take Amos to Bethel and Jerusalem, where he could keep abreast of the happenings of the day.

B. *He had a profound sense of call.* In describing his call, Amos says in substance: "Jehovah took me; he told me; he sent me" (see 7:15). "I was no prophet, neither was I a prophet's son" (7:14). He denied being a member of the guild of professional prophets, who for a price spoke what people wanted to hear. His father was not a prophet. Thus, Amos had not inherited his office. He identified himself with the true prophets.

C. *He had a message from God.* As a result of his commission, Amos said, "Now therefore hear thou the word of the LORD: Thou sayest, Prophesy not against Israel, and drop not thy word against the house of Isaac. Therefore thus saith the LORD" (7:16–17). The source of his message was God. Moreover, there was a powerful simplicity about his words. In some of the best Hebrew in the Old Testament his message was pointed and clear. We have little difficulty understanding what Amos meant by what he said.

D. *He had great courage.* Amos dared to confront the lion in his den, the king in his royal sanctuary. This was an unheard of thing. To ingratiate himself with the people, the demagogue type of politician denounces the opposition and the people and rulers of another land. Amos was no mere politician. He was a spiritual statesman, a seer. He took his life in his hands to declare the word of God wherever, whenever, and to whomever God directed.

E. *He had remarkable faith.* Amos believed there was a future. In the face of the sin within the nation and the impending judgment on the chosen people, Amos did not despair of the purpose of God. He foresaw a time when God would build "as in the days of old" (9:11). The future will see the plan, the purpose, and the dream of God realized, not in the nation itself, but in the remnant. God will raise up the tabernacle of David in the messianic kingdom of the future.

II. Consider the prophecy of Amos.

In addition to the introduction (1:1–2) and the epilogue (9:11–15), the prophecy falls naturally into three parts.

A. *Part 1 (chapters 1–2) is introductory.* The title (1:1) and the introduction (1:2) describe in graphic imagery God's power over all Palestine. Then Amos surveys the nations bordering on Israel—Damascus, the Philistines, Tyre, Edom, the Ammonites, Moab, and Judah—in order to show that, as none of these will escape retribution for their sins, so Israel, for similar or greater sins, will be subject to the same law of righteous government. A terrible military disaster will soon overtake them.

B. *Part 2 (chapters 3–6) consists of three discourses.* Each is introduced by the imperative, "Hear this word" (3:1; 4:1; 5:1). This section expands and enforces what the prophet had said with reference to Israel in 2:6–16.

 1. In the first discourse (3:1–15) there are four distinct lessons. In verses 1 and 2 Amos disillusions the people of Israel about their election. This is not, as they suppose, an unconditional guarantee of their security. To the contrary, this makes their sins the more serious in their consequences. In verse 3–8 the prophet reasons that since no event occurs in nature without sufficient cause, the appearance of a prophet with such a message indicates that God has sent him. In verses 9 and 10 Amos, with fine irony, suggests that even the heathen can bear witness that the sins of Samaria deserve God's judgment. In verses 11–15 we see the foe at the door. Only a small remnant will escape. Altars and palaces will perish together.

 2. In the second discourse (4:1–13) two groups are addressed by the prophet. In verses 1–3 Amos rebukes the women of Samaria for their self-indulgences and cruelty. He predicts their tragic end. In verses 4 and 5 the prophet sarcastically turns to the people at large, bidding them to continue in their ritual since they trust in it to save them. In verses 6–11 Amos expresses surprise that Israel should have neglected to heed the fivefold warning of famine, drought, blasted crops, pestilence, and earthquake. In verses 12 and 13 Amos ends this discourse hinting darkly that God will soon resort to more extreme measures.

 3. In the third discourse (5:1–6:14) there are three divisions. Each draws out, in different terms, the moral grounds of Israel's impending ruin,

and ends with a similar outlook of invasion or exile. In verses 1–17 the prophet sings his elegy over Israel's fall. In verses 18–27 he rebukes those who desire the "day of Jehovah," for if they continue in their present sins, it will be a day not of deliverance but of dire misfortune. In 6:1–14 a second rebuke is addressed to the leaders of the nation.

C. *Part 3 (7:1–9:10) consists of a series of five visions, interrupted (in 7:10–17) by the altercation that took place between Amos and Amaziah.* Each vision is followed by explanatory comments. Their purpose is to reinforce, by means of effective symbolism, the truth that the judgment he had already predicted can no longer be averted. The visions are the devouring locusts (7:1–3), the consuming fire (7:4–6), the plumbline (7:7–9), the basket of summer fruit (8:1–14), and the smitten sanctuary (9:1–10).

The epilogue (9:11–25) promises a brighter future.

III. Finally, note the preaching of Amos.

Where Amos preached, how long his ministry continued, or just what response he received, except for that of Amaziah, we do not know. There was no general revival, and judgment was not averted. Several distinct themes appear in his preaching.

A. *The imminence of judgment.* This theme is to the prophecy of Amos as the motif of a Wagnerian opera. Amos's first words are, "The LORD will roar from Zion, and utter his voice from Jerusalem" (1:2). In 3:8 we read: "The lion hath roared, who will not fear? the Lord GOD hath spoken, who can but prophesy?" To one accustomed to the ways of the desert, the roar of the lion meant that the animal was even then leaping upon its prey. In like manner the prophet sees God coming in judgment, from which there can be no turning back.

B. *The union of justice and righteousness in daily life.* It is possible to find one of the keys to Amos's preaching in the words, "But let justice roll down as waters, and righteousness as a mighty stream" (5:24 ASV). This union of justice and righteousness in daily life was a burden on his heart.

C. *The sovereignty of God.* Amos saw God as personally in control of all the world. He is not only the God of Israel, but of all the world. God is the Lord of history, of nature, of the nations. Amos viewed God as dealing out punishment impartially to all nations according to his standards of righteousness.

D. *The true meaning of God's election of Israel.* In popular Israelite theology, God's election was an unconditional guarantee of their security. In a key passage (5:18–20) the phrase "Day of Yahweh" appears. This expression grew out of the hope that the day of Yahweh was a day of salvation to the people of God. This meant not only the glorification of Israel, but also included the total defeat of Israel's enemies. Amos preached that, because of their sins, the day of Yahweh would be a "day of darkness," that is, destruction and exile. It was to be the end of the northern kingdom.

E. *Privilege imposes responsibility.* As a specially chosen people, Israel must be doubly accountable to God. Their prosperity was not a sign of God's favor. Their place of privilege was not an assurance that all was well. The people were not safe in their affluent society.

F. *The curse of unconcern on the part of God's people.* In the marketplace Amos observed the indifference to the cries of the poor. In the palaces he could see no thought given for the oppressed. Even at the sanctuaries the deepest needs of the downtrodden were ignored. Amos's most devastating condemnation was aimed at this callous disregard for the rights and necessities of others.

G. *The basis of true religion.* The externals of religion were everywhere apparent, but they were divorced from any relationship to moral obligations.

H. *The message of hope.* This is a secondary theme throughout the prophecy. "Seek me and live" (5:4 RSV), "Seek Yahweh and live" (see 5:6), "Seek good, and not evil, that you may live" (5:14 RSV). The possibility of repentance and deliverance still existed (5:15). The hope theology of Amos sounds most clearly in the epilogue (9:11–12). Even though God is to make an end of the northern kingdom, he will not give up the people he has chosen.

Conclusion

The hope of Amos is fulfilled in Christ in his messianic kingdom. Amos's warnings are as applicable to the new Israel as they were to the old.

WEDNESDAY EVENING, JANUARY 30

Title: Man's Extremity, God's Opportunity

Text: "The foolishness of God is wiser than men; and the weakness of God is stronger than men" **(1 Cor. 1:25).**

Scripture Reading: 1 Corinthians 1:25–31

Introduction

The subject of this message is a common cliché. It is used in many facets of life. Two areas of human ability are compared to the abilities of God. One is in the area of mental abilities and the other is strength. Of course strength is found in numerous facets of life.

I. First, consider an analysis of the passage itself.

A. *The wisdom of the world is not of significance to God (1 Cor. 1:27).* Salvation comes in connection with the cross. In verse 18 Paul gave his own testimony. In the language of the New Testament, salvation is a thing of the past (Rom.

8:24), of the present (Eph. 2:5), a progression (1 Cor. 15:2), and a future prospect (Rom. 13:11).

B. *A historical example refers to Israel (1 Cor. 1:19).* "For it is written, I will destroy the wisdom of the wise, and will bring to nothing the understanding of the prudent" (see Isa. 29:14).

First Corinthians 1 states that Ariel—"the city where David dwelt"—referred to in Isaiah 29:1, despised the Word of God and relied on the wisdom of statecraft. The people also made an alliance with Egypt that led to their overthrow.

C. *A major principle is then established.* The world and God are at issue. Each counts the other as folly, but God turns their wisdom to folly, and his folly—according to their terminology—into wisdom. Then after the wisdom of the world has been reduced to ignorance, God, by the foolishness of preaching, saves all who believe. A person is saved through faith, which the world deems folly. The power is seen in the cross.

II. Second, consider some examples from history.

A. *Many biblical references illustrate the text.* The book of Judges records a series of cycles in which man finds himself at his extremity. He calls upon God, and God delivers. Jonah is a classic example of human extremity. Paul suffered opposition and found that his extremity was God's opportunity. Other examples are the woman with an issue of blood and the man at the pool of Bethesda.

B. *Historical examples support the text.* Society lost in the wickedness of sin is a classic example of being at the extremity. When a person calls on God, the Lord God answers and shows that human extremity is God's opportunity. From time to time people find themselves with disastrous financial situations, health problems, or emotional struggles, and God proves sufficient to deliver.

III. Third, consider some facts about human extremity.

A. *It is in Christ that we live, move, and have our being.* Apart from the Lord Jesus, we can do nothing. We are helpless. Jesus said, "I am the vine; you are the branches. If a man remains in me and I in him, he will bear much fruit; apart from me you can do nothing" (John 15:5 NIV).

B. *Each Christian needs to let go of self and let God have his way.* When a person comes to his or her extremity, that is God's opportunity. God wants each of his children to surrender totally and unconditionally to him. Then God makes those who do so his instruments.

Conclusion

If you have never made a total commitment to the Lord Jesus, now is the time. I plead with you to do so right now.

FEBRUARY

■ **Sunday Mornings**

Continue with the "Responding to the Living Word" series from the Gospel of John.

■ **Sunday Evenings**

Continue the messages with the theme "Listen to the Major Messages of the Minor Prophets."

■ **Wednesday Evenings**

Continue the studies based on Paul's first letter to the Corinthian Christians.

SUNDAY MORNING, FEBRUARY 3

Title: Playing Second Fiddle

Text: "John answered them, 'I baptize with water; but among you stands one whom you do not know, even he who comes after me, the thong of whose sandal I am not worthy to untie'" **(John 1:26–27 RSV)**.

Scripture Reading: John 1:6–8, 19–28

Hymns: "Rejoice, the Lord Is King," Wesley
"Like a River Glorious," Havergal
"Take My Life and Let It Be," Havergal

Offertory Prayer: Grant unto us, Lord, a servant heart. The world honors powerful men and women, winners, achievers, those who make it to the top. Teach us, Father, that all your children are important to you. There is not one greater in the kingdom than those who would give their lives in service to you. It is not weakness we bring to you, but strength, harnessed and obedient, to do your will. Accept our offerings as tokens of our love to be used for your work in this world. Through Jesus we seek to serve, and in his name we pray. Amen.

Introduction

Most people do not like playing second fiddle. Most vice presidents dream of being the president. Most back-up quarterbacks eagerly await their chance to be number one. The term "second fiddle" comes from the practice

41

of having the best player of each instrument in an orchestra sit in the first-chair position while the second-best player plays the second part. For instance, the best violinist plays first chair, while the second-best player sits in the second chair and plays "second fiddle" (a fiddle being slang for a violin). To be sure, some people delight in being the back-up person, the substitute, the aide who makes the leader effective in his or her work. But most people have a hard time playing second fiddle to someone else's first violin! Even more difficult is playing second fiddle after you have been the first fiddle!

John the Baptist knew about this, for he had been the one the crowds came to hear. He was the best preacher for God in all the country. And then came Jesus. I wonder how John felt about stepping aside and pointing his disciples to Jesus (see John 1:35–39). No wonder Jesus could say, "Among those born of women none is greater than John" (Luke 7:28 RSV). What do you suppose was John's secret?

I. In order to play second fiddle well, you must know yourself.

John's questioners asked him if he was the Christ, Elijah, or the prophet (1:19–21). "No," he replied. "Then who are you? We want an answer," they demanded (1:22). Is it ever easy to know how to answer that question? Socrates suggested that the key to wisdom is to "know thyself." John's reply is our first clue as to how he was able to play well from the second position. "I am the voice of one crying in the wilderness, 'Make straight the way of the Lord'" (1:23).

Does that answer intrigue you? John, with all his oratorical gifts, his large following, his amazing sense of the righteous call of God, says simply, "I am a voice"—not a man, not a preacher, just a voice. John lived a strong and independent life. He lived in the wilderness, robbed the bees of their honey, and ate locusts. He preached in a fury, calling all Israel to repentance. Even a powerful government official like Philip, Herod's brother, could not frighten him into silence (Matt. 14:3–5). Great crowds gathered to hear John preach, and he baptized many people, but when Jesus came into his life, he knew that he had found his purpose for living—he was a voice preparing the way for the Lamb of God. For John there was no greater truth for his life. He knew why he was alive, who he was.

II. In order to play second fiddle well, you must be willing to lose yourself.

John could say he was unworthy to untie the thong of Jesus' sandal (John 1:27). He would say later about Jesus, "He must increase, but I must decrease" (3:30 RSV). John was willing to lose himself in Jesus Christ. Jesus would say that this is the only way to greatness (12:24–26).

John understood that serving Jesus was the way to receive honor from the Father (12:26). Therefore, he was willing to lose himself that he might find himself; he was willing to give himself away in order for Jesus Christ, the Lamb of God, to be boldly lifted up.

In losing his life, John found it. Every Christian knows about John the Baptist but only because he gave up his place that Jesus might be known. If Jesus had not been the Christ, then who would know of John? Because he was willing to play second fiddle to Jesus, the Christ, John's name is known and honored.

Consider what Jesus our Lord had to say about John's life. *(Read Luke 7:24–28 at this time.)*

Would it be worth everything, even the loss of your life, for Jesus to commend your life in this way when you stand at the final day before God himself?

Before you despair of ever being worthy of such a word, note carefully the closing of Luke 7:28. "Yet he who is least in the kingdom of God is greater than he [John]" (RSV).

Jesus' ministry revolved around this theme of servanthood. Nothing goes more against the grain in our society than this call to be a servant. People struggle with each other to find the key to the next position, the invitation to the next honor. Too many of us are willing to put our foot on someone else's neck if it will get us ahead. But Jesus said that his people must not engage in this kind of behavior. You will find your joy in service, or you will miss the joy completely.

You may be frankly admitting, "I find myself resisting the idea of losing myself, of playing second fiddle. I don't know if I can do this or not. Sometimes it is hard just to do God's will, but you're also suggesting there will be times when I will have to play second fiddle to another person who is human and frail like me. I could play second fiddle to Jesus, but I don't want to be second to any other person."

III. You can find the grace to play second fiddle if you are willing to look for God's plan in it.

You must be willing to see God at work in your life. An evangelist had gone through some rugged terrain before he became an evangelist. It had not been easy for him as pastor in his church, but God moved him into the itinerant ministry of church-to-church evangelism. After some years in evangelism he was able to look back upon his earlier experience and affirm that God had taught him some things he would never have known in any other way. He felt that his experiences had taught him compassion and enabled him to minister in churches where things were sometimes difficult.

That story in itself is not so remarkable. What is remarkable is that that kind of statement comes from Christians again and again as they look back on a difficult period in their lives. They find that "they who trust him wholly, find him wholly true" (from the hymn "Like a River Glorious").

When you understand God's plan, you can accept the role you have, whether it be first violin or second, third, or even last. You find that you are able to be responsible to God in the place he has put you and that you can be effective in doing the task appropriate to that opportunity.

Conclusion

None is great or small in the service of our Lord, for he is concerned only about our faithfulness to the work he gives us. If you want to be great in God's kingdom, you must be a servant (Mark 10:44). By God's grace and the power of the Holy Spirit, we can play second fiddle and harmonize with the whole orchestra. Then all the world can know that Jesus is the Lamb of God who takes away the sin of the world.

SUNDAY EVENING, FEBRUARY 3

Title: Obadiah—Possessing Our Possessions

Text: "And the house of Jacob shall possess their possessions" **(Obad. 17 RSV)**.

Scripture Reading: Obadiah 1–21

Introduction

Fighting among brothers is deplorable, and the results are disastrous. A classic example is that of Esau and Jacob. Although the two brothers were later reconciled, the feud between their descendants went on for generations as the memory of ancient wrong was perpetuated. Petty meanness and open hostility marked Edom's attitude toward Israel. Outbursts of their hatred toward one another punctuated the history of both nations.

On the Israelites' journey to Canaan, the Edomites refused Israel permission to pass through their territory. Later there was hard fighting between the Edomites and King Saul. David took stern measures against them, as did Solomon. Rigorous repression, however, only served to widen the gap and intensify the hatred between the two peoples. Under King Jehoshaphat there was a renewal of hostilities as Moab and Ammon formed a triple alliance with Edom to invade Judah. Under King Amaziah's punitive hand, Edom suffered a crushing blow. Petra was taken, and many of Edom's fighting men were slain. Still unsubdued and implacable, Edom cherished its sum of unpaid scores.

Hatred lived on, intensifying as the years passed. In 587 B.C. when Jerusalem fell before Nebuchadnezzar, the Edomites played the part of a jackal to the Babylonian lion, preying upon the stragglers and rejoicing over the ruin of Jacob. The writer of Psalm 137 remembered that the Edomites said, probably of the temple, "Tear it down, tear it down to its foundations!" (Ps. 137:7 NIV).

This opens up the meaning of the prophecy of Obadiah. This brief prophecy has three parts. The first section (vv. 1–9) denounces the pride of the Edomites, who felt secure in their mountain fastness. Obadiah reminds them that no fortress is secure for those who deserve the judgment of God. In the second section (vv. 10–14) the baseness of Edom's treatment of her sister nation is described and condemned. Obadiah's God was the protector of Israel, and to betray her was to defy him. The third section (vv. 15–21) is the prophet's message of hope for dispossessed and exiled Israel. This prophecy says in effect: "The world will be ruled in righteousness. The sovereignty of God that guarantees the destruction of Edom assures also the eventual restoration of Israel."

Obadiah's eye of faith looked beyond the darkness of the day of their calamity and saw the clear gleam of God's dawn: "And the house of Jacob shall possess their own possessions" (Obad. 17 RSV). Was this not Israel's problem in all her long history? She had not, in any real sense, possessed her possessions. Is this not our problem as a great nation? As we apply this thought, three questions are in order.

I. What are our possessions?

A. *Our material possessions.*
Joyfully, but I fear thoughtlessly, we sing:

> *O beautiful for spacious skies,*
> *For amber waves of grain,*
> *For purple mountain majesties*
> *Above the fruited plain!*

> —Katharine Lee Bates

Ours is a land where wealth accumulates yet where the day laborer can usually enjoy not only the necessities of life but a fair share of luxuries as well.

B. *Our political possessions.* Born and reared and nurtured in the tradition of government "of the people, by the people, and for the people," we cannot grasp the full meaning of the tyranny that others know. The right to vote, to choose those who will serve us in government, to approve those who serve well, and to repudiate those who do not—ah, what a treasure that is!

C. *Our social possessions.* In America we have no royalty, no commoners, no aristocracy, except that of superior ability. The ideal of a society where neither class, caste, creed, gender, nor color shall divide, and where a person shall be accepted upon the face value of his or her demonstrated worth—that is the structure of the society to which we are committed. Even though it has not always been practiced, the ideal that all humans are created equal before God is in the very roots of the first principles of our social order.

E. *Our religious possessions.* Our spiritual heritage is that of a "free church in a free state." And written into the highest law of the land is this safeguard: "Congress shall make no law concerning an establishment of religion." No religious institution shall be favored over any other, and there shall be no approved state religion. Imbedded deep in our history and laws and culture is the guarantee that every person shall have the right to worship God, or not to worship God, as he or she pleases, according to the dictates of his or her own conscience. What a possession that is!

These are our possessions, but have we possessed them? Do we appreciate them as we ought? Do we use them for the best and highest advantage? Do we know what to do with them?

II. How shall we possess our possessions?

A. *It is a matter of appreciation.* If, in the highest sense, we have not possessed these wonderful possessions, it is because we have not appreciated them for their true worth.

One of the famous jewels in the world is the 83.5-carat diamond called The Star of South Africa. It was found by a shepherd boy who sold it to a trader named Van Niekird, from Hopetown, for five sheep, two oxen, and a horse. Three weeks later this trader sold it in Hopetown for $56,000. Later in London this diamond sold for $560,000. Now it is not for sale at any price. And to think it originally sold for five sheep, two oxen, and a horse! The finder had not possessed his possession because he did not know its worth.

B. *It is a matter of utilization.* What we use we keep. It multiplies. But what we fail to use we lose. This is true of all our great blessings. My hope and prayer is that we may raise up a generation genuinely interested in politics, a generation that will sincerely participate in the political process. The bane of our generation is that we have blamed "politics" for many of our ills when we ought to have blamed ourselves. This is just an effort on our part to cover our failure to participate.

C. *It is a matter of correct utilization.* The father and mother in a very wealthy family died together in an airplane crash leaving a tremendous legacy to a spoiled and pampered only son. Within a few months he died a sudden death, dashed to a mangled bundle of bleeding flesh behind the wheel of a massive automobile driven at a furious pace by the press of a drink-numbed foot. An aunt, the only relative, pronounced a benediction upon the tragedy: "Poor John," she said, "he never inherited his inheritance."

Years ago three high school seniors accompanied their pastor on a short trip. On the way home they began to talk about their future plans. "Sure, I'd like to make some money," said one. "but say a man makes a lot of money and has a palatial home, good cars, nice clothes, and all that. So what? Does that make him happy? A lot of people have made a lot of money, and they are miserable. I want to do two things: I want to make some money doing something that will help somebody. And I want to know what to do with my money when I get it." That boy remained true to those sound principles. He possessed his possessions.

III. What if we do not possess our possessions?

A. *Our material possessions may possess us.* How deadly is this peril! Of many people it may be said that they have money and land, houses and cars, stocks and bonds and securities. These things are legally theirs, but they do not actually own them. Their possessions own them and use them and enslave them in terrible bondage. Such a man is Adam Ward in Harold Bell Wright's novel *Helen of the Old House*. In a street-corner conversation one citizen says to another, "Adam Ward retires today." And the other asks, "Retires to what?" That is more than a line from a novel; that is the great American tragedy.

B. *We may lose our possessions if they are unappreciated and unused.* Many years ago a man who was a genius in the use of a lathe made a beautiful solid walnut bedroom suite out of a black walnut tree he had processed himself. As it passed down through the family, two of the three pieces disappeared. When the man died in 1916 his youngest daughter, an antique buff, wanted the solid walnut bed, which someone had painted green. She stored it in the attic of the barn, planning to get it later. But when she went the next spring and couldn't find it, the tenant living on the old home place admitted he had cut it up and used it for firewood during the big snow. He did not know its value. He destroyed it. The woman lost her prized possession.

C. *If our possessions are misused, they may destroy us.* Our country has a vast arsenal of weapons to be used for war. We may ask, "Will we use this possession correctly or, used incorrectly, will it destroy us?"

During World War I the great British scientist Sir Oliver Lodge wrote, "We do not in the least know how to harness the energy locked up in the atoms of matter. If it could be liberated at will, we should experience a violence beside which the suddenness of high explosives is gentle and leisurely." That was in 1918. Reading what Dr. Lodge had written, the British poet Thomas Thornely wrote a poem titled "The Atom," first published in 1919. The last stanza reads,

> *Thy last dread secret, Nature! keep;*
> *Add not to man's tumultuous woes;*
> *Till war and hate are laid to sleep,*
> *Keep those grim forces buried deep,*
> *That in thine atoms still repose.*

In 1945 after the first atomic bomb fell, Thornely wrote this one-stanza poem, which he called "Presage."

> *If, knowing all that now is known*
> *Of power that in an Atom dwells,*
> *We let War's trumpet still be blown,*
> *Its blast may view with Gabriel's;*
> *And Earth, as when its course began,*
> *Be free from its invader—Man.*

Conclusion

Let us pray that we might be able to possess our possessions for the glory of God and for the good of our fellow humans. Let us be on guard lest our possessions enslave us and abuse those about us.

WEDNESDAY EVENING, FEBRUARY 6

Title: That Which Is Prepared for God's Lovers

Text: "As it is written, Eye hath not seen, nor ear heard, neither have entered into the heart of man, the things which God hath prepared for them that love him" (**1 Cor. 2:9**).

Scripture Reading: 1 Corinthians 2:1–9

Introduction

At first glance one might conclude that the promise of this passage of Scripture is referring to heavenly rewards. However, a closer examination of the content will reveal that this is not true. The discussion that precedes these verses relates to the wisdom of the natural man. Now the writer speaks of the spiritual man. Verse 10 confirms that this promise refers to the present and not the future.

I. Some things the Holy Spirit gives to believers.

A. *The first is the divine pardon of sin.* This is first in importance both chronologically and by priority. The natural mind cannot grasp this. The unsaved person does not have the Holy Spirit to make the explanation.

B. *The second thing the Holy Spirit gives is spiritual purity.* God desires that we live clean, wholesome lives. Spiritual purity is a cleanliness that comes as a gift of God.

C. *The third thing the Holy Spirit gives is hope.* This can and does refer to hope beyond the earthly life, but it is not confined to that. It also refers to hope for better things in the present life.

D. *The fourth thing the Holy Spirit gives is the revelation of God.* The Holy Spirit reveals the very essence of God (1 Cor. 2:10). He—the Spirit—tells of the attributes as well as the thoughts of God. He also reveals the purposes, plans, and providence of God.

E. *The fifth thing the Holy Spirit gives is assurance (Rom. 8:16).* Romans 8:28 declares, "All things work together for good to them that love God, to them who are the called according to his purpose."

F. *The sixth thing the Holy Spirit gives is comfort.* The fourteenth chapter of John is truly a masterpiece for human comfort. The Lord Jesus emphatically states, "I will not leave you comfortless: I will come to you" (John 14:18). He also states emphatically that the Holy Spirit is that Comforter (John 14:16–17).

II. The Lord teaches believers these things (1 Cor. 2:10).

A. *In this school the believer is taught "the deep things of God."* These things are deep because they are undiscoverable by human reason. Natural human powers cannot comprehend these things. The "eye" referred to in verse 9 is the equivalent of natural faculties. The things are also deep because they come from the fathomless ocean of divine love.

B. *In this school the believer is instructed by the greatest of teachers—the Holy Spirit.* As the divine one, the Holy Spirit has infinite knowledge about all things.

Conclusion

If you are a believer in the Lord Jesus Christ, having received eternal life as a gift from God that makes you God's child, then I urge you to take inventory of all that is yours because of your relation to God.

SUNDAY MORNING, FEBRUARY 10

Title: Giver of Abundant Life

Text: "Every man serves the good wine first; and when men have drunk freely, then the poor wine; but you have kept the good wine until now" **(John 2:10 RSV).**

Scripture Reading: John 2:1–11

Hymns: "Praise Him! Praise Him!" Crosby
"All That Thrills My Soul Is Jesus," Harris
"Oh, for a Thousand Tongues to Sing," Wesley

Offertory Prayer: Sometimes, Lord, our lives are dull and drab. But we are convinced that is not what you want for us. Help us to be open to the joy that you bring to our lives. Help us not to be preoccupied with our own manufactured and counterfeit joy. The offerings we cheerfully bring to you now are the results of the joy we have come to know. We will be able to give more when we learn to glory in your joy. In the name of Jesus, the joy-bringer, we pray. Amen.

Introduction

The key theme in the gospel of John is "I came that they may have life, and have it abundantly" (10:10 RSV). Early in this gospel we are presented with a sign (2:11) that vividly illustrates the abundance Jesus brings to life.

Jesus, his mother, and his disciples were invited to a wedding feast. It could very well have been the wedding of a relative, since Mary seemed to have some influence on the servants (2:5) and took a personal interest in the embarrassment to the family when the wine ran out (2:3). Every pastor who works with nervous families at wedding celebrations knows how uneasy they can become if everything does not go well.

This wedding celebration was about to be a disaster. It appeared that the groom's family had not made adequate preparation; they had tried to skimp on the expenses. Their social faux pas would be remembered. It would be a long time before they would be able to live down this embarrassment!

I. In a world where things run out, Jesus is the abundance of life (John 2:3).

In John 2–11 the writer tells us of the great signs Jesus did to demonstrate his power over the world. He brings joy to this party (2:1–11); he brings judgment to the temple functionaries (2:13–22); he brings healing to the nobleman's son (4:46–54); and he gives a man sick for thirty-eight years a new chance at life (5:2–18); then he feeds the five thousand (6:1–14); he walks on the water (6:16–21); he gives sight to blind eyes (9:1–17); and he shows his power to give life by raising Lazarus from the dead (11:1–44).

The connecting theme of these signs is that when things run out, whether it's wine, or justice, or health, or hope, or bread, or life itself, Jesus is the true source of abundance for life. In a world where there is never enough, Jesus is all-sufficient.

II. In a world where people are satisfied to just get by, Jesus goes beyond simply providing; he improves on life (John 2:10).

The steward of the feast was obviously surprised as he called to the bridegroom, "Every man serves the good wine first; and when men have drunk freely, then the poor wine; but you have kept the good wine until now" (v. 10 RSV). When the most important celebration in the lives of these two families was about to disintegrate because there was not enough wine, Jesus not only rescued the party, he improved upon it!

If this is not an accurate picture of how Jesus deals with life, there isn't one in all the Gospels. Jesus comes to us when everything appears to be lost and turns what could have been disaster into a miracle of abundance.

Has this ever happened in your life? Perhaps it was the loss of a job, a failed test, a broken promise, a divorce, or a death that left you feeling that life had caved in on you. At these kinds of moments, Jesus brings to our life, not just rescue, but grace sufficient to bring us finally to victory and joy again. He does not simply "help us get through the night," he improves on our situation.

III. In a world living by ritual, Jesus becomes the source of true life and joy (John 2:6).

The six stone jars may represent the Jewish ceremonial laws. They were there for the cleansing rites. The water from them was used to wash the feet and cleanse the hands of the guests. The number six is an incomplete number, being one less than the sacred and complete number seven. It is not wild allegorizing to see Jesus as the one who completes what is lacking in the Jewish ritualistic ceremonies.

B. F. Westcott suggests that the water used to make wine did not come from the stone jars, but from the well. The Greek word for *draw* out (v. 8), Westcott insists, is the word for taking water from a well, not dipping from a jar. The symbol is that after the ceremonial activities had been completed, what was needed was "a spring of water welling up to eternal life" (4:14 RSV).

And so from the well they drew the water that Jesus then transformed into the new wine, the best wine (see Matt. 9:17; Mark 2:22; Luke 5:37). This then is the sign of the gospel—the new wine, which will require new wine skins. The Jewish legal system for righteousness was not able to hold the new wine of grace that was in Jesus Christ, the Giver of abundant life.

Jesus says in John 15:1 (RSV), "I am the true vine." The implication surely is that he is the vine from which the true wine will come.

Jesus does away with all substitutes for the abundant life. He is the true vine giving the new wine that frees people from the wine that runs out. He is the water of life in the ceremonial jars that can cleanse but never satisfy by itself.

IV. In a world where there is little real joy, Jesus brings true joy to the party of life.

Jesus is no killjoy. He enjoys the celebration of life. Wine is a symbol of joy and of the blessings of God (see Ps. 104:15; Eccl. 9:7; Isa. 25:6; Hos. 14:7; Joel 2:19, 24; 3:18; Amos 9:13–14).

Our awareness of the dangers of alcoholic beverages is also biblical (see Prov. 23:29–32; Isa. 28:7; Hab. 2:5; Eph. 5:18). God is in favor of joy, but he is opposed to everything that works against the people he loves. God is for everything that is good, but he is against everything that harms life and tears people apart. When God is against something, it is because he is for us. As long as people become drunkards, as long as alcoholism is a threat to life, as long as drinking drivers are a menace to safety, as long as families are frightened and torn apart by drinking parents, I will choose not to drink any alcoholic beverage at all.

Christians instinctively know that the greatest joy at the party is the presence of Christ who is the new wine that satisfies our every craving for joy and laughter. The disciples saw the glory of God in Jesus as he changed the water into wine. They knew that in Jesus, God was acting to provide abundance for their scarcity, joy for their ordinary lives. "And his disciples believed in him" (John 2:11 RSV).

Conclusion

In Jesus there is the abundance of life, a new way, a new hope, a new gospel, a new freedom for all of life. You, too, may now believe and be invited to join in the joy of the party of life.

SUNDAY EVENING, FEBRUARY 10

Title: Jonah—The God Revealed to Jonah

Text: "He prayed to the LORD, 'O LORD, is this not what I said when I was still at home? That is why I was so quick to flee to Tarshish. I knew that you are a gracious and compassionate God, slow to anger and abounding in love, a God who relents from sending calamity'" **(Jonah 4:2 NIV).**

Scripture Reading: Jonah 4:1–11

Introduction

The literary form of Jonah is that of a short story, wonderfully told and rich in revealed truth. This prophecy may be seen as a drama in four acts, corresponding roughly with the four chapters.

Act 1 we may call "A Prophet in Rebellion" (1:1–16). Called to go to Nineveh, the capital of the Assyrian empire, Jonah headed for Tarshish, a Phoenician town on the southwest coast of Spain, as far from Nineveh as he could go. When a violent storm at sea made it obvious to the superstitious sailors that someone on board had offended some god, Jonah was found to be the culprit. At his suggestion, the sailors, against their will, were persuaded to throw him overboard. There Jonah was swallowed by a "great fish" (not a whale). Disobedience is redeemed by self-sacrifice.

Act 2 we may call "A Prophet Rescued" (1:17–2:10). Jonah prayed to God from inside the great fish. His prayer was later written down in poetic form, a beautiful psalm that comprises chapter 2. God graciously heard his prayer, and upon command the fish "vomited out Jonah upon the dry land" (2:10 ASV).

Act 3 we may call "A Prophet in Revival" (3:1–10). This time, when God called, Jonah went to Nineveh and preached God's impending judgment upon the wickedness of the imperial city. The result was tremendous. The whole city repented. Fasting and sackcloth were the order of the day, and God thus decided to spare the city.

Act 4 we may call "A Prophet's Petulance" (4:1–11). Jonah's preaching had been embarrassingly successful. He was indignant. Personally, he had hoped to see a wholesale holocaust at the divine hand. In chapter 4 God explained to Jonah why he spared the city. He pointed out that mercy is a quality of God. Jonah indicated that he knew this but that personally he was not for it, preferring death, even his own, to such an exhibition of divine forgiveness. And there the writer leaves Jonah.

The prophet Jonah is not the hero of this story. He is rather the villain of the piece. God is the hero. The author's theology echoes John 3:16, "God so loved the world"—Jerusalem, of course, but the wicked Nineveh too. This superb story was written by a man with an accurate view of a great and merciful God. What are the characteristics of the God revealed to Jonah?

I. The God revealed to Jonah is a God of universal love.

God loves all people. The book closes with some painful questions that God asked his loveless prophet. With a soft but pointed sarcasm God asks Jonah: "Have you any right to be angry?" (4:4 NIV). The same question is asked about the vine that the cutworm destroyed. The climax, however, is this: "But Nineveh has more than a hundred and twenty thousand people who cannot tell their right hand from their left, and many cattle as well. Should I not be concerned about that great city?" (4:11 NIV). Jonah was a bigot, selfish and arrogant; the God revealed to him was gracious in love, plenteous in mercy, loving everyone.

Religious people like Jonah put Jesus to death on the cross. Our Lord taught people about a God of universal love. God had a place in his love for the despised Samaritans; for an officer in the occupying Roman army; and for the people of the land of Palestine who would not or could not keep the Jewish law. Had you asked Jesus why he loved these people, he doubtless would have replied, "Because God loves them."

The spirit of the Great Commission, the Christian evangel, saturates the book of Jonah. Through the message of this inspired book God was seeking to reveal the universal scope of his love to Israel.

II. The God revealed to Jonah is sovereign.

A. *God is sovereign in his claims.* Without explanation, "The word of Jehovah came unto Jonah the son of Amittai, saying, Arise, go to Nineveh, that great city, and cry against it" (1:1–2 ASV). The God revealed to Jonah laid the claim of divine ownership upon Jonah's person, his time, and his talents, that he might communicate God's message to the people of Nineveh. Any person trying to get away from God will always find someone else going in his direction, just as Jonah did. There is sure to be a ship sailing for Tarshish on which the runaway can book passage. A college student came to our evening worship service saying that God had called him to preach and he was surrendering to that call. Immediately afterward he started running in the opposite direction. Three years later, in a revival, he came rededicating his life, saying, "I do not yet know where my Nineveh is, but I sure know the way to Tarshish." Don't we all?

B. *God is sovereign in his complete control of things.* The book of Jonah is filled with evidence of this truth. It was God who sent the mighty storm to intercept Jonah. It was God who prepared the great fish that swallowed this disobedient prophet. Jesus did not regard this as a joke or tall tale, for he used it to illustrate his own resurrection: "For as Jonah was three days and three nights in the belly of a huge fish, so the Son of Man will be three days and three nights in the heart of the earth" (Matt. 12:40 NIV). It was God who directed the fish to vomit Jonah out on dry land. It was God who gave Jonah success in his preaching in Nineveh. Jesus also used this as an illustration: "The men of Nineveh shall stand up in the judgment with this generation, and shall condemn it: for they repented at the preaching of Jonah; and behold, a greater than Jonah is here" (Matt. 12:41 ASV). It was God who prepared the gourd vine, and it was God who prepared the worm to destroy it. It was God who prepared the sultry east wind to beat upon Jonah's head. God is in control.

III. The God revealed to Jonah disciplines his own.

God repudiated absolutely Jonah's right to flee to Tarshish. He set a great tempest directly across his path to hinder his selfish purpose. He put Jonah in such a position that he was willing for his body to be used in preaching to Nineveh, though his heart was not in it and his spirit was wrong.

The New Testament teaches that whom the Lord loves, he chastens. The writer of Hebrews tells us, "Endure hardship as discipline; God is treating you as sons. For what son is not disciplined by his father?" (12:7 NIV). This same writer says, "No discipline seems pleasant at the time, but painful. Later on, however, it produces a harvest of righteousness and peace for those who have been trained by it" (12:11 NIV). We can be certain of the chastening hand of God upon us if we are disobedient in Jonah-fashion at the point of communicating his message to others.

IV. The God revealed to Jonah gives a second chance.

There is a thrilling word here: "The word of Jehovah came to Jonah the second time, saying, Arise, go unto Nineveh, that great city, and preach unto it the preaching that I bid thee" (Jonah 3:1–2 ASV). Notice carefully the writer's words. He says, "the second time." There can be no doubt. The Scriptures teach the gospel of the second chance. The God revealed to Jonah did not utterly cast him off because of his disobedience but came to him in love and grace, offering him another opportunity to serve.

And how he served! The chief city of the heathen world was startled by his voice proclaiming its overthrow: "Yet forty days, and Nineveh shall be overthrown" (3:4 ASV). All Nineveh repented at the first summons. No preaching before or since has ever accomplished such results.

God never gives up on us. Jesus described the shepherd hunting all over the mountainside for that hundredth sheep. He was unwilling to give up until he had found it. Jesus portrayed the housewife continuing her search in every crevice and cranny of the house until the lost coin was found. He pictured the father of the prodigal keeping watch until the figure of his disillusioned son appeared on the horizon. Thank God for the gospel of the second chance!

V. Above all, the God revealed to Jonah is eager and willing to save.

Jonah knew that God was merciful and willing to forgive (Jonah 4:2). The reason he disobeyed and fled to Tarshish was the fear that his preaching would be effective! "Now look what you've done!" he railed at God. "You did forgive them; and this makes me mad enough to die."

The leader of a small, impoverished country suggested a war with the United States as a solution to their problem. He said that after they had been defeated, the United States would come in and rebuild the country. But someone raised the question, "But what if we won the war?" That was Jonah's problem. With God using him, he won the war. He didn't want to, and it made him angry!

In its own context, the message of Jonah strikes at the narrow nationalist spirit of religious exclusiveness that characterized the Jewish people after the exile. This spirit, vividly portrayed by Jonah, is severely criticized by the overall impact of the book. God is eager and willing to save all people.

Conclusion

The book of Jonah is also for our times. The book ends abruptly, leaving Jonah "as mad as a wet hen" out there on a hill above Nineveh, with his blistered bald head and his withered gourd vine. Why doesn't the book tell us what this very minor prophet did, or what became of him? That problem was not the writer's; it is the reader's problem. That problem is ours—yours and mine. The question is: Are we willing to face the embarrassment of real religion? Are we willing to allow the battle for spiritual values to be a real war within ourselves? If not, what then?

WEDNESDAY EVENING, FEBRUARY 13

Title: The Mind of Christ

Text: "'For who has known the mind of the Lord that he may instruct him?' But we have the mind of Christ" **(1 Cor. 2:16 NIV).**

Scripture Reading: 1 Corinthians 2:9–16

Introduction

It is odd but interesting how minds are directed toward the same thing. In a small town the Methodist and Baptist churches were on adjoining blocks.

Each had a bulletin board on the street in front of the church building. On successive Sundays each pastor used exactly the same subject for his sermon. It just may be that each pastor "had the mind of Christ." That is the subject of this message.

I. The need of a scriptural analysis is evident.

A. *The text of the message is the first consideration.* The context of the passage is a contrast between those who are spiritually minded and those who are not. In the text itself, a reference is made to Isaiah 40:13: "Who has understood the mind of the LORD, or instructed him as his counselor?" Our text goes on to affirm that believers are able to discern the things of the Lord because they possess the mind of Christ.

B. *Philippians 2:5 commands that the believer have the mind of Christ.* "Let this mind be in you, which was also in Christ Jesus." One will notice this context is similar to 1 Corinthians 2:16. Here it refers to one's attitude. The right and wrong attitudes are contrasted. Philippians 2:2 speaks of love, and verse 3 speaks of lowliness of mind. The contrast in attitudes is seen in verse 3, where the attitude of strife or vainglory is prohibited.

C. *First Peter 4:1 commands believers to arm themselves with the same mind as Christ.* The context here is to have the mind of Christ as it relates suffering to sin. Jesus suffered in the flesh to redeem the sinner. The believer is to be willing to suffer as Christ suffered.

II. The need of determining what was the mind of Jesus is also evident.

A. *The one basic purpose of the Lord Jesus during his earthly life was to do the will of the Father.* "For I came down from heaven, not to do mine own will, but the will of him that sent me" (John 6:38). He prayed, "Not my will, but yours be done" (Luke 22:42 NIV). He made frequent references to his and his Father's relationship (John 15:1–8). Those who have the mind of Christ will have as their chief purpose in life the will of God.

B. *In doing the will of God, Jesus was busy serving humankind.* "The Son of man came not to be ministered unto, but to minister, and to give his life a ransom for many" (Matt. 20:28). A close study of Jesus' life reveals it was totally dedicated to service.

C. *The New Testament reveals several characteristics of Jesus as he did God's will by serving others.* These characteristics were compassion, humility, and suffering.

III. The need of determining some reasons for having the mind of Christ is evident.

A. *Each person is able to determine right or wrong because of this mind.* The Holy Spirit is at work enlightening the mind. The person who has the mind of Christ will be involved in serving others under the leadership of the Holy Spirit.

B. *The spiritual person is superior to others who attempt to give instructions.* The Spirit knows about all relationships at all times and the ultimate consequences. When a believer acts in this light, he or she has a fuller and more meaningful life.

Conclusion

To have the mind of Christ, you will not only think like him but also act like him. This is life's greatest achievement.

SUNDAY MORNING, FEBRUARY 17

Title: The Angry Jesus

Text: "Making a whip of cords, he drove them all, with the sheep and oxen, out of the temple; and he poured out the coins of the money-changers and overturned their tables. And he told those who sold the pigeons, 'Take these things away; you shall not make my Father's house a house of trade'" (**John 2:15–16 RSV**).

Scripture Reading: John 2:13–22

Hymns: "Immortal Invisible, God Only Wise," Smith
        "Oh, Worship the King," Grant
        "Brethren, We Have Met to Worship," Atkins
        "We Are Called to Be God's People," Jackson

Offertory Prayer: Lord, your blessings are full toward us. We have more than we ever thought we would have. Help us not to want more until we have learned to share what we have. When you trust us with much or little, we know we are responsible to you for the way we use all of it. A tithe of what you have provided is in our hands this morning that we might bring it to you for the doing of your work in the world. Make us loving and wise stewards of the resources you place in our hands. In Jesus' name. Amen.

Introduction

Jesus' anger is a sensitive issue. Is not anger a sin? The Scriptures admonish us to be "slow to anger" (James 1:19 RSV). The writer of Ecclesiastes warns, "Be not quick to anger, for anger lodges in the bosom of fools" (Eccl. 7:9 RSV). Paul suggests that we can be angry, but he cautions, "Do not sin; do not let the sun go down on your anger, and give no opportunity to the devil" (Eph. 4:26–27 RSV). Anger in itself is not an inappropriate emotion. Jerome, the early church father, said, "The greatest anger of all is when God is no longer angry with us when we sin." For God to give up on his people is a far greater terror than for him to show his anger toward us. We can be grateful that "the Lord is gracious and merciful, slow to anger and abounding in steadfast love" (Ps. 145:8 RSV; see also Num. 14:18; Neh. 9:17).

Anger is a characteristic of the eternal God, and it is one evidence of a healthy personality. But it must be a disciplined emotion, harnessed and carefully directed against evil wherever it is found. Aristotle observed that it is easy to become angry, but to be angry with the right person to the right degree at the right time for the right purpose in the right way—that is not easy.

When Jesus came to the Jerusalem temple, he was moved by zeal for the house of the Lord (John 2:17). In his anger he drove out the exploiters of God's people using a cord he had made with his own hands (v. 15). What made our Lord so angry? Shouldn't we be watchful so that we do not fall guilty to the same sin that so exercised Jesus' anger?

I. Jesus was angry with those who were content for evil things to remain as they were.

The people Jesus drove from the temple were a part of the religious establishment. They should have known better. But they had fallen into compromise and then into eager cooperation with the exploitation of the pilgrim worshipers who came by the thousands each day to the temple. Two groups felt his wrath that day: the moneychangers and the sacrifice inspectors. They had turned the house of the Lord into "a tourist trap," "a hideout for thieves," a merchandise mart, a house for barter and trade.

The moneychangers were at the temple to perform a useful function: to change the coins of the provinces that bore the graven image of an animal or man into coins suitable to pay the taxes to support the temple worship. The moneychangers had the pilgrims at their mercy. A man's temple tax amounted to two day's wages. The moneychangers would exact another day's wages just for the changing of the money, a 50-percent profit.

The sacrifice inspectors also took advantage of the worshipers. Many people would bring their own turtledoves or lambs for the sacrifice. But if the offerings did not pass the careful examination of the inspector as to their suitability for sacrifice, the owners had to buy a costly replacement from the temple stock. Of course, the animals kept in the temple corral were not examined with the same care. In the trading back and forth, the sacrifice inspectors were making fat profits from their dishonest double standard of inspection.

Our Lord's anger flamed out at these temple thieves, for they not only exploited the people, they were also content to allow things to stay as they were. The prostitution of worship did not trouble them. Injustice was rampant. The moneychangers treated sacred things and feelings with contempt in their rush to line their money pouches with unfair gain.

When God's people see injustice flourish and indecent gain made from the things of God yet do not speak out, then watch for the anger of God. His wrath is kindled against those who are willing to look the other way.

II. Jesus was angry with those who would not pray when they came to God's house.

The three other gospels place the cleansing of the temple at the last of Jesus' ministry rather than at the first as does John. It is not clear whether there were two cleansings of the temple or one cleansing placed by the gospel writers in different chronological order. It is entirely possible that there were two. A moment's reflection reminds us that cleansing temples is not a once-and-for-all job. Like washing dishes, or the need for revival in the church, it must happen again and again. It is likely that before the day was over, the people were back in business. If so, it is not unlikely that Jesus met them again at the close of his ministry with the same anger and hurt in his heart.

Each of the synoptic gospels records that Jesus' anger was in part a reaction to their callous willingness to turn the "house of prayer" into a "den of robbers" (Luke 19:46 RSV). Anyone who comes often to the house of worship needs to be careful not to handle sacred moments with disdain, indifference, or preoccupation with other matters.

What do you do when you come to the house of prayer? Are you more concerned with who sits beside you than you are with getting in touch with God? Do you pray here or do you purposely maintain the barriers between you and God? Are you determined to tune out God and refuse to answer him lest before you know it he has rearranged the furniture in your life? This is a place to pray. Be alert. For God comes in judgment and anger to overturn the tables of our lives, spill our plans on the floor, and call us to worship him!

III. Jesus was angry with those who tied all their religion to a building and to religious rituals.

Surely John's account of the cleansing of the temple at the first of our Lord's ministry is a way of announcing that the end is seen from the beginning. Jesus had come to offer his body as the temple of God (John 2:19–21). He would say to the woman at the well, "The hour is coming when neither on this mountain nor in Jerusalem will you worship the Father. The true worshipers will worship the Father in spirit and truth" (4:21, 23 RSV).

It is not buildings or rituals that finally bring us to God. They may help; they often intrude. But in Jesus, a new day has dawned, the kingdom of God is arriving, and the people of God are to be watching and open to what is about to happen all around them.

A building must never be a substitute for the worship of God. It is only the wrapping that surrounds us as we worship the God who is above all buildings made with hands. Neither can our rituals substitute themselves for God. Anytime a person relies on baptism or church membership for security in God, he or she has worshiped at the wrong altar.

59

Conclusion

God chastens us, not because he doesn't love us, but precisely because he does love us. He moves against us at any place where we exploit or agree to the manipulation of others for personal gain. He is determined to break into our business-as-usual attendance in this place and call us to genuine prayer. He is unwilling to leave us to counterfeit worship or second-rate religion. Of all the things we have to be thankful to God for, don't forget to thank him that he cares enough to become angry with us.

SUNDAY EVENING, FEBRUARY 17

Title: Micah—The Requirements of Real Religion

Text: "He hath shewed thee, O man, what is good; and what doth the LORD require of thee, but to do justly, and to love mercy, and to walk humbly with thy God?" (**Mic. 6:8**).

Scripture Reading: Micah 6:1–8

Introduction

Today you may see our text on the wall in a conspicuous place in the halls of the Library of Congress. Years ago Charles W. Eliot, then president of Harvard University, who had suggested this inscription, said, "Nothing in the history of literature is more worthy than these words from the prophet Micah." There they stand, as true in the twentieth century as when they were first written in the eighth century B.C. Certainly these words are the high-water mark of the prophecy.

Called "the herald of the morn," Micah preached against the sins and injustices of his time in an effort to turn the hearts of his people back to God. He also foretold the coming of "the Anointed One," the Messiah. When King Herod, disturbed by the coming of the Magi seeking the newborn King of the Jews, asked the chief priests and scribes of the people "where Christ should be born" (Matt. 2:4), they answered, "In Bethlehem of Judaea" (Matt. 2:5), and cited Micah 5:2 as their proof text. Moreover, Micah prophesied peace to come as he dreamed of the time when swords would be fashioned into plowshares and spears into pruning hooks and nations would not learn war any more (4:3).

Unlike Isaiah, who was of royal birth and "to the manor born," Micah was "of the people...and for the people," crying out against the oppression of the poor and fighting their battles. His work was carried out during the reigns of Jotham, Ahaz, and Hezekiah, kings of Judah, but principally in the time of Hezekiah.

This book of seven chapters may be divided into three parts. Chapters 1–3 deal with the social conditions of his time. He pointed out the parallel with conditions in Samaria before it fell in 722 B.C. Chapters 4–5 show the pitiable state of the nation, with the people scattered like shepherdless sheep. But in God's providence a divine Shepherd would be raised up. The Messiah would come (5:2). Chapters 6–7 expound the nature of real religion. Though God's purposes are hindered by human folly, God is neither frustrated nor defeated. God and righteousness will prevail.

Micah 6 presents a controversy between God and his people. In verses 1–5 we hear God's protest as he calls the mountains to witness and appeals to history. His experience with his people ought to have awakened gratitude and resulting obedience. In verses 6–7 we hear a question raised that is really their objection to God's charge. They had worshiped faithfully, but their observance had been formal, not from the heart; and God was not pleased. What then would please him? Verse 8 gives the answer: "He hath shewed thee, O man, what is good; and what doth the LORD require of thee, but to do justly, and to love mercy, and to walk humbly with thy God?"

How that question needs to be sounded loud and clear today! The prophet's question is not "What can I get from God?" but "What does the Lord require of me?" The threefold answer to the question sets forth "the requirements of real religion." Micah starts at the outer rim and moves toward the center.

I. The prophet says, "Real religion requires justice in our dealings."

"What doth the LORD require of thee, but *to do justly?*" Our lives must manifest the character of God in all our relationships with others. There must be no inconsistency between our inner life and our open profession, between our worship of God in his temple and our dealings with our fellows in the marketplace. Both Isaiah (1:14–15) and Amos (5:21–24), whom Micah resembles, tell us that religion that does not produce exalted concepts and standards of morality in the individual, and social justice and righteousness in society, is not genuine. Genuine religion and social injustice never march together.

This message was needed in Micah's day, when judges were bought with bribes; when merchants used two sets of weights, one to buy and another to sell; when the rich pillaged the poor but were devout in religious observances. This is not religion, but a gaudy burlesque of the real thing.

This message is needed in our day too. In the mid-twentieth century there was a great upsurge in church attendance in the United States. Unfortunately, however, the effects were not seen in a higher standard of morality nor in a deeper sense of social ethics. That religious upsurge was like someone's description of the Pecos River in Texas: "a mile wide and a foot deep."

Some years ago, speaking to two thousand Methodist ministers at Duke University, the publisher of a newsweekly made a fervent appeal for moral and ethical foundations for our modern society. It was a good speech, though the speaker was rough on those ministers and made strident demands upon the churches. But when I counted the number of column inches of liquor advertisement in the very issue of his magazine that carried the report of his address, I thought, *Who is he to be preaching to preachers about the ethical and moral foundations of our society when for "blood money" he is using his powerful news medium to dig them down?*

II. But moving closer in, the prophet says, "Real religion requires love for mercy and kindness."

"And what doth the LORD require of thee, but to do justly, and *to love mercy?*" As already indicated, these requirements are presented in inverted order as the prophet begins at the outer rim and moves in toward the center. Justice in our outward dealings is based on love of justice and mercy and kindness in our hearts. We are to love the right for right's sake. Religion is character, the character of God in the human being.

In his second epistle Peter describes religion in terms of our being partakers of the divine nature (1:4). If we have God's nature in us, we will love the things he loves; and our God is a God of mercy. Our deeds are an expression of our character. If we love mercy, if we love the right, if we love what God loves, our lives will reflect it. Christian character will exhibit itself; and it is required if religion is to be real religion.

Christian character, the character of God planted in people, is the need of the hour. This is necessary in individual lives, in church life, in government, in business, in education, in all the affairs and realms of the world's life.

One of the most dramatic and emotional scenes in the Old Testament is Samuel's valedictory, his farewell address, after the king had covered himself with glory in the defeat of the Ammonites and the old man at last realized that he must step down. Before all Israel he said, "I have walked before you from my youth unto this day. Here I am: witness against me before Jehovah, and before his anointed" (1 Sam. 12:2–3 ASV). And no one witnessed against him! What was Samuel's secret? How had this one man been able to draw Israel back to God? Through the integrity of his character. Let it be so among us.

III. Coming directly to the heart of the matter, the prophet says, "Real religion requires a genuine experience with God in our hearts."

"What doth the LORD require of thee, but to do justly, and to love mercy, and *to walk humbly with thy God?*" This speaks of an experience with God, an experience growing into an intimate fellowship.

In that dismal list of "begets" in Genesis 5 we find this precious jewel: "Enoch walked with God" (v. 24). These five words are a wonderful biography of a man who knew God and daily increased in his knowledge and likeness until "God took him" to be with himself.

The only way to make a relationship meaningful and real is to spend time in its cultivation. United with God through Christian experience, coming to know God through Jesus Christ, we grow into his likeness as we walk with him, not hurriedly or reluctantly, but humbly.

Conclusion

The refrain of a song we sing may give the wrong idea. We sing:

> *And he walks with me, and he talks with me,*
> *And he tells me I am his own.*

This could be the wrong approach. We are not to demand that God walk with us. Let us make sure that we walk with him, that we find out where he is going and go with him.

WEDNESDAY EVENING, FEBRUARY 20

Title: Things Freely Given Us

Text: "Now we have received, not the spirit of the world, but the spirit which is of God; that we might know the things that are freely given to us of God" (**1 Cor. 2:12**).

Scripture Reading: 1 Corinthians 2:12–16

Introduction

An unusual story was recounted many years ago in a book by Paul S. James entitled *They Gave Their Blood for Their Church*. It seems a church building in Minnesota was in need of some remodeling and repair. The congregation voted to spend $1,900 for the job. The work started, but as it progressed, costs soared. It became apparent to the pastor that some plan was necessary to meet the added expense, and he proposed one that was startlingly unique.

Every three months the pastor and the twenty-two members who responded to his challenge made a trip to the Mayo Clinic in Rochester, Minnesota, where each sold a pint of blood for $25. The church netted more that $2,000 through this enterprise. They were literally paying for their church with their own blood.

Blood, James stated, has always been the life of the church. Christ gave his precious blood for it. "The blood of the martyrs is the seed of the church." Across the centuries the church has flourished in proportion to the sacrifice and dedication of God's people. The present hour calls upon each of us to give nothing less than oneself in a new surrender to Christ and his church"

The subject for this message is "Things Freely Given Us."

I. First, let us look at today's passage.

A. *The meaning of the word "freely" in 1 Corinthians 2:12 means "bestowed."* It is to be distinguished from the word "freely" found in Matthew 10:8, which reads, "Freely ye have received, freely give."

The primary idea of the word here is the spirit of giving, or the spirit in which a thing is given. God's gifts are not given grudgingly, nor with resentment, nor of necessity. They are freely given blessings from heaven, agonies of earth, and blood of life.

B. *Grace is unmerited favor.* "He that spared not his own Son, but delivered him up for us all, how shall he not with him also freely give us all things?" (Rom. 8:32). "For if the inheritance be of the law, it is no more of promise: but God gave it to Abraham by promise (Gal. 3:18). All gifts of God are "without money and without price" (Isa. 55:1).

II. Second, look at the variation of people who are offered God's gifts.

A. *Some people resent the idea of God's giving his Son the way he did.* They feel so secure within themselves that receiving a gift as described in this text is an unheard of thing. These people are lost.

B. *All people need to see that God's giving of his Son is God's plan for our redemption from sin and ruin.* God's redemption would be unfair if it were not free, for some would not be able to purchase it. If it were not free, think how a lost person would feel. This redemption cost Jesus his blood, and there have been many martyrs for his cause since.

C. *All who receive these God's gifts must count the cost of discipleship.* Although we cannot earn or buy our own salvation, which is a free gift from God, we are called upon to commit our lives in Christian living and service. The Christian is to be separated from the things of the world and consecrated to the things of God.

III. Third, look at the Spirit of God who reveals God's gifts to each person.

A. *God's gifts are "freely given," but the recipient is not to take them for granted.* No person is to believe he or she is the recipient of any gift because of merit or worth. The giving is according to the sovereign will and plan of God.

B. *The gifts carry with them responsibility.* The gospel, about which Paul talked earlier in this passage, is to be shared. The good news of Jesus is the privilege and responsibility of God's children to share. Believers are to bear the expense of spreading the gospel.

Conclusion

If you are a Christian, you have been bountifully blessed. You have many gifts bestowed on you. Now you must use them.

SUNDAY MORNING, FEBRUARY 24

Title: Look What Love Does

Text: "For God so loved the world that he gave his only Son, that whoever believes in him should not perish but have eternal life" **(John 3:16 RSV).**

Scripture Reading: John 3:16–21

Hymns: "Love Divine, All Loves Excelling," Wesley
"He Included Me," Oatman
"O, Love That Wilt Not Let Me Go," Matheson

Offertory Prayer: Heavenly Father, we pray that you will be able to receive our offering without pain or embarrassment. We have been greatly loved by you. Our offerings are an expression of our love for you. If anyone has brought less than a gift of love, help him or her not to give it. We have not come to offer a tip to you for services rendered, but an expression of our love. We give what love we can give, and so, dear Lord, accept our lives as well as our gifts of money. Because we love you, Lord, what we bring we bring with cheerful hearts. Through Jesus Christ our Lord. Amen.

Introduction

The man was angry. He muttered to the deacon on his way out of church, "Give, give, give. That's all that preacher knows to talk about!" The deacon called him back and said, "John, I want to thank you. That's one of the best definitions of Christian love I have ever heard."

Right at the heart of this great text is the word "gave." It is the word that expresses what love does. "For God so loved the world that he gave...." Look at what love does.

I. Love gives another chance to the creation.

Like the Bible itself, John 3:16 begins with God. "In the beginning God created" the world and all that is in it. The story of God's love is that he was not content to create a world without beings who could respond to him. He did not want to live in an empty universe alone. So from a love that reached out to bring into being those who could be loved and love in return, God created man and woman. God was willing to cease being everything in order that we could be something.

But all too soon it was clear that human love was flawed. Humankind would not love back with the same devotion and trust God had given them. Mistrust, disobedience, and pride entered the human family, and suddenly life was out of joint. The humans went into hiding.

God did not give up on his creation. He came searching for the man and the woman. The story of Jesus is that God never really found us as he wanted to until he "so loved the world that he gave his only Son." And Jesus came and found us. God has found us in Jesus, not to cast us out of the garden, but to bring us in; not to condemn, but to save (John 3:17).

II. Love gives compassion to all the world.

At unbelievable cost, God's love comes fully to us. He poured all his love out upon us. The warmth of his devotion came cascading down to us in Jesus Christ, the Son. Every religion that talks about sacrifice speaks of the sacrifice that people bring to their god, seeking to appease him and to justify themselves. But not the Christian faith. The Christian gospel states that there is nothing people can offer to God in exchange for their soul (Mark 8:37).

God has himself provided the sacrifice. Jesus is not man's best gift offered to God; he is God's best gift offered to man. God himself has become the sacrifice of atonement. He died in our place, holding nothing back. He emptied his heart, and the love drained out.

Who did the love cover? "Whoever believes in him." God loves the world, not just a certain part of it. His love for the whole world is forever a judgment on our petty prejudices. God's love reaches beyond the outer limits of our telescopes. It reaches down to include the most humble and forgotten person anywhere on the earth.

When the church prays for its missionaries scattered around the world, it is praying with the certainty that God intends for all people to be reached and wants every person to be saved. And in our hands, which have been richly blessed, he has placed the responsibility to go to all people everywhere. Our love will cause us to give our lives as he has given his.

III. Love gives attention to our response.

One of the evidences of God's love is that he pays attention to us and seriously considers our response to his love given freely, but painfully, to us in Jesus Christ. "Believing" in this text means trusting with the whole heart, holding nothing back, casting all that we are in faith upon Jesus Christ. We believe he will save us from death, deliver us from hell, rescue us from the punishment that is due to fall upon our sin (Rom. 6:23). He who believes in Jesus has no other hope. If he drops us, we are lost; if he forgets us, we are alone; if he fails us, we are helpless. Believing in Jesus is trusting that he will hold nothing back. He will be faithful to us and bring us finally home.

Believing is our greatest act of response to God's love (John 3:16, 18). No work of worship or service comes before believing. We can do good all our lives and fail to please God if we turn our backs on his Son. Love for others and ministry to the world is the healthy and necessary response that believers make to the needs around them (John 3:21). But nothing substitutes for believing. God requires us to believe (John 3:18).

IV. Love gives us cause for celebration.

As God's love touches us and we are delivered from death, we are released from fear. We are brought from the darkness to the light (John 3:21). We have cause for celebration.

The promise that we have eternal life (3:16) is the antidote to the poisonous fear people feel when they face eternity without the assurance that they will go to heaven when they die. This terrifying fear comes upon unbelievers at strange and solemn moments when they are suddenly confronted with their doubts and uncertainties about the meaning of their life and the eternal destiny of their soul. And well it might. For without Christ people are dying without hope, perishing without God.

God's promise of eternal life is not only the antidote to our fear, it is the elixir of joy. It is the cup of celebration. The lively and joyful hope of the Christian believer is that eternal life has been given to us now and we may live rejoicing in it today. Eternal life is a new kind of life—Jesus calls it abundant life (John 10:10)—which God intends to bring about in us now. And that kind of life is worth living forever. Eternal life is not just living forever with God; it is living God's kind of life forever, beginning now.

One lovely Christian said it this way, "All the way to heaven is heaven because Jesus said, 'I am the way'" (see John 14:6). When we walk with Jesus, we have light all the way.

> *Shadows around me, shadows above me,*
> *Never conceal my Savior and guide;*
> *He is the light, in him is no darkness;*
> *Ever I'm walking close to his side.*
>
> *Heavenly sunlight, heavenly sunlight*
> *Flooding my soul with glory divine:*
> *Hallelujah, I am rejoicing,*
> *Singing his praises, Jesus is mine.*
>
> —"Heavenly Sunlight," H. J. Zelley

Conclusion

Look what love does. It gives and gives and gives yet more. God's love gives his creation a second chance. God's compassion reaches out to all the world and gives us an invitation. And then God gives attention to our faithful response. He gives us cause for celebration, for he has removed our fear and given us life with him now and forever! Come! Believe in him. And prepare to go in joy!

SUNDAY EVENING, FEBRUARY 24

Title: Nahum—Woe to the Bloody City!

Text: "Woe to the bloody city, full of lies, full of plunder, never without victims!" (**Nah. 3:1** NIV).

Scripture Reading: Nahum 2:8–3:7

Introduction

When the Romans finally conquered Carthage in 146 B.C., they razed the city, thoroughly plowed the site, and sowed it with salt. The spot where the city stood, however, has been well known from that day to this. Not so Nineveh! Its destruction was so complete that even the site was forgotten. So completely had all traces of the glory of the Assyrian empire disappeared that many scholars actually thought the references to it in the Bible and in ancient histories were mythical. They thought that in reality no such city or empire ever existed. It was not until 1845 that the site was definitely identified and the ruins began to be uncovered. The library of Assurbanipal in the palace of Sennacherib, originally containing one hundred thousand volumes, is one of the most important archaeological discoveries ever made. Its wealth of material about Assyrian and Babylonian history serve to confirm much of the Bible record.

Nahum seems bent on self-concealment; and in this he fairly well succeeds. The term "Elkoshite" (1:1) has little meaning for us. We are not told his family, his tribe, or even his nation, though he was undoubtedly from Judah. He wrote sometime between 663 B.C., when Assyria conquered Egypt, and 609 B.C., when Assyria was defeated by Babylon. This was perhaps a hundred years after Jonah had delivered God's message to Nineveh, the capital of Assyria.

The prophecy of Nahum is given to one subject alone—the destruction of Nineveh, capital of Assyria, which is used as a synonym for the entire nation. For the most part this prophecy is pure poetry. This poem of three strophes, which correspond exactly with the chapter divisions, can be summarized in five words: "Woe to the bloody city" (3:1). Unlike others among the prophets, Nahum has not a word to say about Judah's sins. His only references to Judah are words of encouragement, for the destruction of Nineveh will mean deliverance for Judah (1:12–13, 15; 2:2).

In language that is forcible and graphic, the prophet's descriptions are condensed and brilliant. Chapter 1 consists of a question and its answer. The question: "Who can stand before God's indignation?" (v. 6; see vv. 1–6). The answer: "He will make an utter end of the enemies of his people" (v. 15; see vv. 7–15).

Chapter 2 is made up of a threefold description: the siege and defense of the city (vv. 1–5); the capture and sack of the city (vv. 6–10); and the prophet's exultation over the destruction of the ancient den of lions (vv. 11–13), meaning the king and his cohorts.

Chapter 3 is constructed, at least by implication, around four questions: "Who will mourn for [fallen Nineveh]?" (v. 7; see vv. 1–7). "Are you better than Thebes, situated on the Nile, with water around her? The river was her defense, the waters her wall" (v. 8 NIV; see vv. 8–15). Nahum writes that the surrounding nations will rejoice when Nineveh falls. He declares, "Everyone who hears the news about you claps his hands at your fall, for who has not felt your endless cruelty?" (v. 19 NIV; see vv. 16–19).

The book of Nahum is no mere cry of joy over the ruin of Israel's enemy. Nahum is not simply a nationalist exulting over the ruin of his nation's oppressor. He is a prophet with a prophet's deep conviction that the power of God is ruling in all the turmoil of history. It is a hymn of praise for a great manifestation of the power and justice and mercy of the true God. What then, has this little book to say to us in our day? Three things are clear.

I. Militarism is not the way to solve the problems of history.

Thebes is destroyed by the Assyrians; the Assyrians are destroyed by the Babylonians and their allies; the Babylonians are destroyed by the Persians; and so on. When Peter attempted to defend his Lord with a sword, Jesus warned him, "All they that take the sword shall perish with the sword" (Matt. 26:52).

Whenever a mighty nation, becoming rich and powerful by violating the principles of justice, freedom, and right, has appeared on the stage of history, this principle has been demonstrated. The empires of the Caesars, of Charlemagne, and of Napoleon had the elements of decay at the core even in the hour of their brutality and bloodshed. Their end was inevitable.

By military might and tyranny among his own people, Adolf Hitler brought into being his Third Reich, which he predicted would stand a thousand years. "Woe to the bloody city!" He committed suicide in Berlin on April 30, 1945. Napoleon, who bathed the continent of Europe in blood for nearly two decades met his end at Waterloo on June 18, 1815. Genghis Khan conquered Mongolia in 1205 and then most of China, followed by conquests of Turkistan, Transoxania (modern Uzbekistan), and Afghanistan. He even penetrated southeastern Europe. Upon his death, his sons, who succeeded him, started back to Mongolia to regroup. From last reports, they had not returned.

Militarism creates most of the problems of history; it solves none. Trying to solve the world's problems by war is like trying to arrange the household furniture by using a stick of dynamite.

II. Tyranny ultimately recruits the opposition by which it will be destroyed.

Nineveh was really a complex of four cities in one, protected by the confluence of two rivers and a system of moats. It had a one-hundred-foot-high wall broad enough for three chariots to be driven abreast and fortified with fifteen hundred towers, each two hundred feet high. The whole area covered 350 square miles. But the vastness of Nineveh was overshadowed by its wickedness. Nineveh's brutality toward the victims of its conquests was enough to make the blood run cold. Surrounding peoples shuddered with horror at the thought of ever being prey to Nineveh. Its mania for blood and savagery was gruesome. Nahum confirms this as he drags out to view the violence, murder, witchcraft, whoredom, and vile corruption within the harlot city (3:1–7). God's word to Nineveh is, "I will make thy grave; for thou art vile" (1:14). How will he do this? By recruiting all those who have been oppressed by "the bloody city."

A combined policy on the part of those who had been humiliated by the Assyrian conquerors brought about Nineveh's downfall. Forming a compact with nations that had long been tributary to Assyria, Nabopolassar of Babylon headed the conspiracy. Egypt, Media, and Persia joined him. Other peoples joined this confederacy against the common foe. The enemy surrounded Nineveh but were at first driven back. Reinforcements came, and the city was again attacked. The siege lasted two years, for the defenders were valiant. But a new foe, against which they were powerless, had to be reckoned with. The Tigris River, overflowing its banks, undermined and finally swept away a large section of the city walls that had for so long resisted the besiegers (2:6). When the flood subsided, the enemy crossed the river and poured through the gap into the city, and Nineveh was no more.

Page after page of history demonstrates the truth that tyranny ultimately recruits the opposition by which it is destroyed. Search and see.

III. God is the sole ruler of the universe.

Nahum declares his sovereignty and strength. God is jealous of his holy name, recompensing the wrongdoer, and preparing to vent his wrath upon his adversaries. Although slow to anger and so forbearing that his proffered forgiveness might be scorned by some, yet he would by no means clear the guilty. The fact of his omnipotence is beyond controversy (1:3–6).

Judah had suffered intensely at the hands of Assyria. Some godly men felt that Jehovah was no longer interested in Judah's welfare, or if he were, he was powerless to restrain the ferocity and spoliation that marked Assyrian aggression. Nahum was convinced that neither was the case. Nineveh was at the zenith of its power and splendor. The earth rang with the shouts of her armored men as they sacked cities and enslaved peoples. But could Nineveh defy Jehovah with impunity? Could the moral law be set aside indefinitely? God had not abdicated nor had his laws become inoperative. Sentence was already pronounced. Judgment would surely fall upon the ruthless oppressor. In spite of its wealth, display of military power, and strategy of its monarchs and statesmen, it will be overtaken by the righteous anger of the most high God.

Of all the minor prophets, not one seems to equal the loftiness, the fire, and the spirited boldness of Nahum. Let the people of today take a good look at Nineveh of long ago, for it is one of God's special object lessons to rulers and nations and peoples. The same God rules the world today. Nahum speaks the universal voice of humanity. Let all people hear and beware.

Conclusion

In this prophecy there is comfort for the godly. Nineveh proclaims to us the final vindication of right against the wrong; and therein is comfort. God's government is righteous. He is the stronghold of the godly.

Nahum's doom-song on Nineveh is no mere human cry for revenge, nor does it view Nineveh's coming destruction with patriotic gratification from the standpoint of his own nation and countrymen. The predicted requital is viewed solely from the requirements of divine justice. "Shall not the Judge of all the earth do right?" (Gen. 18:25).

WEDNESDAY EVENING, FEBRUARY 27

Title: God's Fellow Workers

Text: "We are God's fellow workers" (**1 Cor. 3:9** NIV).

Scripture Reading: 1 Corinthians 3:1–9

Introduction

The Holy Spirit is at work within God's church to call out laborers for the Lord's harvest. The emphasis of the text for this message is that all who serve their Lord are not just laborers with God, and God with them, but also they are laborers with one another. It is the statement, "We are God's fellow workers" that furnishes the subject for this message.

I. All Christians who are in service for God are God's fellow workers.

A. *The church has its origin in God and is maintained by him.* The Lord established the church for his purpose and declared that the gates of hell would not prevail against it (Matt. 16:18). Because of the purpose and plan of the church, he will see that it goes on and, in so doing, he will use believers as his colaborers.

B. *The Lord, in maintaining the work of the church, requires the work of his children.* If the world is to be evangelized, it must be done by trustworthy human laborers (Mark 16:20). These laborers are God's human instruments, and each one has a specific and definite responsibility to perform. This idea is found in 1 Corinthians 3:6, where Paul speaks of one person planting and another person watering. It is also found in the parable recorded in Matthew 25:14–30.

C. *The Lord, in evangelizing the world through the use of human instruments, supplies their needs.* Even though his human instruments plant and water, it is the Lord who gives the increase (1 Cor. 3:7). He also rewards according to one's labor. The Lord even supplies the teamwork to get the job done.

II. All Christians who are in service for God have their weaknesses, and this will hinder the work (1 Cor. 3:1).

A. *This is not saying that weak people cannot serve; rather, even though there are weaknesses among Christian workers, they can still be used.*

B. *Weak Christians ought to discover their weaknesses and seek to strengthen them.* People are dominated by the lower nature (v. 1). They need to reverence God and his work. Because of weaknesses and the need for the ability to work, each Christian should grow. Paul suggests ways of growth in verse 2. Food for spiritual growth includes good reading, proper fellowship, subjecting oneself to the right kind of influence, and prayer to God for help.

Another way to grow spiritually is to avoid envy and strife (1 Cor. 3:3–6). Each Christian needs to conduct his or her way of life as Christ would (1 Cor. 3:3).

III. All Christians are to rise up and meet the task of serving the Lord.

A. *Christian people are to cooperate with their spiritual leaders.* Cooperation must be grounded in confidence in the leader's judgment. To cooperate, we must have respect for our leader's training, decisions, and knowledge.

B. *Christian people are to cooperate with their peers.* Paul said he planted and Apollos watered (1 Cor. 3:6). The Lord bestows on each the spiritual gifts needed to carry on the work of the church. For the work to be done successfully, each person must do his or her own work in cooperation with others.

C. *Christian people are to consecrate, dedicate, and surrender their all to the Lord.* These actions of consecration, dedication, and surrender will offset human weaknesses and make Christians available for the Lord's use.

Conclusion

The Lord's work is vast and challenging. He has chosen you to be his partner in this work. Now work with him.

Suggested preaching program for the month of

MARCH

■ **Sunday Mornings**

Continue with the "Responding to the Living Word" series from the Gospel of John. The Palm Sunday and Easter sermons are also based on John's gospel.

■ **Sunday Evenings**

Continue the studies with the theme "Listen to the Major Messages of the Minor Prophets."

■ **Wednesday Evenings**

Continue the messages based on Paul's first letter to the Corinthian Christians.

SUNDAY MORNING, MARCH 3

Title: Either He Is or He Isn't

Text: "Therefore the Jews sought the more to kill him, because he not only had broken the sabbath, but said also that God was his Father, making himself equal with God" **(John 5:18).**

Scripture Reading: John 5:17–29 (see also vv. 30–47)

Hymns: "All Hail the Power," Perronet and Rippon
"Fairest Lord Jesus," Anonymous
"Lead Me to Calvary," Hussey

Offertory Prayer: Dear Lord and Father, we have come to seek you today. We are thankful that you have sought us first. We bring our offerings to you for your use and work. But we give to you, in response to your already giving to us. Seeking or giving, loving or finding, we are the tardy ones. You first sought us and gave to us; you loved us before we could love you, and you found us before we found you. Accept, O Lord, our praise and our gifts. In love we bring both. Amen.

Introduction

Occasionally people will say, "I can't accept anything by faith. I have to have reasons for believing." Theology has sometimes been defined as "faith seeking understanding." No Christian would deny that we are saved by faith, but not by faith in faith. We respond to God's gift of salvation by putting faith

73

in Jesus Christ as the Son of God and Savior of the world. Contrary to popular belief, Christianity is not based on "blind faith"; we have reasons for believing in Jesus Christ. Thus, there is such a thing as a "reasonable faith."

The highest task a preacher of the gospel has is to proclaim Jesus Christ as God's Son, given to us for our eternal salvation, and then to ask for decisions from every hearer as to what he or she will do with that knowledge.

At the end of Jesus' earthly life, the Roman governor Pilate asked the crowd, "What shall I do then with Jesus?" (Matt. 27:22). Essentially, that is the question every person must face. And there can be no half-hearted decision. For, as our Scripture reading makes clear, Jesus claims to be the Son who "gives life to whom he will" (John 5:21 RSV). The Jews were ready to kill him precisely because they understood that he was claiming God as his Father, "making himself equal with God" (5:18). Jesus pointedly says, "He who hears my word and believes him who sent me, has eternal life; he does not come into judgment, but has passed from death to life" (John 5:24 RSV).

The issue must be faced squarely. Either Jesus is the Son of God and we must praise him, or he is a liar and deceiver and you are free, even wise, to walk away from him. If that radical choice shakes you, then you understand a little bit of what the Jews felt that day when Jesus would not back away from his startling announcement, "My Father is working still, and I am working" (John 5:17 RSV). "The Father judges no one, but has given all judgment to the Son, that all may honor the Son, even as they honor the Father. He who does not honor the Son does not honor the Father who sent him" (John 5:22–23 RSV).

Pantheists—those who find God in everything—or idolaters who create with their own hands gods for every occasion would have no problem with what Jesus was saying. The god issue for them is very diverse and cheapened by its easy multiplication. But these men and Jesus himself were Jews. The Jews had come painfully to a bedrock conviction that "the LORD our God is one LORD" (Deut. 6:4). They were strict monotheists who knew from their history the awful results of idolatry. For Jesus to claim to be God's Son in a unique and unrepeatable way was either blasphemy or miracle of the highest order. There could be no middle ground.

And you will either decide to come to him and follow him as God's Son, or you will decide to walk away from him, rejecting his claim to be the giver of life. If you walk away, you will face the judgment God has placed in his hands (John 5:25–27).

Jesus does not simply say that he is the Son of man (a messianic title) and Son of God and expect the people to believe it because he said it (John 5:25, 27). He offers witnesses to the truth of his claim.

I. Witnesses Jesus could call to establish his unique place as God's Son (John 5:30–47).

Jesus presents three witnesses as evidence of the integrity of his claims.

A. *John the Baptist has testified on Jesus' behalf (John 5:31–35).* The power of this witness is the courage and integrity that surround the ministry of John. Everyone knew he was a truth teller at whatever cost to himself (see Matt. 14:3–4). In front of the crowds who came to hear him, he had not minced his words or sought to soothe. Like a hot iron his words had pressed the weighty judgment of God down on the minds of the people. John had been the first to see and understand. "Behold, the Lamb of God, who takes away the sin of the world! This is the Son of God" (John 1:29, 34 RSV). And then John did what no other preacher I have ever known could do gracefully: he turned his congregation over to someone else! He said of Jesus, he "ranks before me, for he was before me" (John 1:30 RSV). "He must increase, but I must decrease" (John 3:30).

B. *The mighty works Jesus did also bear witness to Jesus' authenticity (John 5:36).* No magician could do the works Jesus did. He had turned water into wine and signified the new joy he was bringing to life (John 2:1–11). He had told a woman all about her life and given to her living water that brought a joy she had never known (John 4:1–42). Jesus healed a man sick for thirty-eight years (John 5:1–9). He would feed the multitude from a small shared lunch (John 6:5–14), and he would raise a man dead for four days to life (John 11:1–44). Every mighty work was a sign that brought people into an awareness of God's extravagant love for them. These mighty works Jesus offered as a witness to the truth of his claims.

C. *Jesus next cites the witness of the Father himself through the Scriptures (John 5:37–40).* The messianic prophecies of the prophets were often used by early Christian preachers as evidence of Jesus' messiahship. But here Jesus pushes back past the traditional prophets to Moses—the lawgiver himself—the most important religious person in Jewish history. Jesus claims Moses' witness in the Scripture as God's witness to the truth of Jesus' claim to be God's Son. "If you believed Moses, you would believe me, for he wrote of me" (5:46 RSV). Jesus is the seed of the woman who shall indeed bruise the head of the evil one (see Gen. 3:15). Jesus is the fulfillment of the law (Matt. 5:17–18).

Jesus sought to move the faith and worship of the people past the written Word to the living Word, past the Scriptures to the one whom the Scriptures bear witness to. He is the Savior in whom there is eternal life (John 5:24, 39–40). And more can now be added to Jesus' claim.

II. Additional witnesses we can call forth today to establish Jesus' unique place as God's Son.

A. *History.* We have the advantage of two thousand years of experience with the life and teachings of Jesus. The historical argument points to what it has meant to the world that Jesus lived among us. An anonymous poet wrote:

He was born in an obscure village. He worked in a carpenter shop until he was thirty. Then for three years he became an itinerant preacher....

Nineteen centuries have come and gone, and today he is the central figure of the human race. All the armies that ever marched, all the navies that ever sailed, all the parliaments that ever sat, all the kings that ever reigned have not affected the life of man on this earth as much as that one solitary life.

B. *Jesus' life.* There was a wonderful harmony in Jesus' life between what he taught and how he lived, what he said and what he did. One of the awful hurts in a sensitive person's life is the difference between what he wants to be and what he is, between what he knows to be right and what he actually is able to do. In Jesus, what he dreamed to be, he was; what he said was true, he proved out. Jesus said a seed must fall to the ground and die if it is to live, and then he went to the cross and offered himself in death for us. When he said you must love God as you love nothing else, he found that a loving and obedient heart would take him to the cross. "Not my will, but thine, be done" (Luke 22:42). He said you must love your enemies. As he hung on the cross dying, he prayed, "Father, forgive them; for they know not what they do" (Luke 23:34). The ability to fulfill the vision, to live completely as one teaches, is an evidence worthy of your careful consideration.

C. *The church.* The life of the church after the crucifixion of Jesus would lead one to believe Jesus was much more than an ordinary man. If Jesus had not been raised from the dead, there would have been no impetus for the church to live. The disciples were defeated and disheartened until Jesus appeared to them after the resurrection to empower them and send them forth. The existence of the church—baptizing, observing the Lord's Supper, preaching the Word, and seeing lives changed—is both an ancient and a contemporary evidence to the truth of Jesus' claims.

D. *Your inner need.* Each person's life is an open testimony to the reality of Jesus' claims. He offers to meet our deepest needs. Do you experience sin and brokenness as a part of your daily experience? Do you know the dark feelings of guilt that arise not because somebody is trying to lay a guilt trip on you, but because you really are guilty? Do you know about coming to the end of the day and having no reason to live another day? Do you know about loneliness and a need for love that is frustrated again and again by counterfeit imitations of the real thing? Are you afraid to die not knowing what, if anything, lies ahead for you? Have you reached most of your goals in life but are finding with some discomfort that the goals you have achieved may not have been worth what it has cost you to achieve them?

If any of this description of human need touches you at the deep places of your life, then Jesus has come to touch and to heal you at that place.

Jesus is the one who heals our brokenness, forgives our sin, removes our guilt in his own deep acceptance of us. Jesus is our hope that gives purpose to life. It is his love for us that makes us know we are important and valuable to God. He is our eternal life, who fulfills the living of life now, who gives direction in the setting of lifelong goals, and who escorts us through dying into the full and blessed presence of the eternal God.

E.   *The Scriptures.* If you have read the Bible very much, you know that the Bible knows you. The Bible knows what is true about people. I submit that if the Bible can be so right about people, it has an excellent chance of being right about God as well.

These are arguments for you to consider, to help you see that faith is not blind but that there are reasons for believing. At the moment of truth, after you have considered the arguments, you must receive the gift of faith and choose to believe.

Conclusion

If Jesus is not God in the flesh, you are free to walk away, but if he is God in the flesh, you must believe or face the unhappy consequences of your unbelief (John 5:24–29). He either is or he isn't. You either will or you won't. You will either live or you will die. What will you choose? I urge you to believe Jesus and choose life!

SUNDAY EVENING, MARCH 3

Title: Habakkuk—The Just Shall Live by Faith

Text: "The just shall live by his faith" **(Hab. 2:4).**

Scripture Reading: Habakkuk 1:1–2:4

Introduction

A contemporary of Jeremiah, Habakkuk was a prophet during fateful days for Judah. Nineveh had been destroyed, and Babylon was in the ascendancy as the dominating world power. Josiah, Judah's last good king, was dead, and his weak and wicked son, Jehoiakim, was on the throne. Only two or three decades of Judah's existence as a nation remained when Habakkuk began to write.

Habakkuk was one of three prophets used of God to pronounce the doom of the three outstanding enemies of God's people. In the prophecy of Obadiah the fate of Edom is sealed. Nahum tolled the knell over Assyria. God showed Habakkuk that Babylon was digging her own grave. Hence, the focus of Habakkuk's problem and prophecy is Babylon.

All the prophets were conscious of divine inspiration. Their work demonstrates it. Yet this does not erase their individuality, but leaves ample room for it.

Habakkuk is unique in this respect. Unlike the other prophets, he does not address either his own countrymen or a foreign people. His words are for God alone. Autobiographical in flavor, his prophecy is primarily concerned with solving a problem. His inability to understand God's government of the nations vexed his own sensitive soul. Obviously familiar with the work of Amos and Moses, Habakkuk was bewildered by a third book that was constantly before his eyes—the Book of Life. To Habakkuk the declared promises of God, on the one hand, and the experiences of life on the other, seemed hopelessly at variance. Why did the Book of Life seem to contradict the Book of God? The trial of Habakkuk's faith sprang out of the times.

In chapter 2 (vv. 1–4) Habakkuk gets his answer in the keynote of the whole book expressed somewhat in oracular fashion by the words, "The just shall live by his faith." So significant are these words that they are quoted three times in the New Testament (Rom. 1:17; Gal. 3:11; Heb. 10:38). Luther made them the watchword of the Reformation. Habakkuk found faith to be the golden key that brought deliverance to the believer imprisoned in the dungeon of doubt. In his three chapters he goes from a sob to a song, from a cry of doubt to a rapturous song of trust. Three progressive steps correspond exactly with the chapter divisions.

I. In chapter I we see the problem for faith.

A. *The prophet states his problem.* "O Jehovah, how long shall I cry, and thou wilt not hear? I cry out unto thee of violence, and thou wilt not save" (Hab. 1:2 ASV). *(Also read vv. 3–4 here.)*

These verses are a complaint regarding internal conditions in Judah. Habakkuk's problem was God's silence, inactivity, and apparent unconcern. Violence abounded; lawlessness was rife; blatant evils defied all the protests of God's prophets, and God seemed to be doing nothing. With implicit faith in God's goodness came the difficulty of reconciling a bad world with a good God. But God never stifles the sincere questioner. He gives more light.

B. *The prophet's query is answered by a word from God.* "Behold ye among the nations, and look, and wonder marvellously; for I am working a work in your days, which ye will not believe though it be told you. For, lo, I raise up the Chaldeans, that bitter and hasty nation, that march through the breadth of the earth, to possess dwelling-places that are not theirs" (1:5–6 ASV). *(Read verses 7–11 here.)*

To Habakkuk the solution was worse than the problem. The punishment coming to Judah was deserved; but why should God punish her by means of a people far more wicked and ruthless than Judah herself? This seemed hard to reconcile with his belief in God's righteous government over the nations of the earth. The moral problem before the prophet—how God can silently look upon wrong and inhumanity—is not eased, but intensified.

C. *The prophet appeals further to God concerning his problem.* "Art not thou from everlasting, O Jehovah my God, my Holy One? We shall not die. O Jehovah, thou hast ordained him for judgment; and thou, O Rock, hast established him for correction" (1:12 ASV). *(Read vv. 13–17 here.)*

Chaldea was only God's instrument. The prophet was overwhelmed. It was not that the punishment outweighed the offense; it was rather that the Holy One, righteous though his judgments were, should permit a heathen nation to work its cruel will upon the elect. "Wherefore lookest thou upon them that deal treacherously, and holdest thy peace when the wicked swalloweth up the man that is more righteous than he?" (v. 13 ASV). Habakkuk was to learn that chastening is not necessarily a denial of the divine love; it may be proof of it. By the fires of war the nation was to be refined, yet like gold in a crucible, merely the dross would be consumed. Keeping this in mind will help us understand not only the times of the prophet, but also our own times.

II. In chapter 2 we see the pledges of faith.

Habakkuk decided to await God's word. He said, "I will stand upon my watch, and set me upon the tower, and will look forth to see what he will speak with me, and what I shall answer concerning my complaint" (2:1 ASV). Isolation does not always yield a full answer to life's questions, but there is such a thing as the detachment of the exalted life. And so it is here. The prophet's vision was wonderful, offering a solution, not in the logical sense, but a spiritual solution intelligible to faith. In this chapter God gives two great pledges.

A. *In verse 4 (ASV) we read, "Behold, his soul [the Chaldean's] is puffed up, it is not upright in him: but the just shall live by his faith."* These words look beyond the body to the soul. As the first half of the sentence would indicate, the word *soul* betokens the deeper sense in which we are to read the latter half: "The just shall live by his faith." These words look beyond the outward to the inward, beyond the physical to the spiritual, beyond the present to the future, beyond the immediate to the ultimate. God's estimate of the Chaldean is correct. Though God uses him to chastise his people, his soul is all wrong, and he himself shall be brought to woe in the end. But the just shall never perish.

B. *In verse 14 we read, "For the earth shall be filled with the knowledge of the glory of the Lord, as waters cover the sea."* This word of Habakkuk's is one of the most prolific in the Old Testament, though it must be read in the light of the New if we are to grasp its full meaning. Those who by faith in Christ are justified, or made righteous, do "live" by their faith in that they receive new spiritual life here and now. These words have not yet been fulfilled but await the return of Christ to this earth and the consummation of his kingdom. The controversy of history will be resolved in the vindication of the right and true. God's word through Habakkuk is, "For the vision is yet for the appointed time.... Though it tarry, wait for it; because it will surely come, it will not delay" (2:3 ASV).

III. In chapter 3 we see the products of faith.

This chapter, which begins, "A prayer of Habakkuk" (3:1), is a sublime rhapsody of faith. It may be understood as a poem or psalm on the text "The just shall live by his faith" (2:4). There are three parts of the prayer, three products produced by faith.

A. *The prayer begins with an appeal to God to grant a gracious revival "in the midst of the years" (v. 2).* The prayer does not suggest time limits on God. But before his ultimate purpose for history has worked out to its final fulfillment, will he in his mercy and grace grant revival to his people?

B. *From verse 3 to verse 15 there is a glorying in God's mighty doings in the past.* This includes God's coming forth for the emancipation of Israel, his marvels from the time of the exodus onward. Here are two products of faith: praise for the past and confidence for the future. There is one more.

C. *In verses 16 through 19 we have a postlude in which faith soars on wings above all doubts and fears.* Though the prophet be brought to utmost destitution, still he says:

> *Yet I will rejoice in Jehovah,*
> *I will joy in the God of my salvation. (v. 18 ASV)*

How can you defeat a faith like that?

Conclusion

The applicable message of this prophecy is clear. Faith had its problems then; it has them now. If Habakkuk's times seemed draped with dark enigmas, even more so our own. But the book tells us not to judge merely by the appearances of the hour. God has given us great promises. He is working out great purposes. Wait for him!

WEDNESDAY EVENING, MARCH 6

Title: The One Foundation

Text: "For other foundation can no man lay than that is laid, which is Jesus Christ (**1 Cor. 3:11**).

Scripture Reading: 1 Corinthians 3:10–15

Introduction

In the February 24, 1956, issue of *U.S. News and World Report,* an army expert in psychiatry made the startling statement that one-third of the American soldiers taken prisoner in the Korean conflict yielded to brainwashing. By this he meant that they became so-called progressives in the communists' hands or became sympathizers or collaborators with the enemy. This was done not through physical torture, starvation, or the like, but merely by attempting to distort convictions and principles. He further stated that this weakness, in his opinion, was due to a serious weakness in America's character and to shortcomings in American education. In answer to religious questions, he said that no specific data on religion had been obtained, but the indications were that one who had a strong religious background stood the test far better than one who had "fox-hole" religion.

I. Some people have superficial foundations for life.

A. *Some people feel that church membership is a sufficient foundation.* This is good but only if Christ is Savior. Church membership has little meaning until one has repented of sin and believed on the Lord Jesus. Then church membership becomes an aid to growth in salvation.

B. *Lives built on superficial foundations are doomed in spite of appearances.* Jesus illustrated this in the closing words of the Sermon on the Mount.

C. *One must face the unalterable fact that there is only one real foundation.* This foundation is Jesus Christ himself. It is not doctrine, theories, or systems, but Jesus of Nazareth. Myriad people have built on Jesus as the foundation. They have found solace from sorrow, liberation from prison, emancipation from slavery, and salvation from sin.

II. Consider some materials that go into the proper foundation.

A. *This foundation is made of the rocks of the sacrifice, suffering, and vicarious death of Jesus.* In this suffering and death of Jesus, one finds the expressions of divine love, mercy, and pardon. It is at that point one finds God's remedy for human sin.

B. *This foundation is tied together with the cement of God's love.* This love will never let go in the midst of any kind of storm. It grows stronger and stronger in the face of adversity.

C. *This foundation is made solid in the very person of God.* At a certain dinner in London, Dean Stanley asked, "Who will dominate the future?" An answer was given: "The ones who stick most closely to the facts." Another person added, "The greatest fact in history is God."

III. Consider some structures built on such foundations.

A. *The first and most important structure is personal salvation.* Salvation means more than escape from torment. For believers it means saved lives, joyous hearts, devoted service, and resurrected hopes.

B. *The second structure that rests on this foundation is the church.* Jesus said, "Upon this rock I will build my church." Christ died for his bride, the church. We are not to take that lightly or neglect it. The church is the apple of Christ's eye. We are to love and support it.

Conclusion

Satan is busy trying to deceive you about the foundation on which you build your life as well as the kind of life you build. Make sure you are building on the Solid Rock.

SUNDAY MORNING, MARCH 10

Title: What Do You Do for Hungry People?

Text: "Jesus then took the loaves, and when he had given thanks, he distributed them to those who were seated; so also the fish, as much as they wanted" **(John 6:11 RSV).**

Scripture Reading: John 6:1–15

Hymns: "Break Thou the Bread of Life," Lathbury
             "Where Cross the Crowded Ways of Life," North
             "People to People," Reynolds

Offertory Prayer: Holy Father, you have given us bread for our hunger. We eat every day and are filled. We want to thank you for your bountiful provision. We intercede on behalf of those who are hungry and offer our resources for their filling. Part of what we now bring to you we dedicate especially to the feeding of the hungry, the aid of the poor. We thank you too for Jesus who is the Bread of Life and is food enough for our spiritual hungers. In our goings and comings may we be eager and bold to share with others our greatest good gift—the invitation to salvation and new life in Jesus Christ. In his name we live. Amen.

Introduction

Most of us have never seen a desperately hungry person. Because we can't identify with the hungry, we lack compassion for them. Consider the anguish of parents who can't afford enough food to quiet the hunger in their children's stomachs.

The issue is squarely before us. Hunger continues to be a worldwide problem. Even with aid programs, many Americans are hungry in the wealthiest nation on earth! What are Christians called to do in a world where people are hungry? Here are some suggestions.

I. Send the hungry people away.

Although John does not mention this suggestion of the disciples to send the people away to the villages, all three of the synoptic gospels record it (Matt. 14:15; Mark 6:36; Luke 9:12). John does note (6:7) that Philip could see no way to help, since all the disciples had was two hundred denarii (a denarius equaled one day's wage for a common laborer), which could not buy enough bread for each of them to get even a little bite. He was probably about ready to suggest that the people should go elsewhere for help.

We often are tempted to send trouble on down the road to find another person who will help. Those of us who have plenty to eat do not want to be reminded of the hollow-eyed hungry people who peer at us from the TV screen, magazine advertisements, or church reports that call us to Christian response.

Mentally we "send them away" by our crude suggestions that poor people are hungry because they won't work. Not many years ago people proudly displayed the bumper sticker, "I fight poverty. I work." As commendable as it is that people work, the self-righteous attitude of a person who does not understand the complexities of the problem of hunger are revealed in that slogan. By that slogan we announce: "Send them away. It's all their fault. If they would work, they wouldn't be hungry!" But we must not send away the millions who die of starvation every year. Jesus says that we must care for them.

II. Start a revolution.

Ray Summers, in his book *Behold the Lamb* (Nashville: Broadman, 1979), suggests that many in the large crowd would have liked for Jesus to start a revolution against the Roman oppressors. John 6:15 makes it clear that there were men who were insistent that Jesus take up leadership and become king of the Jews in opposition to the hated foreign rule.

By paying close attention to the synoptic accounts of this passage, you can note that Mark often points out that they were in a "lonely" place or a desert place. This would be ideal for a gathering of men who were intent on revolution. Mark also says that there was much "coming and going" (Mark 6:31), suggesting great activity caused by Jesus' appearance. Mark notes Jesus' observation that the crowd was "like sheep without a shepherd" (Mark 6:34 RSV). This could have military allusions, since in Numbers 27:16–17 Moses speaks of his people as "sheep without a shepherd" unless the Lord appoint a man to lead them in and out. The Lord appointed Joshua as the leader of Israel to succeed Moses, and this shepherd was indeed a general of the army. Notice finally that the crowd was almost all men. In a lonely place in an occupied land like Palestine, five thousand men wanting to make the charismatic leader their king would surely present a ready-made opportunity for revolution.

But Jesus would not take the militant revolutionary way. It may be understandable when some do. They take all they can take and then rise up to say, "No more!" It is wise for those who have bread to figure out a way to help those who don't, lest the time come when no one has anything at all.

Jesus, however, with all his compassion and appreciation for the agonies of injustice suffered by his people, knew that he could feed them. And he did.

But the ultimate joy and salvation did not rest in his becoming a revolutionary leader, "a bread-and-guns" messiah. People must have bread (John 6:5–11), but people cannot live by bread alone (Matt. 4:4). Because bread is important, we ask for it each time we pray the Lord's Prayer.

III. Share what they have.

We need to "pass the bread to everyone." We who have so much, even more than the boy who had but five barley loaves and two fish, are called upon to share. Jesus made it clear that he expects us to feed the hungry and give water to the thirsty no matter how small and insignificant they may at first appear to us (Matt. 25:34–46).

When we share, Jesus will hold our gift in his hands and give thanks for it (John 6:11). Jesus knows how much can come from so little. We cooperate with a God who is in the business of multiplying our gifts. What was shared and then blessed was enough and more (6:12–13).

Sharing is not difficult if we remember that all we have comes from God in the first place.

> *Back of the loaf is the snowy flour,*
> *And back of the flour is the mill,*
> *And back of the mill is the wheat,*
> *The shower and the sun and the Father's will.*

> —Anonymous

Mahatma Gandhi lived in the midst of debilitating hunger. Looking about him, he observed, "The earth has enough for every man's need, but not enough for every man's greed." Jesus gave the boy an opportunity to be a partner with him in feeding the hungry multitude. He gives us the same opportunity, but in order to do so meaningfully, "We are going to have to learn to live more simply, in order that others may simply live" (Elizabeth Seaton).

But as Jesus knew—as important as bread is and as necessary as it is that we share our bread—people cannot live fully by bread alone. We are called to share with a hungry world bread for their physical hunger and the Bread of Life for their spiritual hunger.

Conclusion

When we share what we have and know, Jesus blesses and multiplies it and makes it enough. So share what you have; it is all you can do. You cannot give what you do not have. Share what you have; no one else can give what only you have to give. Although what you have to share may not seem to be much or even enough, you never know what God will do when you give him what you have!

SUNDAY EVENING, MARCH 10

Title: Zephaniah—Jerusalem's Sins of Omission

Text: "She obeyed not the voice; she received not correction; she trusted not in Jehovah; she drew not near to her God" **(Zeph. 3:2 ASV).**

Scripture Reading: Zephaniah 3:1–13

Introduction

Zephaniah gave his pedigree more fully than any other prophet. He was the great-great-grandson of King Hezekiah (Zeph. 1:1). He tells us specifically when he prophesied. It was "in the days of Josiah the son of Amon, king of Judah" (1:1). Like Nahum, Zephaniah foresaw the ruin of Assyria, but he did not exult over it. Like Habakkuk, he saw the forces at work in the world revolution going on about him. But he did not seek an answer to the problem raised by God's use of wicked nations as executioners of his judgment. As a prophet with a clear vision of the nature and reality of God, Zephaniah's attention was centered on the life of his nation. The sins he saw there convinced him that the general upheaval of the world meant the coming of Jehovah in judgment on his own people.

It is likely that Zephaniah, along with Jeremiah and even Habakkuk and Nahum, supported the reforms of Josiah, the last attempt at revival in Judah before the end of the kingdom. But he clearly saw that however sincere the young king, the revival itself was a phony, outwardly impressive but inwardly failing to change the hearts of the people (2 Kings 22:15–20). That the king was the chief patron in this new outburst of Jehovah worship did not change the lives of his subjects. In their hearts they were saying, as many are now, "The religious ideas of our fathers are played out," that "Jehovah will not do good, neither will he do evil" (Zeph. 1:12). They were saying, "He is as indifferent to us as we are to him."

Three notes are sounded in Zephaniah: (1) judgment (1:1–2:3), (2) wrath (2:4–3:8), and (3) healing (3:9–20). A key note in this prophecy is, "The great day of Jehovah is near" (1:14). Unlike Jeremiah, who grieved over the misery and shame sin entailed, Zephaniah was pitiless, seeing only the iniquity of his people with not a redeeming feature in their lives. No prophet gives a more vivid picture of God's coming judgment than he.

In part 2 the prophet looks away from Jerusalem and Judah to the surrounding nations: Philistia, Moab and Ammon, Ethiopia, Nineveh and Assyria. God's wrath is upon them all. From this circle of nations the prophet suddenly turns upon Jerusalem again. The thought is if God so smites the surrounding nations with judgment, how certainly will he smite the people of Judah who have had privileges above all others (3:6–8).

In part 3 the prophet, having looked within at Jerusalem and Judah and around at surrounding nations, looks beyond at a time of healing and blessing after the days of judgment have served their purpose. There is to be a regathering of the dispersed (3:11–13) and a decided change in the people (vv. 14–15). God himself will find pleasure in the Holy City and her people (vv. 16–17). All afflictions are to be over, and Israel is to be made "a praise among all the peoples of the earth" (v. 20).

At the heart of Jerusalem's sins are the sins of neglect. In one verse (3:2) we have the sins of omission of which Jerusalem was guilty. How relevant today!

I. The sin of disobedience.

"She obeyed not the voice." Obedience can be either true or false.

A. *False forms of obedience.*

1. Sometimes obedience is born of the pressure of fear or the dread of circumstances or some other outward factor. In the long years of servile obedience to his father, the older brother in Jesus' story of the loving father (Luke 14:25–32) was like that. Outwardly he obeyed; inwardly he rebelled. God cannot accept that.
2. Sometimes obedience is unthinking, mechanical, dead, an obedience in which our moral nature neither responds nor rebels. This is not the obedience God wants.
3. Sometimes obedience is a mere submission to authority whether that authority be legitimate or not.

B. *True forms of obedience.*

1. Sometimes obedience is born of the conviction that obedience is the best policy. "To obey is better than sacrifice," Samuel said to King Saul, "and to hearken than the fat of rams" (1 Sam. 15:22). Far from being optional, obedience to the divine will is the only way we have of proving that we know God. "Why call ye me Lord, Lord," Jesus asked, "and do not the things which I say?" (Luke 6:46).
2. Sometimes obedience is born of love and the inward desire to be conformed to God's will. Obedience is a demonstration of love: "If ye love me," Jesus said, "ye will keep my commandments" (John 14:15 ASV).
3. Sometimes obedience is a reasoned response, rooted in moral motivation. God wants his children to obey because they see that his commands are for their good and given because he loves them. We cannot disobey the voice and still grow in his grace and knowledge. Obedience is the key that unlocks the power of God.

II. The sin of stupidity.

"She received not correction," or as the marginal reading has it, "She received not instruction." The nation had failed to learn from experience. To repeat the same mistakes over and over is stupid.

Geographically, Israel was hemmed in by the great nation of Egypt on the southwest and in succession by the great powers of Syria, Assyria, Babylon, and Persia on the northeast. Time after time Israel's sins had brought God's judgment upon them as one or the other of these great powers laid them in the dust. "Yet," Zephaniah says, "she did not learn. She received not instruction." Israel was a poor scholar, a stupid pupil.

A. *Our world has proved a poor scholar.* We make the same mistakes again and again. Speaking of the repeated mistakes of his own nation, Conrad Adenauer, one-time chancellor of West Germany said, "The good Lord set definite limits on man's wisdom, but set no limits on his stupidity" (*The Encyclopedia of Religious Quotations,* ed. Frank S. Mead [Westwood, N.J.: Revell, 1965], 468).

B. *Our churches have proved to be poor scholars.* We make the same mistakes over and over. In a certain church's liturgy the anthem followed the sermon. One Sunday, just after the close of World War II, the pastor preached on the subject, "What Have We Learned from the War?" The choir sang as their anthem "Search Me, O Lord."

C. *As individuals we have proved to be poor scholars.* On September 2, 1945, when Japan surrendered, police picked up a pickpocket on Times Square in New York City. As they were booking him, he remarked, "You fellows have had me here before under similar circumstances." When asked to explain, he said, "More than twenty-five years ago when the Armistice was signed you brought me in here for picking pockets on Times Square." He was a poor scholar. Aren't we all?

III. The sin of unbelief.

"She trusted not in Jehovah." This is not to say that Israel did not believe in God. She did! But she had not placed her full dependence on him. She had turned first to Egypt, then to Assyria for help, but not to God. That kind of unbelief is deadly. Only a small percentage of people say, "There is no God," and mean it. Unbelief is shown by the person who says, "I believe in God; I am a God-fearing person," then lives as if he or she had never heard of God.

Faith is not only the willingness to put ourselves into God's hands, it is actually doing it. Years ago a frightened but determined girl left her home near Shelbyville, Kentucky, for Louisville to get a job and try to make something of herself. Fortunately, her roommate was a sincere Christian and a member of Walnut Street Baptist Church in Louisville. She took her new roommate to Sunday school and worship. When her new roommate came under conviction, she took her to visit the pastor, Dr. F. F. Gibson. In that interview the girl asked Dr. Gibson what it means to become a Christian." He replied, "It means more than joining the church, or being baptized, or attending services now and then; it means to put yourself, all you are and all you can be into the hands of Christ." The girl did so at that very moment. She went back to school and finished at Georgetown College with honors. She then served several terms as a Southern Baptist missionary in Nigeria. Her name was Isabella Moore. What a story of grace! This is faith: to put oneself into the hands of Christ for life or death, for time and eternity, for good or ill. Have you done this?

IV. The sin of irreligion.

"She drew not near to her God." How contemporary this sounds. When one is disobedient, stupid, and unbelieving, he or she is not apt to take much stock in religion.

A. *Apparently some feel they do not need the church.* In an English setting T. S. Eliot pictures this in Chorus I from "The Rock":

> *And the Church does not seem to be wanted*
> *In country or in suburb; and in the town*
> *Only for important weddings.*
>
> > (*The Questing Spirit,* ed. Halford E. Luccock and Frances
> > Brentano [New York: Coward-McCann, 1947], 397)

Zephaniah said this same thing 2,600 years ago: "She drew not near to her God."

B. *Apparently some feel that they do not need to worship.* There are all manner of excuses, but when you get to the rock bottom of the matter, many seem to feel that worship does not have values to meet their needs. They haven't given it a chance. In his epistle James says, "Come near to God and he will come near to you" (4:8 NIV).

C. *Apparently some feel they do not need to support the church.* If your church should vote to close the church or to keep it open for a while, how would you vote? How have you been voting?

Conclusion

Are not these sins our sins? Are not these failings our failings? In our own lives do we not need disobedience to give way to obedience, stupidity to humility, unbelief to trust, and irreligion to devotion and worship?

WEDNESDAY EVENING, MARCH 13

Title: Everyone's Work Shall Be Made Manifest

Text: "Every man's work shall be made manifest: for the day shall declare it, because it shall be revealed by fire; and the fire shall try every man's work of what sort it is" (**1 Cor. 3:13**).

Scripture Reading: 1 Corinthians 3:10–16

Introduction

This message will develop the rather startling thought that the works of each laborer of God will be made manifest.

I. The positive affirmation that every person's work will be made manifest.

A. *This statement is not referring to salvation; it is referring to works (1 Cor. 3:15).* Numerous Scripture passages confirm this affirmation. "We are his workmanship, created in Christ Jesus unto good works, which God hath before ordained that we should walk in them" (Eph. 2:10). "Even so faith, if it hath not works, is dead, being alone" (James 2:17). "Ye shall know them by their fruits" (Matt. 7:16).

B. *A person can be saved and still bear very little fruit.* "If any man's work shall be burned, he shall suffer loss: but he himself shall be saved; yet so as by fire" (1 Cor. 3:15). Zechariah speaks of Israel as "a brand plucked out of the fire" (Zech. 3:2), and Amos made a similar statement (Amos 4:11).

C. *This affirmation is concerning the work of a Christian.* Different people do different types of building (Eph. 2:20–22). "God's solid foundation stands firm, sealed with this inscription: 'The Lord knows those who are his' " (2 Tim. 2:19 NIV). "We must all appear before the judgment seat of Christ; that every one may receive the things done in his body, according to what he hath done, whether it be good or bad" (2 Cor. 5:10).

II. An affirmation of reward for the right kind of work.

A. *Rewards are a prominent teaching doctrine in the New Testament.* We will be rewarded according to our works (Rev. 22:12), for the Lord judges according to one's faithfulness and spirit.

B. *Rewards are such that each person will want to work for God so as to receive God's praise.* Each person will want to search his or her heart, seek the leadership of the Holy Spirit, and be diligent in determining the will of God in regard to how God's works will be made manifest.

Conclusion

We need to come clean with God in regard to our works. He desires and expects us to work for him, and he knows what we can do. Our rewards will be determined by the quality of our labor for God.

SUNDAY MORNING, MARCH 17

Title: When Grief Comes to Your House

Text: "Martha said to Jesus, 'Lord, if you had been here, my brother would not have died'" **(John 11:21 RSV)**.

Scripture Reading: John 11:17–37

Hymns: "A Mighty Fortress Is Our God," Luther
"O God, Our Help in Ages Past," Watts
"What Wondrous Love Is This?" American Folk Hymn

Offertory Prayer: Lord God, we bring gifts of praise and love as well as the offerings of our material wealth to you today. You have blessed us richly with strength and skills, energy and expertise, and opportunity to work. There is nothing we bring that was not first given to us. You ask for our praise but only after you have praised us. In your own image you made us and of the creation you said, "It is good." You ask for our love, but first you loved us and gave your Son for our salvation. You ask for our tithes and offerings, but first you gave us the bounty of life out of which we give our gifts to you today. Thank you, Lord, for enriching our lives out of the abundant riches we joyfully give. In Jesus' name. Amen.

Introduction

Is there any home where grief has never come? Or never will come? To live is to face the certainty that a time will come when death or some other form of grief will knock at the door where you live. For those who have never known grief, there is sometimes a fearful premonition that grief may come, and we wonder if we will be able to deal with it. Those who have gone through grief know the pain and would not desire it again, but they know they have found in the grace of God courage enough to walk through it. There is a certain strength in that knowledge that is one of the by-products suffering brings to the believing heart. Mary and Martha, even though they knew Jesus, were not spared the grief that comes when a brother dies. Today's text shows the kind of help you can expect when grief comes to your house.

I. Notice that when grief comes to your house, so do your friends (John 11:19).

Many of the Jews came to Martha and Mary to console them concerning their brother's death. If you live within a community of faith where people care for one another and love one another, when grief comes your way, so will the people who love you.

People unfamiliar with grief often think that grieving people must surely get weary of all those who come to them. They think that surely the grief-stricken ones would prefer for everybody to go away and leave them alone. But experience shows us that one of the grandest gifts God gives his people is other people. At times of heartache and sorrow friends come bringing gifts of food and love and presence.

A minister told me this story: "When my brother's child died, I found how important it is that people come when grief comes. We arrived at my brother's house as quickly as we could. Our father is a preacher and I'm a preacher, but my brother did not need us to be his pastors; he needed us to be father and brother. And he needed the friends who came. I will never forget how much it meant to the family when their own pastor came. The pastor was out of town, and he could not come until the day after the child's death, and until he arrived, there was grief work that could not be done. Pastors sometimes wonder if they are intruding on another's grief. We want to help, but we feel so inadequate. It meant a great deal to me as a young pastor to see that the minister's presence was indeed a word from God and a word from his church. But it was not only the pastor who made the difference, it was the people of the church as they gathered round and cared. Pain shared is pain divided. And it is true of grief. Grief that is shared is grief that is divided among those who share it, and one is able to carry it more easily. It is important when grief comes to your house that people come too."

II. When grief comes to your house, different people will handle their grief in different ways.

In verse 20, when Martha heard that Jesus was coming, she went and met him, while Mary remained seated in the house. Martha needed to talk to Jesus. Mary waited quietly. Notice another difference between them. Mary wept openly (v. 33), yet there is no mention that Martha wept. Jesus wept and the Jews wept and Mary wept, but it is not recorded that Martha wept at all. Did that mean that she loved her brother less? Or did it mean stronger faith? I think not.

One of the terrible myths that Christians often force upon one another is that if you love somebody you will weep at his or her loss. Or worse, if you are a strong Christian and have firm faith, you will not weep when death comes to your house. There is another myth that strong men don't cry. Jesus dispelled all three of those inadequate attempts at the truth. Jesus wept. No stronger or more courageous man was ever alive on our earth. And he wept. Men do cry, and that's all right. When grief comes to your house, some will cry. That is how they can express their grief. But people don't need to cry simply for fear people will think they did not love the lost one if they do not cry. Whatever you feel, and however you seek to express it, what's honest with you is all right. Martha loved her brother; she did not weep. Mary loved her brother; she did weep. There is no one way to handle our grief.

Generally, you will find that when you hear the word of impending grief, you will go through stages of grief. First, you will attempt to deny that it is so and perhaps seek isolation. You will want to be by yourself with your grief. There's nothing wrong with that as long as you don't stay alone. To deny impending darkness may be the necessary reaction to keep from being overwhelmed by it. It is reflected in the kind of statement, "Well, Doctor, I think I'll get another opinion." And you ought to. No doctor knows everything. Or you might say when you first hear of a death, "No, it can't be!" The first stage in grief is often denial, and then often we get angry. We don't like it; we don't think it's fair. "I haven't been as bad as so and so, and he is making a million dollars a year and has been healthy all his life! Why me instead of him?" Be careful about your anger, that you don't deny it and bottle it up. Some people are not growing Christians because they are angry at God and are afraid to admit it. If you are angry with God, tell him so; he is quite able to handle it. You're not going to shock him; he is not going to turn in a tantrum and wipe you out like a mosquito. Out of the anger will come questions. It's all right to ask God anything you want to ask him as long as you don't insist that he answer you by your timetable.

After our anger we begin to bargain. "God, if you'll deliver me, I'll serve you for the rest of my life. If you'll let me get well, I'll teach a Sunday school class; I'll go visiting every Tuesday night; I'll give a tenth of my income." After the bargaining, comes depression. Feelings of dark helplessness roll over us. But we understand God has called us to life and we must live. So we move into the final stage of grief, a simple acceptance of life as it is. We begin to live with hope, not giving up, believing God will bring us through it all.

III. When grief comes to your house, most people will ask God, "Why?"

In verses 21 and 32 this is the question that is being asked. Mary and Martha said, "Lord, if you had been here my brother would not have died." The implied question is, "Why weren't you here?" It's the same thing we say to God in our questioning. "Lord, why didn't you do something?" "Why weren't you here when I needed you?"

The truth is that there is no simple answer to suffering. We have struggled with it in Christian theology from the beginning of the faith. Some of the answers we have found are that God permits suffering for our good and his glory; that God teaches his children through suffering; and that God is able to transform life through his suffering on our behalf. God may not always answer our questions of why, but he will give you himself, his presence. We think we want to know why we suffer and why we grieve, but knowing why would not change the reality of the loss, nor would it restore the life. What we need more than answers to why is his presence with us—that is why Jesus came to Mary and Martha in their need. And that is why God the Holy Spirit comes to us in our need. Listen for his presence.

IV. When grief comes to your house, you can remember the words of Jesus.

Jesus quietly but firmly insisted to Mary and Martha, "I am the resurrection and the life. He who believes in me will live, even though he dies; and whoever lives and believes in me will never die" (John 11:25–26). And if you believe that, when grief comes to your house, you will not only survive it, you will not only grow through it, you will be able to look beyond the present pain and anticipate the victory Jesus has won for us over death and its sting.

Conclusion

Do not wait for a great grief to bring you to God's grace. Suffering does not automatically make people better; it often makes people bitter. But those who trust in Jesus are preparing in advance for life with all its strange twists and turns, its dark valleys and painful separations. Those who in faith approach whatever grief life brings to them do so knowing they can feel their pain, own their anger, await the answers, and affirm the victory the word of Jesus promises to those who believe.

SUNDAY EVENING, MARCH 17

Title: Haggai—Rebuilding the Temple

Text: "Go up to the mountain, and bring wood, and build the house; and I will take pleasure in it, and I will be glorified, saith the LORD" **(Hag. 1:8).**

Scripture Reading: Haggai 1:1–11

Introduction

Following World War II, hard-pressed congregations in Britain and Europe worshiped in bombed-out church buildings. Twenty-five centuries earlier, the people of the restored community of Judah were living indoors, for they had rebuilt their own houses, but God was camping out in the ruins of the temple. And then the voice of a prophet rose and echoed "o'er crumbling walls."

In 536 B.C., seventy years after the first deportation to Babylon in 606 B.C., about fifty thousand Jews returned to Judah led by Zerubbabel, who was of royal lineage, and Joshua the high priest. This was primarily a religious pilgrimage, with the purpose of rebuilding the temple. It had lain in ruins since it was sacked and burned in the destruction of Jerusalem in 587 B.C. The people repaired the altar and laid the foundation with great rejoicing. But the harassment of the Samaritans, who also gave false reports to Persian authorities, and the preoccupation of the people with their own affairs soon brought the work to a halt.

From Ezra 4:24–52 and 6:14–15 we learn that Haggai was associated with another prophet, Zechariah, and that these two inspired the returned exiles to rebuild the Jerusalem temple. This was completed in five years, 520–515 B.C. Haggai and Zechariah had a limited but very specific objective—simply to arouse the people to restore the temple. They achieved their goal.

This book of only two chapters contains four messages from the prophet Haggai dated for the exact month and day in the year 520 B.C., which was sixteen years after the end of the exile. There is also a brief historical interlude.

The book of Haggai gives us the people's reaction to Haggai's preaching. It is a report in the third person, not by Haggai, but about him. Whoever this inspired writer may have been, he was both exact and clear. This prophecy is made up of five natural divisions.

I. The first sermon (1:1–11).

After giving the exact date of the event, Haggai made a threefold appeal.

A. *He appealed to the mind (vv. 2–4).* Though the appeal was to Zerubbabel and Joshua, it was through them to the people, who said, "It is not the time." God's answer came, "Is it a time for you yourselves to dwell in your ceiled houses, while this house lieth waste?" Their excuses didn't add up.

B. *He appealed to the heart (vv. 5–7).* "Consider your ways," God challenged. Despite much labor, there were scant harvests, little to eat and drink and wear, so God told them to consider why.

C. *He appealed to the will (vv. 8–11).*
1. God gave three clear imperatives: "Go," "Bring," "Build."
2. He explained the reason for this: God will take pleasure in it and be glorified by it.
3. There is a recapitulation of the whole argument. Abundant sowing had resulted in meager reaping; and when the grain was in the garner, God "did blow upon it." Why? The answer was that they did not put first things first. While God's house lay waste, they built elegant houses for themselves. Because they neglected to build God's house, he withheld the dew and the rain, and this was for their sakes. Drought brought disaster. They must blame themselves.

II. The historical interlude (1:12–15).

Here the writer gave five results of Haggai's first message.

A. *The leaders and the people responded with obedience (v. 12).*
B. *The people felt fear (v. 12).*
C. *The prophet received encouragement (v. 13).*
D. *The Lord gave his approval.*
  "Jehovah stirred up the spirit of Zerubbabel...and the spirit of Joshua...and the spirit of all the remnant" (v. 14 ASV).
E. *The leaders and the people responded with work (v. 15).*
  The writer carefully dated these responses (v. 15).

III. The second sermon (2:1–9).

After the exact date of Haggai's second message was given and those to whom it was addressed were named (vv. 1–2), the prophet did three things.

A. *He recognized the difficulties (v. 3).* Were there not some among them who had seen the temple of Solomon in all its glory? Did they not see the house being erected "as nothing"?

B. *He revealed their duty (vv. 4–5).* Governor, priest, and people were required to "be strong," "to work," and to "fear not." God gave them all the reassurance, "I am with you."

C. *He refuted their disparagement (vv. 6–9).* This unveiling of the future utterly refuted those who were discouraging the builders by their backward looking. "I will disturb the heavens, and the earth, the sea, and the dry land; and I will disturb all nations." This was a declaration that God was going to break in upon earth's history in a supernatural way. He was going to disturb the even tenor of the earth's ways. The supreme reason for, and result of, this disturbing of the universe would be the advent of the Desire of all nations. "The latter glory of this house shall be greater than the former…and in this place I will give peace, saith Jehovah of hosts" (ASV). The latter glory would be as much greater than the former as the reality is greater than the type, and the fact than the symbol. God was unveiling something of his plans for the future to these builders. They were not to be discouraged. God's methods are progressive. Consequently, it was wrong to be hankering after things that were past. It was the utmost folly, for there were to be greater things ahead. Those who walk with God never go backward, for he is ever moving on to glorious consummations.

IV. The third sermon (2:10–19).

After the exact date and the occasion were given (v. 10), Haggai challenged the people by an appeal to the law, called upon them to consider its application, and announced God's grace upon the nation.

A. *He challenged the people by an appeal to the law (vv. 11–13).* Since the people were discontented because they had not become prosperous after several months of faithfulness to Jehovah, Haggai challenged them to ask two questions of the priests.

   1. The first question was, "If one bear holy flesh in the skirt of his garment, and with his skirt do touch bread, or pottage, or wine, or oil, or any food, shall it become holy?" (v. 11 ASV). The answer of the priests was, "No." This had to do with the ceremonial law and, in effect, the question was, "Can the holy make the unholy holy?" It could not!

   2. The second question was, "If one that is unclean by reason of a dead body touch any of these, shall it be unclean?" (v. 13 ASV). In other

words, "Can the unholy make the holy unholy?" The priests answer, "It shall be unclean."

Two principles emerge: holiness in people is not communicable; pollution in people is communicable.

B. *He called upon the nation to apply these principles to themselves.* The prophet said, "So is this people, and so is this nation before me, saith Jehovah; and so is every work of their hands; and that which they offer there is unclean" (v. 14 ASV). The call is twofold.

1. In verses 15–17 the people were asked to consider the fifteen years they had neglected building God's house. The ground and its produce had been affected through their sin. Pollution had been communicated.
2. In verses 18–19 the people were asked to consider the three months during which they had been in harmony with God. Adversity had continued for them. It was a case of holiness uncommunicated.

C. *He announced God's grace upon the nation.* This sermon ends: "From this day will I bless you" (v. 19). These are words of ineffable grace. All that we receive, we receive through God's grace.

V. The fourth sermon (2:20–23).

As with the former sermons, the date and the event were given (v. 20). This fourth message is different, however, in that it is addressed to one individual, Zerubbabel. Here God, through his prophet, revealed a program. Two things were revealed about it.

A. *The plan is this: "I will shake the heavens and the earth" (v. 21).* Everything that follows is included in this great initial utterance. God is reaffirming the plan he spoke of in the second sermon. He is going to disturb the universe.

B. *The purpose is both destructive and constructive (vv. 22–23).*

1. God will overthrow "the throne of kingdoms." This is referring to Satan's throne.
2. He will "destroy the strength of the kingdoms of the nations." This second result stems out of the first. The destruction of "the chariots and those that ride in them" simply means that militarism will destroy militarism. The constructive purpose concerns Zerubbabel. "In that day...will I take thee, and will make thee as a signet: for I have chosen thee." Since he said, "In that day," this could not mean while Zerubbabel was alive. This reference is to the One who should come through the line of David, David's great Son. He who disturbed the heavens and the earth will yet again break into the earth's history, for he who came, comes!

Conclusion

The moral of the prophecy of Haggai is this: "When in disrepair through disaster or neglect, a church building must be rebuilt—to save the whole life of the community from demoralization and to point it toward its destiny."

WEDNESDAY EVENING, MARCH 20

Title: The Temple of God

Text: "Know ye not that ye are the temple of God, and that the Spirit of God dwelleth in you?" (**1 Cor. 3:16**).

Scripture Reading: 1 Corinthians 3:16–17

Introduction

The subject of this message is a metaphor to describe the nature of the Christian. It may apply to the collective group—the church—and it may apply to the individual Christian. We will study the passage in detail, then discuss the subject in detail, and last, make an application.

I. Consider the temple of God.

A. *The phrase "know ye not" is an introduction.* If this were translated into modern terminology, it would probably read, "This is the same thing I have told you before." It is a phrase used by Paul to emphasize an important truth (1 Cor. 5:6; 6:2, 15; 9:13, 24).

B. *The phrase "that ye are" designates the one to whom the words are addressed.* According to Ephesians 2:21, the words can be rightly interpreted collectively or individually. For the Christian, the first thought would probably be toward that of an individual. However, a more careful thought will lead one to see that much of the entire epistle of 1 Corinthians is directed to the church.

C. *The phrase "the temple of God," is the heart of the subject.* The article "the" needs to be noticed. This does not refer to a temple among many temples. It refers to the one and only temple. The word "temple" denotes a shrine where deity resides. So the truth is that human beings are the shrine where God dwells.

II. Consider the temple that Christians are.

A. *The church is the temple of God.* The Spirit of God dwells in people, not buildings built with hands (Acts 7:48; 17:24). The church is the spiritual organism. That is where God dwells. He dwells in the people of the church for the glory of God, not for our glory. The church is to bring people to faith in Christ for salvation. The Spirit builds and dwells in believers as a church.

B. *The individual is the temple of God.* This indwelling is the culmination of the work of grace. The heart must first be quickened, renewed, and purified. The only person in whom the Holy Spirit abides is one who has been born again. The Father and the Son make their abode with the person who loves and obeys the Son (John 14:23).

97

III. Consider how this truth should affect each Christian.

A. *We are warned about the destruction of the temple.* This is true of the church. It is a terrible thing to tear down the church. The word *destroy* means to corrupt morally or defraud in character. One can defile the church by deliberate attack or by negligence. Any abuse given to the human body is applicable here. This is a strong argument against the abusive use of narcotics of any kind. It also applies to lack of rest, overeating, and the like. The Scripture says, "If anyone destroys God's temple, God will destroy him" (1 Cor. 3:17 NIV).

B. *That we are the temple of God should encourage holy living.* One's duties to the church are duties to the Spirit of God. God's temple must not be marred. One's duty to the care of his or her own body is a duty to the Holy Spirit. One must not destroy one's body.

Conclusion

As individual Christians, each of us should take positive steps to remove from our life anything that would be detrimental to the body of the church or to our human body. We should take positive steps to make ourselves pure and acceptable to God.

SUNDAY MORNING, MARCH 24

Title: Moved by the Cross

Text: "I, when I am lifted up from the earth, will draw all men to myself" (**John 12:32 RSV**).

Scripture Reading: John 12:27–36

Hymns: "There Is a Fountain," Cowper

"When I Survey the Wondrous Cross," Watts

"Must Jesus Bear the Cross Alone?" Shepherd

Offertory Prayer: Suffering Lord, while the crowds screamed their praise, you knew the fear that would silence their hosannas before the week was done. We come praising you and giving our tithes and offerings. We do so joyfully and in gratitude that you are our King of Kings and Lord of Lords. Help us to be watchful this week that our praises are not silenced by fear and our gifts are not withheld because of selfishness. Lord, help us to be constant in our love, consistent in our praise, and courageous in our obedience. This we pray in Jesus' name. Amen.

Introduction

Never is the pathos of the journey to the cross more sensitively put than in John's account of our Lord's troubled soul as he approached Calvary. But he would not turn away. Paul said when Jesus found himself in "human form he humbled himself and became obedient unto death, even death on a cross" (Phil. 2:8 RSV). That obedience is tenderly witnessed as John shows Jesus refusing even to pray for deliverance from dying but yielding in deep obedience to the purposes of God for this hour (John 12:27). "Here there met the horror of death and the ardor of obedience" (William Barclay, quoting Bengel in *The Gospel of John*, vol. 2 [Philadelphia: Westminster Press, 1955], 146).

What was the hope in Jesus' heart that prepared him for this journey to death? Jesus expressed his great conviction: "I, when I am lifted up from the earth, will draw all men to myself" (12:32 RSV). Jesus was going to the cross because he wanted more than life to bring all people everywhere to himself that he might present them forgiven and redeemed to God the Father (see 17:12, 24). Not everyone would come to believe, but he would die for everyone. The appeal was to be universal. All people would feel the tug of his great love for them demonstrated at the cross on which he would be lifted up.

William Hull notes, "Judaism offered men a national shrine, a racial circumcision, and the sectarian religious law" (*The Broadman Bible Commentary, Luke–John*, vol. 9 [Nashville: Broadman, 1970], 322). But Jesus offered himself—obedient, gracious, loving, dying—and in that sacrifice we are moved by the cross, drawn to his death, and released by his redemption into a life abundant and accepted, full and forgiven, rich and redeemed.

What draws you to the crucified Christ?

I. Are you moved by the agony you see?

A. *Physical agony arrests us when we consider the cross.* Jesus' back torn to shreds by a flying whip, he was pressed down on a rough and splintery cross. His head was filled with visions of God's love for humanity, and now it was surrounded by a mock crown of thorns that bit painfully into his scalp. Awful nails pierced his flesh and muscles and held him with jagged waves of pain to his makeshift throne. As painful as the wounds were, the most desperate need was for breath. As he hung by his arms, no air could enter his lungs. So he pressed against the nails in his feet to lift himself and breathe. When he could stand that pain no longer, he fell against the cross. Then his weight was suspended by his arms, which were held by the nails in his hands.

B. *Consider the spiritual agony Jesus endured at the cross that day.* Words can get much closer to describing the physical pain than they can to expressing the spiritual suffering Jesus went through. Jesus had never known sin in his own life; now he was covered with it. "For our sake he made him to be sin who knew no sin" (2 Cor. 5:21 RSV). Jesus, who had never known a moment's isolation from the Father, cried out, "My God, my God, why hast thou forsaken me?" (Mark 15:34). Who can illumine for us the spiritual loneliness Jesus felt in that eternal moment when our sin cut him off from the Father and the sacrifice for our sins was offered once and for all (see Rom. 5:8)? I am drawn to Jesus by the agony he suffered on the cross.

II. Are you moved by the love you see?

God has loved us with a love that holds nothing back. For our selfishness he prescribes a death to self and a sharing with others. For our cynicism he prescribes a rebirth of innocence and a new beginning in the new birth. Nothing gets through to us as love can. "A sinner may go to hell unsaved; he cannot go to hell unloved" (Robert L. Moyer, quoted in *Decision*, October 1971, 6). We are dealing with nothing less than the love of God.

In a passage from his journal, Sören Kierkegaard speaks of God as a cook making a dish in which a great many ingredients produce the desired flavor. The cook knows that the dish is not complete without a little pinch of spice.

> A little pinch of spice! Humanly speaking, what a painful thing, thus to be sacrificed, to be the little pinch of spice! But on the other hand, God knows well him whom he elects to use in this way, and then he knows also how, in the inward understanding of it, to make it so blessed a thing for him to be sacrificed that among the thousands of diverse voices which express, each in its own way, the same thing, his also will be heard, and perhaps especially his which is truly *de profundis,* proclaiming: God is love. The birds on the branches, the lilies in the field, the deer in the forest, the fishes in the sea, countless hosts of happy men exultantly proclaim: God is love. But beneath all these sopranos, supporting them as it were, as the bass part does, is audible the *de profundis* which issues from the sacrificed one: God is love. (Quoted by Geddes MacGregor, *Introduction to Religious Philosophy* [Boston: Houghton Mifflin, 1959], 287.)

I am drawn to Jesus by the love he showed to others in his dying.

III. Are you moved by the forgiveness you see?

The willingness to forgive is one of the clearest indicators of the spirit of Christ alive in a person. To be sure, it is not easy to forgive, but the cross gives us our most powerful encouragement to forgive by the example our Lord gave us.

Luke records that Jesus implored the Father to forgive those who had taken him to the cross and in mockery proceeded to hang him there (Luke 23:34). In the moments of his greatest personal darkness, Jesus was eager to hear a penitent's plea and assure him personally of the glory that was to be theirs together at the end of the day (Luke 23:43). And John gives us that ultimate word of courage, "It is finished" (John 19:30). In these three words from the cross, we see an indomitable spirit that refused to retaliate in anger, escape from the needy cry of a dying man, or lay down the task before he had completed it.

Jesus forgave those who nailed him to the tree. He pardoned and received the criminal on his right. His atoning death did not stop short of being adequate to forgive any person or sin. When he cried, "It is finished," he had gone far enough to cover every sin in any person's life.

A young man and his wife had come to church for several weeks. They invited the pastor to visit with them. Karl had never made a commitment to Jesus Christ, and he wanted to talk with the pastor about it. He was afraid God could not forgive him. Years before, as a teenager, he had shot his older brother in a fatal hunting accident. He had not been able to forgive himself, and he could not believe God would forgive him. Everyone said it was an accident, and he believed it to be an accident also. But still his brother was dead and he had shot him. He accepted the blame and could not go free. The pastor shared with him the words of Jesus on the cross and urged him to see that if Jesus had died for every sin but his sin, God had made a terrible mistake and Jesus was misled when he called out, "It is finished." Jesus' death is enough; God's grace is sufficient. We can all be set free. No sin is more powerful than his forgiveness and no hurt can outlast his love. Karl heard the promise of God that night and experienced the cleansing and the relief that comes when we really hear in the deep places of our life—forgiven, accepted, beloved, made new. And it is all because of the cross. I am drawn to Jesus by the forgiveness I experience there.

IV. Are you moved to response when you come to the cross?

Jesus admonishes his listeners to "walk while you have the light, lest the darkness overtake you" (John 12:35 RSV). What response will you make to the cross? It is not enough to consider the cross, not enough to meditate on the cross, not enough to believe in the historical reality of the death of Christ. Jesus calls you to another response: Walk in the light (see John 12:35–36). Be wary lest the darkness overtake you. The darkness can be the fright of failure that prevents you from beginning to follow him. The darkness can be misplaced priorities that detour you away from doing the one thing in your life that is most needful. The darkness can be a reluctance to trust, or bondage to pleasure and desires that are not compatible with obedience to Jesus.

Conclusion

But whatever stands between you and the response of faith in Jesus Christ, I call you to lay it aside, be drawn to the cross, and respond by walking with him while you have the light. His invitation to come, his drawing of your spirit, is God's great gift to you. I am grateful to God that I could respond in faith when Jesus drew me to him at the cross. Will you respond to him?

SUNDAY EVENING, MARCH 24

Title: Zechariah—Rejoice Greatly...Your King Comes to You

Text: "Rejoice greatly, O daughter of Zion; shout, O daughter of Jerusalem: behold thy King cometh unto thee...and he shall speak peace unto the heathen: and his dominion shall be from sea even to sea, and from the river even to the ends of the earth" **(Zech. 9:9–10).**

Scripture Reading: Zechariah 9:1–10; Matthew 21:1–11

Introduction

The fourteen chapters of the prophecy of Zechariah fall naturally into two parts. Chapters 1–8, constructed chiefly around the prophet's eight visions, were intended to encourage the people and their leaders in the rebuilding of the temple. With his older contemporary, the prophet Haggai, Zechariah was eminently successful in this (Ezra 6:14). Chapters 9–14, which record the later ministry of the prophet, contain some of the most remarkably precise messianic predictions in the Old Testament. The entry of Zion's lowly king is described in 9:9; the mourning over the pierced one in 12:10–14; the smiting of the shepherd and the scattering of the flock in 13:7. And there are others.

Our primary concern is with the first of these, the coming of the messianic king riding on a colt into Jerusalem. The fate of the tyrant was sealed, and his reign must inevitably come to an end. But the Messiah's power was to be for all time. "His dominion shall be from sea to sea, and from the river to the ends of the earth" (Zeph. 9:10). The Lord of Hosts would be the redeemer of his people who, cleansed and sanctified, should boast in their unfailing helper. This was the reference in its own historical context.

When Jesus entered Jerusalem on the Sunday before he was crucified, he was careful to fulfill this prophecy in its every detail. This was his "royal entry." He entered Jerusalem as king to make a final appeal to his people, but he was rejected and crucified.

The third fulfillment of this prophecy is yet to come.

Someone has said that deep down in their hearts all people desire a king to rule over them. Whether this be true or not, there is something about the relationship of a good king and his subjects to which no other form of government can compare. In the wisdom of God this is one figure he has chosen to show the relationship between himself and his children.

These haunting words of Zechariah's come down to us over the centuries: "Rejoice greatly...thy king cometh unto thee" (Zech. 9:9). Let us consider this in three applications.

I. The Old Testament says, "The king will come."

A. *Looking back, we can see in the Garden of Eden the first prophecy of Jesus' coming.*
"I will put enmity between thee and the woman, and between thy seed

and her seed: he shall bruise thy head, and thou shalt bruise his heel" (Gen. 3:15 ASV). The patriarchs added their testimony.

B. *The psalmist said: "The LORD is King for ever and ever" (Ps. 10:16 NIV).* The prophets spoke of a "king who would reign in righteousness." He would be of David's line; he would be born in Bethlehem; he would be a man but more than a man; he would save his people.

C. *Of all the prophets, perhaps Isaiah has more statements that are messianic.* He refers to the coming king, God's anointed. In one verse Isaiah uses five names, each suggesting a facet of his character: "For to us a child is born, to us a son is given, and the government will be on his shoulders. And he will be called Wonderful Counselor, Mighty God, Everlasting Father, Prince of Peace" (Isa. 9:6 NIV). There they are, the five names! Then Isaiah says something the centuries have not dimmed but have only served to light up in bold relief: "Of the increase of his government and peace there will be no end. He will reign on David's throne and over his kingdom, establishing and upholding it with justice and righteousness from that time on and forever" (9:7 NIV).

Turn the pages of the Old Testament, and the glow from messianic passages becomes brighter and brighter as the years go by. This revelation is both increasing and progressive. This is the burden of the Old Testament: "The king will come."

II. The New Testament says, "The King has come."

A. *Jesus was born a king when an infant's cry broke the stillness of the night in a rude cattle shed in Bethlehem.* Humble shepherds saw a great light and heard the angels sing.

B. *Jesus was proclaimed a king when in exact fulfillment of Zechariah's prophecy he entered Jerusalem to the plaudits of the multitudes.* They cried, "Blessed is the King that cometh in the name of the Lord" (Luke 19:38 ASV). When the Pharisees urged him to rebuke his disciples, he replied, "I tell you that, if these shall hold their peace, the stones will cry out" (Luke 19:40 ASV). The time had come, as Zechariah had prophesied, for him to be proclaimed king; and nothing could prevent it.

C. *Jesus was crowned king when he came forth as the risen Son of God from the tomb.* Death could not conquer the King of life and death and time and eternity.

D. *Jesus is reigning now.* In one of his great doxologies, Paul said, "Now unto the King eternal, immortal, invisible, the only God, be honor and glory for ever and ever" (1 Tim. 1:17 ASV). Jesus reigns in the spiritual realm. The kingdom of God is not a state or condition of this world, nor an ideal order of nations and life. It centers about a person: the King. "For he must reign," said Paul, "till he hath put all enemies under his feet" (1 Cor. 15:25).

III. Receive your king.

But above all, the Christian gospel says—the Bible says; the Holy Spirit says—to every person everywhere and for all time, "Receive your king."

Jesus' coming forces us to face two alternatives. (1) We may sing his hosannas and cast our palm branches before him with adoring emotions, and then, as the challenge to him grows sharp, let him be led out of another gate to a hill called Calvary. (2) Or we may receive him as the King of our lives and dedicate ourselves to his cause.

A. *What was Jesus doing on the day he entered Jerusalem "riding upon an ass, even upon a colt the foal of an ass"? (Zech. 9:9 ASV).* Heretofore, Jesus has avoided being called "the Son of David" because of the reference to the promised King-Messiah. He did not wish to precipitate the issue with the rulers prematurely. But now the time had come, and he presented himself as king.

B. *What was the reaction?* The Pharisees were indignant and tried to squelch the demonstration but to no avail. The enthusiasm of the multitudes knew no bounds. As long as a year before they had wanted to take Jesus to Jerusalem to make him king (John 6:15), but he would not consent. Now they visualized him throwing the Romans out of Jerusalem and taking the throne. When he did no such thing, their enthusiasm cooled quickly.

C. *What was the immediate result?*
   1. The king was crucified. When the Roman governor surrendered to the pressure to crucify an innocent man, he put a title over the cross in Hebrew, Latin, and Greek: "JESUS OF NAZARETH, THE KING OF THE JEWS" (John 19:19 NIV).
   2. The king was "declared to be the Son of God with power" (Rom. 1:4) by his resurrection from the dead.
   3. Fifty days later, at Pentecost, the king was preached as "both Lord and Christ" (Acts 2:36) and three thousand were converted.

D. *What will be the ultimate result?* Ultimately Jesus will come to rule over all people and all things.
   1. This is the prophet's vision. The prophets dared to dream of a time when nations would beat their swords into plowshares and their spears into pruning hooks; when nation would not lift up sword against nation nor learn war anymore (see Isa. 2:4; Mic. 4:3).
   2. This was the psalmist's dream. One psalmist sang, "The LORD reigns; he is robed in majesty" (93:1 RSV).
   3. This was the great apostle's faith. To Paul, crowning Christ as king was the ultimate significance of the resurrection (1 Cor. 15:24–25).
   4. This is the dynamic of Christian missions, the faith that:

   > *Jesus shall reign where 'ere the sun*
   > *Does his successive journeys run.*

5. This is the substance of John's vision on Patmos. He tells us, "The seventh angel sounded; and there were great voices in heaven, saying, The kingdoms of this world are become the kingdoms of our Lord, and of his Christ; and he shall reign for ever and ever" (Rev. 11:15). On a still higher note, he says, "For he is Lord of lords, and King of kings" (17:14). But the climactic note of John's vision and of the whole Bible is this: "Alleluia: for the Lord God omnipotent reigneth" (19:6).

6. This is the ground of Christian hope. There is no hope except in Jesus, the king. Every other kind of life is bound by the limits of this shrinking world, but Christianity has all the windows open toward the limitless expanse of eternity. "Alleluia: for the Lord God omnipotent reigneth."

Conclusion

This is the Christ who stands at the door of our hearts. What shall be our response to him? God grant that we may say, "Blessed and only Potentate, King of Kings and Lord of Lords, O merciful Christ of God, come! Come now. My life is yours. Enter my heart and reign, both now and forevermore."

WEDNESDAY EVENING, MARCH 27

Title: The Lord Knows the Thoughts of the Wise

Text: "The Lord knoweth the thoughts of the wise, that they are vain" (**1 Cor. 3:20**).

Scripture Reading: 1 Corinthians 3:18–20

Introduction

One of the most deceitful thoughts we can have is that we can depend on our own wisdom alone. The passage of Scripture under consideration in this message emphasizes this.

I. The statement "The Lord knoweth the thoughts of the wise" emphasizes the folly of human wisdom apart from dedication to God.

A. *Human wisdom is deceiving (1 Cor. 3:18).* It leads us to overrate the value of our attainments. Many of our accomplishments are of little value beyond our earthly mind. This kind of wisdom is deceiving inasmuch as it leads us to overrate our own importance. We are vainly puffed up in our earthly mind.

Human wisdom also leads us astray so far as evaluation of things is concerned. The Bible says such a person is a fool. He or she looks for happiness where it cannot be found. It is not found in the brain but in the heart. This person ignores the chief good, which is love for God, resemblance to God, and fellowship with God.

B. *The wisdom of the world leads to trouble.* False wisdom, the kind referred to in this passage, leads to self-conceit, striving, and wrangling in the church. It leads to conceit and trouble among friends and loved ones. And it also leads to distraction from Christ.

II. The statement is followed by a passionate plea.

"Let no man glory in men" (1 Cor. 3:21).

A. *This forms a paradox.* It is Paul's formula for the statement Jesus made when he said, "Whosoever will save his life shall lose it; but whosoever shall lose his life for my sake and the gospel's, the same shall save it" (Mark 8:35).

B. *The opposite of this plea is to glory in self.* This type of glory is comparable to the idea presented in verse 20 in reference to the vanity of human wisdom. It too leads to self-deception or conceit. To glory in man means to boast about self either in word or action. It exalts one's qualities, teaching, attainments, and wisdom apart from Christ and the wisdom of the gospel.

III. The positive statement calls for real humility.

A. *Paul gives a statement of the believer's possessions.* "All things are yours" (1 Cor. 3:21). What are these things? One of the greatest is the church and its leadership. However, these are to be accepted with humility and not with boasting. Another of the possessions is material blessings. Still another is life itself. Death is a possession. It transfers the believer from life on earth to life in heaven. It is a release from sin and temptation.

B. *How does the believer get these things?* They are gracious gifts of God. They are acts of grace. They are appropriated by accepting Christ as Savior and following him in faith.

Conclusion

It is time that each person follows the admonition of the psalmist when he said, "Be still and know that I am God." We need to realize the knowledge God has of us and how weak we are in genuine wisdom.

SUNDAY MORNING, MARCH 31

Title: The Darkness Gave Way

Text: "Now on the first day of the week Mary Magdalene came to the tomb early, while it was still dark, and saw that the stone had been taken away from the tomb" (**John 20:1** RSV).

Scripture Reading: John 20:1–18

Hymns: "Christ the Lord Is Risen Today," Wesley
"The Head That Once Was Crowned," Watts
"I Know That My Redeemer Liveth," Pounds

Offertory Prayer: O, Lord God, your Word says, "If Christ has not been raised, your faith is futile and you are still in your sins." We are totally dependent on your victory for our salvation. For the light that overcomes the darkness, we give you praise and rejoice in your presence. Use the offerings we give to bring life and joy to all who wait for the light to shine in their darkness. Through Jesus Christ, the Light of the World, we pray. Amen.

Introduction

On the evening of November 9, 1965, fifteen minutes and eleven seconds past 5:00, the lights went out all over the northeastern United States. There was a power failure in the great electric lines north of Niagara Falls. The breakdown occurred when the megawatts exceeded the 375 allowable megawatts in that grid. A small metal cup inside a black rectangular box began to revolve until it switched off the line and threw the current onto the four auxiliary lines that also move north. The switches tripped out under the unexpected load of the extra electric current. In 2.7 seconds all the electricity surging toward Toronto, Canada, and the far Northeast had been routed back across Niagara Falls south and east to New York City.

Thirty million people were affected that night, some for as few as three minutes, many for as long as thirteen hours. Eight hundred thousand people were trapped in the subways of New York, reporting later that they were in a darkness so deep they thought they were buried. Two hundred and fifty flights had to be diverted from John F. Kennedy Airport to other landing places. The street traffic jammed up because the traffic lights would not function. In a moment the street lights all flickered out and darkness covered the face of the earth!

On the first Easter morning Mary Magdalene came to the tomb while it was still dark. Just two days before, the earth had quaked and trembled. Fissures had opened in the ground. The skies had turned dark as the sun hid itself, and at midday there was no light—only darkness.

I. All you have to do for darkness to come is remove the light.

Darkness is everywhere. Mary knew about darkness. She had been there with her Lord through Friday's darkness. Patiently, agonizingly, she had stood with the other women and his mother at the cross watching him die. As he died, they felt, as well as saw, the darkness descend upon them. Now, unable to sleep, in the fourth watch, sometime between 3:00 and 6:00 in the morning, she made her way to the tomb in the garden. Nobody much was out at that hour. Mary had known other darkness. She came from the little town of Magdala, a town known for its licentiousness and wickedness, on the shores of the Sea of Galilee. The rabbi said it was because of its evil that Magdala lost its life. Only in recent years have archaeologists begun to excavate the ruins of the little city.

In Luke 8 the gospel writer recalls how Jesus met Mary with her seven demons. Jesus had exorcised the demons and brought light to Mary's darkness. On the dark edge of sanity, Jesus had reached out to bring Mary back to the center of life, back to the light at the heart of life.

Jesus had gone with Mary through the darkness, and now she had come to share for a while the darkness of his burial place. But when she got to the tomb, the stone cover was moved. She peered into the gloom and slowly knew that he was not there.

II. The light removed the darkness in Mary.

Mary didn't know what had happened. She didn't expect a resurrection; she simply knew that Jesus' body was not there. The most logical explanation was that someone had stolen his body away—to do who knows what kind of horrible maliciousness to his earthly frame! So Mary ran and told Peter that someone had taken away her Lord.

Peter came toward the tomb, walking first; then with increasing excitement he began to run. His friend John ran with him. John got there first, only to stop outside. Peter knew no such timidity and immediately rushed into the darkness of the tomb. The light of dawn had begun to disturb the night darkness outside, but in the tomb they hardly knew what to make of it all. Jesus was not there! But still they had no thought of the resurrection. They went back to their homes, but not Mary. Mary would not leave. She stayed behind, weeping.

It may surprise you that Mary mistook Jesus for a gardener. There are two reasons, perhaps. The Scriptures say the angels were there when she came back to the edge of the tomb and looked in. The angels were clothed in white. The Greek word means white, not like a linen cloth, but glistening, shining, and dazzling. Besides the radiance of the light, Mary was in tears. She had been crying since Friday. Dazzled by the light, her eyes washed in tears, she saw Jesus but thought him to be the gardener.

"Woman, why are you weeping? Whom do you seek?" And Mary replied, "Sir, if you have carried him away, tell me where you have laid him and I will take him away." Love and pathos, generosity and courage were enveloped in that statement. Strong men had taken Jesus' body down from the cross and carried it to the tomb in the garden. Some had been afraid to stand with Jesus as he died, but not Mary.

Do you know how Mary realized who Jesus was? Not by sight, nor by the sound of his voice. It was the specific word he spoke—her name. "Mary, Mary," he said. Then she knew who he was. Mary and the disciples believed God had taken up the struggle with darkness and the sin that had held his creation in bondage. They had seen him die. They had helped place him in the tomb.

Now Jesus was alive, and they knew God had only just begun the battle. Out of those clothes that had wrapped our Lord came the resurrected Christ, the Son of the living God, the Savior of the world, the Light for our darkness, Jesus the Savior. All he had to do was call her name, and she knew he was Jesus. The darkness fled from her spirit in the presence of Jesus as darkness flees the earth in the presence of the rising sun.

John uses the theme of light and darkness all the way through this gospel. It is no accident that he tells about Mary coming to the tomb while it was dark. This phrase causes one to think back to the way John began the gospel. "The light shines in the darkness and the darkness has not overcome it" (John 1:5 RSV). It was dark when Mary approached the tomb, but the darkness did not have the last word that day. Jesus had warned earlier in his ministry, "Walk while you have the light, lest the darkness overtake you" (John 12:35 RSV).

The darkness is pervasive just as evil is pervasive. Darkness will swallow us up if the light does not shine. Jesus said that men loved "darkness rather than light, because their deeds were evil" (John 3:19 RSV). Jesus invited people to consider that he was "the light of the world; he who follows me will not walk in darkness, but will have the light of life" (John 8:12 RSV). And then Jesus said, "I have come as light into the world, that whoever believes in me may not remain in darkness" (John 12:46 RSV). Mary knew about believing. She knew about Jesus who had given her another chance at life. She believed, and the darkness had to flee.

III. Where is the darkness in your life?

On the edges of your life, have the dark clouds begun to gather? Or is it already later than that for you? Almost suffocated beneath the weight of your rebellion, sick unto death because of the nature of your sin, have you lost hope in this world? Walking in your own way and stubbornly resisting the grace of God, seeking peace at your own pace and joy at your own price, have you come to the place where you know the darkness is finally going to conquer you?

Think of it this way. Suppose that one day the earth were suddenly to break out of its own orbit, no longer to revolve around the sun, but were to fly farther and farther away into the cold mist of space—spaceship *Earth* run amok. Men and women would wait for the coming of spring, but it would never come. We would wait with weariness for the birds' return and the buds to come to the trees, but never would there be a sign of spring; only deeper and ever deeper into winter we would travel. Meanwhile we would be saying to one another, "Surely tomorrow spring will come." But still nothing happens as we travel faster and faster into the darkness. No spring, no summer, only the deathly coldness that grips the earth as we whirl farther and farther away until at last the truth breaks upon us that we are doomed. And with a great and bitter cry we would know we were lost in the darkness (paraphrased from James S. Stewart, *The Baptist Messenger*, March 27, 1975).

Many people feel darkness like that. For some, it is loss of hope that life can ever be different from what it is. A young man pleads with his pastor, "Tell me how my life can change. I've tried everything to be accepted and find my place, but nothing works!" For others it is the sense of darkness as they look at their country. The faces change, but the broken promises continue. The moral courage required to stand against pornography and racism and drug traffic are sadly lacking. Others are frightened for a world that seems to have lost its moorings and is drifting in dark, uncharted space. Others suffer from loneliness in the midst of a busy world. Most serious of all is the darkness suffered by those who leave God out of their lives. Jesus is the true Light; all other light is temporary and reflected. The darkness cannot forever be kept back by any substitute light pretending to be the Light of the World! To ignore God and his Son Jesus Christ is to run to darkness.

Conclusion

God calls us back to light. Into the dark night of the soul comes the Light of the World.

> *Flourish the trumpets; the living Savior comes.*
> *Roll the victory cadence on a thousand drums,*
> *Let the anthem swell from a thousand tongues,*
> *He is living, He is living, the Lord of light,*
> *He is alive!*

—Anonymous

If you would live, bid the darkness flee. Invite the light of God in Jesus Christ to dispel your darkness. In him there is no darkness at all. In him the darkness gives way. He is risen! He is risen! Hallelujah!

SUNDAY EVENING, MARCH 31

Title: Malachi—Religious Recession and Revival

Text: "Return unto me, and I will return unto you, saith the LORD of hosts" (**Mal. 3:7**).

Scripture Reading: Malachi 3:1–7

Introduction

Three things may be noted about the last of the Old Testament prophets.
A. *Malachi's style was unique among the prophets.* He did not thunder, "Thus saith the Lord!" He has been called the Hebrew Socrates because he

employed that Greek philosopher's method with telling effect. First he presented an accusation against the people. Then we read, "But you say," as the prophet proposed an objection on the part of his hearers. This objection was next refuted in some detail; and in so doing, the truth of his original charge was driven home. Seven distinct examples of this method appear in this fifty-five-verse book.

B. *Malachi's prophecy is remarkable in its originality.* No expression of universalistic monotheism is as clear and far-reaching as that found in Malachi 1:11. While God's name is despised by his people, it is magnified among the heathen. Malachi is also unique in his attitude toward divorce. He presents the Old Testament doctrine of marriage in its highest form. In his admonition regarding the fatherhood of God and the brotherhood of man (2:10), Malachi rises to sublime heights.

C. *Malachi lived in perilous days.* Though the temple of the restoration had been completed in 516 B.C., Judah seemed doomed to obscurity, little touched by the tides of history, their dreams of renewed splendor gone, their zeal for the God of their fathers played out. Ezra visited Jerusalem in 458 B.C. and found conditions there appalling. He made little headway until the coming of Nehemiah, by the authority of the Persian king, to rebuild the walls and carry through the reforms Ezra had begun. Sparked by Ezra's public reading of the law, a genuine revival resulted. During Nehemiah's twelve-year absence in Persia, however, the abuses he had so vigorously suppressed sprang up again. It was at about this time that Malachi began his work.

Accordingly, our text aptly states the theme of this prophecy: "Return unto me, and I will return unto you, saith the LORD of hosts" (3:7). This is a plea for revival. Note three things.

I. The nation's need of revival.

Five evidences may be singled out.

A. *The spirit of ingratitude (1:1–6).* Chosen of God, nurtured with loving care, the people of Judah had neither appreciated their blessings nor thanked the divine Giver. "A son honoreth his father, and a servant his master: If then I am a father, where is mine honor? and if I am a master, where is my fear?" (1:6 ASV).

B. *The spirit of irreverence.* This charge was made against both priests and people (1:7–14). They had held "the table of the LORD" contemptible. They were irreverent in their offerings of polluted bread as well as beasts that were lame, blind, and sick.

C. *The unworthy priesthood (2:1–10).* The priests made their office contemptible. As blind leaders of a blind people, they caused others to stumble with them. The aim of the leaders of the restoration was the creation of a religious community. Consequently, the life of the new Jerusalem was centered around the temple and its services as the life in the old city had never been. High character rooted in a vital faith in God, devotion to the preaching of the truth, patient and loving teaching of the God-given way of life that is life indeed—these are still, as they were in the days of Malachi, the marks of a good minister.

D. *The unfaithfulness of the people (2:10–16).* "Judah hath profaned the holiness of Jehovah which he loveth, and hath married the daughter of a foreign god" (2:11 ASV). This figure is different in form from that of Hosea, but the meaning is almost the same. The people as a whole, and many as individuals, were untrue to God. Not content with their sins of sorcery, perjury, and oppression, they entered into mixed marriages, practiced adultery, and encouraged divorce. This was unfaithfulness with a vengeance.

E. *The spirit of envy (2:17; 3:13–15).* This was a new note in the experience of the Hebrews. Previous generations had turned away from God because they had dallied with some foreign deity; but here, while professing still to serve Jehovah, they complained bitterly against his apparent favoritism to the wicked. For a people as a whole to be moved by envy of evildoers and to flaunt their dissatisfaction with God before the world was an alarming thing.

II. The tokens of revival.

With Malachi the tokens, the harbingers, of revival were not wholly spiritual. They must be with us.

A. *The spirit of liberality.* This is the exact opposite of the sin of ingratitude. To bring into the storehouse the whole tithe (3:10) and only their best in sacrifices was necessary for revival among the people of Judah. So it is for us. Revival can never come to the church of Christ until the whole church brings the whole tithe into the church treasury, which corresponds to the prophet's storehouse.

B. *The spirit of reverence (3:16).* The words "then they that feared Jehovah" indicate that there was a remnant in Judah who held Jehovah in reverence. Such fear is the dominant note of every saintly life. The psalmist said, "The secret of the Lord is with them that fear him" (25:14). If this be slavish fear, may the tribe of slaves increase.

C. *The attitude of meditation.* "For them…that thought upon his name" (3:16). In our evangelistic efforts are we content with the absence of thought? Are we ministers too busy to prepare thoughtful messages based on diligent study of the Bible? As one ancient saint said, "O how love I thy law! it is my meditation all the day" (Ps. 119:97). In former days the mighty power behind the mass meetings held by Moody and Sunday was due largely to Bible study and prayer.

D. *The willingness to serve.* "I will spare them, as a man spareth his own son that serveth him" (3:17). This fourth harbinger of revival goes with the third. Meditation and service are inseparable. They must blend. Meditation without service would soon degenerate into religious day-dreaming; service without meditation would soon smack of materialism. When revival truly comes, God's people are no longer content with thinking, talking, and singing about spiritual things. They begin to serve.

E. *The habit of cordiality.* "They...spake often one to another" (3:16). This harbinger of revival should stand last, for unless the other graces precede, cordiality means little to the kingdom. If all these graces—liberality, reverence, meditation, and service—abound, cordiality and friendliness will also abound. With these graces abounding, God's favor crowns the work of revival.

III. The blessings that will come with revival.

These also are purely spiritual.

A. *The prayers of God's people will be heard.* In a sense our heavenly Father hears all our prayers, but he does not give us all we ask for. When we really learn to pray, all our prayers are heard, and all our prayers are answered according to his will for us.

B. *God's people will be remembered.* The prophet puts it in quaint but beautiful fashion: "A book of remembrance was written before him for them that feared the Lord, and that thought upon his name" (3:16). When revival comes, new names will be written in God's book, and other names, written long since but blotted by sin, will be made as bright as new.

C. *God's possession of his people will be confirmed.* "They shall be mine, saith the LORD" (3:17). They belong to him, and he will keep them safe.

D. *God, as a Father, will spare his children.* "I will spare them, as a man spareth his own son that serveth him" (3:17). God spares his children, not from burdens and trials, but from burdens too heavy and from temptations too strong. He treats them not as pets to be pampered, but as children being trained for eternity.

Conclusion

The appendix (4:5–6) appears to have been written as the conclusion not merely to the book of Malachi but to the whole collection of the twelve minor prophets. In any case, it presents the grim alternatives to revival and the glorious promise of the coming of the forerunner of the Messiah.

Suggested preaching program for the month of

APRIL

■ Sunday Mornings

Messages for the weeks following Easter focus on the power of the resurrection and the power of the Holy Spirit within believers. The series is called "Power to Save."

■ Sunday Evenings

The suggested theme is "The Continuing Adequacy of Jesus Christ." As God promised to be adequate to meet the needs of Moses and the children of Israel, so Jesus also claimed divine adequacy. The great "I Ams" of the Gospel of John serve as the texts for these messages.

■ Wednesday Evenings

Continue the studies based on Paul's first letter to the Corinthian Christians.

WEDNESDAY EVENING, APRIL 3

Title: We Have This Treasure

Text: "All are yours; and ye are Christ's; and Christ is God's" (**1 Cor. 3:22–23**).

Scripture Reading: 1 Corinthians 3:22–23

Introduction

Christians are the wealthiest people in the world. As Christians look up, down, and all around, everything they see is theirs. In this passage of Scripture, Paul begins to enumerate the Christian's possessions. He refers to messengers that deliver the truth; the "world" and all its riches and beauty; "death," the key that unlocks the door to the Christian's eternal reward; "things present," which would include such things as homes, families, friends, and businesses; and "things to come," which would include blessings and curses. These gifts are piled high before believers' eyes and serve as a subject for this message.

I. First, consider the fact that Christians do have these treasures.

A. *These treasures are from God.* Each person who has had an experience with God through Jesus Christ knows that all spiritual possessions are from God. They are marks of love. The recipients should accept the experiences in a spirit of gratitude and not take them for granted.

Each person should also realize that material possessions come from God. They are not merely the result of one's own efforts but are gifts from God.

B. *These treasures are for a holy purpose.* There are three views of material wealth.

1. Material wealth is intended for personal comfort and delight. This is what the parable found in Luke 12 is describing. These gifts are to be used for the divine purpose of honoring God.

2. Material wealth is something that may be hoarded. There is a difference in saving for a holy purpose. Those who hoard violate the principle of having possessions for a holy purpose.

3. Material wealth is a gift for a high and holy purpose. In this view, one realizes God controls all things and does all things for a holy goal.

C. *These treasures are to be surrendered to God.*

1. God is patient. He patiently waits for penitent sinners so that he may give them eternal salvation. He patiently waits for his children to learn vital lessons. And he patiently waits for wayward Christians to return to him.

2. People suffer when they withhold these treasures from God. They build a false sense of security and retard the progress of God's kingdom.

II. Second, consider what Christians have in these treasures.

A. *We have power, especially to evangelize the world.* To utilize this power, we must take our stand for righteousness. We must be busy proclaiming the gospel.

B. *We have influence.* We have an influence for good in a world that is plagued with evil. We can especially influence others to accept Christ as Savior.

C. *We have talents given us by the Lord to accumulate material wealth.* They are talents to be used in specific service for the Lord.

III. Third, consider the use of these talents.

A. *There are different levels of giving.* At the "tip" level, a small gift is given as a token of appreciation for a service rendered. The "entertainment" level is similar to purchasing a ticket at a ball game or theater, or giving only when one goes to church. At the "emotional" level a person gives only when his or her emotions have been stirred. Some people give on the "promise" level: they make a pledge but do not fulfill it. God's way is the giving of tithes and offerings.

B. *Token giving is not pleasing to God.* Token giving is giving only a small portion of what one is capable of giving. It is often used as an excuse for not giving more and a way of redirecting attention. It is used to soothe one's conscience. Token giving is a sin, as it breaks the first commandment.

C. *Love is the basis of all giving.* When we love, we give. When we do not love, we find excuses. Giving is an act of worship. Worship has been defined as self-giving to God.

Conclusion

Paul says that all these things are yours. Because of the bountiful way the Lord gives to us and because of the rich benefits we receive from giving, we should follow God's plan for giving.

SUNDAY MORNING, APRIL 7

Title: The Resurrection and Our Great Salvation

Text: "Consequently he is able for all time to save those who draw near to God through him, since he always lives to make intercession for them" (**Heb. 7:25** RSV).

Scripture Reading: Hebrews 7:23–28

Hymns: "All Hail the Power of Jesus' Name," Perronet
"Oh, for a Thousand Tongues to Sing," Wesley
"Jesus Shall Reign," Watts

Offertory Prayer: Holy Father, we come today to thank you and to praise you for the gift of your love to us revealed supremely in the life, death, and resurrection of Jesus Christ. We thank you for the presence of the living Christ in the person of the Holy Spirit in our midst today. Help us to have the faith to recognize and to respond to his presence. Help us to open our lives fully, not only to his surveillance, but to his sovereignty. We bring gifts as expressions of our love and as indications of our faith and hope that all people everywhere shall come to know Jesus Christ as Lord and Savior. In his name we pray. Amen.

Introduction

The words of our text declare that Jesus Christ is alive from the dead. *Today's English Version* declares it in these words: "He is able, now and always, to save those who come to God through him, because he lives forever to plead with God for them." Phillips paraphrases the content of this verse as follows: "This means that he can save fully and completely those who approach God through him, for he is always living to intercede on their behalf."

We meet today in this house dedicated to worship because of our faith that Jesus Christ was raised from the dead, conquering death, sin, and the grave.

Christianity is the faith that claims a living founder. Jesus Christ was born in Bethlehem and died on a cross outside the walls of Jerusalem. Jesus Christ conquered death and the grave and ascended back to the Father. By his Spirit he is present everywhere in the hearts of those who trust him and love him. Christianity is good news about the Son of God, who came, lived, died, and conquered death, and continues to live.

Our great salvation is made possible and certain by the resurrection of Jesus Christ. Dr. Robert G. Lee has a great sermon entitled "The World's Blackest Assumption." In that sermon he declared that if Christ be not raised, the church has no message for the world; the Christian has nothing to believe; Christian witnesses are telling falsehoods about God; our individual faith is an empty, lifeless shell; and tragedy of tragedies, we are still in our sins. Paul declares that our salvation is based on our belief in the fact that Christ died for our sins, that he was buried, and that he was raised from the dead on the third day according to the Scriptures (1 Cor. 15:3–8). If Christ be not risen, then those who have fallen asleep in Jesus Christ are perished. If Jesus Christ be not risen, we are to be pitied because we are living and building our life on an illusion.

Christianity is based on the faith that Jesus Christ has been raised from the dead as the firstfruits from among the dead.

I. The resurrection vindicates Jesus of Nazareth as being God's unique Son.

During his life and ministry Jesus revealed his unique person, not only by the marvelous words that fell from his lips, but by the miraculous works that came from his hands and from his words. He talked as man had never spoken before. His disciples came to believe that he was more than just a man and more than just a prophet. Peter spoke for them in his remarkable confession of faith in which he expressed his belief that Jesus was the Son of God (Matt. 16:16).

It was the resurrection of Jesus Christ that dramatically declared Jesus to be the unique Son of God.

II. The resurrection of Christ declares the crucifixion to be a revelation of divine love for sinners rather than just a horrible execution.

For the apostles the death of Jesus was a personal catastrophe, a public disgrace, and a political disappointment. For the Father God it was the revealing of his suffering love and his redeeming power to save sinners from the consequences of their sins. It was through the doorway of the empty tomb that the apostles were able to visualize the cross as the instrument of God's redeeming love. Had there been no resurrection, the death of Jesus Christ would never have been understood as a revelation of the great love of God for sinners.

The death of Jesus Christ for sin was a once-and-for-all substitutionary sacrifice that takes care of our sin debts (1 Peter 3:18).

III. The resurrection gives us an intercessor in the presence of God.

Jesus Christ, our great High Priest, has entered into the Holy of Holies with his own sacrificial death as an atonement for our sins.

John, in his first epistle, wrote to encourage believers not to live a life of sin. "My little children, I am writing this to you so that you may not sin; but if any one does sin, we have an advocate with the Father, Jesus Christ the righteous; and he is the expiation for our sins, and not for ours only but also for the sins of the whole world" (1 John 2:1–2 RSV).

All of us need the ministry of this divine advocate.

IV. The resurrection gave to the believers a living Lord and companion.

A. *Jesus began his ministry by saying, "Follow me."* He continues to extend that invitation.

B. *This living Lord walked and talked with his disciples.* He taught them and showed them how they could become makers of disciples. He continues to lead us in helping others to become disciples.

C. *Jesus instructed his disciples that they were to teach new disciples to obey his commandments and to follow his example.* Jesus Christ, the living Lord, continues this same ministry and wants to assist us as we seek to help others.

Conclusion

Yes, Jesus Christ is alive. He walks the road of life with us today as he did with his two disciples on the road to Emmaus. He comes to us in the prayer closet. He comes to us in the place of worship. He comes to us in the needs of those about us.

If you have never yet trusted him as Savior, he comes today to knock at your heart's door. Let him come in as Savior and Lord and teacher and friend. As the living Lord comes to communicate himself to you, let him walk with you along the road of life. Go with him as he leads in the good way.

SUNDAY EVENING, APRIL 7

Title: The Great I AM

Text: "God said to Moses, 'I am who I am. This is what you are to say to the Israelites: I AM has sent me to you'" **(Exod. 3:14 NIV).**

Scripture Reading: Exodus 3:13–15

Introduction

Tonight's message is an introduction to a study of the seven "I am" sayings of Jesus found in John's gospel. John continually demonstrated a keen awareness of the relationship between the revelation of God in the Old Testament and the revelation of Jesus as God in the New Testament era.

As John listened to Jesus' teachings, he sensed a significant parallelism between God's announcement of his name to Moses and Jesus' repeated announcements about his person in the "I am" sayings. Thus, in order to gain the full import of John's design in his gospel account, we must go back to that burning bush at Sinai and examine the great I AM who revealed himself to Moses.

Moses was eighty years old (Exod. 7:7) when he turned aside to examine the strange sight of a bush burning without being consumed. He was startled when the Lord announced to him that he had chosen him to go to Pharaoh and secure the release of his people.

But Moses began making excuses, one of which was, "Suppose I go to the Israelites and say to them, 'The God of your fathers has sent me to you,' and they ask me, 'What is his name?' Then what shall I tell them?" (Exod. 3:13 NIV). God's reply was weighted with meaning. He said, "I AM WHO I AM" (v. 13 NIV), which implied, "I am the God of the past, the present, and the future."

I. I am the God of the present.

The word God used is a verb of being *('ehyeh)*; it can be translated "I am who I am."

A. *God was saying to Moses, "I am the God of now."* He was assuring Moses of his continued presence as he carried out the divine task.

B. *Moses was already concerned about what personal qualities and abilities he had to carry out this task (Exod. 3:11).* People often look only at their own abilities when God calls them to a particular responsibility. God is saying what Jesus said in Matthew 28:20: "I am with you always."

C. *In Moses' day a person's name was the summation of his or her character.* The refusal to share one's name was an unwillingness to give oneself to the other person completely. On the other hand, to give someone your name was to imply that you were giving that person some power over you. Thus, God was willingly giving to Moses a great deal of power to call his name in prayer, proclamation, and prophecy.

D. *God wanted Moses to go and tell the Israelites that he is a very present help.* God is always available to his people. He is not locked in the past with what used to be, nor is he so preoccupied with the future and what might be some day that he cannot be helpful here and now.

Thus, God tells Moses and all succeeding generations that he is "the God of the present."

II. I am the God of the past.

In Exodus 3:15 God also said to Moses, "Say to the Israelites, 'The LORD, the God of your fathers—the God of Abraham, the God of Isaac and the God of Jacob—has sent me to you.' This is my name forever, the name by which I am to be remembered from generation to generation" (NIV).

God wanted his people to know that he was the same God who led, blessed, and made covenants with their forefathers.

A. *He is the God of Abraham.* Abraham was a righteous man. The Israelites were aware of Abraham's significance as the chief patriarch of their nation.

1. Furthermore, Abraham was generally known and respected as a righteous man.

2. Of the three greatest patriarchs, Abraham was the most shining example of good moral and ethical conduct.

3. God was saying to his children, "I am the God your righteous father Abraham worshiped."

B. *He is also the God of Isaac.* Isaac is the least well-known of the three patriarchs.

1. Isaac is overshadowed in Scripture by his father and by his son Jacob. Isaac is given only one chapter in Genesis in which he is mentioned totally for something he alone did. In all other places he is mentioned in relation to either Abraham or Jacob.

2. Thus, Isaac is in reality a nobody compared to the other two patriarchs. He is most remembered as a link between Abraham and Jacob.

3. Isaac was almost a nobody. God was saying to his children, "I am the God of the 'least known,'" of those who are overshadowed by the fame of others.

C. *He is also the God of Jacob.* Jacob was notoriously unrighteous.

1. His life was characterized by deceit and dishonesty.

2. His very name meant "He supplants." His name reflected both his character and his deeds.

3. Yet when Jacob met God at Jabbok (Gen. 32:22–30) his character was forever changed—as was his name. No longer known as "supplanter," he became known as Israel, "prince of God."

4. Thus, God was saying, "I am the God of changed lives—no matter how evil their past."

So God's name also meant that he is the God of the past.

III. I am the God of the future.

Earlier it was mentioned that the Hebrew word God used as his name was *'ehyeh.* It is true that it is a present tense verb of being, but it is also true that the word can be translated, "I will be who I will be."

A. *Thus, God was also saying to Moses that he is a God of the future.* At any time in the near or distant future, he will still be God.

B. *God was telling Moses that he was not only here now, but that Moses, the people of Israel, and their descendants could always count on God being there.*

C. *God has no limit.* He is not bound by time. Whatever promises he has made in the past will be kept in the future. Even if the generation of Moses is not present to see the fulfillment of a promise, the people can be sure that God will always and forever be present to keep his word.

D. *God comes to us today to tell us that he will be present tomorrow, and tomorrow after that, and tomorrow forever.*

Conclusion

Thus, God has said to Moses what he wishes to say to us today: "I am the God of the past." I have spoken to your fathers. I have been with the leadership of your churches in past generations. Even though they were not perfect, I still worked with them, loved them, and saved them.

"I am also the God of the present." I am not locked in an ancient book, tradition, or history. What I did for Moses, I can and want to do for you today. I want to be your God, and I want you to be my people.

Finally, "I am the God of the future." I am going before you. I will not change. I will keep my promises to you, because I will be with you tomorrow and forever.

"I am the great I Am." Respond with faith today to our God who knows your past and your future.

WEDNESDAY EVENING, APRIL 10

Title: Fools for Christ's Sake

Text: "We are fools for Christ's sake" **(1 Cor. 4:10).**

Scripture Reading: 1 Corinthians 4:1–13

Introduction

The apostle Paul was a gifted man in many respects. He used various techniques to get his message across, one of which was irony. That is the technique he was using when he spoke of himself as being a fool for Christ.

I. Examine the words Paul used in this statement.

A. *The word "fool" is the first consideration.* The Greek root is the word from which *moron* comes. It means empty or useless.

B. *The words "for Christ's sake" are the second consideration.* The phrase means "because of Christ." Thus, it does not mean being a fool in order to advance the cause of Christ but rather to be considered a fool by some because of what Christ has done for each person.

C. *The words in Matthew 5:11 are a commentary on the meaning of these words.* "Blessed are ye, when men shall revile you, and persecute you, and shall say all manner of evil against you falsely, for my sake."

II. Examine the irony of Paul's statement.

A. *It stems from the attitude of the Christians at Corinth.* Suffering was the lot of Christians in that day. However, the Corinthians had a different idea.

They spoke as if they needed no instruction from Paul or any other person. They believed they had already attained the highest Christian advantages. They also behaved as if all the trials of Christians were over. They thought they had attained superiority to all disturbances, trials, and need of teaching.

B. *Paul used certain words to scorn such ideas.* Some of the words he used in a general way were derived from *wisdom, power,* and *honor.* They were such words as *full, rich, strong,* and *honorable.* But they were used in scorn and do not depict the normal meaning. Some words Paul used more specifically were *hunger, thirsty, naked, buffeted,* and *no dwelling place.* These words were used to denote the true feeling.

Some words Paul used in this passage that sum up his attitude were *reviled* (1 Cor. 4:12), *persecuted* (v. 12), *defamed* (v. 13), and *made as the filth of the world* (v. 13). Christians are to rise above such things as these, and when they do, they are considered "fools" by some people.

III. Examine a modern-day concept of the same idea.

A. *When people are devoted enough to live by faith and cast aside human wisdom, they may be considered by some as "fools for Christ's sake."* This can be demonstrated by being totally honest in every respect of every business dealing. It is also demonstrated by being willing to let God retaliate on our behalf and by not demanding personal rights. It is that "second mile" that Jesus spoke about. Another application is for Christians to live a life that is completely clean in deed, word, and thought. Living by faith is seen when believers rely on the hidden power of the gospel rather than on using cheap means of impressing people.

B. *When people are devoted enough to take the initiative in doing their Christian duty, they may be considered by some as "fools for Christ's sake."* Christians should separate themselves from things that are wrong or questionable. They should take a positive stand against things that are wrong or for those that are right. All of us should dedicate ourselves to God to the extent that nothing will come between us and God.

Conclusion

You will notice that Paul uses three sets of contrasts to carry out his irony. "We are fools for Christ, but you are so wise in Christ! We are weak, but you are strong! You are honored, we are dishonored!" (1 Cor. 4:10 NIV).

SUNDAY MORNING, APRIL 14

Title: The Resurrection of Christ and Our Resurrection

Text: "Christ has been raised from the dead, the first fruits of those who have fallen asleep" (**1 Cor. 15:20 RSV**).

Scripture Reading: 1 Corinthians 15:20–23, 35–45

Hymns: "Christ the Lord Is Risen Today," Wesley
"Majestic Sweetness Sits Enthroned," Stennett
"My Savior, First of All," Crosby
"O That Will Be Glory," Gabriel

Offertory Prayer: Loving Father, we are the recipients of your gracious and wonderful gifts. Thank you for loving us in Jesus Christ. Thank you for giving us assurance that our sins are forgiven and that we are accepted in Christ as members of your family. Thank you for the fellowship that we enjoy in and through the church. Thank you for the task that is ours of sharing the good news of a risen, living Lord with a needy world. Accept our gifts as tokens of our desire to be dedicated to the proclaiming of the good news of his death, resurrection, and living presence to the ends of the earth. In his saving name we pray. Amen.

Introduction

One of the great truths of Christianity is that death has been defeated, giving us hope for a life beyond this vale of tears in which we live. The word *resurrection* means a "state of standing up" or a "state of standing again." In the New Testament the word refers to the raising up of the body, the victory of the body from the cruel clutches of death. Our belief in resurrection is based solidly on the fact that Jesus Christ has conquered death and the grave.

I. The resurrection of Jesus Christ.

The New Testament writers based their belief in the resurrection of the saints firmly on the resurrection of Jesus Christ. They believed that the victory Jesus experienced over death is a victory that is to be experienced by those who believe in him and follow him as his disciples (1 Cor. 15:56–57; 1 Thess. 4:13–18).

A. *Jesus predicted his own resurrection (Matt. 12:39–40; John 2:19–22).*

B. *The resurrection of Christ.* The resurrection of Christ is the central fact of the New Testament. The Scriptures declare that Jesus' physical body did not decay in the grave. It was made alive again by the power of God. It was gloriously transformed so that it was no longer limited by time or space nor subject to change, decay, and death.

C. *The postresurrection appearances of the living Christ.* We have at least ten recorded instances in which the Christ who experienced crucifixion and death appeared to his disciples. Six of these are most significant for our consideration.

123

1. The appearance to Mary Magdalene in the garden (John 20:11–18).
2. The appearance on the road to Emmaus (Luke 24:13–32).
3. The appearance in the upper room (Luke 24:36–43).
4. The appearance one week later (John 20:26–31).
5. The appearance by the sea (John 21:4–19).
6. The appearance to Saul of Tarsus (Acts 9:1–22).

D. The nature of Jesus' resurrected body.
   1. Jesus' body was tangible.
      a. The disciples saw Jesus.
      b. Jesus talked to the disciples.
      c. Mary clasped the feet of the resurrected Christ.
      d. Jesus ate the bread and honeycomb.
   2. Jesus' body was transcendent.

      The resurrection of Jesus was not a restoration to the natural plane of life. His resurrected body was not subject to time, space, or material objects. As his precrucifixion body had been perfectly adapted to the needs of life in this world, so his resurrection body was adapted to the needs of the new plane of life.

II. The resurrection of believers (1 Cor. 15:20–22).

Christianity's belief in the certainty of a resurrection is based solidly on our belief that Jesus Christ conquered death and as such is the firstfruits from among the dead.

A. *The resurrection of believers is based on the truth of the resurrection of Jesus Christ.* The gospel, stated in capsule form, relates to the truth taught in the Scriptures that Christ died for our sins, that he was buried in a tomb, and that he was raised from the dead on the third day. He was seen by many people, giving indisputable proof of his living presence (Acts 1:3).

    That Christ has been raised from the dead is our proof that the kingdom of death has been invaded and the power of death has been defeated. The message of Christianity is that ultimately death will be completely destroyed.

B. *The resurrection of believers is based on our belief in the power of God (1 Cor. 15: 35–38).* In response to the question of "How are the dead raised?" Paul speaks concerning the power and wisdom of God.
   1. The resurrection is possible because of God's power.
      a. God's power is demonstrated in the world of vegetation, where he is able to make from seeds planted in the ground a variety of plants and trees that are adapted to their habitats.
      b. In the realm of zoology, God the creator has given living creatures bodies adapted to their habitats. Although there are similarities between these living creatures, each is given a body suitable for its surroundings.

    2. God's power is perfectly demonstrated in the creation of the heavenly bodies—the stars, the moon, the sun—for all are unique.

        God's power makes it possible for him to do what he wishes regarding the resurrection of the saints.

C. *The resurrection of believers is possible because of the wisdom of God as well as his power.*

    1. The body, planted in corruption, will be raised in incorruption.

    2. The body is planted in dishonor because of sin, but it will be raised in honor, not subject to sin.

    3. The body is planted in weakness, because it is subject to death, but it will be raised in power, not subject to death.

    4. The body is planted as a natural body, but it will be raised as a spiritual body like unto the body of Jesus Christ.

        The earthly body has been perfectly adapted to the needs of our physical plane of existence. The body in which we will exist in heaven will be perfectly adapted to the needs of that level of spiritual experience. Out of our relationship to Adam, we received a physical body subject to decay and death, but through our relationship with Jesus Christ, we will receive a spiritual body that is subject to neither decay nor death.

III. Responding positively to the prospect of resurrection.

If Jesus Christ be not risen, we are of all people most to be pitied (1 Cor. 15:12–19).

If Jesus Christ be not risen, we are whistling in the dark when we think about the possibility of survival beyond death.

If Jesus Christ be not risen, it is good-bye forever when we go to the cemetery that last time.

If Jesus Christ be not risen, there is absolutely no hope for a life beyond.

The message of Christianity is that Jesus Christ is risen. Consequently, there are four great responses we should make.

A. *We should respond with gratitude (1 Cor. 15:57).*

B. *We would respond with comfort (1 Thess. 4:18).*

C. *We should respond with faithfulness and diligence in service with the conviction that what we do for God is not in vain (1 Cor. 15:58).*

D. *We should respond with joyful obedience to the living Lord as he commands us to carry the good news of his life, death, resurrection, and living presence to the ends of the earth (Matt. 28:18–20).*

Conclusion

Each one needs to respond to the resurrection of Christ by trusting him as Lord and Savior. Jesus Christ arose from the dead to give proof of the fact that his death on the cross was an adequate solution to your sin problem. He conquered death and the grave that he might be able to give you the gift of eternal life (Heb. 7:25). Today is the day in which you can do business with the living Christ. Let him become the Lord of your life now.

SUNDAY EVENING, APRIL 14

Title: I Am the Bread of Life

Text: "Then Jesus declared, 'I am the bread of life. He who comes to me will never go hungry, and he who believes in me will never be thirsty'" **(John 6:35 NIV).**

Scripture Reading: John 6:1–14, 26–27, 32–35

Introduction

A commercial bakery was located not far from a college campus. The aroma of freshly baked bread could be smelled for blocks. It had a mouth-watering effect, and the company made the most of it by opening a cafe where customers could buy warm, fresh bread and other baked goods and sit and enjoy them with a cup of coffee or juice. College students liked to visit the cafe because it was an inexpensive place to take a date or to hang out with friends.

As wonderful as freshly baked bread is, Jesus offers something even greater. Jesus begins the "I am" statements in John by declaring, "I am the bread of life." His statement is uttered after his feeding of the five thousand, when they came seeking him to feed them again. It is here that Jesus encourages the people not only to seek food for the body, but to seek food that can satisfy their souls.

Jesus used a metaphor that we can readily understand. In this text he speaks of how bread can satisfy, how it is sufficient, and how it provides salvation.

I. Jesus offers bread that can satisfy.

A. *Hunger is one of humanity's basic drives.* What begins as a mild discomfort progresses rapidly to become a compelling need.

   Hunger refers to more than just a need for physical food. For example, one can be hungry for affection or for power. Hunger is a craving and desire for anything.

B. *Vast numbers in the world are hungry.* The literal lack of food is frequently flashed before us on our television screens. Emaciated bodies with hollow, hungry eyes stare blankly at us.

   One cannot help but make an analogy with the spiritual hunger that is equally evident. The Christian is moved to compassion for physically hungry souls, but too often we are not as concerned about their spiritual hunger.

C. *Jesus can satisfy the spiritual void in a person's life.* Jesus says, "I am the bread of life." He feeds life. He provides the banquet of life. He offers life beyond death, joy beyond sorrow, hope beyond disappointment, and companionship beyond loneliness.

Christ is not a superficial solution. A look at his own life and that of his followers shows that there were still hardships, opposition, and trials. But Jesus offers a quiet confidence that "right" will be separated from "wrong."

II. Jesus offers bread that is sufficient.

The bread or manna that Moses offered was sufficient only for the one day it was gathered (Exod. 16:19–20). There was always enough for that day, but it had to be gathered each day.

A. *Humankind has an enormous appetite for spiritual matters.* Every culture has a religion. People worship and long for some explanation of their origins and purpose, and they ask such questions as, "If there is a God, who is he and what is he like?" People also want to know what is expected of them. They ask, "Is there life after death? If so, will I be allowed to go on beyond this life?" Jesus provides answers for all of these questions.

B. *Jesus offers an ample solution to life's riddles.* His reasons for living—why to live, how to live—come in superabundance. As the Bread of Life he offers us goals for our lives and then provides us with life beyond this life.

C. *Jesus' offer is not stingy or sparse.* He provides enough "bread" for all of humankind, and each person receives an equal portion. Not only is there room at the banquet for everyone, but there is also enough to satisfy each person's hunger. Some people are filled more quickly and easily than others. Jesus invites each one to come to his table and to eat the bountiful fare of spiritual food he has provided.

III. Jesus offers bread that can provide salvation.

A. *Physical food provides a "kind" of salvation.* It provides the physical nourishment that keeps us from dying. Malnutrition and death occur from an insufficient diet.

B. *The "bread" Jesus offers is like the manna in the wilderness—they both come from heaven.* But Jesus was quick to point out that Moses was not the source of the manna. God is the only one who sends "bread" from heaven. The "bread" of Moses was temporal. The Bread of Life is eternal. Jesus was saying that he is the gift of life.

C. *The "bread" Jesus offers can bring everlasting life.* Those who heard Jesus say this asked him to give them this bread. He declared, "I am the bread of life. He who comes to me will never go hungry."

Conclusion

The aroma of freshly baked bread lured the college students to the bakery. It was always a scene of laughter and anticipation of something good. Likewise, Jesus provides a banquet here and now that draws people who hunger for truth and meaning in life. Jesus wants us to be satisfied, have sufficient suppy for our needs, and have salvation.

Do you have these qualities? Does your soul hunger for nourishment? If it does, I invite you to accept Christ as fulfillment of your needs.

WEDNESDAY EVENING, APRIL 17

Title: The Kingdom of God in Power

Text: "The kingdom of God is not in word, but in power" **(1 Cor. 4:20)**.

Scripture Reading: 1 Corinthians 4:14–20

Introduction

The kingdom of God is a much talked about subject. Many able scholars have written volumes concerning it. There is also a considerable amount of controversy related to the meaning, extent, and so on, of the kingdom. However, it is not the intent of this message to deal with controversial issues but to take Paul's simple statement found in 1 Corinthians 4:20 and deal with it.

I. Why would Paul make such a statement?

A. *Basically, it was because of the attitude of the recipients of the epistle.* The people in the Corinthian church were almost everything Paul believed a Christian should not be. They were puffed up (v. 18), proud, and guilty of holding partisan opinions. This is characteristic of many modern-day Christians. Many fine people in current society think there is power in words, and thus many are spoken, and often very loud.

B. *It was also spoken to remind the reader about more important things.* All Christians need to be reminded of the truth by being confronted with it. The truth needs to be held high and straight. The truth is that just words are an empty display, but the kingdom of God produces true faith, true confession, and true love.

II. What is the kingdom of God?

A. *Paul says it is power (1 Cor. 4:20).* The kingdom is the reign of God in and among people. It is presently among God's people and within them.

B. *The very nature of the kingdom proves it is not in word.* A kingdom implies authority exercised and obedience rendered. Such an idea is incompatible with mere words. It is action or activity.

C. *This kingdom has a real secret.* It is the working of God through his people in right living. Paul spoke of himself as being an example and exhorted the Corinthians to follow him (v. 16). He also spoke of Christ's being the director of his life, which would indicate God's power in action (v. 19). In the same verse, Paul makes a contrast between power and the words of those who are puffed up.

III. How is the kingdom of God manifested? (v. 21).

A. *Sometimes it is in the form of discipline.* Paul makes reference to the rod, which implies punishment or discipline. It refers to disapproval. God's reign does denounce wrongdoing.

B. *All the time it is in the form of love.* Discipline does not exclude, but includes, love. Love is always God's method and never involves such ideas as arrogance, false wisdom, and the like.

C. *It also is in the form of kindness.* In verse 21 Paul speaks of "the spirit of meekness." This is kindness in word and action; it is how the kingdom works.

Conclusion

Each Christian ought to be careful about words. They can be good or bad, but they are not the kingdom of God.

SUNDAY MORNING, APRIL 21

Title: Responding Positively to the Indwelling Holy Spirit

Text: "Therefore, as the Holy Spirit says, 'Today, when you hear his voice, do not harden your hearts as in the rebellion, on the day of testing in the wilderness, where your fathers put me to the test and saw my works for forty years'" (Heb. 3:7–9 RSV).

Scripture Reading: Hebrews 3:7–11; Psalm 95:1–11

Hymns: "Come, Thou Almighty King," Anonymous
"Spirit of God, Our Comforter," Hendricks
"Teach Me Thy Way, O Lord," Ramsey

Offertory Prayer: Heavenly Father, we bow before your presence to thank you for the days of this new year. We thank you for each day as a new page upon which we can write a record of worship and witness and works of love for others. Thank you for these opportunities for living in this time, and for the values of eternity. As we bring tithes and offerings, we pray your blessings upon these indications of our recognition of your ownership and lordship. Help us to give ourselves completely into your service. In Jesus' name. Amen.

Introduction

Have you developed the habit of making an appropriate response to some gift or act of kindness on the part of others?

Many parents put forth a consistent effort to teach an attitude of gratitude to their children by instructing them to always say "thank you" when they are given a gift or rendered some significant service.

Some people always make an affirmative response when they receive a gift. Others never indicate an attitude of gratitude.

How have you responded to God's great gifts? We should think of life itself as a gift from God. How have you responded to God's gift of his Son who came to be our Savior? If you have received Jesus Christ as Savior, how have you responded to God's gift of his indwelling Holy Spirit? It is possible to receive this priceless gift and not even recognize it (1 Cor. 3:16; 12:1).

God's gift of his Holy Spirit is the gift of himself as an abiding presence. This divine Comforter, Counselor, Helper is present to work the work of God in our hearts. It is with his guidance, energy, and assistance that we, as the disciples of Jesus, are able to become Christlike in our character and conduct. This is possible if we make a proper response to the Holy Spirit.

I. We face the peril of making a negative response to the Holy Spirit.

A. *You may grieve the Holy Spirit of God (Eph. 4:30).* This insight into the emotional reaction of God to our failure to respond properly should concern us. In his letter to the Ephesians (4:25–32), Paul details some of the attitudes of mind and actions of life that can bring bitter grief to the Holy Spirit. The opposite side of this coin is that we can bring joy to the Holy Spirit if we cooperate with him in eliminating these bad character traits and these destructive forms of conduct toward others.

B. *You may quench the Holy Spirit (1 Thess. 5:19).* The picture in this imperative is that of pouring water on a fire to put it out. It is a picture of quenching the flame of a candle. It refers to a response toward the Holy Spirit that refuses to cooperate with him as he seeks to do God's good work within us.

C. *You may insult and outrage the Holy Spirit (Heb. 10:29).* This particular section of Scripture, Hebrews 10:25–31, contains a warning that should cause us to tremble if we are tempted to the point of yielding to the forces of evil and to the purposes of Satan.

The Scripture teaches us very forcefully that our Father God chastises his children when they live a life of disobedience growing out of little faith and a rebellious spirit (Heb. 12:5–11).

II. An invitation to respond positively.

A. *"Today."* Some people have a tendency to confine God to the past. They think of him as living in the ancient long ago when the Bible was being written. This is a sad mistake to think of God as some kind of an antique that must be relegated to history.

Others make the mistake of confining God to the future. They think of him as being concerned only about the soul and its safety in heaven.

The God and Father of our Lord Jesus Christ is the God of the living. He is the God of the now. God is the God of current events. He is our contemporary. By means of his Holy Spirit, he wants to speak to us today.

B. *"When you hear his voice."* It is rather shocking to read through the Scripture and to discover both in the Old Testament and the New Testament the recurring refrain, "You would not listen" or "They would not listen." Some people refuse to listen because they are preoccupied with their own pursuits. Others refuse to listen because they disagree, and disagreement often hinders a person from really hearing.

1. The Holy Spirit speaks to us today through the Scriptures.
2. The Holy Spirit speaks to us today through spiritual songs.
3. The Holy Spirit speaks today through pastors, teachers, parents, Christian literature, good books.
4. The Holy Spirit speaks today through the church.
5. The Holy Spirit speaks today through the events of life.

Do you listen? Are you tuned in to hear what God would say to you with the still small voice of his indwelling Spirit?

C. *Notice the warning, "Do not harden your hearts as in the rebellion" (see also Exod. 17:1–7).*

1. You can harden your heart by ignoring God's voice. Have you ever turned off an alarm on your alarm clock morning after morning until finally you could turn it off without being aware that it had sounded?
2. You can harden your heart by disobedience to God's will.
3. You can harden your heart by refusing to listen when God seeks to speak to you.
4. You can harden your heart by making excuses for yourself and by blaming other people.

Conclusion

Let us bow down in worship before the presence of the Holy Spirit of God who has come to dwell within each of us individually and all of us collectively. Let us rejoice in the creative and benevolent purpose of this indwelling presence of God. He has come to enable us to be all that God wants us to be. He is present to reproduce within us the spirit and the character of Jesus Christ (Gal. 5:22–23). Let us trust him for help, for leadership and strength, for divine inner control, and for his help.

If you have not yet come to know Jesus as Savior, the Holy Spirit calls you to him by the great needs in your life. He invites you to Jesus by virtue of your need for forgiveness. He calls you to Christ by your potential for helpfulness to others. He calls you through your responsibility for being helpful to others. He calls you by virtue of the fact that you are on the way toward eternity and you need to be ready. God wants to forgive your sin and give you the gift of eternal life if today you will receive Jesus Christ.

SUNDAY EVENING, APRIL 21

Title: I Am the Light of the World

Text: "Again therefore Jesus spake unto them, saying, I am the light of the world: he that followeth me shall not walk in the darkness, but shall have the light of life" **(John 8:12 ASV)**.

Scripture Reading: John 1:4–5; 8:12; 9:5; 12:46

Introduction

The world of "light" can be divided into artificial light and natural light. Artificial light derives its energy from a manufactured source; light bulbs, flashlights, lanterns, lamps, and heaters are powered by various energy sources. Some natural lights are our sun, stars, lightning, and fireflies. Their light sources are found within themselves.

In the spiritual world there is light that is also artificial or natural. Many kinds of artificial spiritual light have their source in something other than themselves, but there is only one natural spiritual Light, which has its own source of energy. That Light is Jesus, and the light of Jesus dispels darkness.

I. Jesus dispels the darkness of artificiality.

A. *We live in a world of artificiality.* We have soft drinks with artificial color, artificial flavor, and artificial sweeteners. We are surrounded by synthetic fabrics, synthetic rubber, and even synthetic diamonds. In a world of false, fake, and make-believe, we need a true standard. The average person is sometimes not knowledgeable enough to discern the superficial from that which is real. Therefore, we must rely on experts to tells us the difference. For instance, we trust our jeweler to tell us the true quality of a gem.

B. *Christ is the true standard.* Jesus brings light and understanding to life. Everything looks different in the brilliance of sunlight. True color tones are revealed when they are exposed to sunlight. Often artificial light gives off a certain hue. For instance, incandescent light gives off a yellow tint and fluorescent light gives off a blue tint. Sunlight, however, is a white light, and colors are evenly beautiful under its glow.

C. *Humankind offers many forms of spirituality.* Eastern religions and humanitarian enterprises are artificial substitutes for a personal walk with Jesus Christ. They too offer a "light" for humanity, but it is manmade. They are false religions that are shown to be false when they are exposed to the light of Jesus Christ.

II. Jesus dispels the darkness of sin.

Sin is more often than not associated with darkness. Even the secular world makes darkness synonymous with evil thoughts and actions.

A. *Evil deeds seek the cover of darkness.* Even our evil thoughts are often kept private because we do not want others to see us as we really are.

More crime is committed under the cover of darkness than in broad daylight. Dimly lit places of entertainment often are associated with questionable activities. Few people want to walk the streets without the benefit of a street light. Sin finds its best fruit under the cover of darkness.

B. *Jesus is to sin what light is to darkness.* He is the opposite of sin. When he is present, no sin is present. In order to sin, one must put Christ somewhere else. Sin and Christ are not compatible.

C. *Jesus said, "I am the light of the world."* Our sun can only light half of the world at a time. While part of the earth enjoys sunshine, the rest of the world is shrouded in darkness. But Jesus is a Light to all the world. He is not confined by geography or race or national boundaries. His light shines brightly for all humankind.

D. *There is no sin that the light of Christ cannot dispel except, of course, if you reject him.* His light is sufficient to obliterate all shadows.

III. Jesus dispels the darkness of hopelessness.

Life has meaning, but that meaning is not apparent without God.

A. *We are wandering in a moral fog.* Old ways no longer seem to work in our present world. Society is rapidly changing its mores and values. Long-held moral beliefs are ridiculed; marriages are easily dissolved; patriotism is questioned; and respect for God and his church rates very low.

B. *Despair is an enemy of life.* Despondent thoughts choke hope out of life. The tears of anguish are poured out week after week to ministers and professional counselors. All are seeking hope and meaning for life.

C. *Jesus comes to say that he offers "the light of life."* In the midst of difficulty, he offers strength to the weak, comfort to those who mourn, and hope to those who have lost their way. We do not always have the experience necessary to face life's tragedies. Jesus becomes a lighthouse to guide us when we are confused. By knowing Christ, we can know how he would act in a similar circumstance. His Holy Spirit in us witnesses to proper conduct and proper attitudes. Likewise, his Spirit makes us uncomfortable concerning improper conduct.

Conclusion

Thus, Jesus offers true light to a world walking in shadows and darkness. He exposes artificial light as being inferior. He dispels sin and leaves no room for it in a person's life. He adds zest for living by giving us hope in our darkest hours.

This same Jesus can be the Light of your life. Will you take him into your life? Will you let him help you get rid of your sin and give you hope? His light can be the light of life for you.

WEDNESDAY EVENING, APRIL 24

Title: Is There No Wise Among You?

Text: "I speak to your shame. Is it so, that there is not a wise man among you? no, not one that shall be able to judge between his brethren?" (**1 Cor. 6:5**).

Scripture Reading: 1 Corinthians 6:1–8

Introduction

Is it right or wrong for Christians to go to court against one another? Perhaps this has never crossed the minds of most believers in the Lord Jesus Christ, but it is a thought that needs careful consideration. The implications are that Christians should settle their differences out of court.

I. Each Christian should consider the situation at Corinth.

A. *Corinth's situation was somewhat different from today.* Greeks in general were fond of going to the law. They were not only quarrelsome, but the suspense and uncertainty of cases before courts brought excited pleasure to their frivolous nature. Their courts were quite different from modern courts. It seems as if Paul's discussion is not about crimes, but rather about civil cases.

B. *Christians should not take legal action toward one another.* The fact that Paul was not talking about crimes does not lessen this axiom. Every implication of Paul's argument in this passage is that suing one another is wrong. The same argument points out that when Christians do such, they are the losers.

II. Each Christian should consider his or her privileges and responsibilities.

A. *Paul said that the saints will judge the world (1 Cor. 6:2).* If saints are to judge the world, then pagan or civil courts should not be used to make decisions for Christians. Here Paul makes his argument from the greater to the lesser. He moves from the "world" to the "smallest matters." The proper use of the Word of God judges the world, and that honestly. In the last days, the saints shall be associates of Christ in the matter of judging.

B. *Paul's whole argument is that any time a Christian goes before the court to settle an issue, he or she is going from the highest court to a lesser one.*

III. Each Christian should consider what is wrong with going to court against a fellow Christian.

A. *The first wrong is the admission of a lack of competence on the part of those who have the light of Christ.*

B. *The second wrong is that it is a recognition of defeat.* The scale on which these matters work is a descending one. To have disputes is bad. To go to court with one another is worse. And to do it before unbelievers is even worse. The very question of courts indicates there is something wrong. Disputes ought not to arise, but if they do, they should be settled by a mutual friend. It should be done in the spirit of love and forgiveness.

C. *The third wrong is that it causes an adverse effect on the church.* Christians cannot go to court against Christians without having a harmful effect on the fellowship of the church. The fellowship of the church should always be based on love, brotherhood, and forgiveness.

Conclusion

In modern society some things must be settled in civil courts, but Christians should take every precaution to avoid using them. They should never do so unless it is the law of the land.

SUNDAY MORNING, APRIL 28

Title: The Holy Spirit and Our Great Salvation

Text: "Do you not know that your body is a temple of the Holy Spirit within you, which you have from God? You are not your own; you were bought with a price. So glorify God in your body" **(1 Cor. 6:19–20 RSV).**

Scripture Reading: 1 Corinthians 6:12–20

Hymns: "All Hail the Power of Jesus' Name," Perronet
"Grace Greater Than Our Sin," Johnson
"O Spirit of the Living God," Tweedy

Offertory Prayer: Heavenly Father, we thank you for again calling us together that we might worship you in spirit and in truth and rejoice with one another in the bounty of your rich gifts to each of us. We thank you for the manner in which your Spirit indwells the church to lead us into paths of righteousness. Lead us now as we give our tithes and offerings for the advancement of your kingdom's work. In Jesus' name, we pray. Amen.

Introduction

Jesus Christ came to take away the sins of his people (Matt. 1:21). John the Baptist declared that Jesus was the Lamb of God who came to take away the sin of the world (John 1:29). Paul declared that "Christ died for our sins in accordance with the scriptures" (1 Cor. 15:3 RSV). And Peter emphasized the substitutionary nature of the death of Jesus Christ (1 Peter 3:18).

Many people think of salvation only in terms of forgiveness for the guilt of sin and the removal of the penalty of sin. This is to fall far short of the great salvation Jesus Christ came to provide. He came not only to save us from the penalty of sin, but also to save us from the power and the practice of sin.

The Father God wants us to be living, powerful demonstrations of what Jesus Christ can do in the life of those who trust him as Savior and Lord. God is interested in saving us in the present from the power and the practices of sin. To accomplish this great purpose he has given us the precious, personal gift of his Holy Spirit as an indwelling presence.

In the Scripture passage for today we have heard the instructions that God sent through the apostle Paul to the church at Corinth in which it is declared that we are to glorify God in our bodies. The closing challenge in verse 20 places before us an imperative. It is as if Paul is saying, "Honor God in your body." He is requesting that you "reveal the graciousness of God in your body." He is demanding that we "demonstrate the presence of God in our body." He is inviting us to "introduce God to others by our very being." To make this response is a part of the great salvation God wants us to experience through faith in Jesus Christ.

The Father God, through the apostle, called upon the people in the church of Corinth to be the place where God dwelled so that the other people of that pagan city could be saved. To live a profane life of immorality was to defile and to degrade the temple—the residence, the meeting place where people could experience the very presence of God.

It is through the Holy Spirit that the people of God experience the presence of God in the present.

I. The Holy Spirit came to continue the work of Christ.

There is a shyness about the Holy Spirit that causes him to never call attention to himself. Like John the Baptist, the Holy Spirit is always pointing to Jesus Christ (John 16:14).

As Luke opens the book we know as the Acts of the Apostles, he states, "I have dealt with all that Jesus began to do and teach," in reference to the gospel that we know as the Gospel of Luke. The Acts of the Apostles would be more correctly thought of if it were entitled "The Acts of the Holy Spirit." The Holy Spirit continues to do what Jesus began to do.

II. The Holy Spirit convinced each of us of our need for salvation from sin (John 16:8–11).

III. The Holy Spirit brought about the new birth when we responded to the gospel by faith (Titus 3:5–7).

This same precious Spirit—who brought about conviction of sin and conversion from sin and the miracle of the new birth—wants to lead us in a manner of life that will demonstrate to the world that we are the people of God (Titus 2:11–14).

IV. The Holy Spirit works in creating conflict between our lower fleshly nature and our new nature (Gal. 5:6–21).

Some new converts experience a great deal of inward tension as they struggle with the presence of evil within them. Some are quite disappointed to find that the life of faith is not a life of comfort and relief from tension. Perhaps some feel this experience of disappointment because they responded to only a fraction of God's great plan for them when they received Jesus Christ as Savior.

V. The indwelling Spirit is God's seal of ownership.

The Holy Spirit is also God's guarantee of our final and ultimate salvation from death and the grave. Paul affirms this divine seal of ownership in his letter to the Ephesians (1:13–14). In his letter to the Romans, Paul declares that the gift of God's Holy Spirit is his guarantee that he will give us ultimate and complete victory over death and the grave (Rom. 8:11).

VI. The Holy Spirit has been given to us in order that, with our cooperation, he can produce the fruit that will indicate that we are indeed children of God (Gal. 5:22–23).

A. *We give our consent to Jesus Christ to become our Savior.*
B. *We must give not only our consent but our continuous cooperation with the Holy Spirit if we are to experience God's full salvation for us.* By so doing, it is possible for us to glorify God, that is, to make him known to others.

Living the Christian life is something much more than lifting ourselves by our own bootstraps. In reality it is a life of joyful cooperation as the Holy Spirit works within us. When we recognize him and cooperate with him, it is possible for us to glorify God in our body in the here and now.

Conclusion

Yours is the peril of making a negative response to God's great plan for you. Yours can be the joyous privilege of making a proper response to Jesus Christ. Trust him as Savior. Listen to him and obey him as your Lord. Trust in the abiding presence and power of the Holy Spirit to help you become all that God wants you to be.

SUNDAY EVENING, APRIL 28

Title: I Am the Gate for the Sheep

Text: "Therefore Jesus said again, 'I tell you the truth, I am the gate for the sheep'" **(John 10:7 NIV).**

Scripture Reading: John 10:7–10

Introduction

Doors are necessary to any enclosure. Some doors are elaborate and some are simple. Some are ornate and intricate, while others are plain and simply functional. Doors and gates have been made from almost every known material: stone, wood, glass, various metals, bamboo, plastic, and many others. Doors have handles, hinges, removable panels or screens, door knockers, peepholes, and locks. And there are various kinds of doors: screen doors, storm doors, front doors, back doors, garage doors, gate doors, side doors, as well as doors for rooms, storm cellars, vehicles, and closets.

The familiarity of this "door idea" is exactly what Jesus had in mind when he told his followers, "I am the door of the sheepfold." Building on all we know about doors and their function, we can readily see what Jesus was trying to say about himself and God's kingdom.

I. A door is for coming and going.

A. *Jesus is the doorway to God and his kingdom.* Jesus makes this plain in John 10:9: "I am the gate; whoever enters through me will be saved" (NIV). Humankind is looking for the way to eternal life. Jesus is the entryway. He declares this because so many claim to be the true avenue to God.

   In the previous chapter in John a man has been excommunicated from organized religion. To many Jews this was the same as having been cut off from God. Jesus reassures this man and the disciples that the way to come to God is through Jesus.

B. *Jesus further calls himself the "doorway of the sheep."* The sheep did not just come into the sheepfold to spend the rest of their lives in the sheepfold. Again in verse 9 Jesus continues by saying that his sheep "will come in and go out, and find pasture." This refers to the sheepfold as a place for rest and restoration of strength during the night or during a storm. But on the morrow they go back out to pasture.

C. *It is a grand analogy.* We enter God's kingdom through Jesus. There is no thought here of losing one's salvation. Instead, the analogy shifts from salvation to growing as a Christian "sheep."

   You come to Christ for rest, restoration, and comfort. Then you go back out into the world. He is the source of your strength and spiritual health. You are allowed to come in and go out. Doorways are for coming and going.

II. A door is for protection and safety.

A. *In the first century there were two kinds of sheepfolds.* One kind was located in the village and was a community shelter where several shepherds might leave their flocks overnight or for several days. This sheepfold usually had a strong door and also a guardian or keeper of the door.

But a second, more modest sheepfold was located in the countryside. It was usually a stone wall or fenced enclosure without any door or gate. The shepherd slept in the doorway. No sheep could go out without his notice, and no wild beast could get in without his being awakened. In the most literal sense, the shepherd was the door.

B. *Whether Jesus had reference to the village sheepfold door that was strong and well guarded or whether he was referring to the rural sheepfold with the shepherd as the door is almost immaterial.* In either case, the sheep are well protected and can rest in peace knowing that they are safe.

C. *We live in a frustrating world.* The anxiety of life is a constant threat to our safety and well-being. Jesus offers us the reassurance that he is our protector. As David said, "The Lord is my shepherd" (Ps. 23:1). He cares and provides for us. We are his sheep, so he gladly lays down his life for us.

During the night, a sheep might be startled and awakened. If so, it would surely look toward the gate. If it could see the shepherd sitting or lying at the gate, the sheep would know, even in its fear, that the shepherd was there.

III. A door is for opening and closing.

A. *Jesus is the only—absolutely only—way to God.* There is a door, or way, into God's favor. It is a door that is as broad as the heart of God, a door that is open to all races, all ages, both sexes, and persons from every strata of society. It is a door open to rich or poor, important people or forgotten souls, powerful potentates and enslaved serfs.

In Revelation 21:12–13 heaven is described as having a great high wall. In the wall are twelve gates: three on the east, three on the north, three on the south, and three on the west. Through these gates, persons who trust in Christ stream from every nation on earth.

The door is open and the invitation is clear. Here in John 10 Jesus says, "I am the door." Everyone who enters through him will be saved.

B. *But there are two implications here.*

1. All other doors are closed. Those who seek to enter into God's kingdom will find a dead end. Those doors lead nowhere. Some will not open, and those who find doors that do open will find that they are useless.

2. A second implication is that the true door does not stay open forever. Death is the end of life. There is no more chance to seek the doorway to eternal life. That door closes at death. That door also closes if Jesus returns before you die. When the Bridegroom comes, those who are prepared will enter with him, and the door will be shut. In Matthew 25:11 those who were unprepared for the Bridegroom begged him to open the door, but the response was negative.

Conclusion

It is obvious from this passage that Jesus saw himself as the only and true gateway to God. He offers us eternal life if we believe that he is God's way to heaven. He further provides us with safety and protection from the wild enemies of life.

But while God's door is open, it will also close someday. This is said not to frighten you, but rather to demonstrate the urgency of responding to him.

There is no other door to God. Would you come and receive Jesus as the true doorway to God?

Suggested preaching program for the month of

MAY

■ **Sunday Mornings**

Prepare a series of messages designed to strengthen and enrich family living. The suggested theme is "The Living Christ and His Concern for Family Living."

■ **Sunday Evenings**

Complete the series "The Continuing Adequacy of Jesus Christ" based on the great "I Ams" of the Gospel of John.

■ **Wednesday Evenings**

Continue the studies based on Paul's first letter to the Corinthian Christians.

WEDNESDAY EVENING, MAY 1

Title: Kingdom Heirs

Text: "Know ye not that the unrighteous shall not inherit the kingdom of God?" **(1 Cor. 6:9).**

Scripture Reading: 1 Corinthians 6:9–11

Introduction

Just who will inherit the kingdom of God? Perhaps in the terminology of the average person of today, the question would be: Who will enter the kingdom of God?

I. Some terms need to be clarified.

A. *What is the meaning of the "kingdom of God"?* The definition that is commonly given for the kingdom of God is that it is the rule or reign of God in the hearts and lives of human beings. This concept means that the rule is on earth here and now. For practical purposes, the blessings of God are for the redeemed here on earth now. It is righteousness, or right living.

However, the definition used in 1 Corinthians seems to have some variations, for Paul seems to refer to the new Jerusalem and not the present. He is referring to the reign of God when there will be no night, no sin, no curses, and no pain.

B. *What is the meaning of "inherit"?* The literal meaning of the word is "to receive; to take or hold a possession or rights by inheritance." It is to take possession of by receiving. In order to inherit God's kingdom, one must be made a child of God, and he or she will then become an heir.

II. Some warnings should be mentioned.

A. *In 1 Corinthians 6:9 Paul said, "Be not deceived."* This is a common warning in the Bible. Jesus said, "Take heed lest any man deceive you" (Mark 13:5). John said, "Little children, let no man deceive you" (1 John 3:7). Paul said in another place, "Be not deceived" (Gal. 6:7).

B. *This is a warning that is justifiable.* The Corinthians were wrong in their thinking. They needed a warning. Their thinking had led them to loose morals and sinful habits. People's behavior today is very similar. There is a great danger in thinking lightly of sin. An example of this wrong thinking is believing that being admitted into the church by baptism is sufficient.

C. *This warning involves the simple statement that profession must be supported by action.* James wrote, "Faith, if it hath not works, is dead" (James 2:17). Christians are to be distinguished by righteous living.

III. Who will inherit the kingdom should be made known.

A. *Jesus placed prime importance on inheriting the kingdom.* He said, "Seek ye first the kingdom" (Matt. 6:33). He also said, "The kingdom of heaven is like unto treasure hid in a field; the which when a man hath found, he hideth, and for joy thereof goeth and selleth all that he hath, and buyeth that field" (Matt. 13:44).

B. *Paul mentions three things in 1 Corinthians 6:11 that indicate how one inherits the kingdom.*

1. "Ye are washed." This literally means, "Get yourself washed," or "Let yourself be washed." The sinner is washed in the blood. This cleansing is symbolized in baptism.

2. "Ye are sanctified." Sanctification means consecrated to holiness. It means separated from sin unto God and thus made holy. It is the removal of sin and guilt.

3. "Ye are justified." This is a judicial term. The sinner is declared to be in the right relationship with God through the work of the Lord Jesus Christ.

Conclusion

Our Scripture reading lists a number of things that keep one from inheriting the kingdom (1 Cor. 6:9–10). Then we find how one can be free of all these and inherit the kingdom (1 Cor. 6:11). Go to God to make sure you are washed, sanctified, and justified.

SUNDAY MORNING, MAY 5

Title: Christ Lives within My Heart

Text: "I have been crucified with Christ; it is no longer I who live, but Christ who lives in me; and the life I now live in the flesh I live by faith in the Son of God, who loved me and gave himself for me" **(Gal. 2:20 RSV).**

Scripture Reading: Colossians 1:24–27

Hymns: "Great Redeemer, We Adore Thee," Harris
"Crown Him with Many Crowns," Bridges
"Jesus Is All the World to Me," Thompson

Offertory Prayer: Heavenly Father, we bow down before you today in our hearts to acknowledge you as our sovereign Creator, Lord, and Redeemer. We come acknowledging you as the giver of every good and perfect gift. We thank you for life, for love, and for hope. We thank you for your forgiveness and for the gift of new life. We thank you for the privilege of worshiping you with our material substance. Accept it as an expression of the gratitude of our hearts. Bless it to the end that others shall experience your love. In Jesus' name. Amen.

Introduction

Christianity is wonderful news about a Christ who came and died for our sins. He then arose from the dead—triumphant over death and the grave—and brought to light the reality of eternal life and the gift of immortality (2 Tim. 1:8–10).

The living Christ came during his earthly life to the Jewish people. Many of them rejected him. But to those who did receive him, he gave the privilege of becoming children of God (John 1:11–13). He came to live in the hearts and lives of those who received him by faith (Gal. 2:20; Eph. 3:17). The presence of the indwelling Christ is the basis for our hope of experiencing God's full plan for our lives (Col. 1:27). Affirming the fact of the presence of the living Christ, a song writer has said very beautifully:

> *I serve a risen Savior, he's in the world today;*
> *I know that he is living, whatever men may say;*
> *I see his hand of mercy, I hear his voice of cheer,*
> *And just the time I need him he's always near.*
>
> *He lives, he lives, Christ Jesus lives today!*
> *He walks with me and talks with me along life's narrow way.*
> *He lives, he lives, salvation to impart!*
> *You ask me how I know he lives? He lives within my heart.*
>
> —A. H. Ackley

Belief in the resurrection of Jesus Christ was based on the solid evidence of his repeated appearances to his apostles and other followers during the days after his resurrection and preceding his ascension.

He appeared to Mary Magdalene and to the other women with her. He walked with two of his followers on the road to Emmaus. He appeared to the apostle Peter. He appeared in the upper room when Thomas was absent. A week later he appeared again when Thomas was present. He appeared and talked with seven by the sea. He appeared to eleven on the mount in Galilee and gave voice to the Great Commission. He appeared to over five hundred at one time. He appeared to James. As the glorified but living Christ, he appeared on the road to Damascus when Saul was converted.

The very existence of the church can be ascribed to the unwavering faith of eleven men who marched throughout their world affirming that Jesus Christ was alive. There are millions in the world today who would join the poet and say, "You ask me how I know he lives? He lives within my heart."

I. The living Christ, by means of his Spirit, is in the world seeking to save people from sin (see Acts 8:26–40; 10:19–48; 13:1–4).

II. The living Christ comes to live in the believer (see Gal. 2:20; Eph. 3:17; Col. 1:27).
A. *The living Christ enters the heart of the believer through faith.*
B. *It is through faith that the living Christ dwells within.*

III. The living Christ lives in our hearts today.
A. *He lives within as the forgiver of sin.*
B. *He lives within as the giver of life.*
C. *He lives within as the disturber and rebuker of evil.*
D. *He lives within as a trustworthy leader.*
E. *He lives within as an adequate source of energy.*
F. *He lives within as a conqueror of death.*

It is impossible to separate the living Christ from the indwelling Holy Spirit. What Christ came to accomplish, the Holy Spirit works continuously to achieve (John 14:16–28).

IV. The living Christ wants to live in your heart.
A. *The living Christ can bring to you the peace of knowing that your sins have been forgiven.*
B. *The living Christ gives you the joy of being alive with an eternal life.*
C. *The living Christ wants to live within to assure you that divine help will be available when it is needed.*

Conclusion

Jesus Christ must not be thought of as limited to the time of his physical and visible manifestation in the long ago. In his ascension our Lord stepped behind a curtain where he is no longer visible to us in physical form. In the Holy Spirit he comes to be everywhere present at all times.

The living Christ wants to forgive your sin today and to bestow upon you the gift of eternal life. He will become real to you today if by faith you will invite him to come in and if you mean it with all of your heart (Rev. 3:20).

SUNDAY EVENING, MAY 5

Title: I Am the Good Shepherd

Text: "I am the good shepherd. The good shepherd lays down his life for the sheep" **(John 10:11 NIV).**

Scripture Reading: John 10:1–6, 11–18

Introduction

One of the most familiar scenes in first-century Palestine was the figure of a shepherd tending his sheep. The land was given more to pastoral livestock than to agricultural farming. Most of the land is like western Texas and Oklahoma—stony and without enough rainfall to support farm crops. Thus, goat herds and flocks of sheep were common sights and had been for centuries.

The shepherd's life was not one to be envied. It was hard and constant. Two-week paid vacations were unheard of. The shepherd's work week was twenty-four hours a day seven days a week. He faced the elements of nature in all their fury. He endured the dangers of thieves, poachers, and wild beasts. Because there was little grass, he was bound to lead the sheep in constant search of food. Veterinary skills were a part of his trade.

Many who listened to Jesus were well acquainted with the life of a shepherd, so he used their knowledge of the shepherd and the sheep to illustrate his own relation to God's true believers.

Let us look closely at this illustration.

I. The good shepherd knows his sheep by name.

A. *The sheep of Palestine were not used primarily for slaughter in the marketplace.* Their principle function was to produce wool for the loom. Thus, each sheep might be with the shepherd for years. It was common for shepherds to name their sheep based on physical markings, characteristics, or disposition.

Jesus, speaking of the shepherd, says, "The sheep listen to his voice. He calls his own sheep by name and leads them out" (John 10:3 NIV). Jesus knows the name of each of his followers.

B. *We live in a world where we are more often a number than a name.* A number is dehumanizing. It has no personality. It is cold, indifferent, and apathetic. But our name is personal, because it was given to us by those who love us. Jesus seizes on our need to have a name and calls us by name and leads us.

C. *Not only does the good shepherd call the names of his sheep, but the sheep know his voice and respond to him.* Voices and names are intertwined in this passage.

We can be in a crowd, and with everyone talking at once, many of us can hear our own name being called. It is readily evident to us whether it is the voice of a stranger calling us or a loved one whose voice we easily recognize.

II. The good shepherd is more than a hired hand.

A. *There were two kinds of shepherds in Jesus' day.*
  1. One kind of shepherd was a member of the household that owned the herd of sheep. It might be a son, a daughter (as in the case of Rachel in Genesis 29:9), or a servant who was considered part of the family unit.
  2. A second kind of shepherd was hired to care for the sheep. His devotion to duty and to the welfare of the sheep was tempered by his own self-preservation. Jesus points out that if the hireling sees a band of thieves or some wild beast attacking, he may well abandon the flock in order to protect himself.

B. *The good shepherd, however, does not run away.* He cares for the sheep and willingly stays to defend them, for they are his. Whether the herd is large or small means little to the good shepherd. He cares for them all. The good shepherd knows that sheep are defenseless creatures that cannot protect themselves. His strength and weapons are the only hope the sheep have. The sheep look to their shepherd for protection.

C. *The good shepherd is not pastoring the sheep for money.* He does it because they belong to him and his father.

Jesus will not abandon us in the face of the enemy. He is not a hireling. He stands with us and fights for us. He provides for our safety.

III. The good shepherd is willing to die for his sheep.

A. *The ultimate test of love and devotion is how far one will go in practicing such love.* It is one thing to talk of how good a shepherd one is or how much he is willing to do, but it is quite another to be willing to risk certain death in order that the sheep can escape.

King David appears first in Scripture as a shepherd. Scripture tells of his courage in killing a lion and a bear that came to ravage his father's flocks (1 Sam. 17:34–35). At the risk of personal injury and death, he willingly put his life on the line for them.

B. *But the case of Jesus goes one step beyond the story of David.* David believed he did not necessarily have to die in order to save the sheep. As a matter of fact, David most probably believed that in any conflict of one on one (even with the giant Goliath), he would not lose his life.

Jesus, however, knew for a certainty that for him to be the Good Shepherd, he would have to die for God's sheep.

C. *Furthermore, this was a death in which Jesus would have to bear the full weight of sin for all of humanity.* It was not just that Jesus would have to die, but the meaning of his death was also part of his decision. He said, "The good shepherd lays down his life for the sheep" (John 10:11 NIV), and he did exactly that.

Conclusion

Most of us would willingly sacrifice our lives for the sake of our families. Human history is filled with such stories of love and devotion. People who run into burning houses or people who swim into deep water to save loved ones are not uncommon.

Jesus is trying to say that about his relationship to us. He loves us, knows our names, and willingly gives himself on our behalf. He is no coward. He does not find excuses to keep from aiding us. He comes quickly and voluntarily to our defense and takes our place in death so that we might live.

This is a great love, and it calls us to respond with great love and loyalty. Will you do that? Will you let Jesus become the Shepherd of your life?

WEDNESDAY EVENING, MAY 8

Title: You Were Bought at a Price

Text: "You were bought at a price. Therefore honor God with your body" (1 Cor. 6:20 NIV).

Scripture Reading: 1 Corinthians 6:12–20

Introduction

Every noble life is based on self-renunciation. To make a worthwhile mark on the world, we must lose ourselves in a great cause. Christians have found the cause: they live for God in Christ. They have been bought at a price and thus are owned by the Son of God.

I. Consider the state of bondage from which Christians are ransomed.

A. *Paul says in 1 Corinthians 6:19, "You are not your own" (NIV).* There was a time in the lives of the Corinthians, as well as all others, when they thought they were "their own." When they thought that, they followed their own ways.

B. *In reality these Corinthians were in bondage to the law and its sentence of condemnation.* All unsaved persons are in bondage to sin and its cruel letters. All are in bondage to Satan and his wretched service.

C. *This power of evil fostered the delusion of liberty, pride, and selfishness.* All the while, Satan was drawing tighter and tighter the chains of spiritual bondage.

II. Consider to whom Christians are indebted for redemption.

Christians are indebted to:

A. *The one whose laws and service were forsaken and despised.*

B. *The one without whose help all sinners would be in eternal bondage.*

C. *The one upon whom sinners had no claim so far as justice and right are concerned.*

D. *The one whose heart was moved with pity by the spectacle of the sinner's slavery.*

E. *The one who graciously resolved to suffer all that was involved in the work of deliverance.*

F. *The one who was ordained of God and who came into the world to save sinners— the Lord Jesus Christ.*

III. Consider the cost at which Christians were ransomed from slavery and purchased as free bondmen and bondwomen of God.

A. *It was a price no mortal was capable of paying.*

B. *It was a price that could not be counted in an earthly equivalent.*

C. *It was a price so high that the Son of God had to become incarnate and empty himself of heavenly glory.*

D. *It was the price of the precious blood of Jesus Christ, the Son of God.* "You know that it was not with perishable things such as silver or gold that you were redeemed from the empty way of life handed down to you from your forefathers, but with the precious blood of Christ, a lamb without blemish or defect" (1 Peter 1:18–19 NIV).

"Christ redeemed us from the curse of the law by becoming a curse for us, for it is written: 'Cursed is everyone who is hung on a tree'" (Gal. 3:13 NIV).

IV. Consider the obligations this deliverance places on Christians.

A. *There are some negative obligations.* "Ye are not your own." The heart is not the Christian's—it is Christ's. The thoughts are not the Christian's— they are Christ's. Time is not the Christian's—it is Christ's. Abilities are not the Christian's—they are Christ's. All these are to be consecrated to him. Property is not the Christian's—it is Christ's. He should be honored with it.

B. *There are some positive obligations.* "Therefore glorify God in your body, and in your spirit." To love the Lord Jesus is of necessity to serve him. All the faculties and opportunities are to be laid on the altar.

Conclusion

It is time for each of us to take a spiritual inventory. When we have done this, we will see the price our Lord paid for our redemption and we will want to reconsecrate ourselves to him.

SUNDAY MORNING, MAY 12

Title: What Is a Christian Mother?

Text: "The disciples were called Christians first in Antioch" **(Acts 11:26).**

Scripture Reading: Isaiah 55:6–9

Hymns: "Holy, Holy, Holy," Heber
         "God, Give Us Christian Homes!" McKinney
         "More about Jesus," Hewitt

Offertory Prayer: Gracious and loving Father, we come into your presence because you have been so good to us and because we need a continuing awareness of your abiding presence. We come thanking you for inviting us into your throne room to pray and worship. We thank you for inclining your ear to us in our times of need. We thank you for being so generous in giving your rich and wonderful gifts to us. We come now returning tithes and offerings as expressions of our love and gratitude. Bless these gifts to the end that others will come to know Jesus Christ as Savior. Amen.

Introduction

On this date that is celebrated as Mother's Day throughout the United States, it is interesting to note the definition of a mother by an unknown author who wrote:

A mother can be almost any size or any age, but she won't admit to anything over thirty.

A mother has soft hands and smells good.

A mother likes new dresses, music, a clean house, her children's kisses, a dishwasher, and Daddy.

A mother doesn't like having her children sick, muddy feet, temper tantrums, loud noise, or bad report cards.

A mother can read a thermometer (much to the amazement of Daddy) and, like magic, can kiss a hurt away.

A mother can bake good cakes and pies but likes to see her children eat vegetables.

A mother can stuff a fat baby into a snowsuit in seconds and can kiss sad little faces and make them smile.

A mother is underpaid, has long hours, and gets very little rest. She worries too much about her children, but she says she doesn't mind at all.

And no matter how old her children are, she still likes to think of them as her little babies.

She is the guardian angel of the family, the queen, the tender hand of love.
A mother is the best friend anyone ever has.
A mother is love.

What is a Christian mother? Someone has said, "A Christian is a person through whom Christ thinks, a heart through which Christ loves, a voice through which Christ sings, and a hand through which Christ helps."

I. A Christian mother is one through whom Christ thinks.

We become disciples of Jesus Christ by receiving him into our life as Lord and Savior. We experience the miracle of the new birth through faith in him as the one whom God has sent for the salvation of the world (John 3:16). Disciples of Jesus become truly Christian when they begin to think as Christ thought. The apostle Paul challenged the disciples in Philippi to seek for and to highly prize "the mind of Christ" (Phil. 2:5–8). In Paul's letter to the believers in Rome, he speaks of the need for and the urgency of experiencing "the renewing of your mind" (Rom. 12:1–2).

We cannot become like Jesus Christ in our attitudes and actions until we accept the very thoughts of God as the way in which we will do our thinking. Through the prophet Isaiah, God urged the people of that day to forsake their wicked ways and their unrighteous thoughts (Isa. 55:6–8). Because the thoughts of God are so much higher than our thoughts, we must think as Jesus thought if our ways would be comparable to his (Isa. 55:8–9). A Christian mother is a mother through whom Christ thinks.

II. A Christian mother is a mother with a heart through which Christ loves.

There are different kinds of love in the world. Romantic love is the type of love that is always seeking its own satisfaction. Philanthropic love or respect love is based on worth and expresses itself in kindness. The love that Jesus Christ had for God and man is *agape* love—the love that helps. This love is characterized by a persistent, unbreakable spirit of good will and is devoted to the highest possible good of the person being loved.

Christian mothers are those who have something more than a maternal type of love. They are those who have permitted the Holy Spirit to pour out within them the very love of God for the members of their family (Rom. 5:5). A Christian mother is a mother with a heart through which Christ loves.

III. A Christian mother is one through whose voice Christ speaks and sings.

During our Lord's earthly ministry, some mothers brought their children to him that he might bless them. It is easy to imagine the Christ, with great love, talking in affectionate terms with a child on his knee. It doesn't take too much imagination to believe that he might sing to children.

Some of us are fortunate in that we have memories from early childhood of a mother who would sing to us some of the great songs of faith expressing God's love.

Genuine Christianity affects the speech of true believers. The Christian mother will be a good steward of her tongue, using it to speak words of kindness, affection, and encouragement, as well as correction. The Christian mother will be generous with words of praise and commendation and very sparing in words of criticism that might create a sense of low self-esteem in her child. The Christian mother will certainly communicate her faith to her children and encourage them to not only trust Christ as Savior but to follow him as Lord. A Christian mother is a mother with a voice through which Christ speaks.

IV.A Christian mother is a mother through whose hands Christ helps.

An old proverb says, "A father works from sun to sun, but a mother's work is never done."

In the wise man's great tribute to a good woman, he describes her as one who "stretcheth out her hand to the poor; yea, she reacheth forth her hands to the needy. She is not afraid of the snow for her household: for all her household are clothed with scarlet" (Prov. 31:20–21).

The Christian mother is a true helpmate to her husband and a great helper to her children. She is a worker and an achiever who finds her strength and help in the Lord.

Conclusion

What is a Christian mother? She is one who believes in Jesus Christ as Lord and Savior. She loves him and seeks to obey him day by day. She sees the home as a place in which to honor God and serve her generation.

May each husband seek to help his wife be a good Christian mother.

Each mother can be a Christian mother with the help of Jesus Christ. May God bless you in your efforts in that direction.

SUNDAY EVENING, MAY 12

Title: I Am the Resurrection

Text: "Jesus said to her, 'I am the resurrection and the life. He who believes in me will live, even though he dies; and whoever lives and believes in me will never die. Do you believe this?'" **(John 11:25 NIV).**

Scripture Reading: John 11:1–44

Introduction

Some scholars have estimated that in the gospel accounts we have only fifty days out of the earthly life of Jesus. Fifty days out of approximately thirty-three years is not very much. Therefore, we do not have a lot of knowledge about the lives of some of the people whom Jesus knew.

However, in the case of Mary, Martha, and their brother Lazarus, the gospel writers provide a number of intimate and personal details. In John's account of the resurrection of Lazarus, he tells us that "Jesus loved Martha and her sister and Lazarus" (John 11:5 NIV). Nowhere in the Gospels does Jesus say directly to anyone, "I love you." This is not to say that he never said that; it only points out that the phrase never appears.

Yet people knew Jesus loved them, and Jesus loved these three friends of his. When he heard that Lazarus was ill, Jesus arrived at their home in Bethany to call Lazarus back from the dead. It was during the performance of this miracle that Jesus pointed out to Martha that he had power over death.

I. Because Jesus is the Resurrection, death is banished.

A. *Death is the foremost enemy of humankind.* It separates us from our loved ones, cuts down young and old indiscriminately, and casts dark shadows over what lies beyond the grave. Classical art and literature portray death as a cape-clad figure with a skull for a face and bony fingers for hands. Death carries the scythe with its gleaming curved blade and rides a horse whose eyes are fearsome and whose nostrils are wide from snorting. All in all, death is not pictured as our friend.

B. *For Martha and Mary death had taken their brother.* The tears and grief are evident in our Scripture reading (John 11:19, 31, 33). Although Martha showed some faith in a resurrection far out in the future (v. 24), she saw the present situation as hopeless (vv. 38–40).

C. *But Jesus made a startling announcement.* He declared not only that Lazarus would live again, but that he would live again that day. The emphasis is on the present tense in the text, "I *am* the resurrection." He does not say, "I *will be* the resurrection."

Jesus promises that death has no power over the one who believes in him. Although one may die, he or she only dies physically.

II. Because Jesus is the Resurrection, graves are empty today.

A. *Without the resurrection, humankind would be left in a terrible condition.* The grave would have the last triumph, for life would cease at death. But Jesus is the Resurrection. He raised Lazarus from the dead and arose from the grave himself. All those who believe in Jesus never cease to live.

B. *When we drive past a cemetery, we can wonder how many of the graves are empty.* Oh, I don't mean that the earthly remains are not still there. I'm speaking of the souls of those people, for all who trust in Jesus Christ for their salvation never die. I believe that at death believers pass from this life to eternal reward immediately.

C. *Some believe that Christians fall asleep at death and simply remain in "soul sleep" until Christ's return.* But Jesus promised the thief on the cross, "Today you will be with me in paradise" (Luke 23:43 NIV). In Revelation 6:9–11 the saints who have died because of their faith in Jesus are pictured under the altar in heaven.

Jesus makes the grave empty, even as his grave is empty.

III. Because Jesus is the Resurrection, eternal life is a reality.

A. *Life has a new meaning in Jesus.* This life—here and now—takes on a new perspective. The fear of death is diminished, and we become absolutely certain that God who raised Lazarus from the dead will also raise us.

The text says that Jesus loved Martha, Mary, and Lazarus. He raised Lazarus to demonstrate that even though a man had been dead four days, Jesus could bring him back to full health.

B. *Life is no longer viewed as threescore and ten.* Life no longer has a limit. It begins not at birth, but at the new birth. And every life that begins at the new birth never dies; it will live eternally. Thus, everlasting life is a reality. Life continues beyond death. Death is no longer a dead end but a bridge. Death means meeting Jesus face to face and joining all the saints of all the years before us.

C. *Heaven is within our grasp.* It is no longer just a wish or a dream. Jesus brings God and man together again and puts away the wages of sin—death.

Conclusion

Jesus summarizes his own teaching in this text. He asks Martha a direct question: "Do you believe this?"

That is the question Jesus asks all of us who claim to be his followers. Sometimes it is hard to believe. We want to believe, but death seems so real. Martha wanted to believe, so she said, "Yes." But later at the tomb when Jesus ordered the stone rolled away, Martha protested. "But Lord, he has been dead four days."

Jesus seeks to reassure us. Jesus reminded Martha that she claimed to believe. Now he called on her to maintain her faith and she would see the glory of God. When we waver, Jesus calls on us to maintain our faith. If we believe—truly believe—we shall be saved to everlasting life.

"Do you believe this?"

WEDNESDAY EVENING, MAY 15

Title: Keeping God's Commandments Is Everything

Text: "Circumcision is nothing and uncircumcision is nothing. Keeping God's commands is what counts" (**1 Cor. 7:19** NIV).

Scripture Reading: 1 Corinthians 7:1–40

Introduction

The text of this message leaps from the pages of God's Word. It is a diamond buried in the mountains of great truth. Paul has entered into a discussion of Christianity as it relates to life problems. In connection with his discussion, he mentions that the thing that really matters in relation to all other concerns is keeping the law of God. This is seen in the matters of circumcision, marriage, divorce, and all other areas of life.

I. The most important law to obey is to have saving faith.

A. *Paul commands that one believe on the name of God's Son Jesus Christ (see 1 John 3:23).* Faith is necessary to please God (Heb. 11:6) and for justification (Rom. 5:1). It is necessary to receive answered prayers (James 1:6), to be assured of God's blessings (2 Chron. 20:20), and to obtain everlasting life (John 5:24).

B. *Faith binds together things on earth with things of heaven.* Faith is a person's reliance on the heavenly Father for all his or her earthly life as well as the life beyond.

II. Laws to obey are the laws related to 1 Corinthians 7.

A. *Laws concerning the marriage relationship.* Marriage is the fundamental institution of society. Husbands and wives have specific duties toward each other (1 Cor. 7:3–16). Divorce is forbidden except when a nonbelieving spouse leaves his or her Christian marriage partner. The Christian partner should strive to win the non-Christian spouse.

B. *Laws concerning the use of divine gifts (1 Cor. 7:17).* Paul says in Ephesians 4:1 to "walk worthy of the vocation wherewith ye are called." So obedience to the law also applies to one's vocation in life.

C. *Commandments involving the things of the world (1 Cor. 7:29–34).* Things of the world are temporary and will pass away. They are not worth distraction from the Lord.

III. The third consideration is the reason given for obeying the laws of God.

A. *We should reflect on all God has done for us.* Out of appreciation for redemption from sin, we should be diligent in obeying the commandments of

God. Out of appreciation for his blessings upon us, we should keep his commandments.

B. *We should reflect on the fact that every commandment the Lord has given is for our own good.* This applies to every facet of life (1 John 5:3).

Conclusion

The laws of God are designed for our good. They are laid out in the Bible in such a way that each of us can understand them. Keeping God's commandments is vital to our earthly well-being and eternal happiness.

SUNDAY MORNING, MAY 19

Title: Ten Ways to Guarantee Unhappiness

Text: "Whoever knows what is right to do and fails to do it, for him it is sin" **(James 4:17 RSV).**

Scripture Reading: James 4:13–17

Hymns: "God, Our Father, We Adore Thee," Frazer
"Holy Bible, Book Divine," Burton
"Take Time to Be Holy," Longstaff

Offertory Prayer: Thank you, Father, for drawing us to this place of prayer and worship on this Lord's Day. Thank you for the presence of your people who have come to praise you and to rejoice in your goodness. Help us this day to confess our sins. Grant to us the joy of forgiveness. Help us to give our lives totally to you as we bring tithes and offerings indicating our love for you and our desire that your kingdom should come in the hearts and lives of others. In Jesus' name we pray. Amen.

Introduction

As we think in terms of enriching family life, we should be on guard against the peril of neglecting the things that are of supreme importance. Benjamin Franklin has said, "A little neglect may breed great mischief; for want of a nail the shoe was lost; for want of a shoe, the horse was lost; and for want of a horse the rider was lost, being overtaken and slain by an enemy. All for want of a little care about a horseshoe nail." By neglecting certain basic ingredients we can guarantee the breakdown of family values.

I. Neglecting the Bible hurts the family.

Every family should have a Bible—and not for display purposes only. The Bible should be read. It should be loved and reverenced. Its teachings should be obeyed by parents as they seek to set a good example for their children.

II. Neglecting prayer hurts the family.

Each day the family should be led in prayer together as well as each individual member praying privately. These prayers should include adoration of God, confession of sin, expressions of thanksgiving, and intercessions for others.

III. Neglecting public worship hurts the family.

The best investment a family can make of its time is attending church. No other investment of a similar amount of time will produce such rich dividends for the family's well-being, for God's strength and guidance come in a superlative manner through public worship. Parents should set an example by declaring their reverence for God and their love for the church. Children should not be sent to church; they should be led to church.

IV. Neglecting to build Christian friendships hurts the family.

"He who would have friends must show himself friendly," says the wise man in the book of Proverbs. Each Christian family should put forth continuous effort to develop friendships with other Christian families. This should be done for mutual helpfulness in times of stress and need. Other families need the blessing that can come to them through you, and you may someday need the strength and help that can come to you through your Christian friends.

V. Neglecting one's neighbors is to harm the family.

In many parts of the world a neighbor is considered to be a person who lives close by. Jesus defined a neighbor as someone who is in need. We act neighborly when we show compassion for those who are suffering (Luke 10:25–37). Family life can be enriched by meaningful relationships with those who live nearby, and family values will be increased if the family ministers to those in need.

VI. Neglecting the opportunity to serve others hurts family life.

Jesus warned about the person who hears the Word but then lets the cares of the world and preoccupation with riches choke the Word so that it becomes unfruitful (Matt. 13:22). It is exceedingly easy in our materialistic and competitive society for parents to become so pressured by material values that they neglect to give time to their family. Time for the church and community also suffers, which in turn has a negative impact on family values.

VII. Neglecting to become a tither hinders family values.

Most believers who are exposed to the teachings of God's Word learn that they are supposed to return to God a portion of their income. Some families are so pressured by the desire for economic security and possessions that they postpone becoming significant givers. They do this to their own spiritual impoverishment and to their economic misfortune. People were made to be givers. Each of us needs to let God enter into our economic affairs by acknowledging God's ownership and our trusteeship by giving a minimum of a tithe to the Lord's work.

VIII. Neglecting to praise and thank God hurts family life.

A significant economic event took place in the life of a poor family. The father was able to secure a loan, making it possible for him to provide a farm home for his family. At the first meal following this good news, the mother suggested that it would be appropriate to thank God and to praise him. It wasn't the family's custom to pray together, but the father mustered up the courage to offer thanks before the meal, and prayer became a regular part of the family routine, enriching the lives of the children as well as the parents.

IX. Neglecting the Lord's Day hurts the family.

As one-tenth of our income given to God indicates his ownership, so the dedication of one-seventh of our days for rest and worship emphasizes our spiritual nature. People were not made to live by bread alone. The Lord's Day should be special for God and for the family.

X. Neglecting to respond to the indwelling Spirit impoverishes family life.

Conversion to Christ brings with it the gift of God's Holy Spirit as a personal presence and power in the life of each believer. When there are Christians in the home, they need to make a proper response to the Holy Spirit so that all of family life might be lived under the grace and guidance of God. To neglect the Holy Spirit is to live an impoverished life.

Conclusion

This message has been rather negative in emphasis. It has pointed out some dangers to family values. I hope a positive response can be made to a negative emphasis.

It is said that an ounce of prevention is worth a pound of cure. A conscious and continuous effort must be put forth by each family against the peril of neglecting the basic essentials that produce happiness in the family.

SUNDAY EVENING, MAY 19

Title: I Am the Way, the Truth, and the Life

Text: "Jesus answered, 'I am the way and the truth and the life. No one comes to the Father except through me'" **(John 14:6 NIV).**

Scripture Reading: John 14:1–7

Introduction

Summer vacations that involve long trips often include the need for a map. This is particularly true when you are traveling to a city or state that is unfamiliar to you.

Because it is nearly impossible to drive and read a map at the same time, the driver either has to rely on someone else to read and give instructions or must stop periodically to check the map. But even with the benefit of a map, it is still possible to get lost. It is easy to take a wrong turn or fail to see some highway marker. When that happens, one either has to backtrack or consult the map for a new route to his or her destination. The best possible scenario is to travel with someone who knows the way, because that nearly eliminates the chances of missing a turn or taking a wrong turn.

In our text for this evening, Jesus had been instructing his disciples that he must leave. But he reminded them that they knew where he was going. Thomas interrupted Jesus to ask, "Lord, we don't know where you are going, so how can we know the way?" (John 14:5 NIV). To this Jesus answered with our selected text and made three statements about himself.

I. Jesus is the only way.

A. *Christianity is an exclusive religion.* It rules out the possibility that one can come to eternal life by any other means. Many people wish this were not so. They want God to admit people into heaven in spite of the fact that they have never committed their lives to Jesus Christ. This would solve so many problems. It would mean that we would not need missions. Nor would we need churches. If one could be saved through ignorance or never hearing about Jesus, then it would be best to eliminate all missions, churches, and Christian outreach programs. But Jesus is the only way to be saved.

B. *Some people believe that all religions are basically the same.* They say, "We are all traveling different roads, but all roads lead to one God." The most elementary student of comparative religions knows that there is indeed some similarity in various religions. The differences, however, are what convince me that someone is wrong.

C. *Jesus is either the only way to the Father or he was a liar.* If he was a liar, then he wasn't God. And if he wasn't God, then everything he taught is suspect, because he told us he was God. Jesus is the only way to the Father. That means we must tell every person on earth that Jesus is the only way. "No one comes to the Father except through me" (John 14:6 NIV).

II. Jesus is the only truth.

A. *Truth is a valuable commodity in our world.* We live in a time when humankind desperately needs a true standard. Science, mathematics, music, and other disciplines offer true standards, but these are not helpful to us in establishing moral and spiritual behavior. We need a standard outside ourselves that is true for our spiritual lives.

B. *Many people may teach truth, but only one person is Truth.* Jesus not only teaches truth, he embodies it. He is the Truth by word, action, and thought.

C. *The revelation of God in Christ is the sole standard for moral and spiritual conduct.* All claims to truth must be judged by the life and teachings of Jesus. Some teachings in other religions are true by the standards of Jesus, but no religion outside of Christianity can stand the complete scrutiny of Jesus. False ideas about God, eternal life, and moral conduct will be exposed when Jesus is the standard by which they are judged.

III. Jesus is the only life.

A. *Life for many people is a poor existence at best.* Life is going to work at a job they hate, living in a marriage or family they find hard to tolerate, and seeking material possessions they cannot afford and which do not make them happy. Life has no meaning, no purpose, no joy, no assurance, no satisfaction.

We live in a country with one of the highest standards of living in the world. We have fine health care, freedom, possessions, and a world of entertainment possibilities. Yet people are not happy. They seek meaning in drugs, alcohol, sex, technology, corporate advancement—and still those things do not satisfy.

B. *Jesus announces to every age and every generation that he offers the only life worth living.* It is the only life that has meaning and satisfaction that lasts not just a lifetime, but forever.

Jesus said, "I have come that they may have life, and have it to the full" (John 10:10 NIV). He promises a satisfactory answer to why you are here. Millions have given their lives to Christ and have found unlimited reasons to go on living.

C. *A popular chorus of the past says something that is always true.* The words go like this: "If you want joy, real joy, wonderful joy, Let Jesus come into your life!" Jesus does not offer a life without hardship or struggle. But he does offer meaning for why you must struggle.

Conclusion

Many people want to make God a benevolent, loving deity who could never bear to see anyone go to hell. These people have seized on one attribute of God—his love—and have blocked out any other teaching about God's nature. God does love you, and he loves you dearly. In his love he has provided a means whereby all people everywhere can be saved. Jesus is the Way to God; he is the Truth about God; and he is the Life with God. No man can come to God except by Jesus. Do not go looking for some other way. There is none.

Such truth demands that we come to God by accepting Jesus. It also demands that we tell all people everywhere that we want them to come to eternal life by trusting in Jesus. Will you do that tonight? Will you trust in Jesus and then help us to tell others how to trust in Jesus?

WEDNESDAY EVENING, MAY 22

Title: Christian Influence

Text: "If what I eat causes my brother to fall into sin, I will never eat meat again, so that I will not cause him to fall" **(1 Cor. 8:13 NIV).**

Scripture Reading: 1 Corinthians 8:1–13

Introduction

The subject of this message should be of interest to everyone who has a desire to exercise a good influence on others. The matter of influence will be considered from three directions.

I. The first consideration is a discussion of conscience and love.

A. *First Corinthians 7:1–2 introduces chapters 7 and 8 with the issue of whether it is best to be married or to stay single.* This is a question that needs serious consideration in our day.

B. *Another matter concerns abstaining from eating certain foods.* Paul's argument is based on a person's influence. Paul places knowledge beside influence and shows that knowledge is overridden by love. Love is the essential element, not knowledge.

C. *The matter of eating or not eating has nothing to do with commending one to God (1 Cor. 8:8).* Some people consider themselves strong in comparison to others. They think that eating anything they want will make no difference. They are not aware of the influence they exercise. They may think that because they are strong in their relationship to God they have an advantage over others. This is a mistake. The question is: How does eating meat offered in a pagan temple affect others? It is evil and wrong if the weaker person thinks it is wrong. The warning is to take heed that one does not cause his brother to stumble.

II. The second consideration is the fact that each person does exert an influence on others.

The question is: What kind of influence do I exert on others?

A. *The Lord gives each person a great deal of liberty.* We can use that liberty for good or evil. The question is the responsibility of liberty.

B. *Some things are not wrong for an individual as such, but because of an evil influence on someone else, they become wrong.* Many traditional taboos come under this category.

III. The third consideration is how much does one care?

A. *The matter of caring or loving is the determining factor as to whether a particular thing should be done or not done.* Some matters worthy of consideration are social drinking, observance of the Lord's Day, and gambling.

B. *Christians should honestly ask themselves whether they can justify their actions in the sight of God.* This will enable them to determine whether or not they should continue in certain practices.

Conclusion

You, as a Christian, need to constantly examine every activity in the light of its effect on your brothers and sisters in Christ.

SUNDAY MORNING, MAY 26

Title: The Increase of Love in the Family

Text: "May the Lord make you increase and abound in love to one another and to all men, as we do to you, so that he may establish your hearts unblamable in holiness before our God and Father, at the coming of our Lord Jesus with his saints" **(1 Thess. 3:12–13 rsv).**

Scripture Reading: 1 Thessalonians 3:1–13

Hymns: "Love Divine, All Loves Excelling," Wesley
"The King of Love My Shepherd Is," Baker
"I Love Thee," Anonymous

Offertory Prayer: Heavenly Father, we come today to thank you for all of your blessings to us, but especially we thank you for family blessings. Those of us who have Christian parents owe you a great debt of gratitude. We thank you for their example and instruction. We thank you for the love they gave us. Today we come bringing tithes and offerings that we might express our love for you and our concern that others will come to know Jesus Christ as Lord and Savior. Accept these gifts and bless them to that end. In Jesus' name. Amen.

Introduction

In Paul's second letter to the Thessalonians he rejoiced and commended them because "the love of every one of you for one another is increasing" (2 Thess. 1:3 RSV). It is the will of God that we grow in love for one another. This should especially be true within the family circle.

At least three different kinds of love should be experienced in the family. In many instances the precipitating cause for marriage is romantic love. It is expected that young people will "fall in love" and get married. Romantic love is love on the level of the instincts. It is the chemical reaction of a male to a female, and vice versa. Marriage based only on this kind of love often experiences great disappointment.

A second kind of love that is essential in the family is "respect love." This kind of love is brotherly love or philanthropic love. It is love based on worth and integrity, character and reliability. It is social love that exists between friends. A husband and wife should sincerely like each other and be best friends.

The third kind of love that is essential for the well-being of the family is "help" love. This is the sacrificial love God demonstrated in the gift of his Son Jesus Christ for us.

Happy indeed is the home where husband and wife are romantically attracted to each other. Happier is the home where husband and wife also genuinely respect each other. The happiest home is the home where every area of thought and activity is saturated with "help" love.

Each person needs more love. Each person needs to love more.

Each family needs more love. Each family needs to love more.

A poet tells how to put love into practice in the family relationship:

> *Put love in your eyes*
> *like light in the skies;*
> *Put love in your words*
> *like the song of the birds.*
> *Put love in your mind*
> *and true love you will find.*

How can love grow and increase in the family?

I. Let the love of God for each family member be recognized and appreciated (John 3:16).

God so loved the world—that means husband, wife, son, daughter, brother, sister, parents, grandparents. Each of us is the object of God's supreme concern. He loves us and wants to provide for us and protect us. He wants each of us to experience his great salvation. Because God loves each member of our family, we need to love each of them because of their infinite worth in his sight.

II. We must love ourselves properly, positively, and permanently.

If you do not properly appreciate and respect yourself, it will be impossible for you to properly love and appreciate others. When Jesus said, "Thou shalt love thy neighbor as thyself," he was affirming that we should have a proper love for ourselves. If you suffer from a sense of low self-esteem, it follows that you will look upon others in a similar manner. Each of us needs to accept and rejoice in the truth that God loves us, that God is concerned about us, that God has high hopes for us. As we recognize this, it will help us also to respond to the truth that God loves the other members of our family.

III. We need to put love into practice in our families.

A pastor was kind to a young lady in his congregation. He encouraged her and affirmed her in some decisions that she was making. Later in a crafts class, she made for him a beautiful plaque that contained the letters, one above the other, T-A-L-K, with the message printed in beautiful color, "Try A Little Kindness." This was her way of saying thank you for the kindness that she had experienced as a result of her pastor's ministry.

How long has it been since you tried a little kindness on your companion? your children? your parents? Kindness is an expression of love that even deaf people can hear and blind people can see.

IV. We can increase love in our family by practicing forgiveness (Eph. 4:31–5:2).

It is inevitable that family members will bring pain to one another. The only solution to this problem is the practice of forgiveness. Forgiveness is a gift in which the injured one repudiates the right to retaliate and is willing to restore a warm relationship.

Conclusion

There are many ways by which we can increase the practice of love in family living. We should trust the Holy Spirit of God to pour out God's love within our hearts (Rom. 5:5). If we would increase love within the family, we need to let the love of God for us become more real and personal. God loves you and wants to come into your heart today. Let him in.

SUNDAY EVENING, MAY 26

Title: I Am the True Vine

Text: "I am the true vine; you are the branches. If a man remains in me and I in him, he will bear much fruit; apart from me you can do nothing" (**John 15:5** NIV).

Scripture Reading: John 15:1–8

Introduction

Farming is still big business in the United States, but fewer and fewer people are involved in it. At the beginning of this century, we were still a rural country, only semi-industrial. But today the scene has changed. Most people live in the cities, and those who do live in rural areas are no longer farming.

In Palestine, where Jesus lived, vinedressing was a prominent occupation. Although most people were not vineyard keepers, they were familiar with that line of work. In this environment Jesus made his last great "I am" statement. "I am the true vine," he said, "and my Father is the gardener" (John 15:1 NIV).

Vines were grown on terraces and required a lot of attention. A young vine was not allowed to bear fruit within the first three years. It was pruned drastically to develop a strong root system. Even after the vine began to bear grapes, it was still pruned, because some branches would produce fruit while others were only sucklings that sapped the vine of its strength and productivity.

Into this setting Jesus gave a dramatic lesson about those who claimed to be followers of God. Jesus is the only true vine; his Father is the gardener; and we are the branches. Let us look at each of these statements and see what truth they have for us.

I. Jesus is the only true vine.

A. *The vine is the means of life for the branches.* The roots gather water and nutrients from the earth, and these flow through the vine and give life to the branches. Apart from the vine, the branches will wither and die. No fruit will be produced on any branch that detaches itself or is broken off from the vine.

B. *Some persons claim to be Christian but seek to receive their Christian growth from a variety of sources.* It is not that they cut themselves off completely from Christ. They want to be nurtured by Jesus, but they also want to receive sustenance from other sources. They try to have an attachment with more than one vine, so to speak. They want eternal life from Jesus, success from their business, happiness from a bottle of booze or drugs, love from immoral sexual relations, security from the government, and healing from medicine. They are people of divided loyalties and splintered commitments.

C. *Jesus says, "I am the only true vine."* Jesus offers not only eternal life, but true success, true happiness, true love, genuine security, and healing for body and soul. This is not to say that you should not find satisfaction in your business or healing from a physician. It is to say that when your love relationship is in line with your faith in Jesus, you have a more secure chance of real success. Jesus is the guideline for solid business ethics. He is the foundation of good government. He is the doctor's teacher and nurse's aide. Jesus is the true vine—he is the true fountain of all that is good and wholesome about life.

II. The Father is the vinedresser.

A. *If a branch could think, it would still be difficult for it to comprehend the overall scheme of the gardener.* Gardeners just know more than branches. This statement is not intended to be overly simplistic; it is intended to be instructional. Sometimes we forget who God is and who we are. Like Adam and Eve, we want to believe that we either know as much as God or that we should have the right to know as much as God.

   If the branch could think aloud, it might wonder why the vinedresser will not allow it to bear fruit for the first three years. *Why all this pruning? If the vine is put here to bear grapes, then why does he hinder it or hold it back?* None of this pruning makes sense to a branch. Looking at the vineyard in this fashion might help us to better appreciate the role of God in our lives.

B. *In the overall plan of God, it is necessary to prepare the follower for his role as bearer of fruit.* Abraham began his work for God late in life. Still later—when he was one hundred—Abraham's son Isaac was born. Moses was eighty when God met him at the burning bush. David was thirty when he became king; Jesus was about thirty when he began his ministry; Saul of Tarsus was already out of rabbinical training when he met Christ on the road to Damascus. It was another fourteen years before he was accepted by the early church. Yet most of us want to begin sharing the good news of Christ before God's Spirit has properly trained us. (And some Christians use this as a weak excuse for never serving as an active witness for Christ.)

C. *We need to recognize the wisdom and plan of God for a fruitful branch.* That period of preparation is to be where God can mold us, teach us, and train us in his Word. No branch, or follower of Christ, will ever be an effective branch until he or she comes under the discipline and instruction of God. The Vinedresser cultivates the vine so that good fruit will grow on the branch. His sole objective is to care for the vine and the branch. We must trust him to lead us.

III. We are the branches.

A. *Branches are the fruit-bearing part of the grapevine.* Apart from the vine, they cannot bear fruit and thus are withering sticks suitable only for burning. As we have seen, some branches that do not bear fruit are cut off from the vine. But what about the branches that remain? Jesus reminds us, "If a man remains in me and I in him, he will bear much fruit; apart from me you can do nothing" (John 15:5 NIV).

B. *Society is filled with plans for the social betterment of humanity.* Most of these are launched from humanitarian philosophies instead of from Christ. But the world will only be changed by changing people. If we change only the environment, working conditions, and human rights, we still have not dealt with the basic problem of human sin. Jesus is the source of strength for his followers. All of his gospel must be preached and acted on. There is no need for debate about social ethics and evangelistic zeal. Christians should feed the body as well as the soul. It is not a case of either/or. This balanced gospel finds its source in Jesus and will bear much fruit.

C. *Another thing for Christians to remember about bearing fruit is that a "lot of green branch growth" does not necessarily equate a lot of fruit.* The ministry of the church today has never been more active. If things around the church slow down, we usually just grind out another activity with the hope of rejuvenating participation.

Activity does not equal spiritual growth. Sometimes churches are so busy in the new gymnasium that they have no time to be in the neighborhood. It is not that recreation is not important, but it hardly stands on a par with the conversion of the lost or the teaching of God's Word. Youth ministries often benefit from recreation, but not at the expense of enlistment of new disciples. Again we see the need for balance. The church should have both activity and growth—not one or the other. Our ultimate goal is to bear more fruit.

Conclusion

Thus, we come to the end of the great "I Am" sayings of Jesus. Here in this last sermon is a message for the church. Jesus is the true vine, God the Father is the gardener, and we are the branches. I know how well the true vine functions. I also know how well the gardener does his work. But the question that is still to be answered is, "How well do the branches bear fruit?"

Are you a fruit-bearing branch? Do you abide in Christ and receive your strength from him? If you do not, perhaps now is the time to set matters right and become the kind of branch you were saved to be.

WEDNESDAY EVENING, MAY 29

Title: All Things to All People

Text: "To the weak became I as weak, that I might gain the weak: I am made all things to all men, that I might by all means save some" (**1 Cor. 9:22**).

Scripture Reading: 1 Corinthians 9:1–27

Introduction

The apostle Paul is a prime example of one who had an intense desire to see others saved. It is hoped that as this chapter in the Bible is examined, everyone will catch that spirit. The main thought of this message is that of soulwinning.

I. Winning the lost is Jesus' concern.

A. *He was made flesh and dwelt among men (John 1:14).* This is known as the incarnation. The fact that Jesus left heaven and came to earth as a human establishes the urgency of salvation for everyone. Luke says that the Lord's mission was to seek and save the lost.

B. *He was made sin that sinners might be made the righteousness of God (2 Cor. 5:21).* Jesus was not made a sinner, but he was made sin. Jesus never sinned. By being made sin, he became the victim of God's wrath. He was made a curse and was separated from God.

II. Winning the lost is the concern of the apostle Paul.

A. *Paul made a personal sacrifice.* He was educated for business. He was successful in other endeavors. Yet he gave up all of it to be a soulwinner.

B. *Paul became a great traveler.* He traveled untiringly from country to country, city to city, and village to village to win the lost.

C. *Paul underwent extreme suffering.* He was ridiculed, beaten, and imprisoned. He underwent all of this because he wanted to win souls.

D. *Paul was exposed to death constantly and was eventually put to death.* Why? Because he had a concern for the lost. Paul became all things to all people that he might win some.

III. Winning the lost is the concern of the present-day Christian.

A. *Why should Christians today be desirous of winning souls?* Because of the value of a soul. Because of the fate of a soul. Because of the future of a saved soul. Because of the glory of Christ.

B. *How are present-day Christians to win souls?* By using all things at hand. We must use our speaking ability to preach, teach, invite, and pray. We must let our lives be Christian examples and show compassion and concern for the well-being of others by sacrificing our time, talents, and finances for their benefit.

Conclusion

You, as a Christian, have the privilege and responsibility to be a soulwinner. I hope you will follow the example of Paul and do all you can to win others.

Suggested preaching program for the month of

JUNE

■ Sunday Mornings

Continue the series of messages designed to strengthen family life, using the theme "The Living Christ and His Concern for Family Living." Interrupt the series on the last Sunday of the month to present an Independence Day message.

■ Sunday Evenings

"Messages for the Modern World from an Ancient Prophet" is the suggested theme for a series of sermons based on Ezekiel's prophecies. This prophet lived in a foreign country during perilous times. He found God to be very real and present, just as we can find him to be today.

■ Wednesday Evenings

Continue the studies based on Paul's first letter to the Corinthian Christians.

SUNDAY MORNING, JUNE 2

Title: Being Christian in the Home

Text: "In Antioch the disciples were for the first time called Christians" (**Acts 11:26 RSV**).

Scripture Reading: Ephesians 5:21–6:4

Hymns: "All Creatures of Our God and King," Francis of Assisi
"Love Divine, All Loves Excelling," Wesley
"God Give Us Christian Homes!" McKinney

Offertory Prayer: Holy Father, we bow before your throne of grace and mercy today to thank you for the generosity of your heart toward us. We thank you for the gift of salvation from sin and for your Holy Spirit who lives within us. We thank you for this good day. We accept it as a gift from you, and we will rejoice and be glad in it. We thank you for drawing us to this house of prayer and worship that we might hear your voice and that we might sing and proclaim your praises. Accept our gifts and bless them to the end that your kingdom might come in the hearts and lives of all people everywhere. In Jesus' name we pray. Amen.

Introduction

The acid test of our profession of faith is revealed by the manner in which we conduct ourselves as followers of Christ within the family circle. To be genuinely Christian in the home requires more than merely believing in God's existence. It requires even more than being a church member and going to church from time to time. It requires a genuine conversion experience and walking daily with the Holy Spirit.

I. Being genuinely Christian involves a real faith in Jesus Christ.

The basic root of the word *faith* means to unite. Genuine faith in God brings about a unity with God. A genuine faith in Jesus Christ causes us to unite ourselves with him to the extent that we follow him (Luke 9:23). Thus, faith is more than an intellectual belief in the existence of God as a presence or power. Genuine faith brings us to God as he has revealed himself in Jesus Christ.

II. Being genuinely Christian involves a willingness to be corrected so as to bring about change in our lives.

Jesus spent much time in concentrated effort with his disciples. He sought to bring about changes in their thought patterns and in their decision-making processes. He sought to place within them a new set of values. This need for change is dramatically illustrated in our Lord's experience with Peter. Peter sought to turn his Lord from the road that led to the cross. Jesus said to him rather abruptly, "Get behind me, Satan! You are a hindrance to me; for you are not on the side of God, but of men" (Matt. 16:23 RSV).

The apostle Paul challenges believers in Rome to dedicate themselves completely to God. Then they will experience the inward transformation making it possible to discover that God's plan for his people is best (Rom. 12:1–2).

In the seven epistles from John to the churches of Asia Minor, our Lord continued to challenge them to change. Repeatedly he encouraged them to listen to the voice of the Spirit (Rev. 2:1–3:22).

III. Being genuinely Christian requires that we relate to each other in terms of "helping love."

Jesus, in speaking to his disciples concerning the manner in which they would become recognized as his disciples, said, "A new commandment I give to you, that you love one another; even as I have loved you, that you also love one another. By this all men will know that you are my disciples, if you have love for one another" (John 13:34–35 RSV). Our Lord is not referring to romantic attraction in this command. He is talking about self-giving love that always relates to others in terms of the highest possible good for them. It is this same kind of love that Paul speaks of in our Scripture passage when he encourages husbands to "love your wives, as Christ loved the church and gave himself up for her" (Eph. 5:25 RSV). Jesus demonstrated his love for his church by dying on the cross. We must practice this manner of love within the family if we truly are going to be what the Father God would have us to be.

Peter wrote, "Above all hold unfailing your love for one another, since love covers a multitude of sins" (1 Peter 4:8 RSV). In no place is this kind of love needed more than within the family circle.

IV. Being genuinely Christian in the home requires a willingness to be forgiving.

Peter raised the question about forgiveness. Jesus encouraged him to place no limits upon forgiveness in family relationships (Matt. 18:21–22).

Forgiveness involves the repudiation of the right to retaliate for injury. Forgiveness is a decision not to harbor hostility toward the person who has acted as an enemy. Forgiveness involves a positive effort to reestablish a warm relationship with a person who has brought you pain.

V. Being genuinely Christian involves obedience to God out of love (John 14:15).

Jesus encourages us to be obedient to all of God's commandments. The motive for this obedience is not fear of the consequences of disobedience; rather, our obedience is to be based on love and gratitude for God's goodness to us.

The Christian home is a home where God is trusted sincerely and steadfastly and where he is lovingly obeyed in all matters.

Conclusion

Let each of us determine to be genuinely Christian in our hearts and in our homes. Let us begin the day with a prayer of gratitude for the privilege of being alive. Let us invite God to fill our hearts with love. Let us ask God for divine wisdom as we face each day. Let us pray that God's Spirit will control us and help us to be helpful, especially to those within our own families.

If you have not yet received Jesus Christ into your heart, you would be extremely wise to seek him today while you have opportunity. He waits at the door and is eager to come into your life.

SUNDAY EVENING, JUNE 2

Title: Finding God in the Storm

Text: "I looked, and, behold, a whirlwind came out of the north, a great cloud, and a fire infolding itself, and a brightness was about it, and out of the midst thereof as the colour of amber, out of the midst of the fire" **(Ezek. 1:4).**

Scripture Reading: Ezekiel 1:1–28

Introduction

The next nine Sunday evening studies will be based on a contemporary application of the ancient preaching of Ezekiel. If we were to take a poll among Bible students to discover which is the strangest and most difficult book in the Bible to understand, the prophecy of Ezekiel would be among those vying for the top spot. Ezekiel was a young Hebrew priest who was a visionary and who had a vivid imagination. He was a descendant of the family of Zadok, the notable Hebrew priest who could trace his lineage directly to Aaron, the brother of Moses. The family of Zadok was one of the best and noblest families in Jerusalem. Thus, born into this priestly family, Ezekiel became a priest when he was just a young man. He was well educated and exposed to the highest culture Jerusalem afforded.

Then one day King Nebuchadnezzar of Babylon came with his armies and laid siege against Jerusalem. King Jehoiachin of Judah surrendered the city to Nebuchadnezzar, and seven thousand of the best people in the city—including members of the priestly families, the nobility, the artisans, the skilled people—were taken away captive to Babylon. Among these captives was the young priest, Ezekiel. Apparently Ezekiel was a man of some wealth, and doubtlessly he took a considerable portion of his wealth with him. He had a home, a wife, and possibly a family. He lived in comparative ease and comfort on the banks of the Chebar River near a placed called Tel-abib, not many miles from the city of Babylon.

The fact that these Hebrew exiles in Babylon were being treated well did not compensate for the inner agony of soul, the frustration of being torn away from their homeland. They had to leave their beloved Jerusalem, the temple, and the presence of their God in the Holy of Holies. In our day it is a bit difficult to understand the agony of young Ezekiel and his fellow countrymen. But they were God's unique and chosen people; even though they had sinned against him repeatedly and now were suffering the consequences of their disobedience, they knew they were a people of destiny.

I. First, let's see if we cannot sense something of Ezekiel's agony.

A. *The opening scene is striking.* The time is late in what we would call the month of June, 593 years before Christ was born. A dust storm had swirled out of the desert into the flat, irrigated plain where, we might imagine, Ezekiel was tilling the small garden plot in which he raised vegetables for his family. When a dust storm comes, most people hide their faces lest those smarting, gritty particles of dust get in their eyes. But Ezekiel faced the storm, and while it buffeted him in its fury, he saw light, and motion, and glory. As the vivid imagination of this young priest was activated, God revealed himself to him out of this storm cloud!

B. *As the Chebar River flowed through the fertile plains of Babylonia, it seemed to be silently mocking Ezekiel.* "Your God has failed you! Where is the God of

Abraham, Isaac, and Jacob? Where is the God who lives in your precious temple in Jerusalem?" As Ezekiel faced the river, this is what it seemed to shout in derision to him. It was as though he was doomed to a biological existence until he died and his family laid his body in this alien soil. He had grown up believing himself to be an heir of God's promise to Abraham, but the future contained for him no promise, no hope, no God.

Crises that are almost intolerable come into all of our lives. Eventually we adjust to the tragedy of losing a loved one. But "living trouble" never goes away. This was Ezekiel's plight. He could not turn away from his bitterness—this loneliness for his homeland and for his God. But many of his people were adjusting, and it seemed to Ezekiel that the terrible cancer of complacency was eating away at them.

But wait! Let's look again at this despondent, brokenhearted young man. Suddenly we see him square his shoulders as if to say, "No! I will not give in to my feelings! I will not say, 'It's all over'! Our God is the only God, and he is all-powerful, and he knows where we are!"

II. Thus, we have the ecstasy of Ezekiel.

A. *As this lonely young exile stood on the river bank, he saw a dark cloud coming down from the north.* The storm cloud was what people now call a "dust devil." There are times during the day when a dust devil may be filled with strange, iridescent colors as the sun glints against the sand particles filling the cloud. Ezekiel watched, afraid but fascinated, while the storm cloud drew nearer. Slowly, with the eyes of spiritual vision, he began to see shining through this dust cloud the infinite glory of God! And to Ezekiel it was the blazing, dazzling flame of hope. Most of chapter 1 describes the chariot-throne upon which this glory rode. Kings rode in chariots in those days, so Ezekiel saw a conqueror's chariot coming down from the home of the Babylonian gods who dwelt, according to pagan belief, in the mysterious mountains to the north.

B. *With the Spirit of God activating the creative imagination of this young priest, Ezekiel set about to describe what he saw.* Sometimes it is difficult for us to understand the poetic, oriental symbolism of Ezekiel. But we need to remember that Ezekiel was using all that he had—human words, words invented to describe what a person sees and feels around himself or herself—to describe the glory of God. Can you imagine the frustration he felt as he began to probe into his vocabulary trying to come up with words with which to describe God? What does it boil down to? Man cannot describe God! But we can experience him and can commune with him in our souls. We can know that he knows us and can reveal himself to us in his own unique way, even in a dust devil of a storm!

C. *So the first chapter in Ezekiel's book is symbolism.* It is designed to help us think about the majesty, the glory, and the magnificence of God. What is a symbol? It is the use of one thing to suggest another. There are three things we need to remember about symbols that will help us understand not only Ezekiel, but many other portions of the Bible.

1. First, a symbol doesn't need to look, sound, smell, or taste like the thing symbolized. All it must do is suggest an idea.
2. Second, a symbol speaks to our imagination. When the captain of a ship sees a green light in the darkness, he imagines another ship and can tell in what direction it is going.
3. Third, a symbol can have many meanings, and not always does it symbolize the same thing. Jesus used symbols often: "I am the door," he said. We understand that. Symbols of God in Scripture bring us close to him.

III. God in the storm as Ezekiel describes him to us.

A. *All through the Bible we find rich symbolism in numbers.* The number "four" usually represents this world: the four corners of the earth, the four winds, the four seasons. This chariot-throne Ezekiel saw in the mist of the storm cloud is described in terms of four. There were four living creatures, each with four faces and four wings. They were piloting a four-wheeled vehicle. What did it mean? It meant that the glory of God filled the whole earth. He was not confined to a temple or a church, nor was he enthroned in some distant heaven. He was here, by the Chebar River, ready to comfort and strengthen Ezekiel. He is here, by my river of crisis, of trouble, of heartbreak, whatever the name!

B. *And what else do we see about Ezekiel's chariot?* It had wheels. The wheel is a symbol of motion. We do not worship a God who is impassive. He is a God of personality, who loves us and knows us by name. He is a God of action, of accomplishment. The eyes in Ezekiel's vision symbolized the all-seeing God, a God of total awareness concerning his creatures. Through this experience, Ezekiel came to know God—not just "about" him.

Conclusion

Ezekiel and his people knew the facts of faith. But when they came to the Chebar River and all that it represented, facts were not enough. They needed a firsthand meeting with God. You see, when we surrender to him, he teaches us to open our eyes while the sandstorm is blowing, and through all of that chaos and horror, he shows us his glory, and we hear him say, "I am with you always, even to the end of the world."

WEDNESDAY EVENING, JUNE 5

Title: A Lesson from History

Text: "Now these things were our examples, to the intent we should not lust after evil things, as they also lusted" **(1 Cor. 10:6).**

Scripture Reading: 1 Corinthians 10:1–11

Introduction

One can learn in many ways. One can learn by study, experience, and observation. The way to learn, as will be discussed in this message, is that of learning from history. Events that occur serve as examples.

I. To whom did these things happen?

A. *They were a group of people especially chosen through Abraham.* The Lord spoke to Abraham and said, "If you will obey me, I will make of you a great nation. I will bless you and protect you." Abraham obeyed, was blessed, and became a lesson in obedience for history.

B. *They were a people with a strange history.* The descendants of Abraham did not obey their Lord. As a result of disobedience, they drifted from the Lord and became slaves in Egypt. They are a lesson in disobedience.

C. *They were a people who experienced a miraculous deliverance.* God manifested his presence in a powerful way. His presence was seen through the plagues brought on by Moses, the parting of the waters, and the leadership by the pillar of cloud by day and the pillar of fire by night. This was a lesson in God's grace.

II. What did these people do that provoked God's displeasure?

A. *They lusted after evil things (1 Cor. 10:6).* That for which they lusted was inferior morally. As a result, they were overthrown. This is a lesson on priorities. They refused to rejoice over all the good things.

B. *They were idolatrous (1 Cor. 10:7).* This is the direct breaking of the first commandment (Exod. 20:3). They broke this commandment when they worshiped the golden calf. Idolatry is a danger in every life.

C. *They were guilty of fornication (1 Cor. 10:8).* Fornication is the breaking of another one of God's commandments (Exod. 20:14). This commandment was broken when they committed whoredom with the daughters of Moab (Num. 25:1).

D. *They tried the Lord (1 Cor. 10:9).* They spoke against God, and serpents were sent for punishment (Num. 21:4–6), but the Lord manifested his mercy by providing the brass serpent for healing. The Lord is equally as merciful today.

E. *They were guilty of murmuring (1 Cor. 10:10).* This record is found in Numbers 14 and 15. To murmur is to give audible expression to unwarranted dissatisfaction. Back of it is the fact that God is no longer trusted. The Lord dealt with them very severely for this.

III. What can contemporary Christians learn from these lessons?

A. *Taking issue with God is a serious matter.* Anytime people oppose the will of God, they are losers. God's plan is always best.

B. *Doing the will of God is the best for individuals and groups.* The eleventh chapter of Hebrews has been referred to as "Faith's Hall of Fame." It gives good examples of people doing God's will.

C. *The Lord's presence is with each believer today.* There has never been a time in history when God was not with his people.

Conclusion

You are urged to study the Word of God and learn from history the things that are profitable and nonprofitable in your relationship with God.

SUNDAY MORNING, JUNE 9

Title: The Practice of Forgiveness in the Family

Text: "Forgive us for our sins, for we ourselves forgive every one who is indebted to us" **(Luke 11:4 RSV).**

Scripture Reading: Matthew 6:14–15; 18:21–22

Hymns: "Great Is Thy Faithfulness," Chisholm
           "Though Your Sins Be as Scarlet," Crosby
           "Dear Lord and Father of Mankind," Whittier

Offertory Prayer: Holy Father, help us to recognize how rich we are in our relationship with you and in the resources that you make available to us. Help us to recognize you as the giver of every good and perfect gift. Help us to be good managers of the talents and treasures that have come under our supervision. Today as we bring tithes and offerings, use them for your honor and for the good of those you love. In Jesus' name. Amen.

Introduction

Jesus Christ came into this world to be our Savior (Matt. 1:21). He came to save us from the consequences of sin, the control of sin, and the terrible penalty of sin. Jesus came to Christianize the disposition of those who receive him as Savior and Lord. He came to deliver us from attitudes, ambitions, and activities that are harmful to ourselves and others. Jesus wants to save us from the destructiveness of resentment and bitterness, hate and hostility within family relationships. To harbor hate and hostility is contradictory to the spirit of being Christian. But in reality such attitudes are possible within the family circle.

Jesus, as heaven's infallible teacher, provides us with a technique for dealing with injury and mistreatment in family relationships. In Matthew 28:18 our Lord claims to have authority both in heaven and on earth. This means that we must listen to him. His is the authority of perfect love, total wisdom, and absolute truth. We need to recognize and respond to his authority as he teaches us how we are to handle mistreatment and injury in family relationships.

I. How do you respond to mistreatment and injury within the family?

Let us not be so naïve as to believe that injury and mistreatment do not occur among those who have trusted Jesus Christ as Savior. To respond with anger, hostility, bitterness, and retaliation is to follow the devil's way for destroying your home life, your family, and your fellowship. But many people are stingy with the grace of forgiveness. They assume that forgiveness is to be granted only when it is merited. They fail to recognize that forgiveness is always a gift. To neglect, to refuse, or to fail to forgive is to open the door for our satanic enemy to come in and destroy that which is very precious in family relationships.

Paul warned the believers in Corinth against the peril of an unforgiving spirit when he commended the church for their attitude of forgiveness toward the wayward brother (2 Cor. 2:5–11). He called attention to the fact that when we do not practice forgiveness, we leave the door open for Satan to gain an advantage over us (v. 11). There is no place where the practice of forgiveness is more essential than in family relationships.

Peter asked a question that all of us should ask. How often shall we practice forgiveness toward the brother who sins against us? Peter was being very generous by extending the limit to as many as seven times. Jesus responded by saying, "I do not say to you seven times, but seventy times seven" (Matt. 18:22 RSV). To interpret Jesus' reply as an oriental hyperbole is to miss the point. Injured persons must practice forgiveness every time they hurt because of an injury inflicted upon them. Accepting these words of Jesus about forgiveness literally will have a positive healing effect within the family.

II. The benefits of practicing forgiveness in the family.

The practice of forgiveness is absolutely essential if your family is to experience any degree of happiness and stability. There are various kinds of forgiveness that we each need to experience. Each of us needs to forgive ourselves and accept forgiveness for mistakes made in the past. Each of us needs the forgiveness of others against whom we have sinned. And each of us needs the forgiveness of God. Each of us also must grant the gift of forgiveness to others. Not to do so brings harmful repercussions into our lives.

A. *A forgiving spirit prevents the acid of hate from collecting as a corrosive force in your heart.* Hate does more harm to the vessel that holds it than it does to the victim upon which it is poured.

Joseph provides us with a beautiful example of the grace of forgiveness in his treatment of his brothers who sold him into slavery. They expected him to retaliate following the death of Jacob (Gen. 50:15–17). Joseph revealed by his actions that he had forgiven them fully and freely (Gen. 50:18–21). While the brothers benefited as a result of this act of forgiveness, Joseph had responded to injury in such a manner as to prevent the acid of hate from corroding his heart.

B. *A forgiving spirit delivers one from becoming involved in a vicious cycle of self-destructiveness.* Repeatedly throughout the New Testament we are warned against following the policy of retaliation when we are injured. Paul states this dramatically in his epistle to the Roman Christians (Rom. 12:19–21). To be eager for revenge brings harm to others, but it brings greatest harm to the person who appoints himself or herself as the prosecuting attorney, jury, judge, and executioner.

C. *A forgiving spirit brings healing to the broken heart and injured spirit.* Perhaps there was some wound in Peter's heart that caused him to ask, "Lord, how often shall my brother sin against me, and I forgive him? As many as seven times?" (Matt. 18:21 RSV). In Jesus' response to this question, his primary concern is for the injured one. He is declaring that the only way to healing and health and happiness is through forgiveness. There are some people in nearly every congregation who are quivering with pain caused by the cruelty of someone near and dear to them. How are they to deal with this problem of pain? Jesus tells us that healing is through the grace of forgiveness.

D. *A forgiving spirit permits you to reveal the love of God in Jesus Christ to your friends.* An attitude that demands retaliation makes it impossible to reveal the love of God simultaneously. As we practice Christian love toward our enemies, even within the family circle, we manifest the fact that we are the sons and daughters of God (Matt. 5:44–48).

E. *A forgiving spirit prevents the devil from establishing a beachhead in your mind and in your thought processes (2 Cor. 2:11).*

F. *A forgiving spirit toward those who have injured you enables you to experience God's continuing forgiveness (Matt. 6:14–15).* The practice of forgiveness is not a price to be paid but a condition to be met. To experience forgiveness, the forgiven must forgive. To be unforgiving toward those who injure us is to remain unforgiven because one thus makes oneself unforgivable. To close the door on the opportunity of forgiving is to close the door on the receiving of forgiveness.

The basic idea in forgiveness when used in connection with sin is that of canceling a debt. It removes the barrier to reconciliation.

Conclusion

Alexander Pope said, "To err is human; to forgive, divine." Forgiveness is a divine work that stands at the beginning of our salvation experience. The practice of forgiveness on our part makes it possible for us to experience God's full salvation in the present. Forgiveness is not indulgence and tolerance. Forgiveness is overcoming evil with good.

To experience forgiveness we must recognize and forsake our sin. We need to repent of our sin and return to God to experience the joy of forgiveness.

SUNDAY EVENING, JUNE 9

Title: Walking the Hard Road

Text: "He said unto me, Son of man, stand upon thy feet, and I will speak unto thee. And he said unto me, Son of man, I send thee to the children of Israel, to a rebellious nation that hath rebelled against me: they and their fathers have transgressed against me, even unto this very day" **(Ezek. 2:1, 3).**

Scripture Reading: Ezekiel 2:1–3:3

Introduction

Last week we observed a despondent, disillusioned young Hebrew priest, Ezekiel, standing by the Chebar River in a strange and alien land where he and his people were captives. He was at the point of saying, "What's the use? God doesn't even care anymore!" Then God sent a vicious dust storm down from the mountains, and Ezekiel saw the glory of God in a way that it is found nowhere else in the Bible. Through strange and weird symbols, God revealed himself to his wondering servant.

After having had that incomparable experience, Ezekiel fell on his face before God. He would like to have stayed by the river to "soak in" all of that glory and radiance of God's self-revelation. But God said, "No you don't! Stand up on your feet, Ezekiel! There's work to be done. There's a long road ahead with some rough stretches, and you must get prepared for it!" Mountaintop experiences with God are wonderful beyond expression, but the valley is inevitable, and we must be prepared to walk there in the strength of the Lord.

I. First, in our text passage, we find Ezekiel's commission from God.

A. *Ezekiel's task was to deliver to his people a message of judgment.* It was a message to a people who believed they had already been judged too harshly. Judgment does not necessarily mean condemnation. When Christians read the Bible with honesty and openness, they will find mirrors everywhere in which they see their shortcomings and sins. This is God's way of saying, "All right, you've grown a little here, but look at *that* area of your life. You have a long way to go there! Some pruning and spiritual surgery are needed!" This is not always a pleasant experience.

These Hebrew exiles to whom Ezekiel was instructed to deliver a message of judgment did not want to face their sins. They felt sorry for themselves, and they wanted pity instead. Many of them were suffering; and to make matters worse, their brothers who had been left in Jerusalem were not having to bear the trials and heartbreak in this pagan land where they were being held captive. So they were prone to say, "Lord, I'm having enough trouble as it is! I need your consolation, not your judgment! Don't send more fire, Lord; I need healing salve on the wounds I already have!"

B. *But there is a danger involved in expressions of comfort and consolation, for we tend to want more than we need.* The truth is that there come those times in the lives of God's people when we must be forced to examine ourselves, face our shortcomings and sins, and repent. So Ezekiel had a problem. His people, like many today, were quite willing to believe in God as long as he was willing to sympathize with them in their hard times. But they didn't want to be told to repent of their sins, to examine themselves, to face up to their shortcomings. They had had enough trouble already. The lesson here for us, as well as for them, is that we are called upon to live our faith, not just under ideal conditions, but under whatever circumstances we find ourselves, even in the valley of the shadow of death.

C. *And how did Ezekiel begin his bold program of preaching judgment and self-examination to his people?* His first step was to call them back to a private and individual practice of their faith. He stressed strongly a proper diet, prayer, and respect for the Sabbath. Ezekiel knew that these things, while not ends in themselves, were vital aids to an inward and spiritual relationship with God. We live in a day when there are many great and sometimes almost overwhelming issues facing us. These issues are complex, but before we can be effective at all in exerting any significant influence as Christians within our society, we must see to our individual, personal, private lives and our relationship with God.

II. Second, after Ezekiel received his commission from God, we read of his equipment for service.

A. *God had told Ezekiel what to do, and it wasn't a very pleasant task.* But God didn't leave Ezekiel there. He said, "Here's your equipment. Here is your power. Here is the strength in which you are to go." Note God's honesty with Ezekiel. He told him, in so many words, that it would not be easy to preach a message of repentance to a people who did not want to listen. In a very vivid and graphic way, God warned Ezekiel that there would be "briers, thorns, and scorpions." By that, God meant that the people would often reject Ezekiel's preaching, and there would be times when he would actually experience physical danger. The "hand" represented God, and the "roll" (scroll), the holy Word of God (2:9). God told Ezekiel to "eat" the scroll (3:1). When he did, it was as sweet as honey to the taste.

B.   *It is often the case that before we can taste "the sweetness of honey" in the Word of God, we must first apply the "bitter parts."* They are the parts of God's message that call for repentance and self-examination. The Bible presents a frank, realistic picture of human weakness and of the divine strength available. See how the Bible describes the weaknesses, as well as the strengths, of great men? Abraham was a liar; Jacob was a cheat; and Esau, a fool. But that is not the whole story. God touched these weak men and made them great. They were not great within themselves. This says, simply, that man has sinned. This is precisely what man does not want to hear. "I am *not* bad!" he retaliates. "I am essentially good! Give me a good environment, give me food for my stomach and money in my pocketbook, and I will be good!" But not so; sin is not just a "conditioned response to man's environment." It is not just hereditary. It is man's fallen nature expressing itself.

C.   *There is one person in the world for whose life and destiny I am uniquely responsible.* Is that person measuring up to the full stature of which he is capable with God's help? If not, that person ought to repent. And I am that person! This is the message of Ezekiel, and the same message runs throughout the Bible. People do not like this message; they never have, and they probably never will. But it is our only hope.

Conclusion

Over a dangerous reef the Coast Guard anchors a large buoy with a light that blinks by night and a bell that tolls with every wave. The buoy is placed there not to deprive mariners of any freedom, but to show them the way to freedom. To ignore the buoy could mean destruction. The standards set forth in God's Word are high ones. In fact, Jesus told his followers on one occasion, "Be ye therefore perfect, even as your Father which is in heaven is perfect" (Matt. 5:48). It would be difficult to find a standard higher than that one!

But what does a person want? He or she wants a relaxed, easy-going moral code that makes no strenuous demands, a benevolent "grandfather God" in heaven who will smile on sins and shortcomings. But instead of that, God sets a standard for us that is so high we can attain it only with his help. When we are striving to reach that standard, we are possessors of a radiant joy and peace that the world can neither give nor take away.

Thus, the message of Ezekiel is fantastically relevant today. He said to his people, "Wherever you are, in the valley of the shadow or on the sunny highlands, it is your duty to live your faith. And if you fail, then it is your duty to repent and to move back into a right relationship with God." And today it is through such Christians that God's love is channeled into every corner, every nook and cranny, of this world.

WEDNESDAY EVENING, JUNE 12

Title: Beware of Temptations

Text: "There hath no temptation taken you but such as is common to man: but God is faithful, who will not suffer you to be tempted above that ye are able; but will with the temptation also make a way to escape, that ye may be able to bear it" (**1 Cor. 10:13**).

Scripture Reading: 1 Corinthians 10:12–14

Introduction

Yielding to temptation is devastating. It is one of the worst things that can happen to the human race. What happened to Adam and Eve is a classic example of all that can happen to a person when he or she yields to temptation.

I. A fair warning about temptation (1 Cor. 10:12).

A. *Temptation is universal.* The devil, who is the tempter, is no respecter of persons. He is described as a roaring lion walking about seeking those he can devour (1 Peter 5:8). He is the archenemy of everyone and seeks nothing but bad for all he can tempt. He is subtle in his approach and hits at the weakest point when a person is least expecting it. He uses many different tactics.

B. *Temptations need to be constantly guarded against.* No one is ever to flirt with temptation. People should watch every move in regard to it. Each person is to be vigilant all the time. There are no moral holidays. There is no freedom from Satan's attack. The warning is, "Take heed."

II. A solemn statement (1 Cor. 10:13).

A. *God is always conscious of our temptation.* The Lord himself never tempts anyone to do wrong. He does not promise to remove it. He only promises grace to withstand it.

B. *Individual temptations are not unique as such.* They are common to all. No one will be tempted above that which he or she is able to stand.

III. A passionate plea (1 Cor. 10:12, 14).

A. *Take heed (1 Cor. 10:12).* To take heed is to listen to the warnings of those who know and are concerned about one's welfare. It is to listen and adhere to the words of the Bible. It is to respond favorably in regard to the warning.

B. *Flee from idolatry (1 Cor. 10:14).* An idol is anything that stands between us and God. Idolatry is a breaking of the first commandment (Exod. 20:3). To flee from idolatry is to be so close to God that there is no room for an idol to exist between us and God. To flee is to spend time in prayer and fellowship with the Lord. It is to seek high and noble things. When we flee from idolatry, we cultivate good relationships and right attitudes. We rededicate ourselves to the Lord daily.

Conclusion

You are being tempted right this very minute. The devil is after you. Listen to the admonition of Scripture and gain victory over Satan.

SUNDAY MORNING, JUNE 16

Title: Parents Who Are Worthy of Honor

Text: "'Honor your father and mother' (this is the first commandment with a promise), 'that it may be well with you and that you may live long on the earth'" **(Eph. 6:2–3 RSV).**

Scripture Reading: Ephesians 5:21–6:4

Hymns: "Faith of Our Fathers," Faber
           "Tell Me the Old, Old Story," Hankey
           "Happy the Home When God Is There," Ware

Offertory Prayer: Loving Father, we thank you today for revealing yourself through Jesus Christ. We come into your presence with joy and faith and hope. Give us ears to hear your voice. Give us eyes of faith to see your truth. Give us hearts that will not only receive but hearts that will give to others. As we come bringing tithes and offerings, accept these gifts and bless them to the end that others will come to know Jesus Christ as Lord and Savior. In Jesus' name. Amen.

Introduction

In this section of Paul's epistle to the Ephesians (5:21–6:4), the apostle gives some great guidelines for abundant living within the home. These are the most important relationships of life. We can be thankful that God has given guidelines to husbands and wives. He has given guidelines to parents regarding their children and guidelines to children concerning the manner in which they should relate to their parents.

Today we will focus on the parental responsibility to God as well as the parental responsibility to children.

Phillips translates the words that are addressed to fathers—but are applicable to mothers as well—as follows: "Fathers, don't overcorrect your children or make it difficult for them to obey the commandments. Bring them up with Christian teaching in Christian discipline" (Eph. 6:4 PHILLIPS).

Dr. Kenneth Taylor has paraphrased in *The Living Bible* as follows: "And now a word to you parents. Don't keep on scolding and nagging your children, making them angry and resentful. Rather, bring them up with the loving discipline the Lord himself approves, with suggestions and godly advice."

On this day, which in America is called Father's Day, it would be helpful for us as parents to recognize that we need to be worthy of the honor and the respect of our children. This day, Father's Day, was first observed in the United States on June 17, 1910. In 1923 the third Sunday in June was fixed as the official day, and in 1924 President Coolidge recommended its national observance. Today it has a fixed place in the calendar of special days in our country.

Devotion to and pride in fathers does not need to wait for an official approval. The word *father* is defined as "the source or prototype." That is, the father is the one from whom I get my strength. The reverse can also be true. One can receive weaknesses from a father.

As fathers and mothers we should be tremendously concerned about the impact of our lives on the lives of our children. Across the length and breadth of our country, mayors, ministers, senators, judges, law enforcement officers, physicians, and psychiatrists are in agreement that marriage and family living are in serious trouble. Many young people are having problems. As parents we need to be as certain as we can that youth problems are not the result of parental problems.

In the larger passage of Scripture read for today, we saw some instructions specifically for husbands and wives (Eph. 5:21–24), some for wives only (5:22–24), some for husbands only (5:25–33), and some for children (6:1–3). The passage closes with further instructions to parents (6:4).

I. To be parents worthy of honor, we need to subordinate ourselves to the Lord (Eph. 5:21).

The husband is responsible to God for the manner in which he relates to his wife. The wife is responsible to God for the manner in which she relates to her husband. Both husbands and wives should conduct themselves in such a way as to please the Father God in this important relationship of being progenitors and of rearing those children to maturity.

II. If we would be worthy parents, we must accept the authority of God.

A. *The wife should recognize and accept the authority of the husband.*
B. *The husband must recognize the supreme authority of God over his life.* God holds him responsible for the well-being of his family.
C. *The children should recognize and respond to the parents' authority.*

III. To be worthy parents we need a quality of character that is worthy of reverence.

Children are not commanded to honor parents who are dishonorable.

A. *Children need to be able to reverence parents who are not phonies.*
B. *Loving obedience should be deserved on the part of parents rather than being something that is coerced.*

IV. To be parents worthy of honor, we must practice love that is genuine.

A. *It is erotic love or romantic love that often attracts a couple toward each other to the extent that they enter into marriage.* To achieve the highest possible happiness, a couple needs to have something more than romantic attraction for each other.
B. *A husband and wife need to relate to each other in such a manner as to deserve the "respect" love of the other.*
C. *Parents need to practice* agape *love, which is sacrificial, self-giving love.* It is love that expresses itself in helpfulness, not only to the companion, but also to the children.

V. To be parents worthy of honor, we must not be guilty of exasperating our children (6:4).

The imperative in this verse is applicable to both mothers and fathers. As such we have been appointed as teachers and protectors and exemplars for our children. We have a stake in their happiness and well-being and success. Many parents are paralyzed with fear to the extent that they are overcorrective concerning what their children might do.

On the other hand, the apostle is not suggesting that we grant every wish that our children might have. He is not advising us to never cross them. He is not implying that we are always to approve their goals and ambitions.

We must accept the responsibility for being teachers, guides, and exemplars for our children. We must be on guard lest we break their spirit with a destructive, negative, and critical spirit. There are a number of ways by which we can be guilty of doing this.

A. *We can exasperate them by providing an incomplete and inadequate home life in which love and affection and forgiveness and kindness are not the order of the day.*
B. *We can exasperate them by hypocritical, phony lives.*
C. *We can exasperate them by being preoccupied with outside interests to the extent that we never give them any time.*
D. *We can exasperate them by a refusal to listen when they need to talk with us.* Children often spell parental love with the great big letters T-I-M-E.
E. *Perhaps we exasperate them most by making hasty and incorrect judgments concerning their motives and conduct.*

We are strongly prohibited against contributing to a broken spirit on the part of our children that would cause them to react with anger, hostility and self-destructiveness.

Conclusion

We all need help if we are to be parents worthy of honor. We can be confident that God wants to help us improve the quality of our family life. We need to read the Bible and pray daily in the presence of our family. We need to let the church really be the church if we are going to be the finest Christian parents that we are capable of being. Let us earnestly seek to give our children parents that they find easy to honor and respect.

SUNDAY EVENING, JUNE 16

Title: Practicing Your Faith Where You Are

Text: "Son of man, I have made thee a watchman unto the house of Israel: therefore hear the word at my mouth, and give them warning from me" **(Ezek. 3:17).**

Scripture Reading: Ezekiel 3:4–27

Introduction

Tonight we are going to "sit in" on an ordination service—Ezekiel's. But then, perhaps we need to understand what an "ordination service" really is. Most of us have attended at one time or another the ordination service for one about to become a minister or for a group of people in the church set aside by the congregation to serve as deacons.

These are impressive and memorable exercises. They are especially hallowed experiences for the persons involved. And they are appropriate and proper rituals, for they are designed to impress on those being ordained the unique servant roles that are theirs among the people of God.

But at the same time, we must keep this business of earthly ordination in proper perspective. Ordination does not establish "Class A" Christians, as opposed to all those unordained members who must forever and always remain in "Class B." For in a very real sense, every believer was ordained "a priest and a minister of God" when he or she was born again.

Now we as priests of God have many and varied functions in life. Some of us lay bricks; some plant corn; some rock cradles and prepare meals; some teach school; others repair cars. Still others preach sermons from pulpits on Sunday. But all of us are called to be God's special agents wherever we are, all of the time!

Thus, what happened to Ezekiel happens to every believer in the Lord Jesus Christ. It happens in a different way and for different purposes perhaps; yet we all, as Christians, share in this mysterious and divine ritual of ordination. It is God's special way of equipping us for and making us acutely aware of our responsibility to practice our faith where we are.

I. First, in examining Ezekiel's ordination experience, we shall see the meaning of the hand of God upon him.

A. *"The hand of the LORD was strong upon me,"* said Ezekiel (3:14). Throughout this book there are two words that have the same meaning: *hand* and *Spirit.* Both represent the mystery of God at work in the world. This would compare today to the Holy Spirit who lives within every believer.

In the Old Testament the word *spirit* also means "breath." This is an excellent way to describe the life principle God has given to us. So there we have it: "The hand of God, the Spirit of God, the holy breath of God, was upon me!" said Ezekiel.

B. *Already, in those early days of his special relationship with God, Ezekiel had had some unspeakably wonderful experiences.* In the midst of those exhilarating moments, Ezekiel was totally secure in his faith. He was not being challenged by the cold, profane, obscene world. But then, almost anybody can be an exuberant, effervescent, overflowing Christian when things are going well and he or she is having all kinds of great experiences such as Ezekiel was having. But God was about to impart to Ezekiel a peculiar ability and talent every believer must have. Ezekiel was about to learn that the Spirit of God, the hand of God, is still at work even when everything seems to be going wrong. For we read, "So the spirit lifted me up, and took me away, and I went in bitterness, in the heat of my spirit; but the hand of the Lord was strong upon me" (3:14). Ezekiel learned, just as God wants all of his children to learn, that he is with us in the glory moments of our faith, and he is also with us in the times of drudgery, of boredom, of pressure, and yes, even of agony.

II. Now that we have seen the hand of God come to rest upon Ezekiel, let's note the performance of the prophet.

A. *Did Ezekiel's personality match his task?* How did he relate to these people to whom God sent him to preach and to minister? To begin with, we must remember that God had called Ezekiel to serve as the preacher and pastor of a lonely, frightened, depressed, and disillusioned group of Hebrew exiles living in a pagan land as captives. And these were the people of God, the specially chosen people through whom God had intended to work out his purposes for the salvation of humankind. They were frustrated, bewildered, and bitter people. They were about to the point of wondering whether or not their God was as powerful as they had always believed him to be.

B. *It is doubtful that any preacher would deliberately choose such a pastorate as this for his field of service.* The "First Church of Tel-abib on the Chebar" was not the most desirable pastorate for a young preacher just fresh from his ordination service! Nor did Ezekiel always manifest the gift of a good personality and charm; but he was God's servant, and he served God to the fullest with the gifts and abilities he had. Ezekiel had some shortcomings, and it is good that we know about them. It gives us hope that God can use us in spite of all of our imperfections and strange quirks and idiosyncrasies—if we honestly and completely give ourselves to God as did Ezekiel.

C. *Let's imagine Ezekiel, this young prophet, sitting in his home.* His mind is whirling; he is trying to sort out all of the experiences he has had during these days. On the one hand, he thinks of the glory and majesty of God he has experienced, and his soul soars into a state of unbounded ecstasy. For the rest of his life, he will never forget the glory of God in that swirling dust storm! But then, at the other extreme, the evidence all around him indicates failure, shattered dreams, a weak and powerless religion. And with a growing sense of horror, he realizes as God speaks to him that things are going to get worse before they get better! All of this failure is going to be compounded; Jerusalem is going to fall, and God is telling him that he must be the messenger to carry this terrible news to his people.

D. *But just before he throws up his hands in despair, he remembers again the overwhelming glory of God which he has just seen.* He realizes that the faith God has given him is more than just a personal, selfish thing to carry him through the rough days ahead. This new faith he has received will give him the strength and the courage to preach both judgment and repentance, and the glory of God to his people.

Then it was that God gave this young prophet a new title to add to his job description: "Son of man, I have made thee a watchman unto the house of Israel: therefore hear the word at my mouth, and give them warning from me" (3:17). High watchtowers stood at measured intervals along the massive walls of Babylon. When the exiles went into the city on their various errands of business, they could see the watchmen in their towers watching them. When the people returned to their homes, the watchmen were still at their posts of duty. These watchmen knew what was going on in their world all of the time. This is very much a part of a pastor's task. The true pastor whom God calls needs to know what is going on in this world and in the world of his people. He needs to know when there is dissension in the flock and when false doctrine is being taught.

E. *So with a rugged sense of determination, Ezekiel accepted his assignment as a watchman over his people.* Then God gave him an example of what he was to do in this role. He described four individuals and Ezekiel's relation as a watchman to each of them.

   1. The first illustration shows an evil man whom the watchman fails to warn, and the evil man dies in his sin. The Lord says sternly to Ezekiel: "If you fail to warn him, then I will require his blood at your hand!"

2. The second illustration is of an evil man who will not listen. But if the watchman does his duty, then he is not responsible for the spiritual death that follows.

3. The third illustration presents to every pastor a painfully familiar scene. Here is a good man whose outward life and conduct are beyond reproach. But he is going away from God; he is becoming totally confident in himself. Perhaps he has money, position, influence, and security. But eventually he comes to that point where he has shut the door, finally and conclusively, on God. If the watchman fails to warn this "good man" of his collision course with disaster, the watchman will share in the guilt of this man.

4. The fourth illustration presents the ideal. Here is a person who is faithful to God. The watchman-pastor helps him, encourages him, and supports him as he practices his faith.

Thus, to be a watchman is not an easy job. It was not easy in Ezekiel's day, nor is it in our day.

Conclusion

Are you practicing your faith where you are? Only a few, comparatively, are called to serve God within the framework of the organized church in a professional status. But all of us, as believers, are called to serve God where we are. "Doctor, lawyer, merchant, chief," whatever your vocation, is your ministry to God. Ezekiel's message to us, then, is simply this: The glory of God is found wherever faith in him exists; God is in charge of this world, and he will be victorious over it; your part and mine in the final victory is to practice our faith to the utmost wherever we are and to the glory of God.

WEDNESDAY EVENING, JUNE 19

Title: Seeking Our Neighbor's Good

Text: "Let no man seek his own, but every man another's wealth" (**1 Cor. 10:24**).

Scripture Reading: 1 Corinthians 10:15–33

Introduction

A great and underlying principle that runs throughout the Bible is that of seeking good for one's neighbor. This is basically what Jesus meant when he said that one who saves his life shall lose it, but the one who loses his life for the sake of the gospel shall find it. People also need to realize that when they seek the good of their neighbor, they are seeking their own good. In this passage there are three thoughts projected that call for consideration.

I. The first thought is a caution—"let no man seek his own" (1 Cor. 10:24).

A. *That which is condemned in this passage is that of which most people are guilty.* At this point an individual becomes a victim of society. As a whole, society encourages people to seek their own benefit, and when they do, they are praised for it. The normal tendency is to look out for oneself.

B. *That which is condemned in this passage is sanctioned by a certain view of religion.* A good example of this is when certain people of a particular religious philosophy retire from the world to make sure of their own spiritual welfare. It is easy to overlook the interests of others while promoting one's own salvation.

C. *That which is condemned in this passage does not mean that each person is not to look out for self.* The whole message of the Bible is that every person is to be a responsible person. The Bible says, "They made me the keeper of the vineyards; but mine own vineyard have I not kept" (Song 1:6). It also says each person is to remove the beam from his own eye before he seeks to pull the mote from the other person's.

II. The second thought is a rule—let every man seek another's good.

A. *This rule expressly applies to every person.* The text says "every man." Paul says in Galatians 6:2, "Bear ye one another's burdens, and so fulfil the law of Christ." Whatever a person's position is in life, whether it be in the church, the family, or society in general, he is under the obligation of self-denial, benevolence, and helpfulness.

B. *There is a great need in society for such helpfulness.* People are sick, sin-ridden, lonesome, suffering, and lost. They all need help.

C. *The one best way this rule can be followed is by spreading the gospel.*

III. The third thought is a motive.

This is implied but not specifically expressed.

A. *The example of Jesus' life and death is an example of unselfishness.*

B. *His love and sacrifice constitute the moral power of benevolence.* He died that others may live.

Conclusion

Many of the ills and woes of the world today could be remedied if all people would take the admonition of this passage of Scripture—that is, live responsible and useful lives.

SUNDAY MORNING, JUNE 23

Title: Responding Properly When Trouble Comes

Text: "God is our refuge and strength, a very present help in trouble" **(Ps. 46:1 RSV).**

Scripture Reading: Psalm 46:1–7

Hymns: "Have Faith in God," McKinney
"'Tis So Sweet to Trust in Jesus," Stead
"It Is Well with My Soul," Spafford

Offertory Prayer: Precious Father, thank you for inviting us to this house of prayer and worship today that we might have fellowship with you and fellowship with our brothers and sisters in Jesus Christ. We come as children whom you have blessed greatly. We thank you and praise you for the abundance of your blessings upon us. Thank you for health and for the opportunity to have an income. We pray your blessings upon these gifts that they shall bring honor to your name and blessings to others. In Jesus' name. Amen.

Introduction

How can we be sure that we will be genuinely Christian when trouble crosses our pathway?

The Christian has no immunity from catastrophe. Believers experience disappointments in their careers. Some believers experience great heartbreak because of differences of opinion with their spouses. Sometimes children are the occasion for great distress of mind and heart. Conditions and circumstances in the community often contribute to an unhappy state of affairs. Disease can strike down the best among us.

To cope with trouble, many secure hospitalization insurance. Still others secure liability insurance. Many people purchase life insurance. These are forms of coping with financial difficulty.

Have you developed a technique for handling trouble when it comes?

I. Avoid faulty ways of dealing with trouble.

A. *Do not hold God responsible for any trouble that might come into your life.* God is not a mean God who takes delight in our trouble.
B. *Do not resort to resentment and hatred toward people.*
C. *Do not surrender to self-pity and despair.* This can be destructive, and it never provides the pathway to healing and happiness.
D. *Do not seek escape through the anesthesia of alcohol or drugs.*

II. Face trouble with in God (Ps. 121:1–2).

A. *Trust in the goodness and power of God for help (Phil. 4:13).* Paul affirms that God works in all things to bring out good for those who love and trust

190

him (Rom. 8:28). Paul also affirms that God will not permit any trouble to come to us that we cannot endure with his help (1 Cor. 10:13).

B. *Discover and depend on the promises of God.* The psalmist repeatedly encourages us to "wait upon the LORD."

C. *Accept God's forgiveness and be forgiving toward others.* If your trouble comes because of some fault of your own, accept God's forgiveness. If trouble has come because of someone else's fault, practice forgiveness toward that person.

D. *Live life one day at a time.*

E. *Search for the good at all times.* Something good can be found even in the darkest of days.

III. Develop a plan for enduring the pain of trouble.

A. *Listen to God in Bible study.*

B. *Let God speak to you through beautiful sacred music.*

C. *Praise God and be thankful for his blessings upon you.*

D. *Recognize God's angels who come to you in the form of helpers.*

E. *Grow your faith daily by trusting God.*

F. *Let a friend be a friend to you in a time of trouble.*

G. *Follow the light that Jesus Christ gives (John 8:12).*

Conclusion

All of us would like to avoid trouble. Much trouble can be avoided if we will trust Jesus Christ and follow his guidance and help day by day. Sometimes trouble comes upon us in the form of a catastrophe over which we have no control. God can help. Let's trust him.

SUNDAY EVENING, JUNE 23

Title: Our Refuge and Our Fortress

Text: "Therefore say, Thus saith the Lord GOD; Although I have cast them far off among the heathen, and although I have scattered them among the countries, yet will I be to them as a little sanctuary in the countries where they shall come" **(Ezek. 11:16).**

Scripture Reading: Ezekiel 11:14–20

Introduction

It is very difficult for American Christians to understand what persecution really means. In the course of the great wars in our nation's history, some in the armed forces were captured and languished, some for many years, in unspeakably horrible prison camps. But we have never experienced alien armies coming to our shores and taking thousands of our people off to a foreign country as exiles. Neither have we experienced the nightmare of having enemy troops storm into our towns and cities, take over our homes and businesses, and force us to take what belongings we could carry with us and flee for our lives—only to become miserable refugees, unwanted, living like animals instead of human beings, finally existing only to scrounge enough scraps of food to keep our starving children alive.

This was the situation when God called this young priest Ezekiel. Whereas the people had not suffered to a great extent physically, still most of them had no joy, no song in their hearts. When they arrived in Babylon they had hung up their harps, with which they had accompanied themselves when they sang the psalms of David. They had no song, no hope.

Our Scripture reading introduces another blow for these already wounded people. God revealed to Ezekiel the attitude that prevailed among the Hebrews who remained in Jerusalem, those who had not been forced to leave their homeland. "Son of man, your brethren, even your brethren, your fellow exiles, the whole house of Israel, all of them, are those of whom the inhabitants of Jerusalem have said, 'They have gone far from the LORD; to us this land is given for a possession'" (11:15 RSV).

I. The test of true faith.

A. *It isn't easy to bear the taunts and harassments of one's enemies; but when one's friends, or worse still, one's own people, begin to attack, to find fault, to criticize, to say contemptible things—that's something else!* This is especially hard to bear when they are not suffering and we are. And it becomes unbearably hard when it seems apparent that we who are suffering are more righteous than they are! You recall that the Babylonians under Nebuchadnezzar had taken away "the cream of Israel's crop." They had captured the leaders, the aristocracy, and had left behind, for the most part, the followers, many of whom doubtless had secretly envied these leaders who had been captured. Those left behind had never dreamed of being able to step into places of leadership and run the country as they had always thought it should be run! Then, also, there was the age-old concept among the Hebrews that whenever tragedy struck, it signified that the one it struck was being punished for his or her sins. Sometimes this is true; but we also know that often those who suffer are the best, not the worst, among us.

B. *So what was happening back home?* The exiles were not receiving spiritual care packages with messages saying: "We are praying for you! Your names are being called daily in prayer, and our hearts and thoughts are with you continually. We weep for you, and we do not know why you were taken and we were spared, for we are no better than you are!" Instead, word came from those snobs back at home in Jerusalem, saying: "You know, Jerusalem is where God lives. These brothers of ours in exile are away from this holy city, and therefore they are away from God! This means only one thing: They have sinned. They were not as good and gifted as we thought they were—and as they thought they were!"

Sadly, the "religious snobs" didn't vanish with the Old Testament era. We still have them today, those who are ready to say when a brother hits a rough stretch on the road: "Well! Look who's having trouble now! Mr. High and Mighty! Looks like he wasn't so spiritual after all." They never stop to think that God may simply be firing him a little in the heavenly kiln so that the beauty of Jesus can be seen a bit more clearly in his life.

C. *So what do we have here?* We have some of God's immature children, some of his spiritual kindergartners, covering up their envy and littleness with some wrong theology. They were saying: "Our brothers in Babylon suffer because they have sinned. We are blessed because we have been good!" And people, by nature, love that kind of theology. Thus, we have two groups of God's children here. One group was composed of "spiritual snobs" who believed that their favored position at the moment was because they were "good and righteous." Then the other group—those in exile, feeling the fire of persecution and trouble—were about to lose their faith through despair.

How sad that many Christians today are usually in one or the other of these two groups. Either they are proud of their spirituality and feel that good things are happening to them because they are such valuable members of God's family, or else they are in the midst of some fiery trial, some deep, distressing trouble, and they feel that God has forsaken them. It is never easy when God sees fit to test our faith. Yet it is during these tests, these "check points" along the way, that we discover whether or not we are really growing as believers in the Lord Jesus Christ.

II. The reward of faithfulness.

A. *But however dark and impossible the nighttime of trouble and testing may be, we can be certain, as the children of God, that "joy cometh in the morning."* (Read Ezekiel 11:16.) The Israelites had a problem in regard to their concept of worship. They believed that one could not worship God away from the temple. They believed people had to have all the forms and accouterments of worship before they could truly communicate with God. As far as they were concerned, God lived in the temple, in the Holy of Holies. That is where they went to worship him, to offer sacrifices to him, to discharge their obligations to him, "to be religious."

Even Jesus' own disciples had a similar problem. On the night before Jesus' crucifixion, they panicked because he told them he was going away. He told them carefully and explicitly that he would not leave them without a Comforter. He promised that the Holy Spirit would come. In fact, he said, "Lo, I am with you always [wherever you are in this world, and under whatever circumstances you may find yourself], even to the end of the world."

B. *What did Jesus mean by "the end of the world"?* Certainly he had in mind the end of this age, the end of time. But there are other situations in which people find themselves, which are to them "the end of the world." Sometimes it is a geographical experience, as it was for these fellow countrymen of Ezekiel in Babylon. "The end of the world" is sometimes a deep, bitter sorrow that so devastates a person that he feels indeed that the end of his world has come. It is exceedingly difficult sometimes for us to conceive of the omnipresence of God—the "everywhereness" of God. How ridiculous of us to believe that God is always comfortably and permanently established in a hallowed, stained-glass sanctuary, waiting to dispense blessings upon those who visit him there on the Lord's Day! It is often the case that we need the sense of God's presence far more desperately on Monday in the marketplace, in the abrasive atmosphere of temptation, than we do in the security of the Lord's house on Sunday.

C. *What, then, is a "sanctuary"?* It is a holy place, a place where a person is conscious of God's presence. But then, "sanctuary" has a secondary meaning. In 1 Kings we read of two instances where an accused man went to the tabernacle and grasped the horns of the altar. While he was there, the authorities were not free to take him. The "sanctuary" was to him a place of asylum, a spiritual fortress. So God was saying through Ezekiel to these poor people of his trapped in this foreign land: "My dear people, you do not have to wait until you can assemble with all of your brothers and sisters in the magnificent temple in Jerusalem to worship me, to sense my presence. I will be a little sanctuary to you wherever you are in this world—even here in this pagan land of Babylon."

D. *But where is this "little sanctuary" God has promised in regard to us today?* Paul said, "Know ye not that your body is the temple of the Holy Spirit which is in you, which ye have of God, and ye are not your own? For ye are bought with a price: therefore glorify God in your body, and in your spirit, which are God's" (1 Cor. 6:19–20). Every believer in the Lord Jesus Christ is "a little sanctuary" where God dwells. Truly God is with us "always, even to the end of the world."

Conclusion

We need always to learn well the lesson Ezekiel's people learned. The sanctuary of God is not just a building with a steeple on it. It is the awareness of God's presence wherever we are. God knows that we need the "visible institutions." When his people could no longer worship in the temple, he led them to establish the synagogue. Jesus established the church. But God does not need a sanctuary. He simply says, "Where two or three are gathered together in my name, there am I in the midst of them."

WEDNESDAY EVENING, JUNE 26

Title: The Design and Importance of the Lord's Supper

Text: "For as often as ye eat this bread, and drink this cup, ye do shew the Lord's death till he come" **(1 Cor. 11:26)**.

Scripture Reading: 1 Corinthians 11:23–27

Introduction

For every Christian body the observance of the Lord's Supper is a worshipful experience. Different denominations use different terms to describe it, but for all it is worship. The church at Corinth, like many contemporary churches, abused the ordinance. That is the context of our Scripture reading.

I. The design of the Lord's Supper.

A. *It is designed to keep believers "in remembrance" of the death of Jesus (1 Cor. 11:24).* Jesus said, "This do in remembrance of me." Paul said that we show forth the Lord's death. It is somewhat strange that those who have been saved by the death of Jesus would need something to remind them of it, but that is the way it is.

B. *It is designed to remind believers of the nature of the death of Jesus.* The Passover feast is an example of a reminder. The story connected with it is the passing of the death angel. The celebration of it was a declaration. In the partaking of the bread and wine, the Christian celebrates the manner of Jesus' death. It was excruciatingly painful and bloody. The end of it was a sacrifice for human sin. Its sufficiency is salvation from sin.

C. *It is designed to show forth Jesus' death "till he come" (1 Cor. 11:26).* In due time Christ will come again. When he does come believers will not need a reminder of the death, because then we will enjoy Jesus' constant presence and the blessings he brings.

II. The importance of observing the ordinance.

A. *It is important to be obedient.* The Lord's command is specific. Each Christian should observe the ordinance. There are differences of opinion as to the frequency, but most people believe without question that it is commanded.

B. *It is important because each Christian needs to be reminded of Christ's death.* Again, true students of God's Word will find several different interpretations of the meaning of the bread and wine. Most all interpretations still hold to the fact that the observance of this ordinance is to remind us of the broken body and shed blood of Jesus. It also reminds us that one day Jesus is coming again.

Conclusion

It is my hope and prayer that each time you worship your Lord in your church by observing this ordinance, it will be a real worship experience for you.

SUNDAY MORNING, JUNE 30

Title: Responsible Christian Citizenship

Text: "First of all, then, I urge that supplications, prayers, intercessions, and thanksgivings be made for all men, for kings and all who are in high positions, that we may lead a quiet and peaceable life, godly and respectful in every way" **(1 Tim. 2:1–2 rsv).**

Scripture Reading: 1 Timothy 2:1–7; Romans 13:1–7

Hymns: "God of Our Fathers," Daniel C. Roberts
"This Is My Father's World," Babcock
"Let Others See Jesus in You," McKinney

Offertory Prayer: Loving heavenly Father, we come today to thank you for your blessings on our country and its government. We pray for all elected officials and those appointed to positions of high responsibility that they might conduct themselves with reverence toward you and with respect for law and order. We pray that as individual citizens each of us will be responsible to you and helpful to others. As we bring our tithes and offerings, accept them and bless them to the end that your kingdom might come in the hearts and lives of people everywhere. In Jesus' name. Amen.

Introduction

This year we celebrate the 226th birthday of our great republic. Let us be thankful to God for his blessings on our past and our present and let us trust him for his blessings in the future.

What is our Christian responsibility toward our country, our state, our community? From our text and the larger Scripture passage, we can find at least four conclusions.

A. We have a duty to pray for all government officials that they might enjoy the blessings of God and conduct themselves in a manner pleasing to him (1 Tim. 2:1–2).

B. A condition of peace is the hope of God for us (2:2–3).

C. The salvation of all citizens is one of the great goals of God's loving heart (2:4).

D. From this passage we can conclude that the Christian training of all believers is a worthy ideal.

Paul encouraged the early Christians to follow the discreet policy of obeying the laws of the country, paying their taxes, and praying for those in positions of government authority. It is significant that these instructions were given at a time when the government was cruel, domineering, and idolatrous.

In the modern day the average Christian is likely to feel that citizenship responsibilities consist of paying taxes, obeying the laws, and voting on election day. Christian commitment to the lordship of Christ means involvement in and not withdrawal from all of the great issues of life.

I. The first demand of Christian citizenship is involvement.

A. *We must not withdraw from an imperfect situation.* We must not excuse our noninvolvement by saying that "politics are dirty."

B. *Our government never has been perfect.* Our government never will be perfect. We must recognize the human situation and strive for the best.

C. *The governmental process in our country is a struggle between those with differences of opinion.* We strive to achieve the better of what is good and the lesser of the evils that threaten us.

If we are going to be the salt of the earth, we must get involved in the process. As long as the salt is in the shaker, it doesn't do much good. It must be scattered to perform its function.

II. A second requirement for responsible Christian citizenship is voluntary self-discipline.

A. *We need to engage in the discipline of study.* Some people say, "I do not enjoy history." We must have some knowledge of the past to understand the present. Many of the issues of the day grow out of issues of the past. Only as we solve issues today can we hope for a better future.

B. *We must engage in the discipline of work.* Each citizen must be willing to work in the government process right down to the precinct level. We must not wait until the national election to work for the good of our government.

C. *We must engage in the discipline of self-restraint.* There are always private vested interests at work seeking to pass laws that are for the good of a specific group. To be responsible, all of us must practice some self-restraint.

D. *We must engage in the discipline of persistence.* In the government process we must continue to work for the good of our community and our country on a regular basis. The task is never finished.

E. *We must practice the discipline of concern for the unfortunate.* In some manner, collectively, we must minister to the unfortunate whose needs are far greater than what we can meet on an individual or even on a local basis.

III. The Christian has a higher loyalty than his loyalty to the state.

"But Peter and the apostles answered, 'We must obey God rather than men'" (Acts 5:29 RSV).

The committed Christian is obligated to try to be obedient to all of the laws of his country—unless those laws contradict the laws of his God.

A. *Only when we maintain this higher loyalty to God can we really keep pressure on the state to do what is right.*

B. *The laws of the state are to be obeyed, the Bible teaches, only so long as these laws stay within the bounds of that which is morally right.*

C. *God, not Caesar, has the final say in deciding what is to be rendered to Caesar and what is to be rendered to God.*

   1. As followers of Christ, we are obligated to pay taxes to the government (Luke 20:25; Rom. 13:6–7).
   2. Christians are always to pray for those who are in places of governmental authority.
   3. As followers of Christ, we are to love our neighbors as ourselves (Matt. 22:37–40).
   4. As followers of Christ, we are to be the salt of the earth, which preserves from decay (Matt. 5:13).
   5. As followers of Christ, we are to be the light of the world (Matt. 5:14–16). Our influence in the community is to be for the good of all.
   6. As responsible citizens, we should share the good news of God's love for all people, including those of all colors and classes (1 Tim. 2:3–4).

Conclusion

As the followers of Christ, we are citizens of two worlds. We become a citizen of our country either by birth or by naturalization. We become citizens of the kingdom of heaven by a spiritual birth, which takes place within our heart and life when we receive Jesus Christ as Savior.

Today you can become a citizen of the kingdom of heaven if you will receive Jesus Christ as Lord and Savior.

SUNDAY EVENING, JUNE 30

Title: Responsibility: Individual or Collective?

Text: "The soul that sinneth, it shall die. The son shall not bear the iniquity of the father, neither shall the father bear the iniquity of the son: the righteousness of the righteous shall be upon him, and the wickedness of the wicked shall be upon him" **(Ezek. 18:20).**

Scripture Reading: Ezekiel 18:1–23

Introduction

Responsibility is a battle-scarred word in our vocabulary. It has been misunderstood, misapplied, manipulated, and kicked around in general. It has been the victim of extreme fickleness. One day we love it, praise it, defend it, and cherish it; the next day, under a different set of circumstances, we ignore it, evade it, run from it, and pretend it doesn't exist. At times responsibility is terribly hard to live with—but there is no escaping it. Run away from it, and it catches up with you. Pretend that it's not there, and when you round the next corner, it will be staring you in the face. This is God's sovereign plan. So whether the focus is on our country, our God, or ourselves, we must deal with the matter of responsibility.

In spite of all the problems that beset us today, those of Ezekiel and his people, ten thousand strong and miles away from their homeland, were far worse. It was time for God to "come to grips" with the issue. Thus, in a private audience with his young prophet Ezekiel, God dealt with responsibility.

I. First, God dealt with the past.

A. *There is an attribute of God that is baffling to us humans, for whom life and time are divided into past, present, and future.* With God, there is no past—and in a manner of speaking, no future! He is above and beyond time. Because he is the eternal God, who had no beginning and will have no ending, he exists in the eternal present. When Jesus was defending his deity before his enemies, he said, "Before Abraham was, I am" (John 8:58), not "I was." But nonetheless, a human being has a past; and though it is folded like a dried flower between the pages of yesterday's chapter, it is very much there, and often it demands to be heard, to be dealt with.

B. *Any way you look at it, when we are born, we come into a world that is filled with circumstances we did not create.* The heavy hand of the past rests upon us. Many times a young lad will grow into manhood and go off to fight and die in a war he did not start and may know very little about. Likewise, Ezekiel and his people in exile were caught in a situation they did not create. But in that almost impossible dilemma, God had called them to make their lives count for him. Because of the compounded sins of their fathers before them, they were shut away from their homeland and from all they had counted dear. It was easy for them to become cynical. They had a proverb that went like this: "The fathers have eaten sour grapes, and the children's teeth are set on edge" (Ezek. 18:2). And when these Hebrews quoted this proverb to each other, they were trying to cover up their guilt with some barbed jokes against God and his justice.

C. *God wants us to forget the past.* God said to Ezekiel: "I am tired of hearing the people quote their sarcastic little proverb. I am weary with hearing them live in the past and feel sorry for themselves because of the consequences they are suffering as a result of their fathers' sins. True enough, their fathers may have eaten sour grapes. But tell your people, Ezekiel, that they cannot escape responsibility for themselves and for their own sins and shortcomings!"

II. This brings us, then, to the way in which God deals with the present and the corresponding responsibility he has placed upon us.

A. *When children are born into this world, they must be cared for immediately or they will die.* Nevertheless, a baby is an individual who is different from every other individual in the world. When the child reaches the age of responsible choice, he or she must make moral decisions. It is not always easy to make choices, and most of the time we had rather have other people make them for us. This is the situation Ezekiel faced. His people were shirking their moral responsibilities. They wanted to accept the "neighborhood standards," to drift with the tide. They were in Babylon. "Let's live like the Babylonians!" they were saying. They felt God had failed them and was punishing them for their fathers' sins. So they had decided quietly to forget about God.

B. *Then it was that God gave Ezekiel a word for his people.* "Behold, all souls are mine; the soul of the father as well as the soul of the son is mine: the soul that sins shall die" (18:4 RSV). And we can state that same truth positively and say, "The soul that is righteous will live." What is life? It can mean mere biological existence, or it can mean an awareness of God and of his desire to become involved in a person's life. What is death? It can mean the end of one's biological functions, one's physical life, or it can mean alienation and separation from God. Here, of course, God is speaking to his people about spiritual life and death.

C. *It is a tragic fallacy of human nature that in times of prosperity a person is tempted to credit himself with the blessings he enjoys.* But in times of adversity, he is tempted to blame all of his trouble on his forefathers, his enemies, or God. Certainly there is nothing wrong with examining as carefully as possible the historical events that have brought about a particular tragedy whose consequences we are suffering. But in the midst of the tragedy, we must remember that individuals are still responsible before God for their actions. Nobody can be righteous for you—not parents, church, or state. And you can't be righteous for anyone else. But neither can one generation keep another generation from receiving spiritual life from God. No person can hide spiritually behind his family, his tribe, or his nation. Each one of us is individually responsible to God for the way we live in a world we did not create.

III. Finally, let's see how God deals with the future in regard to our relationship with him.

A. *In our day of massive organization, we as individuals sometimes wonder if our life matters much one way or the other.* It does. A left-fielder on a baseball team is unquestionably a part of the team. Yet when the ball is coming his way and the sun is in his eyes, what he does as an individual is what counts. And here is a more serious illustration: a man, a husband, a father says,

"My wife takes care of the religion in our family." What is he doing? He is destroying his own spiritual life, and he is endangering the spiritual lives of his children—all in an easy, gracious, and charming manner. He is not an evil man by society's standards. His personal ethics may be up to the standards of his community. But he has simply not made room for the Almighty God in his life. Spiritually, he is dying on his feet!

B. *Ezekiel was preaching to a group of people, most of whom were pleasant and charming.* They were not cursing God, but neither were they willing to accept the responsibility of serving him. But listen to God's word to them— words that apply as much to us today as they did to those people in ancient Babylon: "But if the wicked will turn from all his sins that he hath committed, and keep all my statutes, and do that which is lawful and right, he shall surely live, he shall not die.... For I have no pleasure in the death of him that dieth, saith the Lord GOD: wherefore turn yourselves, and live ye" (18:21, 32). In all of this God was saying, "I care for you! I made you so that you can respond to my love. Indeed, you may live at a time in history when things are bad. And the consequences you are suffering may stem from problems you did not create. But wherever you are right now, in whatever valley of shadow you may find yourself, you can make life count if you will turn to me!"

Conclusion

In one way of speaking we can call these events in which Ezekiel participated a "dress rehearsal" for God's final triumph on earth. These people to whom Ezekiel prophesied and through whom God had chosen to bring his Son into the world, were not important socially or politically. They were exiles! But God promised he would return them to their home. Before they could return, however, they had to become spiritually fit. They had to receive a new kind of life that only God could give them. And so it is with us. God wants to bring humankind back to him, but he will not, he cannot, until people repent of their sins and receive God's free gift of eternal life. That is the personal responsibility of each one of us. We stand alone in this choice.

JULY

■ Sunday Mornings

Complete the series "The Living Christ and His Concern for Family Living" on the first Sunday of the month. Follow this with "The Master Speaks to the Present through the Parables," a series of messages based on Jesus' parables that describe the nature of the kingdom of God.

■ Sunday Evenings

Continue the series "Messages for the Modern World from an Ancient Prophet."

■ Wednesday Evenings

Continue the studies based on Paul's first letter to the Corinthian Christians.

WEDNESDAY EVENING, JULY 3

Title: Examining Self

Text: "But let a man examine himself, and so let him eat of that bread, and drink of that cup" (**1 Cor. 11:28**).

Scripture Reading: 1 Corinthians 11:17–34

Introduction

There is a great need in every person's life for a close personal examination of self. This is true in one's social, academic, and business life, but especially in one's spiritual life.

I. First, examine the context of this passage.

A. *The historical background is that of a connection between a love feast and the Lord's Supper.* The love feast should have been one of fellowship and sharing; however, it had been abused and wrong conduct had been manifested. It became a time of drunkenness and bad morals, a feast of gluttony and selfishness. The Lord's Supper was a time of expressing love and appreciation to the Lord. The two feasts were incompatible.

B. *The application for Paul's day has a message for today.* Paul gave fair warning about the frame of mind we should have when in real worship. It is not a matter of our worthiness that we sit at the Lord's table.

II. Second, examine the concept in everyday life.

A. *Self-examination is not always a pleasant thing when done honestly.* Many times it is very painful. We often discover things about ourselves that we do not like.

B. *Self-examination can be a wholesome thing.* It can be used to expose evil and undesirable habits, which can then be repented of. It can be an instrument of finding what is lacking in our lives and enabling us to make amends.

III. Third, consider some ways we can examine ourselves.

A. *Bible reading and prayer are measures to be used.* We need to determine how sensitive our spirit is and how genuine our character is as it relates to Christ. We need to determine if we resist all wrong and dislike the unholy. Do we shrink from the deception of this world and do we worship at the foot of the cross? Do we let the Spirit of Christ control our lives?

B. *A self-examination must be free from comparing one's life with that of another.* It should be an honest, soul-searching, sincere testing.

Conclusion

Right now I am asking you to examine your life in relation to the Lord Jesus. Examine every facet of your life and find the things that need to be corrected.

SUNDAY MORNING, JULY 7

Title: Where Is the Far Country?

Text: "Not many days after the younger son gathered all together, and took his journey into a far country, and there wasted his substance with riotous living" **(Luke 15:13).**

Scripture Reading: Luke 15:11–20

Hymns: "Love Divine, All Loves Excelling," Wesley
"There Is a Green Hill Far Away," Alexander
"I Will Arise and Go to Jesus," Hart

Offertory Prayer: Father in heaven, thank you for your great generosity to us. Thank you for giving yourself to us in Jesus Christ. Thank you for abiding in us by your Holy Spirit. Thank you for your blessings to us through the church. Thank you for your message to us through the Bible. Thank you for giving us the opportunity of sharing the good news of your love to a needy world. Accept our tithes and offerings and bless them to the end that many people around the world will come to know Jesus Christ as Lord and Savior. In his name we pray. Amen.

Introduction

Several years ago newspapers and television programs carried the news of identical triplets who had been separated at birth and were reunited at age twenty-three. Through a unique set of circumstances, mutual acquaintances brought them together. They were indeed shocked and pleased to discover that they were triplets.

Have you ever studied the Bible to discover persons with whom you have identical problems or circumstances or needs? Studying the Bible in this manner can be very helpful. It gives us insight into how God worked to bring good into their lives. He will do the same for us if we respond with faith and commitment.

The account of the prodigal son and the waiting father is the most famous short story in all literature. The primary character in this story is not the prodigal son who wasted his inheritance. The main actor in this exciting short story is the waiting father who yearned for the return of his foolish child.

Today let us look at the characters in this short story to see if this passage of Scripture can speak to our hearts. Most of us do not look for ourselves in this story. We live as close as possible to our roots. We have never journeyed into a far country to live. We do not make it a practice to waste our money and tarnish our reputation by reveling with people of low morals. At least we are not on skid row. We have not received an inheritance to waste. Consequently, we remove ourselves from this passage of Scripture.

I. Where is the far country?

The far country has been designated as any place that is "one step away from God." The far country is marked by an attitude of distrust in the Father's will and good plan. The far country is located in an attitude of self-interest that defines one's purpose for living in terms of getting and having.

The elder brother who was living with his father was living in the far country even though he never changed his address. In reality the far country is located in the heart of the person who does not trust the Father.

II. Are you living in a far country?

You can be living in a far country without being aware of it. Do you have the attitude of the younger son who went to his father and said, "Father, give me the portion of goods that falleth to me"? In reality he was saying to the father, "Drop dead. I want what is mine. I want it now. I want to live my own life according to my own plan."

A. *Are you saying, "Give me the freedom to go and do as I please without any controls on my appetites or ambitions"?*

B. *Are you saying, "Give me the pleasure that the world has to offer"?* Is your only concern for the satisfaction of the appetites of your human nature?

C. *Are you saying, "Give me the position that I want?"* This could refer to a place in the home, or on the team, or in the orchestra, or in the place of business. Selfish seeking for a position of privilege and power without accepting the responsibility that goes with that position identifies us as a twin brother or sister of the younger son.

D. *Are you saying, "Give me the popularity I want"?* There is a little bit of the "ham" in all of us. There is something about human nature that likes to be in the spotlight. People hunger for acceptance and recognition. When the desire for approval becomes the dominating motive of life, we find ourselves identified with the younger son.

E. *Are you saying, "Give me the treasure I can acquire"?* It is so easy to measure success in terms of the things that we acquire. Without being aware of it, we can find ourselves in the far country as we achieve one success after another in our business or vocational life.

F. *Are you saying to the Father God, "Give me," in the realm of religion?* Some people see God as being their servant. They desire his forgiveness without any concern about receiving his grace to forgive others.

Are you asking God for guidance so that you can get rich rather than asking him for guidance so that you might be righteous? Are you asking God for protection without any thought at all of fulfilling his purpose for your life? Are you saying to God, "Give me heaven," without any concern at all for working with him to help others escape hell?

It is very possible to be nothing more than a parasite in God's family. To be a parasite places you in the far country without your being aware of it.

III. The disappointments of the far country.

A. *Living the self-centered life does not lift us to our highest potential.* In fact, living the self-centered life lowers us from our position of dignity as a member of the human family.

B. *Living the self-centered life does not honor God or fulfill his purpose for us.* Our chief purpose in life is to honor God and serve him forever. Only what we do for God is going to have any significance for us or for others a hundred years from now.

C. *Living the self-centered life does not benefit others.* It hurts and hinders them. It prevents them from becoming what God wants them to be.

D. *Living the self-centered life leads to a famine in the soul.* Those who focus attention only on themselves may achieve success, popularity, and position. They may be able to enjoy many of the world's pleasures, but they will experience a bleak, desolate famine in their innermost being.

E. *Living the self-centered life leads to a life of crushing slavery.* Those who become a slave to their appetites and ambitions become possessed by their possessions rather than being effective stewards of all that comes under their sphere of influence.

IV. Returning home from the far country.

The so-called prodigal son was a stupid, ungrateful, selfish, immature, and self-destructive young man. Let it be said to his credit that though he was very foolish he did not remain a fool. He did not remain in the far country. He did not remain in the place of blight and desolation and hunger and loneliness.

A. *He came to his senses.* He stopped and took inventory.

B. *He recognized his mistakes.* He was wise enough to recognize that he had chosen the wrong road that led to the wrong destination.

C. *He accepted responsibility for his condition.* He did not blame his father. There is no suggestion that he blamed his brother or his mother. He was honest with himself and did not pass the buck by blaming society.

D. *He was wise in that he resolved to return to his father.* The decision was made in his mind and heart before there was a change in the direction of his body.

E. *He adjusted his attitude from being a parasite to being a contributor.* He began his journey into the far country with the demand, "Give me." He began his return home while still in the far country when he decided he would say to his father, "Make me as one of your hired servants."

Conclusion

The exciting return of the wayward son from the far country brought about a great change in his status and in his situation.

The father had waited in agony and prayer. Day after day he had fed the fatted calf, looking forward to the time when the son would come home. As the son met his father, he cried out, "I have sinned against God and against you. I am no longer fit to be called your son." The father dealt with the son in terms of mercy, forgiveness, and sonship. The Father will deal with you in a similar manner today if you will return from the far country and alter your attitudes and ambitions.

Each of us should pray to the Father, "Make me a giver rather than a getter. Make me a helper rather than a hinderer. Make me a healer rather than a hurter. Make me a contributor rather than a parasite. Make me an encourager rather than a discourager."

A great welcome is waiting for you. The Father God and Christ the Son want to welcome you as do the saints who have gone on before you.

SUNDAY EVENING, JULY 7

Title: The Price of Success

Text: "Thine heart was lifted up because of thy beauty, thou hast corrupted thy wisdom by reason of thy brightness: I will cast thee to the ground, I will lay thee before kings, that they may behold thee" **(Ezek. 28:17).**

Scripture Reading: Ezekiel 28:1–19

Introduction

Before the Israelites were carried away captive into Babylon, they prided themselves on being the most religious people on earth. They had the most magnificent temple the world had ever seen in which to worship God. They had a "holy city" that was known the world over as the city where the God of the Israelites—the God of Abraham, Isaac, and Jacob—lived. They had their holy days, their specified times for prayer and the offering of sacrifices. But gradually, inevitably, all of this worship had become mere ritual and formality. God was in the temple, and what they did between their stated times of worship, how they reacted toward their fellow humans in their business dealings and in their personal relationships, was beside the point.

But now they are away from their precious temple and their holy city. And they can't do anything about it! Because of their wrong and restrictive concept of worshiping God, they have come to think that they really can't worship him anymore, and that it is all his fault! Therefore, in this highly symbolic and imaginative passage, Ezekiel is showing them that worshiping God is a total experience. And here he focuses on, of all things, the business world—the world of commerce. He uses the "prince of Tyre" as a type of person who is endowed with certain skills and talents that are vital for any successful businessperson.

I. First, let's identify the prince of Tyre.

A. *Who is this man whom Ezekiel describes so graphically for us?* To begin with, Tyre was the capital city of the Phoenicians. It lay in the shadow of the Lebanon mountains at the eastern end of the Mediterranean Sea. The city of Tyre was built on a rocky island about one-half mile from the shore. Between the island and the mainland was a deep harbor. Behind Tyre lay the mountains, with their rich supply of ship-building timber. And before Tyre lay the world. Yet the peculiar genius of Tyre was not so much in sailing and building, but in commerce. In Ezekiel's day Ithobaal II ruled over Tyre. But he is not necessarily the man whom Ezekiel is describing in this twenty-eighth chapter. Most probably he is presenting a symbol of the whole Phoenician culture—its strengths and its weaknesses—in order to drive home the lesson he is trying to teach his people.

B. *Ezekiel understood—and he wanted desperately for his people to understand—that the entire economic system of a people is an important part of spiritual life.* The qualities that make for success in business are good—it is the abuse of them that is evil. By and large the Phoenicians had been a people of resource, daring, and imagination. They took the natural gifts with which they had been endowed and used them with intelligence. But these Phoenicians, with all of their natural talents and abilities, did not know the true God. They had no relationship with him, and therefore those talents they had in the area of business and commerce were destined to go sour. They were amazingly successful, but because they did not recognize from whom their success came and for what it was intended, they were destined, like all of the enemies of God, to "go down the drain."

C. *Note what this prince of Tyre, representing his successful country, is saying.* He takes inventory and finds that he has been immensely successful. He has made money hand over fist. His bank accounts are overflowing. Everywhere he turns, he is a success. And so he says, "Move over, God! I've learned your secret now! I've learned how to work this thing called 'success,' and I don't need you or anybody! From now on I'll pilot this ship, and while I am doing it, I'll run the lives of all those around me to my advantage!"

Ezekiel tells us that this man did possess great potential; he could have been such a useful servant of God. But he let pride take over. And the essence of pride is putting self in the place of God. This sin comes easily to successful people—in fact, it comes easily to all of us, whether or not we are the receivers of material success.

II. Second, let's define the word *success*.

A. *The word* success *has been dragged through the muck and mire of self-centeredness.* In some cases, achieving success has meant trampling on others to reach a pinnacle—only to find it a lonely place. Satan has taken something that God intended to be good in a person's life and made it an evil, destructive thing. Nonetheless, it is God who gives a person the potential to be successful and then expects that person to use that success for God's glory and for the blessing of God's people. There is nothing evil about wanting to be successful in whatever life-work God leads one to pursue—even materially successful, as long as one has a clear definition of what the word means from God's perspective.

B. *In the past few decades God has allowed people to make fantastic strides in knowledge and technical skills.* Think, for example, of the vast complex of highways and airlines and railways in our country that joins farms and mines and factories to the distributors, which in turn deliver their life-sustaining products to the people. All of this has happened because of the knowledge and discipline and skill of people who have dreamed and planned and built. Humans have broken loose from the firm grip of the earth's gravity, have soared through space to walk on the moon's surface, and have even developed technology that allows people to live in space for lengthy periods of time. In medical science, unbelievable strides are being made in corrective and life-sustaining surgical techniques because of the uncanny skills God has allowed people to develop. But comes the question: Has all of this "success" been dedicated to the service of God—or, like a preening peacock, has man become proud and haughty and, like Ezekiel's prince of Tyre, "corrupted his wisdom for the sake of his splendor"?

III. Finally, let's determine God's assessment of success.

A. *What is the way to success?* A statement in the book of Proverbs simply but clearly points the way for us: "The fear of the LORD is the beginning of wisdom." But the prince of Tyre, like many other successful people in every generation, chose "splendor," or self-glory, as his goal instead of allowing his success to be a means of worshiping God. And the final result for him was spiritual shipwreck.

Jesus asked a question one day that ought to burn into the heart of every ambitious person: "What shall it profit a man, if he shall gain the whole world, and lose his own soul?" (Mark 8:36). This is what Ezekiel was saying in his own way. He was preaching for a verdict. His congregation consisted of alert, intelligent, ambitious people whose homeland lay in ruins. They were trying to carve out a new life for themselves and their children in Babylon. What goals should they seek? In answer, Ezekiel drew for them the picture of this man who sought, and reached, the wrong goal.

B. *Why did God give us abilities?* He did so that we might serve him with all of our heart, soul, mind, and strength. And how do we do that? It is chiefly by loving—which means respecting—our neighbor with the same kind of wisdom that we show in respecting ourselves. Any economic system in the world that puts profit ahead of justice is in danger. God will not have it! Great empires and nations in the world's history have tried it—and for a season have flourished and reveled in their own splendor. But inevitably their foundations have crumbled, and they have come crashing down in humiliation and defeat. The engineers and architects of those systems failed to remember that the God who gave them the ability to be successful demands equal time! He demands that they worship him, not only in the temples they have built, but also in the marketplace where they work. When we fail to do this, whether we are in Phoenicia or in America, we destroy ourselves.

Conclusion

Any true success story—whether it be about the life of an individual, a nation, or an empire—is beautiful. There is a lyrical beauty in the way Ezekiel described the success of the prince of Tyre. But there is a lethal danger when humans reach the point in their climb toward success when they wave good-bye to God and decide that they can make it the rest of the way by themselves. The Spanish people have a beautiful saying they use as a parting word. It is *Vaya con Dios*—"Go with God." Go with God to his house on the Lord's day and worship him, to be sure. But also go with God to the marketplace on Monday and let the fruit of your labor, of your mind and your hands, bring ultimate honor and glory to the God who made you and endowed you with your talents and abilities.

WEDNESDAY EVENING, JULY 10

Title: Spiritual Gifts

Text: "The manifestation of the Spirit is given to every man to profit withal" **(1 Cor. 12:7).**

Scripture Reading: 1 Corinthians 12:1–30

Introduction

The Bible clearly shows us that God always endows enough people with the necessary gifts to carry on his work. If everyone would do his or her part, there would never be a shortage of workers in any area of kingdom work. In this message we will consider the gifts the Spirit gives.

I. We must discern what our gifts are.

A. *The Holy Spirit inspires people and imparts faith.* Apart from the working of the Holy Spirit, no one can call Jesus Lord. No one can be saved (1 Cor. 12:3). Unless the Holy Spirit is the giver, all people are ignorant and are subject to idol worship (1 Cor. 12:2). The greatest gift ever given is the gift of gifts, the gift of the Spirit.

B. *We need to be discerning and find out what the Holy Spirit wants to bestow on us.* The gifts are available according to God's sovereign plan. These gifts often lie dormant because our faith is insufficient to determine them.

II. God bestows a vast diversity of spiritual gifts.

A. *All gifts are from the same God, though the gifts differ in purpose.* This is true of gifts other than spiritual ones. Take, for example, a building. One person—an architect—has the gift of planning, and another—a contractor—has the gift of construction, but the end result is a building. The end result of spiritual gifts is the work of God, although some people have one type of gift and others another type.

B. *All gifts are given for the purpose of serving God.*

1. There are different ways of serving God (1 Cor. 12:5). Some can sing, some can give, some can teach, and so on.

2. These differences are the ways through which the Lord works (1 Cor. 12:6). All gifts are for a common good. We all should determine our gifts and use them for God's glory.

3. This diversity of gifts is partially enumerated. This enumeration is to teach that there are sufficient gifts for every cause. Some are given the gift of wisdom and others the gift of knowledge (1 Cor. 12:8). There are gifts for such offices as pastors and teachers. There are other gifts of healing, miraculous power, prophecy, discernment of spirits, tongues, and interpretation of tongues.

III. The use of these spiritual gifts makes for unity in the church.

A. *True spiritual unity makes jealousy impossible (1 Cor. 12:14–26).* All Christians form a body through the working of God for a purpose and plan (1 Cor. 12:18). Each part of the body has a special function, as do the various parts of the human body.

B. *True spiritual unity excludes pride and contempt.* There should be no division in the body. Each member should have concern for the others. An arrogant attitude or a feeling of importance over another is not in keeping with spiritual gifts.

C. *True spiritual unity involves mutual dependence (1 Cor. 12:27–30).* This is illustrated by reference to the human body. The foot is dependent on the leg. The tongue is dependent on the ear. If one part of the body is honored, then all parts are honored.

Conclusion

Exercise the use of the gift or gifts God has given you. Use them for unity in the church and for the building up of the kingdom.

SUNDAY MORNING, JULY 14

Title: How Well Do You Hear?

Text: "Who hath ears to hear, let him hear" **(Matt. 13:9).**

Scripture Reading: Matthew 13:1–9, 18–23

Hymns: "Bringing in the Sheaves," Shaw
"Higher Ground," Oatman
"The Master Hath Come," Doudney

Offertory Prayer: Our Father, through the indwelling of your Holy Spirit, cleanse us within so that we may learn to think as you think until we are able to choose as you choose, judge as you judge, and see as you see in order that our priorities may be according to your divine will. Bless us as we give. May we always listen to the still small voice within that reminds us that giving is a responsibility of the believer. We know that it is one of the highest privileges of those who have linked themselves by faith to the Savior. We pray in Jesus' name. Amen.

Introduction

Although this Scripture passage is often called "The Parable of the Sower," perhaps a more nearly accurate title would be "The Four Kinds of Ground," or "The Parable of the Soils." Jesus began with an urgent call for the disciples to listen. He concluded with a challenge that those who have ears should hear. We need to realize that hearing is an important matter. Often we assume that because a speaker takes the initiative, he or she controls the hearer. Actually the opposite is more often true. No matter how well a person speaks, unless the person addressed gives his or her attention, both hearing and heeding, the best message in the world is in vain.

Those who heard Jesus constituted a motley throng. Some came from curiosity, while others were there with self-seeking motives. A large number wished to make him king and thus used him as a rallying point to revolt against the Roman army. Some came with quick but shallow enthusiasm. Others, however, came with deep longing, desiring to find the answer to their life needs.

Jesus knew that the crowd would receive his words as differently as the various soils of the Galilean hillsides received the seeds. He had seen the sower at work. Perhaps the sower was busy even as he stood in the ship and spoke to the crowds. This is the first of seven parables delivered "back to back," with four being given from the ship and three in the house to which they retired. All of the parables deal with the same subject, the kingdom of heaven, but each one approaches it from a different angle. This first parable underscores one of the most important parts of understanding God's will—hearing correctly the Savior's message. He listed four types of soil, symbolizing the four ways that people receive God's Word.

I. The "don't bother me; I'm busy" crowd.

The seed that fell at the edge of the beaten path rolled away before the wind. Birds came and gathered it as they wished. The narrow aisles between the fields were rights of way, and anybody could walk up and down them. They became hardened like pavement by the feet of many people. Seed that fell on them might just as well have fallen on a public road.

Many people today are so hardened to the gospel message that they have no interest in giving it even slight consideration. One day a visiting evangelist went with the local minister to talk to a man whose wife and daughter were active members of the church. The man stood at the door not even inviting them in and said, "Preacher, I appreciate your coming to see me, but frankly, I'm not interested." The two ministers got no farther than the porch. As far as they knew, he never changed. Approximately ten years later the family called upon the minister to conduct his funeral.

What can a minister do with such an attitude? At the present time, nothing! Even if people with such an attitude come to church, their minds are elsewhere. This parable illustrates people whose insensibility to God's Word is caused by outward things that have made a thoroughfare of their natures. Worldly interests have trodden them down until they are incapable of receiving any type of spiritual message. Notice what happens with the seed that lies bare on the pathway. Even a bird can come and take it away. So with this type of hearer. The most insignificant matter can take this person's attention away from any thought about God. The whirl of traffic begins again, and the path is soon beaten a little harder. Any impression made is quickly rubbed out. Some twittering, new excitement or trivial item of gossip eats up all that has been said about the Lord.

We sometimes say of a person, "You might as well talk to a brick wall as to him." When one's mind is set, the truth cannot gain entry. Mental laziness makes people refuse to think; mental arrogance causes them to feel they know everything already. Mental fear causes people to indulge in wishful thinking and, because their lifestyle conflicts with divine standards, they retreat into a type of atheism that denies God. They deny God, not because they are intellectually convinced that God does not exist, but because they do not want God to exist. They know that if God is real, they must bring their lives into harmony with divine principles or suffer the inevitable consequences.

II. The "hip-hip-hurrah for Jesus" crowd.

The "stony ground" was a thin surface of soil over a shelf or slab of rock, like skin stretched tightly on the bone. If seeds fell on it, they would sprout quickly, but no roots could get through the rock or find nourishment in it. Thus, the heat of the sun caused the plant to wither quickly and die. Perhaps even the heat of the underlying stone accelerated the growth, causing premature and feeble sprouts. The fierce Eastern sun blistered the growth quickly.

This soil represents people who are easily stirred emotionally, people of excitable temper whose feelings lie on the surface. A message gets to them quickly, skipping the understanding or the conscience and going directly to the emotions. These people get "religion" the same way a person gets sickness during an epidemic. Any prevalent enthusiasm causes them great joy, a much speedier and more boisterous type than those whose Christian experience is deep and genuine. They have sentimental fervor and, therefore, an instant response, but their zeal soon flags. Their emotional excitability and inconsiderate compulsiveness produce a melancholy conclusion. Religious movements of this type have produced many converts but few stable Christians, many blossoms but little fruit coming to maturity.

III. The "I love Jesus but love the world more" crowd.

Picture a field, or a part of it, where once there had been thorns. The farmer had cut them down but had not dug up the seed. He planted a crop, and the two grew together. The latent "weed-seed" could not be seen when the crop was sown. At that moment the ground looked good because it is easy to make a garden look clean by simply turning over the soil. But the weeds or thorns were still there, and they always grow more strongly than the good seed! The inevitable happened. The bad seed choked the life out of the good seed.

Jesus pointed out clearly two things that he regarded as thorns—anxiety and wealth. We must admit there is a gradual ascent in quality as Jesus listed the three types of hearers. The first one was unreachable, the second one was shallow, but the third had possibilities of a good harvest. The problem was, however, that the man pictured by the "thorny places" lacked the ability to be completely loyal. He tried to serve both God and mammon, or things. Too much anxiety about worldly things is as bad, and sometimes can be worse, than thinking that material things bring security. In fact, the two are very closely related. The great Scottish preacher Alexander Maclaren once said, "The man who is burdened with the cares of poverty, and the man who is deceived by the false promises of wealth, are really the same man. The one is the other turned inside out. We make the world our god, whether we worship it by saying 'I'm desolate without thee' or by fancying that we are secure with it."

IV. The "I'm willing to grow" crowd.

The parable does not tell us what percentage of people fit each category. Jesus never stressed statistics nor emphasized the proportion of success or failure. Rather, he showed interest in revealing to people the importance of attitudes.

The constant and consistent teaching of the New Testament is that Christians grow because a supernatural seed has been planted within them. The fruit they bear comes from the seed that has been implanted. Paul said, "I live; yet not I, but Christ liveth in me" (Gal. 2:20). The degree of fruitfulness varies because each of us is different. The Lord does not demand that our fertility be uniform. He even listed the percentage of productivity in ascending order, as though he recognized even the scantiest fruitage. He promised elsewhere that he would, in love, purge every branch in order that it might bring forth more fruit.

All planting is done in hope. The business of sowing seed possesses no glamour. The sower tramps the earth alone. No band plays for him and no cheerleaders encourage him with their enthusiasm. This is quite a contrast to the harvest field, where one finds happiness and cooperative delight in gathering the results. Thank God for the slow and steady growth that characterizes the true Christian. The growth process, like that of the sowing experience, can be lonely and discouraging, but its end result is fruitful contribution to God's kingdom.

Conclusion

No one parable teaches us everything. Analogy is not proof, and neither can a figure of speech or a story be pressed to find a meaning in every detailed point. We find a great difference in the soil of life and the soil of the earth. No matter how hard we work, some soil cannot be cultivated. There are ice fields in the Arctic and sand in the desert. Also, soil cannot change the climate. The human soul, or soil, however, can work at creating its own environment. A person can plow up the paths and pluck out the thorns. He or she can blast away the rocks or remove other problems that exist to defy and defeat cultivation. Jesus reminded us of our responsibility with his concluding, pungent remark, "Who hath ears to hear, let him hear" (Matt. 13:9).

SUNDAY EVENING, JULY 14

Title: The Shepherds and the Flock

Text: "Thus saith the LORD GOD; Behold, I, even I, will both search my sheep, and seek them out. As a shepherd seeketh out his flock in the day that he is among his sheep that are scattered; so will I seek out my sheep, and will deliver them out of all places where they have been scattered in the cloudy and dark day" **(Ezek. 34:11–12).**

Scripture Reading: Ezekiel 34:2–30

Introduction

If Ezekiel were to enter our modern churches, exchange his Eastern robes for a twenty-first-century business suit, and speak to us the message recorded in the thirty-fourth chapter of his prophecy, we would be certain that he had been reading this morning's newspaper.

The piercing message of this chapter deals with, of all things, politics! Now "politics" to Ezekiel didn't mean what it has come to mean in our generation. His concern was with the art or science of government, both from the standpoint of the governor and the governed. And the shocking revelation he would deliver is that God is intimately concerned with this kind of politics. Not only, says Ezekiel, is God concerned when shepherds—mayors and governors and presidents—abuse their power, he is equally concerned when the sheep—people like you and me—fail to respect the divinely ordained powers that govern us, or when we make life miserable for one another. God judges the shepherd, and he also judges the sheep.

The emphasis of Ezekiel's message is simple. He deals first with the shepherds—the rulers, the overseers of the people. And especially scalding are his words to those rulers who neglect their sheep, exploit them, manipulate them, and even abandon them. Second, Ezekiel deals with the sheep themselves. While the people were nodding their heads vigorously in approval of all that he was saying about the rulers, the searchlight was abruptly turned on them. In painful and specific detail, Ezekiel dealt with the attitudes and the conduct of the people, the sheep.

I. First, let's consider the shepherds.

The shepherds are those charged with the awesome responsibility of governing the people and providing some semblance of security and stability.

A. *In one of his letters, the apostle Paul made this rather strange statement: "The powers that be are ordained of God."* When Paul wrote that, Christians all over the Roman Empire were being persecuted because of their faith in God. They were being discriminated against socially. Yet Paul wrote to these maligned followers of Christ, "The powers that be are ordained of God"! And who was the emperor of Rome at that time? Nero—one of the bloodiest and most inhumane rulers who ever sat on a throne. Of course, Paul did not mean that Nero's actions and methods of ruling were inspired of God. He meant simply that civil government is a necessary, important part of God's plan for the world.

B. *But what kind of civil government does God smile upon?* In a rather brilliant analysis, Aristotle wrote that three forms of civil government are possible. First, in a *monarchy,* one person rules. Second, in a *democracy,* all rule. And third, in an *aristocracy,* (ideally) the few who are best qualified govern. After showing the strengths and weaknesses in each of these systems, Aristotle went on to declare that any form of government is endangered by an excess of itself. The monarchy can degenerate into a tyranny. Democracy can become the fickle, impulsive whim of a mob, and the aristocracy can fritter out its life in an endless series of committee meetings. Yet in spite of the inevitable human imperfections of government, it is a part of God's plan for the world that his children live under some kind of civil government.

C. *But hear Ezekiel again: "Ho, shepherds of Israel who have been feeding yourselves! Should not shepherds feed the sheep?" (34:2 RSV).* Under God, the first task of civil government is to provide order—to create a climate, an atmosphere, in which the people can pursue their lives peaceably. It is rather interesting that nowhere in his instructions does Ezekiel suggest that government should manage business or agriculture. Businesspeople and farmers, by and large, do a much better job of it than the government. But always, in every society, there are those who fall by the wayside. They are weak; they are not sure of themselves; they cannot fend for themselves. Ezekiel tells us that society is responsible to care for those who cannot care for themselves—the handicapped, the sick, and the weak. But alas! a public servant is elected; he enters his arena of service like a shining knight on a white charger, with every good intention of serving the people who elected him. But many times—not every time, thank God!—this shepherd discovers that he can feed himself while he feeds his sheep. And, inevitably, it becomes increasingly enjoyable to add to his own comfort and strengthen his own security while his sheep start to suffer, to be neglected, and ultimately to be hungry themselves.

II. After Ezekiel is finished with the shepherds, he turns to the sheep.

A. *This brings us to the balancing side of Ezekiel's message.* The "sheep" who had been listening from the sidelines while Ezekiel took their leaders to task were, by this time, probably feeling smug and justified. But then I can imagine Ezekiel turning on his heel and facing the cheering mob with these words: "And as for *you*, O my flock. . . ." It was their time now, and the laughter was gone. We might paraphrase Ezekiel's words to fit the jargon of our day: "Now hear this, you who call yourselves the children of God: The time has come for me to determine who will be men, and who will be mice—those who will shoulder responsibility, and those who will pass the buck!"

B. *Already Ezekiel had exposed the false and hypocritical shepherds who had scattered the flock.* They had sown seeds of distrust and had caused disillusionment with life in general. They had created a yawning credibility gap between the people and their leaders. A moral twilight had settled over the land, and no one trusted his brother. So, through his prophet, God was saying to the society of the cynical: "Don't sit in the seat of the scornful! You may indeed have come to the time when you feel you cannot trust anyone. But remember: I have not forsaken you. I will seek out those who have lost their way; I will lead back to the fold those who have strayed. Those who have been deeply hurt, I will heal. And the time will come when those who have made themselves fat and strong through deceit and wrongdoing will be destroyed."

C. *In the New Testament, Jesus took Ezekiel's beautiful picture of the shepherd and the sheep—God's sheep—and gave to us some of his most beautiful and beloved parables.* And what is the lesson behind it all? God knows what is going on in his world! He is not an "absentee landlord," a powerless God who must forever stand idly by and watch evil men destroy all that is good and decent and moral in human affairs. But at the same time, the sheep, the people, must share in the responsibility. As much as we would prefer it, we cannot heap all of the blame for our current dilemma on the heads of our leaders. We are part of the fabric of our nation. The threads of our lives are interwoven, and the strength of our nation is dependent on the interlocking faith of the people of God.

Conclusion

But what can I do? I can search my own heart and life. I can examine my own attitudes. And I can pray that God will begin to do a work in my heart that will change my life and my attitudes toward my country and toward my fellow humans. And when that happens, the influence of my changed life will touch another life, and the irreversible chain reaction will have begun.

What of the future? Has the momentum of our irresponsibility gained such speed in its toboggan slide toward self-destruction that we have passed the point of no return? Have so many so deified self and so committed themselves to the accumulating of things that there is no way to stem the tide? Have we lost altogether the true meaning of sacrifice?

No one knows what tomorrow holds—for you, for me, for our nation. But we do know that there are two paths we can travel. One path offers tantalizing visions of material plenty, of luxury, of prosperity. But then comes the dark. That is the pathway of "self." The other way is the pathway of faith. That way may well lead to a cross—but after the cross will come eternal light and eternal life. God is at work in his world. He wants to involve us in his plans. What about it?

WEDNESDAY EVENING, JULY 17

Title: The Church, the Body of Christ

Text: "Now ye are the body of Christ, and members in particular" **(1 Cor. 12:27).**

Scripture Reading: 1 Corinthians 12:1–31

Introduction

Of the many figures of speech Paul used for the church, none has been more captivating to the human mind than the metaphor of the body. The purpose of this message is to help understand this concept.

I. The church, as the body of Christ, has many members with various functions, but it is still the body of Christ.

A. *The Scriptures are the best illustration of this (1 Cor. 12:12–26).* The body has many different parts, such as the hand, head, foot, arm, and eye. Each of these parts has its individual function, but all are important. Each one is dependent to a large degree on the way the others function.

B. *The Scriptures tell us that various types of work must be done in the church.* As members of the church, Christians are endowed by God to perform specific tasks, just like the members of the human body. As members of the church, Christians are to develop their potentiality and use, or their usefulness will diminish. As members of the church, all Christians are to follow the law of cooperation.

II. The church, as the body of Christ, has one head, which is the unifying factor, and that head is the Lord Jesus Christ.

A. *The church has been defined as "the local and voluntary fellowship of baptized believers, bonded together in the Holy Spirit to find and do the will of Christ, their head."* A breakdown of this definition enables one to see the church as a body. The church membership is made up of a local, voluntary fellowship of baptized believers. It is bonded together in the Holy Spirit to find and do the will of Christ, the head. Believers find that will through prayer, Bible study, and human experience. The doing of that will is known as Christian service.

B. *The church, then, has Christ as its head and is to be controlled by him.* The church is to hear and obey the divine word. No one is to argue or deny this truth. No one is to change the gospel of Christ into human philosophy, nor is anyone to surrender the divine truth to errorists.

III. The church, as the body of Christ, has one major objective— namely, to bring people to Christ for salvation.

A. *To do this, the church needs to use everything available that is scriptural and right.* Lost people cannot be brought to Christ if things are not right. People are brought to Christ through personal work, public preaching, and organizational activities.

B. *To do this, the head of the church must be placed above human desires and petty ideas.* An application of this thought is that Christ is to come before some personal feeling or idea. Some people might seek to justify not working in the church because they don't like some other person. But this is not scriptural or practical.

Conclusion

See what your personal function in the church is and do it with all your might.

SUNDAY MORNING, JULY 21

Title: Only God Knows and He Refuses to Tell

Text: "Let both grow together until the harvest: and in the time of harvest I will say to the reapers, Gather ye together first the tares, and bind them in bundles to burn them: but gather the wheat into my barn" **(Matt. 13:30).**

Scripture Reading: Matthew 13:24–30

Hymns: "Stand Up, Stand Up for Jesus," Duffield
"Work, for the Night Is Coming," Coghill
"All Things Are Thine," Whittier

Offertory Prayer: Our Father, we are grateful that your divine power protects us and your divine resources provide for our needs. We pray for forgiveness where we have sinned and for faith to believe that the way of life you have shown us will work even in a crooked and perverse generation. We give back to you a portion of the money that you have enabled us to earn. We do not offer our money as a substitute for the dedication of ourselves, but as a method of channeling our efforts in a practical way toward the preaching of your good news to those who are enslaved by sin. Bless us as we give. Use our gifts to your glory. We pray for Jesus' sake. Amen.

Introduction

An old cynical cliché says, "If God is God, he's not good. And if he's good, he's not God." If these words seem to apply anywhere in the Bible, it is here! Although couched in a different literary style, that of a parable, the endless question is echoed, "Why doesn't God do something about all this evil in the world?" As after the first parable, the parable of the sower, the disciples needed Jesus to explain the meaning. Jesus readily obliged them. In fact, he did something that we hesitate to do in exegeting parables. He gave multiple identifications, listing six persons or things with symbolic meanings. This parable borders on allegory!

I. This parable in history.

The Donatists of the early fourth century used this story of Jesus to reinforce their position for a pure church. They justified separating from the early "catholic body" on the grounds that holiness is not merely one of the church's basic characteristics, but the essential one, the exclusive trait. Of course, they said, hypocrites might live somewhere within the church, but when people are plainly living out of harmony with the principles for which the church stands, the faithful in Christ must withdraw from them or be defiled. The purists, like the poor, we have with us always!

Martin Luther had an interesting, though slightly inconsistent, approach to this parable. He claimed that the church may exclude heretics but not kill them. The state may do both, he said, because Jesus prohibited Christians from uprooting tares. He did not forbid the civil authorities! Beza, a friend of John Calvin, went further and challenged Luther. He argued that the parable does not deal with church discipline, for the church had not yet been formed and, therefore, both church and state may use appropriate punishment in dealing with the "heretic-tares." With this reasoning he justified the burning of Cervantes. We must "pour a little salt" on such interpretations!

Nonconformists and zealots in all generations have continued the argument and struggle. Both Arnot and French interpreted the parable from their own biases; both Armenian and Arestian accused the other of being biased. Chaucer put his finger on our tender spot. Too often we take any heresy and justify it with a text!

II. Let's be honest.

What does Jesus think about all of this striving to vindicate our position? Can we not imagine him looking with grievous and incredulous eyes and wondering why people feel honest when they forge fratricidal weapons from his simplest words about eternal life? One scholar says with tongue in cheek that some people "are more religious than God himself." To some, perfection seems so biblical! After all, God has placed in our hearts a discontent with anything that is second rate. When national life loses its idealism, disintegration comes rapidly. If we need anything, we need to keep within us a sense of our destiny and refuse to compromise by accepting shallow substitutes.

Yet the drive for perfection can easily turn into an overbearing intolerance. Jesus presented both sides of the picture, and we must be honest enough to realize that our zeal can, if we are not careful, become a projection of our own ego. Only rarely do people so wholeheartedly embrace evil that they are entirely beyond the influence of good. Likewise, most people have within their motivation a pride that can become a satanic tool that will, unless care is exercised, become an instrument of self-destruction. We should keep our convictions strong and our spirits sweet. We should seek, as best we can, in the words of Henry Van Dyke, "to act from honest motives purely."

III. Why not do it now?

Weeding out wrongdoers is a popular method of dealing with evil. Although Jesus refused to sanction it, his followers have practiced it in all generations. This method, however, is as dangerous as it is foolish. Think a moment and you will see why Jesus refused to approve it. For one thing, we do not have enough wisdom to distinguish wheat from tares. Many times a movement, which at the outset seemed to be a menace, actually turned out to be a blessing. Another reason to avoid this method is that it endangers the wheat. If the tare puller is wheat (see Matt. 13:38), he begins to set himself up as a judge of his brother. When we pull up the tares, we are in danger of pulling up the wheat that grows beside it. If you have ever chopped weeds near corn, you know how easy it is to cut the corn also. The tares and wheat are so interrelated that it is difficult to pull up one without doing injury to the other. Furthermore, tare pulling is negative, and God's kingdom is never built on an "anti" program.

A building demolition firm in a large city advertised, "We can wreck anything." Perhaps they can, but God's people are not in the wrecking business. Tare pulling smacks too much of being judgmental with no constructive program.

IV. Let God handle it.

The Christian must take the future on faith. It is hard, of course, to see the wicked prosper while the righteous are in pain or poverty. Seeds, however, require time to reveal what they are. At the start we simply cannot do much about it. God has reserved some things for himself. The mystery of evil is not a mystery to him. Wicked people do not usurp his sovereignty. Judgment will come in God's time because God will not endlessly tolerate wrongdoing.

V. What Jesus did not say.

Let it be underscored again and again that Jesus nowhere advocated compromising with evil or wicked people. He was not suggesting any form of truce with weeds, because he knew that human peace can never be harvested by a reconciliation with treachery, hate, lust, or greed.

Jesus knew, on the other hand, that many times, perhaps always, the only way we can find peace of mind is to accept life the way it is and try to do the best we can with it. Wickedness shocks good people, and our righteous indignation is raised often even if we are too tender to struggle against entrenched evil. It is completely naïve for us to hope for any field without weeds. Life lacks a lot to make it beautiful all the time. We cannot, however, afford to drain our energies in combating every iniquity that we see in someone else.

VI. The fruit is the proof.

Many times in life we cannot distinguish between the genuine things and those that pretend to be real. The world offers many substitutes. Advertising often suggests that something is "just as good," and people fall for this line. If we are not careful, we will think that people are actually doing what the advertisers claim.

The plain, unvarnished truth, however, is not in the advertisement but in the "delivery of the goods." The thing that comes from a tree is the best definition of a tree. An apple tree does not produce oranges. Blackberry bushes do not produce strawberries.

Wisdom comes when we study the past. We need to learn lessons from those who have gone before and make an honest effort to apply them in our lives. Sometimes we are told the world is different today, but the burden of proof is on those who make such statements. Human life is short, but history is a long story that gives a broad basis of judgment for every generation. If history proves anything, it affirms that the weeds are always gathered into bundles and burned. Harvest time comes! We must never pretend there is no difference between wheat and tares, but we must be careful about taking it upon ourselves to distinguish between them. Vengeance belongs to the Lord!

Conclusion

Though the main thrust of this parable is a warning against premature weeding, another application cries for attention. When Christ comes with his sickle and crown, surprises are in store for us. In another parable, Jesus spoke of separating sheep from goats.

The main question for us is whether or not we ourselves have had a personal experience with Jesus or whether we are one of the "tares."

Are you a phony? This is a sharp question, but we need to ask it of ourselves every once in a while. Have you ever said of a person, "I wonder if he has really been saved?" Why not turn the spotlight on yourself periodically? This is perhaps the greatest thought from this parable.

SUNDAY EVENING, JULY 21

Title: Can These Bones Live?

Text: "He said unto me, Son of man, can these bones live? And I answered, O Lord God, thou knowest" (**Ezek. 37:3**).

Scripture Reading: Ezekiel 37:1–10

Introduction

Ezekiel 37 is one of the most solemn and utterly serious chapters in the entire prophecy of this young priest. It describes a most unusual scene and a most incredible happening. The scene is a valley filled with disjointed, bleaching human bones. The happening is the coming of four winds that converge upon this valley. As those mysterious winds sweep across that eerie boneyard, fantastic things start to happen. Bones come together, sinew stretches like elastic across them, then flesh appears and the blowing wind enters the nostrils of those lifeless bodies, and suddenly they live! Then they stand up on their feet, a mighty, organized army.

But what have we done with that story? We have caricatured it. We have parodied it. We have composed funny songs and hilarious skits about it. In short, and for the most part, we have turned Ezekiel's most serious and profound vision into a cheap joke! Tonight I want us to forget that "the head bone was connected to the neck bone, and the ankle bone to the foot bone," and with the microscope of biblical interpretation, see if we cannot discover the true and lasting message in Ezekiel's vision.

When Ezekiel looked to his left and to his right, as far as his eyes could see, there were the dried, bleached bones of soldiers who had fallen in battle. There was no movement, no sound, no indication of life at all. There was no wind, no breeze—just abandoned, forsaken, utter stillness.

I. First, there is a divine question.

The Lord Jehovah, who is Ezekiel's "tour director," asks this stunned prophet a strange question.

A. *"Son of man, can these bones live?"* Or, to paraphrase, God might have said something like this to Ezekiel: "Ezekiel, you've got the picture. You've had the 'grand tour.' You've seen this whole valley filled with bones. Now what do you think? Do you catch even the faintest glint of hope here? Do you think that there is any chance, any possibility, that these bones could ever live again?" What a strange question! Slowly this young man who possessed by nature a vivid imagination began to let God push this question through his mind. Again and again it rang in his ears, echoing and reverberating through that valley of death.

B. *Like the slowly rising sun, like the gentle unfolding of a rosebud, Ezekiel began to see.* Suddenly those dry, dead, bleached bones began to take on eerie and familiar resemblances. Those grotesque, staring skulls began to look like his own people back in the pagan land of Babylon. Then, the longer Ezekiel allowed the Spirit of God to bombard his mind with this scene, the more he began to perceive the picture God was painting before him. "O Lord, this must be how you see them—while they are physically alive and active in their world, they are spiritually dead! And now you ask, 'Can these bones live?' O my God! Only you can know that! The answer, from my human standpoint, O Lord, is 'No!' Death has won in this valley, Lord. The Grim Reaper is supreme here. But I've learned a long time ago, Lord, that your ways are not our ways, and that your power far exceeds our power. Only you hold the answer to that question, Lord!"

II. This brings us to the human dilemma Ezekiel faced in this symbolic vision God had given him.

A. *What is "spiritual death"?* It is a figure of speech, not a medical report. A person who is spiritually dead may be vibrant with physical health and energy. She may be intellectually brilliant and successful. Yet spiritually, as far as her relationship with God is concerned, she may be as dead and void of life as Ezekiel's boneyard. But when we speak of spiritual death, we are describing someone who has no basis for genuine hope unless she responds to the Spirit of God. What about Ezekiel's people? If you had asked them if they believed in God, they would have replied, with a shrug of their shoulders, "Sure. We believe in God." Statistics reveal that if asked today, 90 percent of Americans would also answer, "Sure. We believe in God."

B. *Now let's look around our neighborhood.* Here is a man who is holding down a responsible position. He may be earning a good salary, living in a comfortable home, driving a nice car. He has never been in a jail, nor has he been involved in a scandal. He doesn't drink—at least not to excess. He doesn't use narcotics. He is faithful to his wife, and he provides for his children. Once, long ago, he joined a church. And today he will tell you with a quiet, disarming smile, "Well, church is fine. My wife and children attend. It just really isn't important to me. Don't get me wrong—I think it's good for those who need it." Yet when Ezekiel described his friends and neighbors as a collection of dry bones, he was talking about nice, successful people—but a people whose faith had fizzled out.

III. But then, there must be an ultimate solution to this problem.

God gave the solution to Ezekiel in an unforgettable way.

A. *Once again, Ezekiel had reached a new plateau of understanding.* His first step was to comprehend the symbolism of the valley of dry bones. They were his people, God's people, those for whom God had a purpose and a plan. But they had turned from that plan and were following their own schemes. The result was that they were spiritually dead. There was no vital, living relationship. Then Ezekiel reached a second plateau of understanding. He saw his people as victims of spiritual death. Suddenly he was overcome with the hopelessness of the situation. "Dear God! Is this all there is? Is this the end of your plan and purpose for your people? What of my mission, O God? They will not hear me! They will not listen!"

B. *For what did Ezekiel see among his people?* In the years of their captivity in Babylon, they had become comfortable and some of them even materially successful. They were learning to love that pagan land. Archaeological discoveries have confirmed this, as indications of Hebrew prosperity in Babylon have been found among the ruins of that ancient pagan civilization. So, in the midst of this hopeless twilight, God spoke to Ezekiel again. He said to that distressed prophet: "Ezekiel, preach to the wind!" What a humbling experience for Ezekiel! We do not know what he said, but the winds responded. From north, south, east, and west they came. Gently at first, like whispering zephyrs, they blew across that valley of bones. Then, slowly, the velocity increased. The winds reached gale intensity as they rushed through those bones.

C. *Ezekiel saw his miracle.* The bones began to move, and bone found its bone. Out of chaos and hopelessness and despair there came order and purpose and meaning. Out of the impossible came the possible. Then, as the speechless Ezekiel watched, sinew and flesh came upon the bones. Though the bones had come together to form skeletons with purpose and design, they lacked cohesiveness and unity until the sinews and the flesh appeared. But wait a moment! Although a fantastic transformation had taken place, something vital was missing. These perfectly formed bodies were still lifeless. Everything was there except that which spelled the difference between life and death—the breath of God, or God's Spirit.

D. *Ezekiel's people in Babylon knew the Hebrew Scriptures.* They knew the law of God, for the scribes had continued to teach it faithfully in the synagogues they had established. They had the form of religion, the institution for religion, even the divine law itself. But they were still victims of spiritual death. "Preach to the wind, Ezekiel! Breathe upon these bodies, O Wind of God!" And once again the winds came and filled the nostrils and lungs of these bodies, and Ezekiel saw them stand upon their feet, by ranks, companies, battalions, a mighty army for the Lord.

Conclusion

The Spirit gives life. The songwriter said, "All is vain unless the Spirit of the Holy One come down." And what is the application for us today? We, too, have the superstructure. We have the bones and the sinew and the flesh. We have the institution, the organization, the intellectual know-how. And yet the impact of the church on its community and on the world is pitifully weak. The influence of many Christians on those with whom they associate is heartbreakingly ineffective.

The church needs desperately to be alive, breathing, pulsating with the Spirit of God in this day in which we live. As a nation, our affluence has honeycombed us spiritually. We lie on our battlefield, for the most part, like Ezekiel's lifeless army. But all is not lost. There is hope; the stench of spiritual death can be taken away by the wind of God's Spirit moving among us.

WEDNESDAY EVENING, JULY 24

Title: The More Excellent Way

Text: "And yet shew I unto you a more excellent way" (**1 Cor. 12:31**).

Scripture Reading: 1 Corinthians 13:1–13

Introduction

The words found in 1 Corinthians 13 are those of a great theologian. He stressed such doctrines as justification, sanctification, and glorification. This chapter is one of his masterpieces. It is on the greatest of all themes—love.

I. We must notice the introduction in order to get the message.

A. *First Corinthians 12:31 says, "Eagerly desire the greater gifts"* (NIV). These words refer to gifts mentioned in the entire chapter of 1 Corinthians 12—teaching, preaching, healing, and administration—but in this one phrase, Paul stated there was something greater than any of these.

B. *Several kinds of love are good.* There is parental love for children, children's love for parents, one's love for country, the love between a husband and wife, but the greatest of them all is Christian love.

II. We need to recognize the supremacy of Christian love.

A. *The supremacy is discovered by contrast (1 Cor. 13:1–3).*

   1. Paul lists the things the Corinthians thought were great. Others think the same thing. But when these things are compared to Christian love, love is more important. Some of these important things are public speaking, sacred learning, mighty faith, general sharing, and Christian martyrdom.

2. We all can make our own lists, such as material things that include money, power, pleasure, culture, and health; and spiritual things that include tithing, church attendance, Bible reading, and visitation.

B. *The supremacy is realized in love itself (1 Cor. 13:4–8).* Love is described by the way it works and as being like the Lord Jesus himself.

C. *The supremacy is also found in its permanence (1 Cor. 13:8–13).* Love lasts when other things do not, and the older it gets, the sweeter it is.

III. We need to think about the relationship of love.

A. *Each Christian is challenged to strive for Christian love (1 Cor. 14:1).* To attain this Christian love, we must keep sin out and cultivate love. We must live close to the cross on which Jesus died.

B. *Each Christian is challenged to practice Christian love.* This starts with those to whom we are the closest and moves out to all people of the world. It starts with relatively small and simple things, then ultimately envelops the mighty and complicated.

Conclusion

I challenge you to read and reread 1 Corinthians 13 and then make it your business to love like this.

SUNDAY MORNING, JULY 28

Title: Whatever Happens, God's Work Will Go On

Text: "A grain of mustard seed... the least of all seeds: but when it is grown, it is the greatest among herbs" **(Matt. 13:31–32).**

Scripture Reading: Matthew 13:31–32

Hymns: "Faith Is the Victory," Yates
"'Tis So Sweet to Trust in Jesus," Stead
"Trusting Jesus," Stites

Offertory Prayer: Our Father, we pray that you would help us to serve you as you deserve to be served. We ask that you will help us to fight without heeding the wounds, to toil without seeking to rest, and to labor without expecting any reward except the joy of knowing that we are doing your will. We pray that your love might fill our lives in such a way that we may count nothing too small to do for you nor nothing too large to attempt for you. Fill us with your light and your life in order that we may reveal to others your wondrous glory. Bless us now in the giving of gifts that your work might be carried on in this world. Help us to give sacrificially and joyfully. We pray this in our Savior's name. Amen.

Introduction

No one really understands the mystery of growth. How does a seed change into a flower? Tennyson said:

> *Flower in the crannied wall,*
> *I pluck you out of the crannies:*
> *Hold you here, root and all, in my hand,*
> *Little flower—but if I could understand*
> *What you are, root and all, and all in all,*
> *I should know what God and man is.*

In this parable of the mustard seed, Jesus said that the kingdom of God, like a seed, contains spontaneity and divine vitality, the inherent forces of a life that can fashion its own self. This parable is one of the simplest, yet it contains one of the most profound messages. No one can predict how big something will grow. We should never "despise the day of little things," because God has a way of multiplying our small endeavors and giving us tremendous results.

I. The kingdom belongs to God.

Years ago a young man went to serve in a church in a rapidly expanding area of the city. In talking to an older minister, he said, "The awesomeness of the responsibility frightens me. There is so much to be done in this area. So many people need a spiritual ministry. I pray that I can be big enough for the task." The older minister said to the younger one, "Let me share a verse of Scripture with you." Then he quoted, "Fear not, little flock; for it is your Father's good pleasure to give you the kingdom" (Luke 12:32). The young minister then realized that God was far more interested in the Lord's work than any minister could ever be. This brought a sense of security and assurance that has remained with that man through the years.

God's kingdom did not begin in New Testament days. God had a people in the Old Testament, those who allowed him to rule in their hearts. In a very special way, the kingdom of God came into being when Jesus Christ revealed the Father in all of his fullness. Let us never forget when things are gloomy and when we are discouraged that God stands within the shadow, "keeping watch above his own" and making certain that his kingdom will never be destroyed by wicked people.

II. Do not despise small things.

If anything ever began in miniature, it was the Christian movement. A baby in a manger! A Roman ruler issuing an edict to kill him! A little boy in a carpenter's shop in a small village! This was the start of it all. Yet from that small beginning, God's kingdom, based on love and righteousness, has extended and become worldwide in its scope.

Of course, there are problems. Every good movement has counterfeit people attached to it. Who said there are no hypocrites in the local churches? Or in denomination and independent movements? There are phonies everywhere. One cannot disparage a whole cause, however, because people have joined themselves to it for ambitious reasons or have failed to live up to the standards of the founder.

Another lesson comes to us as we think of how God's kingdom has expanded. Those who attach themselves to Jesus will grow. Many times a person who had a flat personality suddenly developed into an individual with great charisma because Jesus Christ came into his or her heart as Savior and Lord. If we have to give up anything in order to become a Christian, God gives back far more to us. Often, that "much more" is more than the presence of peace in the heart. Many times our personalities take on new meaning. We have great success in personal living because of the transformation that has come through a dynamic experience with Jesus.

A pastor once told how men in his congregation said that the business world missed a great executive when he went into the ministry. They said, "You surely gave up a lot to serve the Lord." He said later: "I began to think about it and began to feel sorry for myself, thinking what I had given up for the Lord. Then I did a little serious reflection and remembered where I was when I became a Christian and where I was when I dedicated my life to the ministry. I was a little farm boy who probably never would have gone to college but would have stayed right on that farm and might have been a tenant farmer like my dad. I decided that the only thing I gave up to follow the Lord was a bull-tongued plow, a flop-eared mule, and a patch of new ground." His experience is true for most of us. Very few really give up much. We're small when we come to Jesus, but he makes us greater, far greater than we ever could have been without him.

III. Have you been to Jesus?

Let's forget the worldwide application for now, although it's true. Let's come home and think about our own possibilities if we will give our lives to Jesus. If you've never been saved, the first step is to become a Christian. If you have been saved but are not fully committed, your need is to face the matter of what a life can do when it is completely surrendered to the will of God.

Four university students in Great Britain had a happy-go-lucky approach to life. They were not wicked, but they were self-sufficient, cocksure, and lacking in life goals. On the spur of the moment, they decided to go hear Dwight L. Moody, the itinerant evangelist from America. Something happened to them that night. They met the Lord and their lives were changed. Those four university students were Henry Drummond, who became a writer and preacher; George Adam Smith, a scholar and teacher; John Watson, the Ian Maclaren of the literary world; and Donald McLeach, a medical missionary. God has a way of taking a mustard seed and making it into a herb and even a tree.

Conclusion

This parable has a double application. Christianity will never be stamped out. Jesus was not teaching that human effort will win the world to Christ. He was not saying that the kingdoms of this world will become the kingdom of our Lord before Jesus comes again. Of course, sin will always be with us. We must remember, however, that righteousness will also be with us. Although sin is rampant in today's world, there are more agencies for good and God today than ever before. More people are preaching the gospel and witnessing for Jesus now than ever before in the history of our world. The kingdom has grown and will continue to grow until Jesus comes again. Are you a part of that kingdom?

The other application is, of course, what Jesus can do in our individual lives when we are surrendered to him. I am not suggesting that God will make a millionaire or successful businessperson or famous personality out of everyone who becomes a Christian. He never promised to do that! But he will give us new life, new personality, new motivation, and a new reason for living if we will come to him in repentance and faith. Whatever happens, God's work will go on. Are you with him or still on the outside?

SUNDAY EVENING, JULY 28

Title: A River in the Wilderness

Text: "It was a river that I could not pass over: for the waters were risen, waters to swim in, a river that could not be passed over" **(Ezek. 47:5).**

Scripture Reading: Ezekiel 47:1–12

Introduction

With this evening's sermon we come to the conclusion of this series of studies from the strange and penetrating prophecy of Ezekiel. It cannot be truthfully said that we enjoy the oftentimes scathing words of this young prophet. For even though this highly imaginative and visionary young man wrote his prophecy six centuries before the birth of Christ, it seems that he has been reading our mail! For with the incisiveness of a surgeon's scalpel, Ezekiel has probed deeply into our hearts. He has shown us ourselves as individuals, as a community of God's people, and as a nation. He has set forth clearly the unchangeable law of God—his demand for righteousness, for truth, for honesty in our dealings both with God and with each other. Yet at the same time, there has run through this hard and piercing prophecy an undeniable message of hope.

In this last message from Ezekiel, we find the vivid description of another vision God gave to this prophet. In this last recorded vision, God showed

Ezekiel the temple in Jerusalem. Out from under the foundation of that magnificent house of worship there flowed a river. This mighty river flowed down through the Arabah to the Dead Sea. As the water flowed, it changed that bleak, arid, blistering desert into a fertile and verdant garden. In previous messages we have listened as this versatile prophet dealt with commerce and politics and sociological issues. But now, in this last vision of the book, he speaks of the geography of the land.

I. First, in the dry desert area between Jerusalem and the Dead Sea, let's see the symbol of the destitution of a people.

A. *To the east of Jerusalem the land of Palestine is rugged.* A great geological fault runs through central Palestine. At the lowest depth of this fault, eighteen miles east of Jerusalem, is the Dead Sea, which is the lowest known spot on the surface of the earth. The Dead Sea is 1,292 feet below the level of the Mediterranean Sea. Jerusalem is located on a ridge about a half-mile above sea level. To the west of Jerusalem, where there are mountains and gullies, moisture-laden clouds from the Mediterranean blow over Palestine. But east of the city, on the side of the ridge where the terrain drops steadily down to the Dead Sea, there is practically no rainfall.

Thus, the desert, or Arabah, that Ezekiel saw in his vision was rugged, barren, empty land. Through the Arabah, this dry, desolate stretch of land, flows the Jordan River. From the air the Jordan Valley is one of the most impressive sights you can imagine. It is a jagged streak of emerald green water cutting through the desert. Here and there a skillful engineer has channeled some life-giving water to a relatively flat field, which is verdant and fruitful. This, then, is a brief, bird's-eye view of the natural geography of the land. Perhaps it will help us understand that Ezekiel is talking about spiritual truth in geographical terms.

B. *The river that transforms the wilderness into a veritable garden—the river Ezekiel saw in his vision—is not the Jordan.* And the wilderness he saw is not really the Arabah at all. It is a symbol of the spiritual desolation in which Ezekiel's people were living and in which millions of people are living today. What Ezekiel is trying to say to us—and what the Bible declares to us—is that a person's first need is for a right relationship with God.

The inner person, without Christ, is desolate and unproductive. His or her hope is to be changed and redeemed by the grace of God. The arid desert must be made to blossom like a rose. The soil of the Arabah was rich in minerals but poor in water. We are told that the oranges grown in those parts of the Arabah where engineers have diverted the waters of the Jordan to irrigate it are more luscious than our own Florida oranges. The soil in our own land cannot compare in mineral content with the soil in the Arabah. But all of the potentially good soil in the Arabah is of no avail without the water.

II. This brings us to the river Ezekiel describes.

A. *It is a most unusual river. It has no tributaries—only a source—yet it flows through dry, thirsty country.* And as it does, it grows deeper and wider. And another peculiarity about this river is that it flows both uphill and downhill! What does this river represent in Ezekiel's vision as it flows through this dry, destitute wilderness? This river that flows from the temple of God is obviously the love of God. The phrase "the love of God" has two meanings. It means that you love him and that he loves you. Like Ezekiel, we live in a time when people have grown cynical about many things. In Ezekiel's day, people were making clever and flippant remarks about God and religion to cover up their own spiritual emptiness. And we are hearing the same things today. Even nominal Christians do not take God and Christianity very seriously. They make crude jokes about God and the church. They flippantly refer to him as "the Big Guy" or "the Man Upstairs."

B. *What is it that brings true joy to a Christian?* It is the realization and the confidence that in the midst of this muddle and mess society has made of things, God is working out his purposes for eternity—and nothing or no one is going to stop him! If we truly believe that, then in the midst of the most devastating set of circumstances, we have something to be joyful about. But that isn't all. Ours is a day of tension. The storms of uncertainty swirl about us on every front—a "quiet center"—like the eye of the hurricane—around which the storm can blow as fiercely as it pleases. Ezekiel is talking about our "quiet center with God." And he likens it to the river—the love of God—that brings fruitfulness and healing to the rich soil of our souls.

C. *There is something else about our love for God.* It ought to bring direction and purpose into our lives. Our love for God can be called "faith," whereas his love for us is called "grace." It doesn't much matter whether we call Ezekiel's river the stream of "faith" or of "grace." In Christ the two are bound into one. You love God—that means that you know where the river is flowing. God loves you—that means the river will reach its destination no matter what. At Christmas time we sing, "Joy to the World, the Lord Is Come!" A line in the lyrics of that carol says, "He rules the world with truth and grace." Sometimes we forget this, for the desert is so wild and frightening. Sometimes we lose our way. But God isn't lost! He knows the way. He has told us to "overcome evil with good." And he is in the process of helping us do just that.

III. Finally, let's see the temple in this last vision of Ezekiel—the temple from which flowed this life-giving river.

A. *We remember that Ezekiel saw in his vision that the river flowing out from this temple transformed the desert.* The last eight chapters of Ezekiel's prophecy are about the temple of God that stood in the midst of the land. And through it all, Ezekiel is telling us that worship is a person's central business in life. If you remember, back in the opening vision in chapter 1, Ezekiel showed us that the reality of worshiping God can take place anywhere, even down by the Chebar River. But at the same time, common sense and the evidence of history show that true worship most often takes place in the hearts of people who have formed the valuable habit of coming to worship in a place dedicated to that purpose. Ezekiel tells us this by describing in careful detail the temple building.

B. *Now here is something interesting—and it is the heart of this message and of this closing vision in Ezekiel's prophecy.* With all of Ezekiel's emphasis on the temple, one would think that this river flowing from it would be its deepest in the area of the temple, right beside the sacred altar.

But Ezekiel knew better than that! In the temple area, where the river began, it was just a trickle. This stream of divine love shimmered across the courtyard and through the Eastern Gate. A quarter of a mile away that little trickle of divine love was beginning to be a recognizable stream. Another quarter of a mile and it was up to Ezekiel's knees. Twice more the guide measured the stream, and at a distance of a little more than a mile, it was too deep to wade. Ezekiel saw lush vegetation along the banks, and the guide told him that those waters grew wider and wider, and deeper and deeper. They brought healing to the land and produced unbelievably lush vegetation.

C. *Where does the love of God really count?* Does it count most in the worship assembly? Certainly it counts here as we worship together. But the point is, when we have sung our hymns, said our prayers, and listened to our sermons, we are not done with God! He wants our total lives, not just an hour of our time doled out to him on Sunday morning and evening!

Conclusion

What is Ezekiel saying? He is not saying that the temple—the church and its worship services—are not important. For the miracle of worship is more likely to begin right here than in any other spot on earth. But the point is, if our worship ends here, then there is no miracle. Nothing is going to be accomplished. What happens in this building is worship if it is fulfilled in your office, on your farm, in your shop, on your job, in the school room, and in your home.

How deep is your river—your love for God, and his love for you? Has it transformed the wilderness of your life?

WEDNESDAY EVENING, JULY 31

Title: The God of Order

Text: "For God is not the author of confusion" **(1 Cor. 14:33).**

Scripture Reading: 1 Corinthians 14:1–40

Introduction

The subject under consideration in this message has to do with confusion in the order of worship. Although the message deals with speaking in tongues, the main focus is not on speaking in tongues, but on strife in the church.

I. God is a God of peace.

A. *The whole Bible and all of human experience testify to the fact that God is love.* It was love that caused God to create humankind for fellowship. It was love that caused him to call Abram. It was love that sent Jesus into the world.

B. *The special message of the Bible is that God sent Jesus into the world to bring peace.* At the birth of Jesus the heavenly host sang, "Peace on earth, good will toward men." Jesus' life was spent in teaching and preaching love and kindness. The church of today is the instrument of the same message.

C. *The greatest act of Christ to establish peace was his death on the cross.* God was in Christ reconciling the world unto himself. Sin had made and still makes humans the enemies of Christ. Reconciliation removes that enmity.

II. The Christian is the instrument of peace.

A. *Pursue love, which is the more excellent way.* To pursue love is to be like God. We become unchristian when we think like fallen humans instead of like God. The opening verse also exhorts Christians to prophesy. This means to speak forth in such a way that people can understand. The messenger of God should speak forth in such a way so as to build up.

B. *Excel in spiritual gifts for the upbuilding of the church.* The church of the Lord Jesus Christ is the hope for order and peace in the world. The church of today is to do what Jesus did in his earthly life. Two things are mentioned for the church to do—pray and praise (1 Cor. 14:15).

C. *Become mature spiritually.* A mature person is one who is convicted of sin and looks to Christ for cleansing. A mature person is one who fulfills his or her office according to God's will.

III. Each Christian must respond to God in order to have peace.

A. *The church at Corinth was guilty of doing the reverse of God's will.* This is the reason there is disorder in the world today. The same is true of the church. Men and women in the church need to be right with God.

234

B. *World peace waits on the children of God.* "If my people, which are called by my name, shall humble themselves, and pray, and seek my face, and turn from their wicked ways; then will I hear from heaven, and will forgive their sin, and will heal their land" (2 Chron. 7:14).

Conclusion

You, as a Christian, are urged to become an instrument of peace. Surrender to your Lord completely.

Suggested preaching program for the month of

AUGUST

■ **Sunday Mornings**

Continue with the theme "The Master Speaks to the Present through the Parables."

■ **Sunday Evenings**

The suggested theme is "Jesus Came Preaching." What did he preach about? These sermon outlines provide many Scripture references for a series of messages on the great subjects about which Jesus taught.

■ **Wednesday Evenings**

Continue the studies based on Paul's first letter to the Corinthian Christians.

On the last Wednesday evening of the month begin a new series entitled "Warnings from the Past" based on incidents in the lives of men who lived in the very dawn of redemptive history. These biographical messages speak to present-day needs.

SUNDAY MORNING, AUGUST 4

Title: Silent Forces Are Often the Strongest

Text: "The kingdom of heaven is like unto leaven, which a woman took, and hid in three measures of meal, till the whole was leavened" **(Matt. 13:33).**

Scripture Reading: Matthew 13:33–35

Hymns: "Break Thou the Bread of Life," Lathbury
          "All Hail the Power of Jesus' Name," Perronet
          "Softly and Tenderly," Thompson

Offertory Prayer: Our Father, we are grateful that you wrote our name in the Lamb's book of life when we accepted Jesus as Savior. We pray that you will engrave your name on our hearts so indelibly that neither prosperity nor adversity shall ever move us from your love. Be to us a strong tower of defense and a comforter in tribulation. Guide us through the many temptations and dangers of this life by making us strong to resist evil and live victoriously in your strength. We bring gifts to you that were earned by abilities that you bestowed upon us out of the rich bounties of your grace. We bring these gifts to help further your work, since we can do collectively, as a community of believers, what we cannot do individually. Pour out your power on this church, granting us wisdom to use good judgment in the expending of funds. May we receive a blessing as we give. We pray this in the Master's name. Amen.

Introduction

Jesus turned to everyday life in Galilee in order to illustrate the kingdom of God. Smaller towns and villages had no bakeries; women made bread in their homes. Jesus had, no doubt, often seen his mother use leaven—dough that had been kept from a previous baking and had fermented. When the leaven was mixed into the new batch of dough, it changed the characteristics of the dough—that is, the dough rose and made full loaves of bread when baked. Jesus observed that just as leaven changes the dough into which it is mixed, God's kingdom likewise changes everything with which it comes into contact.

I. A difficulty of interpretation.

This is a controversial parable. Often leaven symbolized for the Jewish people an evil influence. In fact, elsewhere in the New Testament this is true. Jesus advised his disciples to beware of the leaven of the Pharisees and of Herod (Mark 8:15). Paul twice used the phrase, "A little leaven leavens the whole lot," as he exhorted Christian people to separate themselves from all things that can in any way influence for evil (1 Cor. 5:6; Gal. 5:9). If a Jewish proselyte relapsed into pagan ways, the rabbis spoke of it as a "return to his leaven."

On the other hand, it is not fair to say that the Jews always used leaven as a synonym for wickedness or bad influence. One rabbi said, "Great is peace when that peace is to the earth as the leaven is to the dough." The point of this parable is not whether leaven is good or bad; rather, it is used to illustrate that the most silent of forces may be the strongest.

II. Take the long look.

Too many people today want to see their success immediately. They do not want to wait for rewards. They believe that Christianity means all of our problems are immediately solved and prosperity will come by tomorrow afternoon. This is simply not true!

Of course, when we receive Jesus as our Savior, the guilt of our sin is dealt with on the basis of Christ's death on Calvary and his resurrection from the grave. This should bring immediate peace with God, because we know that we shall not come into condemnation and that our sins are under the blood of Christ. Personal problems, however, still must be dealt with on a day-to-day basis.

The glorious truth, however, is that ultimately we have assurance of victory. Knowing that we are going to "win the game" provides help in time of need, strength for every inning. The apostle John wrote to a struggling church in Asia Minor that "the devil shall cast some of you into prison, that ye may be tried; and ye shall have tribulation ten days: be thou faithful unto death, and I will give thee a crown of life" (Rev. 2:10). John was saying: "Take the long look. Do not set your eyes on short-term goals. Give God time, and he will work out your problems. In the meantime, be faithful and live up to the light you possess."

III. History renders strange verdicts.

If you had been alive in 1809, you would have been tempted to join the group of pessimists who called it "the world's blackest year." Everything seemed to indicate the world had no future. Europe was on the borderline of complete frustration, ready to throw in the towel and call it quits. Napoleon was dominating the entire continent and making plans for further conquests. The cause of freedom and social progress seemed hopeless. The truth is, however, that God was at work. In that year Abraham Lincoln, William Gladstone, Alfred Tennyson, Oliver Wendell Holmes, Cyrus Hall McCormick, and Felix Mendelssohn were born.

As Christians we can put our faith in the fact that history will vindicate our trust in Christ. Polycarp, a Christian martyr, was put to death about the middle of the second century. The group of struggling Christians were terrified by the persecution under the proconsulship of a man named Statius Quadratus. The historian who recorded the death of Polycarp concentrated a great truth into a few words when he wrote of the event and attached the date to it. He penned, "Statius Quadratus, proconsul; Jesus Christ, King forever." He could not possibly have known that 1,850 years later people would still be reading his words. Who was Statius Quadratus? Who knows? In fact, who cares? But above the turmoil of the world and the chaotic conditions that exist now and have existed through the centuries, his affirmation resounds, "Jesus Christ, King forever."

IV. God is always there.

If one were to ask what is the chief appeal of the gospel to so many people in so many generations and in so many countries, what would you say? Is it not the influence of Jesus as a person? Others have come and gone. Military men have conquered large portions of the world but have had to give it up. Merchants have cornered the market on certain products, but they could not hold out forever. Entertainers have become a household word but have perished, some of them tragically. Jesus Christ, however, is stronger today than he was in the first century. His kingdom is greater and more people claim allegiance to him than ever before in the history of the world. Napoleon is reported to have once said, "Caesar, Charlemagne, and I built kingdoms on force and they have crumbled. Jesus Christ built a kingdom on love, and today there are countless thousands that would gladly die for his sake."

Conclusion

Do not let the obvious fool you. Forces are at work for God when we least expect. To celebrate the one hundredth anniversary of Abraham Lincoln's birth, a cartoonist drew a picture of two men talking in a rural section of Kentucky. One said, "What's new?" The other replied, "Nothing. This is an out-of-the-way place. Oh, by the way, there was a new boy born over at Tom Lincoln's last night. But nothing new ever happens around here." One wonders if somebody in the outskirts of Bethlehem might have said one day, "Nothing new ever happens around here. We're just a hick town. Oh, by the way, some girl from Galilee had a baby out in the stable last night. But nothing new ever happens around here." Be careful about believing that the forces making the loudest noise are the most enduring or the more important.

> *How silently, how silently the wondrous gift is given!*
> *So God imparts to human hearts the blessings of his heaven.*
> *No ear may hear his coming, but in this world of sin,*
> *Where meek souls will receive him still, the dear Christ enters in.*

God is on the field when he seems most invisible. Trust him by receiving his death on the cross as payment for your sin and his resurrection from the grave as your power. Commit yourself to share his goals and purposes in life.

SUNDAY EVENING, AUGUST 4

Title: What Jesus Preached about God

Text: "No man hath seen God at any time; the only begotten Son, which is in the bosom of the Father, he hath declared him" **(John 1:18).**

Scripture Reading: John 14:8–12

Introduction

The desire to know God seems to be universal. We all cry with Philip, "Show us the Father, and it sufficeth us" (John 14:8). "As the hart panteth after the water brooks, so panteth my soul after thee, O God. My soul thirsteth for God, for the living God" (Ps. 42:1–2). This earnest cry of the psalmist made centuries ago was echoed in the heart of a six-year-old girl who said earnestly, "Daddy, I want you to show me God."

This desire to know God must have been implanted in our hearts as a part of creation. If God has given us the desire to search for him, it is antecedently probable that he would provide some appropriate revelation of himself.

Such partial revelation of God one does indeed find in nature. "The heavens declare the glory of God; and the firmament sheweth his handiwork"

(Ps. 19:1; see also vv. 2–6). Hear Paul: "For the wrath of God is revealed from heaven against all ungodliness and unrighteousness of men, who hold the truth in unrighteousness; because that which may be known of God is manifest in them; for God hath shewed it unto them. For the invisible things of him from the creation of the world are clearly seen, being understood by the things that are made, even his eternal power and Godhead" (Rom. 1:18–20). Even more significant is the inner voice of the Creator affirming that God exists and that he is righteous. Hear Paul again, "For when the Gentiles, which have not the law, do by nature the things contained in the law, these, having not the law, are a law unto themselves: Which shew the work of the law written in their hearts, their conscience also bearing witness, and their thoughts the mean while accusing or else excusing one another; In the day when God shall judge the secrets of men by Jesus Christ according to my gospel" (Rom. 2:14–16).

These partial revelations are fulfilled in Jesus who is the final revelation of God. In him God took the witness stand and testified about himself. "God, who at sundry times and in divers manners spake in time past unto the fathers by the prophets, hath in these days spoken unto us by his son, whom he hath appointed heir of all things, by whom also he made the worlds; who being the brightness of his glory, and the express image of his person, and upholding all things by the word of his power, when he had by himself purged our sins, sat down at the right hand of the Majesty on high" (Heb. 1:1–3).

I. Jesus is the good news about God.

Jesus was no speculator about God. He was no seeker after God.

A. *He was God incarnate.* He came from the glory with the Father to whom he would return. (See John 1:1–5, 14, 18; 5:19–20; 8:28–38; 10:30; 14:9–12; 17:4–8.)

B. *He held communion with the Father.* (Note his prayers: Matt. 11:25–27; Luke 22:31–32; John 11:41–42; 12:27–28.)

C. *His words and deeds were more Godlike than you could possibly imagine.* "For God, who commanded the light to shine out of darkness, hath shined in our hearts, to give the light of the knowledge of the glory of God in the face of Jesus Christ" (2 Cor. 4:6).

D. *It is a most significant fact that Jesus was absolutely sure about God.* He did not speculate about God. He affirmed what he knew.

II. Jesus was sure as to the character of God.

A. *According to Jesus, God is the heavenly Father.* He is love. In every prayer, Jesus addresses God as "Father." This must have been the reflection of a beautiful affection between his mother, Mary, and his foster father, Joseph. The Old Testament had in a general way indicated God as a Father to the nation. Jesus so personalized God's fatherly attitude for each individual as practically to make it a new concept. Here are some examples: "The Father loveth the Son, and hath given all things into his hand" (John 3:35). "For the Father himself loveth you, because ye have loved me, and have believed that I came out from God" (John 16:27). "God so loved the world" (John 3:16). "If ye then, being evil, know how to give good gifts unto your children, how much more shall your Father which is in heaven give good things to them that ask him?" (Matt. 7:11). Additional examples can be found in the parables of the Father's love in Luke 15.

B. *Jesus reveals God as righteous.* Jesus addressed him as "Holy Father" (John 17:11). He is a God so even-handed and just that he will not coerce obedience nor faith. His Holy Spirit will come to convict "the world of sin, and of righteousness, and of judgment" (John 16:8). Disciples are commanded, "But seek ye first the kingdom of God, and his righteousness" (Matt. 6:33).

The way of the Father may lead through pain, but if it be the Father's will, it must be just and right. Did anyone ever suffer as Jesus did? Yet he did not doubt God. "The cup which my Father hath given me, shall I not drink it?" (John 18:11). His prayer at Gethsemane was not, "Abba, Father, all things are possible unto thee; take away this cup from me"; rather, it was, "Nevertheless not what I will, but what thou wilt" (Mark 14:36). Jesus proved by experience that God's will is always best even when it leads to a cross. He fulfilled the word spoken by the Lord through Isaiah about the Messiah, "He shall see of the travail of his soul, and shall be satisfied: by his knowledge shall my righteous servant justify many; for he shall bear their iniquities" (Isa. 53:11).

III. Jesus brings the good news that God, as righteous love, has provided salvation from sin.

God's holiness demanded that the sinner perish. God's love yearned for his salvation. Wisdom and love provided the atonement that holiness demanded: "And as Moses lifted up the serpent in the wilderness, even so must the Son of man be lifted up: That whosoever believeth in him should not perish, but have eternal life. For God so loved the world, that he gave his only begotten Son, that whosoever believeth in him should not perish, but have everlasting life" (John 3:14–16).

Conclusion

There are many practical applications.

A. *God knows and loves each individual soul.*

B. *One can come directly to God in prayer, in repentance, in faith.* No special form or ceremony is necessary. There is no need of a human mediator.

C. *One becomes a child of God by a spiritual birth.*

D. *Children of God.*
   1. Take as the norm of right and wrong the fatherly character of God (see Matt. 5:48; 22:37–40).
   2. Obedience of a son is right and pleasant (see Matt. 21:28–31).
   3. Prayer is natural from a child to the Father (Matt. 6:6–15).
   4. Forgiveness is logical. Children need to be forgiven. God has provided the way "that he might be just, and the justifier of him which believeth in Jesus" (Rom. 3:26). The only barrier would be unwillingness to repent.
   5. God administers chastisement in love. His concern is for his child (see Heb. 12:1–13).
   6. A child is secure. The Father will not send away a son whom he loves. He is not interested in punishment, but in his son (see John 3:17; 10:27–30).

WEDNESDAY EVENING, AUGUST 7

Title: The Gospel We Preach

Text: "Moreover, brethren, I declare unto you the gospel which I preached unto you, which also ye have received, and wherein ye stand" (**1 Cor. 15:1**).

Scripture Reading: 1 Corinthians 15:1–11

Introduction

A great deal has been said about the gospel that is being preached. Some people are accused of not preaching the gospel, and some are known to be great gospel preachers. The subject "The Gospel We Preach" is Paul's terminology.

I. The gospel is the good news of the death and resurrection of Christ.

A. *The cross of Jesus is the central act of God in the redemption of sinners from their sin.* The writer of the book of Hebrews stated it succinctly when he said, "Without the shedding of blood is no remission" (Heb. 9:22). This has always been true and always will be. John the Baptist said, referring to Jesus, "Behold the Lamb of God, which taketh away the sin of the world" (John 1:29). The cross was where the love of God was poured out, the wrath of God satisfied, and the justice of God fulfilled. Paul declared in Romans 6:23 that the wages of sin is death. Jesus died for sin. Peter said, "Who his own self bare our sins in his own body on the tree" (1 Peter 2:24). Jesus was the substitute for human sin. A person is redeemed by the precious blood of that Lamb.

B. *After Jesus was crucified he was buried, and he then arose from the grave.* The resurrection makes the death of Jesus the good news. This is the gospel. The

242

resurrection of Jesus is the victory of God over the powers of evil. He conquered the sin that killed him and humankind. He conquered death, the last enemy. He became victorious over the grave.

II. This glorious gospel is to be received.

Paul said, "That which I preached, you received" (see 1 Cor. 15:1).

A. *This good news is to be preached.* The preaching of the good news is to proclaim by word and deed. Paul said he was an apostle, one sent to speak the good news (1 Cor. 15:9). People must hear to believe, and they must have preachers in order to hear (Rom. 10:14–15).

B. *This good news is to be received by faith (Rom. 10:9–10).* God takes the initiative in making a way for sinners to hear; he gives us ears and hearts, faculties for receiving. When we receive the Son, we receive eternal life (John 1:12).

III. The gospel is that on which Christians stand today.

Paul said not only have you received, but you stand on it (1 Cor. 15:1).

A. *Standing on the gospel is the hope of the world.* It is the only hope of a lost person. It is the only hope for a world in confusion. It is the only hope for life after death and the blessed reunion with loved ones.

B. *Standing on the gospel is the way one stands against the forces of evil.* Evil is the device of Satan. It may take the form of persecution or temptation. We fight by doing good.

Conclusion

You, as Christians, are asked to preach the gospel. You, who are lost, are asked to receive the gospel.

SUNDAY MORNING, AUGUST II

Title: To Be a Christian Is Worth More Than All Else

Text: "The kingdom of heaven is like unto treasure hid in a field; the which when a man hath found, he hideth, and for joy… selleth all that he hath, and buyeth that field" **(Matt. 13:44).**

Scripture Reading: Mark 10:17–30

Hymns: "A Child of the King," Buell
"He Hideth My Soul," Crosby
"I've Found a Friend, Oh, Such a Friend," Small

Offertory Prayer: Our Father, help us as long as we live on this earth to seek you daily and to walk in a believing and affectionate fellowship with you continually. We pray that when the Lord comes we will not be found hiding our talents, nor serving the flesh, nor asleep with our lamps unfurnished. May we be waiting and longing, but at the same time working, busy about the daily chores that are so necessary for the building of a well-rounded Christian life. A part of our daily duties is the bringing of our gifts into the storehouse. Yet giving is more than an obligation. We give because we love and count it a privilege to invest a part of ourselves in the work of your kingdom. Use our gifts to your glory and use our lives likewise to bring honor to your name. We pray for Jesus' sake. Amen.

Introduction

The kingdom of God is both personal and social. The parables we have studied thus far have emphasized the universal aspect of the kingdom, setting forth its growth and development in the world. This parable and the one following stress the value of God's kingdom to the individual.

The gospel is a great influence to everyone in the community. Even those who have never personally accepted Jesus as Savior share in the benefits that have accrued to community life because the gospel message has been preached. The hospital, orphans' home, and humanitarian agencies of all kind are a product of the compassion that people possess because Jesus has influenced civilization. Yet the treasure of the gospel is primarily a personal possession. Jesus told this story to illustrate the worth of the kingdom of God to an individual life.

I. A word of caution.

This parable was not given to instruct people in business ethics. We get into great danger when we try to press every detail of a parable for a symbolic meaning. If we did so in this parable, we would be in trouble. Would it be honest if we found treasure in another person's field, to slip around behind his back, secure money in some way, and buy the field? Some might say it's "slick business," but we know better! When I posed this question to a man once, he laughingly said, "It depends on whether I'm buying the field from you or you are buying it from me as to whether it's dishonest or not." We may joke about the matter, but deep down we know it would be wrong. Also, a little sober reflection will cause us to realize immediately that this question of ethics is not related to the parable at all. Jesus was telling the parable to illustrate one great truth: Jesus is worth more than anything else or everything else in the world.

II. An accidental discovery.

The story Jesus told easily could have happened in his day. Palestine was invaded often because of its strategic location as the bridge between three continents. When a man accumulated a treasure, he did not know where to hide it because invading armies looted homes indiscriminately and thoroughly. An old tradition said that in the East, because of the frequent revolutions and changes of rulers, many rich men divided their goods into three parts. One-third they used in commerce or for their necessary support; one-third they turned into jewels, which if they had to flee quickly, could be easily carried with them; and one-third they buried. A hireling could be plowing in another man's field and come across the hidden treasure of a previous owner who had been killed. What would he do? He might quickly bury it and seek to raise sufficient cash to buy the man's field.

This parable, in contrast to the one that follows, suggests that some people come upon God's kingdom unexpectedly. The Samaritan woman is such an example. She went to the well to draw water, never expecting to find the Water of Life. Some people find Jesus unexpectedly at a worship service. Perhaps the person went for some other reason than to engage in meaningful spiritual activity, but the Holy Spirit operated through the singing and preaching. The individual discovered the hidden treasure of a personal experience with Jesus Christ. A number of years ago a frivolous young girl—not immoral, but shallow and superficial—went to a church service. Actually, she went to make fun, but as a result of the message and the Holy Spirit's work, she accepted Christ. Someone later wrote of her that she "went to scoff but remained to pray." That girl grew up, matured in the Christian faith, and became an outstanding foreign missionary.

III. Give all you have.

"Life Has Loveliness to Sell" by Sarah Teasdale is a beautiful poem. The last stanza begins, "Sell all you have for loveliness. Buy it and never count the cost." So it is with God's kingdom. Don't miss it because you hold onto something you refuse to give up.

No two people come to Jesus in exactly the same way. Today millions throughout the world suffer physical persecution for their faith in Jesus Christ. In our country we sometimes must endure social ostracism or break family ties, but that is rare. Frequently, however, we are called upon to give up ambitions and lifestyles that are inconsistent with the Christian life. This is a part of the act and process known as repentance. The point of this parable is that if we have to give up everything we have, or are, to be a Christian, it is worth it.

Conclusion

Notice that the man in the parable seized the crucial moment when it came. He did not linger to debate the matter but acted on the moment. James Russell Lowell said, "Once to every man and nation comes the moment to decide." One of life's greatest dangers is that when we are moved by some high impulse we shall not act at once. When we delay the impulse often dies. We must seize the great moments of opportunity while they are present. Someone said it well: "Lord, help us to take advantage of the opportunities of our lifetime during the lifetime of our opportunities."

SUNDAY EVENING, AUGUST 11

Title: What Jesus Preached about Himself

Text: "Believe me that I am in the Father, and the Father in me: or else believe me for the very works' sake" **(John 14:11).**

Scripture Reading: Matthew 11:27–30; John 14:1–11

Introduction

The most distinctive feature of Christianity is its teaching about the person and work of Jesus Christ. John, Peter, and Paul unquestionably teach his deity, preexistence, incarnation, sinless life, messiahship, atoning death, resurrection, ascension, continued intercession, and return in glory. What did Jesus preach about himself?

I. Jesus' preexistence.

A. *Jesus replied to the Jews who said that he was not even fifty years old and could not have seen Abraham, "Verily, verily, I say unto you, Before Abraham was, I am" (John 8:58; see vv. 56–59).* "Before Abraham was born, I existed," he affirmed. He used the same verb "to be" with reference to himself as is used of Jehovah in Exodus 3:14.

B. *Jesus prayed, "And now, O Father, glorify thou me with thine own self with the glory which I had with thee before the world was" (John 17:5).*

II. Jesus' messiahship.

Jesus was the one anointed by God to be the Savior.

A. *His baptism and temptation are meaningless on any other assumption (Matt. 3:13–17; 4:1–11).* At baptism he dedicated himself to the Father's will, which would culminate in his death and resurrection. The voice from heaven saying, "This is my beloved Son, in whom I am well pleased" (Matt. 3:17) combined Psalm 2:7 and Isaiah 42:1. The latter is about the "servant of Jehovah" who is the Messiah. In the temptations, Satan acknowledged that Jesus was the Son of God and urged him to go some way other than that of the cross.

B. *The woman of Samaria said to him, "I know that Messias cometh which is called Christ: when he is come, he will tell us all things. Jesus saith unto her, I that speak unto thee am he" (John 4:25–26).*

C. *Jesus quoted Isaiah 61:1–2 and affirmed that he is the one of whom Isaiah wrote (Luke 4:16–19).* All of the servant passages in Isaiah can therefore be applied to Jesus, including Isaiah 52:13–53:12.

D. *At Caesarea Philippi "Simon Peter answered and said, Thou art the Christ, the Son of the living God" (Matt. 16:16; see vv. 13–20).* Jesus was manifestly pleased with Peter's confession and accepted it as true.

E. *Jesus deliberately fulfilled Zechariah 9:9 (Matt. 21:1–11).* This was a passage understood to be messianic. He proclaimed himself as the Messiah.

F. *Jesus unfolded to his disciples that he was the Messiah of whom God had spoken throughout the Old Testament Scriptures (Luke 24:25–29, 44–49).*

III. Jesus' humanity.

"Son of man" was a term often used by Jesus in reference to himself. For examples, see Matthew 9:6; 12:8, 40; 16:27; 17:22; 25:31; and many others. No one else used this term when referring to him. In Psalm 8:4 the term is a synonym for humankind. Jesus used the term to identify himself with humankind. It emphasized his humility, patience, and suffering.

IV. Jesus' deity.

"Son of God" is a term that expresses ethical likeness to God the Father. Christians are "sons of God" (see John 1:11–13). Jesus is the "Son of God" in a unique sense. John used the term "the only begotten Son" (John 1:18) to express this distinction. Jesus was called the Son of God by others: by the voice of God at his baptism (Matt. 3:17), by Satan (Matt. 4:3, 6), by the demonized (Mark 3:11), by Peter (Matt. 16:16), and by the centurion (Matt. 27:54). Did Jesus conceive of himself as the Son of God? The answer is "Yes," and in a unique sense.

A. *Jesus did not say, "our Father," but "my Father" and "your Father."* As, for example, to Mary Magdalene, "I ascend unto my Father, and your Father; and to my God, and your God" (John 20:17). The model prayer appears to be an exception in which Jesus instructs, "When ye pray, say, Our Father" (Luke 11:2). This prayer, however, is not a prayer that Jesus prays, but rather a model prayer for believers.

B. *In discussing the time of the consummation of the age, Jesus said, "But of that day and that hour knoweth no man, no, not the angels which are in heaven, neither the Son, but the Father" (Mark 13:32).* "The Son" is distinctive. He is calling himself the Son of God in a unique sense.

C. *Similarly in the parable of the vineyard "the son" is different from all who have gone before (Mark 12:1–12).* "Having yet therefore one son, his wellbeloved, he sent him also unto them, saying, They will reverence my son" (Mark 12:6).

D. *Jesus presents himself as the only way to God (Matt. 11:27–30).* He alone knows the Father, and the Father alone completely knows him.

E. *Jesus taught in the temple (Matt. 22:41–46).* The scribes recognized the Messiah as David's son. Jesus said unto them, "How then doth David in spirit call him Lord, saying, The LORD said unto my Lord, Sit thou on my right hand, till I make thine enemies thy footstool? If David then call him Lord, how is he his son? And no man was able to answer him a word"

(Matt. 22:43–46). The answer, of course, is that the Messiah is "the Son of God." Note how Paul expressed it in Romans 1:3–4.

F. *Jesus before the high priest affirmed on oath that he was "the Christ, the Son of the Blessed" (Mark 14:61–64).* Either Jesus was/is the Son of God in a unique sense or he allowed himself to be condemned to death for a misunderstanding.

V. Jesus claimed prerogatives that belong to God.

A. *The power to forgive sins (see Mark 2:5–12; Luke 7:47–50).*
B. *Atonement for sin (see Matt. 26:26; Mark 10:45).*
C. *The gift of eternal life (see Matt. 11:27–30; John 3:14–16; 6:37; 12:32).*
D. *Judge of the world (see Matt. 25:31–46).*
E. *His words the basis of judgment (see Matt. 7:24–27).*
F. *His great "I ams."*
   1. "I am the bread of life" (John 6:35).
   2. "I am the light of the world" (John 8:12).
   3. "I am the door of the sheep" (John 10:7).
   4. "I am the good shepherd" (John 10:11).
   5. "I am the resurrection, and the life" (John 11:25).
   6. "I am the way, the truth, and the life" (John 14:6).
   7. "I am the vine, ye are the branches" (John 15:5).
   8. "I am Alpha and Omega, the beginning and the ending, saith the Lord, which is, and which was, and which is to come, the Almighty" (Rev. 1:8).

Conclusion

These claims on the lips of any other person would be preposterous. They seem natural on the lips of Jesus. They are backed by his life, his character, his power, continuing from his resurrection and ascension until the present time.

WEDNESDAY EVENING, AUGUST 14

Title: The Body That Pleases God

Text: "But God gives [a seed] a body as he has determined, and to each kind of seed he gives its own body" (**1 Cor. 15:38 NIV**).

Scripture Reading: 1 Corinthians 15:35–52

Introduction

The subject of this message is the resurrected body. This subject has been one of much talk and study. It has also been a subject of controversy. Some basic ideas will be presented.

I. In order to have a resurrected body, one of two things must happen.

A. *One must die (1 Cor. 15:36).* This is universally true for all of God's creation. To reach its maximum, it must die. Paul uses the seed as a classic example. A tree, to reach its maximum, must be converted into something other than just a tree—such as lumber. So it is with Christians. In order for them to arrive at God's best, death becomes an entrance.

B. *The Lord will return.* Everyone will not die (1 Cor. 15:51). Some Christians will be alive when the Lord returns. When he does come back, the bodies of those who are still alive will have the same transformation as the dead in Christ (1 Thess. 4:16–17).

II. The resurrected body of the Christian will be pleasing to God and suitable to its environment (1 Cor. 15:38–56).

A. *Paul uses earthly illustrations to prove his point.* People have flesh suitable for their environment according to the plan of God. So do beasts, fish, and birds.

B. *The Christian draws his own conclusions (1 Cor. 15:42–49).*
    1. An age-old question must be considered. Will Christians know each other in heaven? People recognized the glorified body of Jesus. The parable of Lazarus and the rich man seems to teach that same thing. The Lord has arranged for the best, whatever it is.
    2. The resurrected body is part of God's plan. Every change is for the best. Corruptible will put on incorruption and mortal will put on immortality. All defects will be done away with.

III. This glorious resurrected body comes through the power of the resurrected Christ (1 Cor. 15:57).

A. *Jesus came from heaven to take his followers to heaven.* He went through the natural to make humans spiritual.

B. *Because this resurrected body is of Christ, all Christians should take courage.* Believers should take a Christian view of death in time of sorrow. They should rejoice in hope.

Conclusion

You who have lost Christian loved ones by death, rejoice in their welfare. You who are Christians, rejoice in the hope of your future welfare.

SUNDAY MORNING, AUGUST 18

Title: Compare Honestly and You Will Choose Jesus

Text: "When [the merchant] had found [a pearl] of great value, he went away and sold everything he had and bought it" **(Matt. 13:46 NIV).**

Scripture Reading: Matthew 13:45–46

Hymns: "Is Your All on the Altar?" Hoffman
"I Surrender All," Van DeVenter
"Blessed Assurance, Jesus Is Mine," Crosby

Offertory Prayer: Our Father, we know what you would have us to become. Strengthen us that we may be pure, gentle, truthful, high-minded, courteous, and generous. Yet we know that we cannot be these things in our own power. We will fail miserably if we depend on human strength. You have saved us through your death on the cross. Help us to grow in grace, becoming more like you every day that we live. Strengthen us when we are weak and forgive us when we are sinful. Help us to know that a part of our growth in grace is learning to bring material possessions into God's house so that the work of Christ might be carried on.

Accept these gifts today and help us as we channel them into the proper places for the greatest effectiveness in preaching the gospel of Christ. Make us not only generous givers but givers who find happiness in their giving. We pray this in Jesus' name. Amen.

Introduction

In our day gold and silver are precious metals. In Jesus' day, however, pearls were the things most desired. Jewish writers in Old Testament days spoke of the pearl as being "beyond price." Merchants looked the world over for beautiful specimens, and new stories were always circulating about the "greatest pearl of all." In Jesus' story a man finds it.

I. Life is a quest.

Writers have described our time on this earth with many figures of speech. One of the most popular and most meaningful is that of a search. The psalmist said, "O God, thou art my God; early will I seek thee" (Ps. 63:1). Jesus told us to "seek ye first the kingdom of God" (Matt. 6:33).

Our parable today represents the quest for that which would bring us the highest happiness. Often we hear someone say, "She is trying to find herself," which is another way of saying that a person is looking for the one "pearl of great price" that will bring happiness and joy. Too often that person does not realize that happiness will come not in a philosophy nor in a commitment to a superficial cause, but rather it will come when she has found someone big enough to deserve her loyalty and claim her allegiance. We Christians know that this person is Jesus. Only he can bring fulfillment and put an end to the quest.

II. Jesus encourages investigation.

If one person in all the world could cope successfully with his competitors, it was our Savior. He at no time showed any fear of anyone who sought to rival his claim. Jesus knew that if a person made an honest attempt to discover whether or not he was all he claimed, that person would be convinced and become a follower.

When two of the early disciples of John asked Jesus where he lived, he replied, "Come and see" (John 1:39). This has been called the scientific approach. Christianity has always said, "Investigate and decide for yourself." Jesus said on another occasion, "If any man do his will, he shall know of the doctrine, whether it be of God, or whether I speak of myself" (John 7:17).

An outstanding Christian of our day said, "I challenge any person to investigate fully the claims of Christ. I am certain that if he will make an honest survey of the facts and act with integrity, he will give himself in complete commitment to Jesus as Savior and Lord."

III. More than the mind.

In the parable the man seems to have acted merely on business principles. He had heard that somewhere there was a pearl far greater than all others. When he saw it, he knew he wanted it. Perhaps the motivations of both pride and selfishness entered into the decision. We must always, of course, be careful about our motivation in becoming a Christian. In the early stages of our religious impulses, we likewise often act from lesser motives, but God accepts those lesser motives until we can rise to higher ones. The prodigal son came home because he was hungry. In coming, he learned more about his father's love, but it took the "hunger motive" to set him forward on his journey.

In coming to Jesus, we must remember that the heart must make a decision even though the mind is convinced. One attorney said to another, "I know you are a Christian. I am not. I want you to prepare a brief concerning Jesus and present it to me." The Christian lawyer obliged. It was a well drawn up, thoroughly documented brief with the facts clearly stated concerning the validity of Christ's claims. The non-Christian lawyer studied the brief carefully for several days. One morning he said to his attorney friend, "I had an unusual experience. I thought my problem was mental and intellectual. I studied your brief. I found that everything you said about Jesus stood up under critical investigation. I was thoroughly convinced, but then I learned something. My problem was not with my mind. It was with my heart." The man who saw the pearl realized its value, but the deciding factor was that his heart desired it.

IV.A purchase or a gift?

One question has puzzled people: How can God's kingdom be a gift of grace, and yet the parable pictures it as a man's purchase? Again, we can see the error of trying to press every detail in a parable to give us a doctrinal statement. This parable emphasizes the great truth, as does the parable of the hidden treasure, that to be in God's kingdom is greater than having everything else in all the world. Both stories point to the great worth of God's kingdom, but its value is so far beyond all reckoning that any cost of purchase is still a gift.

Whether we come upon Jesus suddenly and unexpectedly—like the hidden treasure in the field—or whether we decide for him after years of search, accompanied by examination and evaluation, the truth is still the same. Bernard of Clairvaux put it beautifully:

> *Thou hope of every contrite heart,*
> *Thou joy of all the meek,*
> *To those who fall how kind thou art,*
> *How good to those who seek.*
>
> *But what to those who find? Ah, this—*
> *Nor tongue nor pen can show!*
> *The love of Jesus, what it is,*
> *None but his loved ones know.*

Conclusion

Joshua gathered Israel before him and recited the history of God's providential healing of the people. He then challenged, "Choose you this day whom ye will serve" (Josh. 24:15). He spoke to the multitudes, but he used the second person singular form when he told them that they must choose. Each one is responsible for his or her own destiny.

Why is it so important to compare and decide? The basic reason is that we cannot have two masters. John Ruskin once said about books, "If I read *this* book, I cannot read *that* book." Likewise, Jesus must be Lord of all or he will not be Lord at all. We cannot mingle our loyalties. We must make every effort to know all the issues and know the final result of our choices. Then we make our decisions based on the evidence. The merchant, once he saw the pearl of great price, knew that he could not live unless he possessed it. Thousands of people have had this experience with Jesus. Once you see him in all of his grace and glory, you know that you must not, yea, you cannot, live without him!

SUNDAY EVENING, AUGUST 18

Title: What Jesus Preached about the Holy Spirit

Text: "If ye love me, keep my commandments. And I will pray the Father, and he shall give you another Comforter, that he may abide with you for ever; even the Spirit of truth; whom the world cannot receive, because it seeth him not, neither knoweth him: but ye know him; for he dwelleth with you, and shall be in you. I will not leave you comfortless: I will come to you" **(John 14:15–18).**

Scripture Reading: John 14:15–31; 16:6–16

Introduction

Almost all Christians from the first century to the present have believed in the Trinity. No one of us has ever entirely understood the doctrine. The word *Trinity* is not in the Scripture, yet the Trinity certainly exists. Jesus' revelation of himself, and of the Holy Spirit as preexistent and divine, forces such an explanation. It ought not to surprise us that God is too wonderful for us to understand. If he were small enough for us to comprehend, he would not be great enough to worship. The doctrine of the Trinity did not come from logical reasoning. It was revealed. It is not contrary to reason, but it is beyond reason. It accords with our Christian experience. We know God as Father, Son, and Holy Spirit. We pray to the Father, or to the Son, or to the Holy Spirit with perfect understanding that we are praying to the one God who has so revealed himself.

Christians must guard against the error of tritheism. Christianity is as monotheistic as Judaism. If one must err, better to err toward the view that God, the Supreme Person, adopts the modes of Father, Son, and Holy Spirit than to believe the error that the three persons of the Godhead are three Gods. Our purpose in this message is to note what Jesus preached about the Holy Spirit.

I. The Holy Spirit is a person.

A. *He thinks, feels, wills, teaches, guides, can be grieved, and so on.* In fact, he has all of the qualities of a person. (In a few instances in the King James Version the Holy Spirit is referred to as "it," but the translators were strictly following grammatical rules because "spirit" or "ghost" in the original language was neuter.) The Holy Spirit, or Holy Ghost, is not an impersonal power or influence.

B. *He is God, now acting directly on the hearts of persons.* "Spirit of God," "Spirit of Jesus," "Spirit of Truth," "Spirit of Christ," "the Comforter," "the Paraclete," are all synonymous names for the Holy Spirit.

II. The Holy Spirit is eternal but came at Pentecost as Jesus had promised.

A. *Jesus talked with his disciples about the Holy Spirit on the night before his crucifixion.* We are indebted to the apostle John for the record in John 13–17. A major theme was the coming of the Holy Spirit to inaugurate the gospel age. Hear Jesus in our text, John 14:15–18. This theme also was continued that night as recorded in John 14:26; 15:25–27; 16:14–16. Just prior to his ascension Jesus renewed the Great Commission and said, "Behold, I send the promise of my Father upon you: but tarry ye in the city of Jerusalem, until ye be endued with power from on high" (Luke 24:49; see also Acts 1:4–8).

B. *At Pentecost the Holy Spirit manifested himself as Jesus had promised.* Just as Jesus did not begin to exist at his miraculous birth in Bethlehem, the Holy Spirit did not begin to exist at Pentecost. The Word and the Holy Spirit existed before creation. At Pentecost the Holy Spirit entered a new phase of his work as had Jesus at the incarnation. Appropriate miracles accompanied the incarnation, such as the miraculous birth, the angelic choir, and the guiding star. Appropriate miracles accompanied the coming of the Holy Spirit including the sound as of a mighty wind, tongues like as of fire, and the gift of languages.

III. The Holy Spirit has work to do.

A. *He glorifies Jesus.* Luke wrote his gospel "of all that Jesus began both to do and teach, until the day he was taken up, after that he through the Holy Ghost had given commandments unto the apostles whom he had chosen" (Acts 1:1–2). He wrote the book of Acts concerning all that the Holy Spirit continued to do and teach. The Holy Spirit glorifies Jesus. He brings to remembrance the teachings of Jesus just as Jesus had promised in John 14:26; 15:26–27; 16:12–15. The Holy Spirit executes the testament of Jesus. The mission enterprise is directed by him. God the Father thought it; God the Son brought it; God the Holy Spirit wrought it.

B. *He works for the unsaved.*

1. He convicts us of the sin of not believing in Jesus. He convicts us concerning the righteousness of believing in Jesus because Jesus is deity and goes to the Father. The Holy Spirit convicts us concerning the judgment and the folly of believing in Satan who already stands condemned (see John 16:8–11).

2. He invites sinners to turn to Jesus for salvation, "Wherefore, as the Holy Ghost saith, To day if ye will hear his voice, Harden not your hearts" (Heb. 3:7–8). "And the Spirit and the bride say, Come. And let him that heareth say, Come. And let him that is athirst come. And whosoever will, let him take the water of life freely" (Rev. 22:17).

3. The Holy Spirit is the agent in regeneration (see John 3:3–8). "The wind bloweth where it listeth, and thou hearest the sound thereof, but canst not tell whence it cometh, and whither it goeth; so is every one that is born of the Spirit" (John 3:8; see also Rom. 8:9, 14; Titus 3:5).

C. *He works for the Christian.*

1. He takes the place of Jesus. Jesus promised, "Lo, I am with you alway, even unto the end of the world" (Matt. 28:20), and again, "I will not leave you comfortless: I will come to you" (John 14:18). He said, "And I will pray the Father, and he shall give you another Comforter, that he may abide with you for ever" (John 14:16). "Another Comforter" means another of the same kind. Would you go so far as to say that Jesus departed from his incarnate state that he might return as the Holy Spirit? In the days of his flesh he was limited to one locality by his body. Now he can be everywhere.

2. He abides in every believer. "Now if any man have not the Spirit of Christ, he is none of his" (Rom. 8:9).

   a. The Holy Spirit bears witness to one's salvation. "And hope maketh not ashamed; because the love of God is shed abroad in our hearts by the Holy Ghost which is given unto us" (Rom. 5:5; see also Rom. 8:15–17).

   b. The Holy Spirit helps the Christian to pray. "Likewise the Spirit also helpeth our infirmities: for we know not what we should pray for as we ought: but the Spirit, itself maketh intercession for us with groanings which cannot be uttered. And he that searcheth the hearts knoweth what is the mind of the Spirit, because he maketh intercession for the saints according to the will of God" (Rom. 8:26–27).

   c. The Holy Spirit helps in warfare against the carnal life (see Gal. 5:16–17, 25).

   d. The Holy Spirit gives wisdom and direction in witnessing. He guided Philip to the Ethiopian eunuch (see Acts 8:26–40). He directed Peter to Cornelius and prepared both for their encounter (see Acts 10:1–11:18). The Spirit would not allow Paul to go into Bithynia, then opened the door to the larger opportunity in Europe (see Acts 16:6–12).

3. The Holy Spirit is sovereign. He gives gifts as he will and to whom he will. He gives different persons different gifts. In different ages, he gives gifts as he will (see 1 Cor. 12).

Conclusion

Let us think of the Holy Spirit as God himself rather than as some power of God. We pray not that we may have more of the Holy Spirit, but rather that the Holy Spirit may have all of us.

The Holy Spirit respects our free will. We may sometimes pray that God's Holy Spirit will force stubborn sinful hearts, but he never does. As does Jesus, he knocks on the heart's door but will not break it down.

"Be filled with the Spirit," Paul pleads (Eph. 5:18). The verb is present tense, continuous action, meaning, "Keep on being filled." God does the filling, and our part is to let him do so.

The Holy Spirit speaks. "He that hath ears, let him hear what the Spirit saith unto the churches" (Rev. 2:7). We hear that for which we listen. On the city street the naturalist may hear a cricket chirp. The parent says, "I hear my child." Let the child of God listen for the voice of the Holy Spirit.

WEDNESDAY EVENING, AUGUST 21

Title: Concerning the Collection

Text: "Now concerning the collection for the saints, as I have given order" **(1 Cor. 16:1).**

Scripture Reading: 1 Corinthians 16:1–4

Introduction

God is concerned about the collection. This truth is found in both the Old Testament and the New Testament. Failure to follow the scriptural plan for money to provide for the Lord's work brings on chaos. Every Christian, whether a pastor or some other church worker, should be interested in the offering. Six ideas are mentioned in this passage that each follower of Christ needs to grasp.

I. The period of the collection.

"Upon the first day of the week" (1 Cor. 16:2).

A. *The day of worship and spiritual recuperation is the time for worship in giving.* In the Old Testament it was the Lord's Sabbath. In the New Testament, it is the Lord's day. Followers of the Lord Jesus are not to bring their offerings to the house of the Lord merely at their own convenience, but as the Lord says.

B. *This period of time when Christians worship in giving provides for the needs of kingdom work throughout the year.* If all of God's children gave only once a year, it could mean chaos to the financing of the Lord's work.

II. The person of the collection.

"Let every one of you" (1 Cor. 16:2).

A. *The Lord wants the giver.* The almighty God to whom all things belong does not need our money as such. What he wants is our whole self.

B. *There is a real democracy in spiritual giving.* People are not saved in masses, but as individuals. People also receive God's providential care and blessings as individuals and not in a mass. People are to give as individuals. Every person should participate.

III. The place of the collection.

"Lay by him in store" (1 Cor. 16:2).

A. *The storehouse, as a biblical term, needs careful consideration.* In the Old Testament it was the tabernacle or temple. In the New Testament it is the church.

B. *The storehouse for Christians today is the church.* Giving in and through the church is the best way to bring honor and glory to God. Other things to which people give should be over and beyond what one gives through the church.

IV. The portion of the collection.

"As God hath prospered him" (1 Cor. 16:2). Basically this is the tithe.

A. *The tithe is the most equitable standard of giving.*

B. *The tithe is to be brought to the storehouse.*

C. *The portion is as God has prospered.*

V. The purpose of the collection.

"That there be no gatherings" (1 Cor. 16:2).

A. *Giving should be done in order.* This is an orderly and systematic way of giving, rather than spasmodic giving according to one's whims.

B. *Giving should be done in order that the Lord's works can be carried on according to his plan (Mal. 3:10).*

VI. The protection of the collection.

"Whomsoever ye shall approve" (1 Cor. 16:3).

A. *Christian people should have a system for handling God's money.* This applies to the collecting and the counting of the money. It also applies to a church budget.

B. *There should be honesty in the administration of the money.*

Conclusion

Scriptural giving is a distinct mark of a Bible-believing Christian. It is my plea that you will follow God's plan in this matter.

SUNDAY MORNING, AUGUST 25

Title: God's Kingdom Excludes Only the Unbeliever

Text: "Which, when [the net] was full, they drew to shore, and sat down, and gathered the good into vessels, but cast the bad away" **(Matt. 13:48).**

Scripture Reading: Matthew 13:47–50

Hymns: "The Master Hath Come," Doudney
"Must I Go, and Empty-Handed," Luther
"Bring Them In," Thomas

Offertory Prayer: Our Father, help us remember that you are always present to give help in times of our struggles. Help us to live our days in such a way that we have no regrets when the evenings come. Help us to fix our eyes on you as our help, as our aim, as the very center of our being, and as our everlasting Friend. Guide us in whatever path you see fit, and help us to accept your purposes for us even when we do not understand why it is your will for us to walk in a certain way. Give us the faith that we need to go forward, but give us the patience that we need so that we may wait when that is necessary. Accept our gifts this morning and use them to do the things that we cannot do ourselves. Bless the many people who will be affected by these gifts, and help us to realize that we have not discharged our entire duty merely because we have brought our money into the storehouse. Make us vessels that can be used effectively in personal living and daily witnessing. Make this part of the worship service vital and meaningful to each of us—as sacred and holy as the preaching, the praying, and the singing. We pray in Jesus' name. Amen.

Introduction

This parable has a close connection with the parable of the wheat and tares. In both, the thought is put forward that we will know the difference between the genuine Christian and one who merely claims to be a Christian when our Lord makes the distinction at the end of time as we know it. Both parables should teach us patience in dealing with people and tolerance concerning those who do not share every conviction we hold. Let the Master decide who the counterfeit people are, who are Christians but may be wrong on certain points, and who are the genuinely devoted Christians who understand the will of God in all things. Indeed, can any of us be bold and boastful enough to claim infallibility in discerning the truths of God and sinless in implementing his commandments?

I.A parable of everyday life.

A.   *The dragnet is what we usually call the seine net.* In New Testament days it probably had corks at the top and weights at the bottom, making it stand upright in the water. The fishermen would attach ropes to the four corners and draw it through the sea. Into it were swept all kinds of things including, of course, great numbers of fish. When it was brought to shore, the men sorted out the things caught in the net. The usable fish were delivered to the market. The useless things were thrown away.

B. *Most of the disciples lived in the general area where the fishing business prospered.* They would identify quickly with this story, for they had often seen what has been called the "drama of the dragnet." We can almost imagine as we read the parable that we see the squirming, leaping mass of fish with the sun shining on their iridescent scales. Jesus admired wholesome toil and no doubt took great delight in telling a simple story of everyday life to the masses in order that they might profit spiritually. We should not seek to attach special significance to every part of the story nor attach special meanings to the net, sea, or beach, or try to force the parable into precise analogies. The simple and obvious meaning in the parable must have been what Jesus intended. He did not expect his hearers in that day, or our day, to look for deep and hidden meanings to his stories. Indeed, the simplicity of Jesus in his teaching was, and is, one of the things that makes him universally attractive to and accepted by all people, especially the simple and unsophisticated masses.

II. Diversity of the kingdom's members.

One thing stands out as quite significant in our Savior's ministry. He had an "across-the-board" approach that reached men and women of all temperaments and lifestyles. Christ has a "universality" of appeal. No other religious leader had the ability to reach people at all levels of life—educational, cultural, emotional, economic. The oriental religious leaders could not do it, because they were too mystical. Greek philosophy could not do it, for it was too academic. Islam could not do it, because it was too militant. Only Jesus had the ability to pull together all things in the world around himself. He was the source of creation and is the goal of creation. When we grasp the centrality of Jesus, we see all other things in relationship to him. One of our poets expressed it this way:

> *I see his blood upon the rose;*
> > *And in the stars the glory of his eyes,*
> *His body gleams amid eternal snows,*
> > *His tears fall from the skies.*

> *I see his face in every flower;*
> > *The thunder and the singing of the birds,*
> *Are but his voice... and carved by his power,*
> > *Rocks are his written words.*

All pathways by his feet are worn;
His strong heart stirs the ever-beating sea,
His crown of thorns entwined with every thorn,
His cross is every tree.

—Joseph Mary Plunkett

III. Don't be left out.

When the gospel net is flung into the world, it attracts people in great abundance. Some, of course, do not respond. They excuse themselves! They choose to be unbelievers and resist every impression the Holy Spirit makes upon their hearts.

Another group is excluded—those who come into the "net" but are never actually transformed by the Holy Spirit. Analogies often overlap and fail to state exactly in detail everything that refers to the matter. For instance, this parable is similar to the parable of the wheat and tares in that it points to the harvest, or judgment, when a separation will take place. In this parable, the casting away of the "bad" fish seems to symbolize the testing of the believer to ascertain whether or not his works prove the genuineness of his salvation experience.

One simple fact stands out clearly! The kingdom is for everybody, but unless one is a genuine believer, he or she is not truly a child of God and will not receive the rewards of the Christian life at the end of time. Many touchstones may be suggested to prove one's experience is real. Is our life in harmony with the principles taught by Jesus? Do we keep ourselves pure from the polluting influence of sin? Are we genuinely concerned about those who have needs in the world? In a sense, every day is a judgment day. As we live, our works are tested. The swiftly passing moments reveal our character to those with whom we associate in day-by-day relationships. The full story, however, will not be told until the King separates the sheep from the goats. Don't miss out on the greatest privilege in the world, that of being a member of God's kingdom! Respond to the gospel call! Also, be sure that your response is a genuine surrender to Christ, accepting all the implications of being a member of God's kingdom.

Conclusion

This parable emphasizes the importance of all Christians working together to assure maximum results in God's kingdom. Divisions in Christ's work tear the net apart and should be avoided. This does not mean that we are to compromise basic convictions, but it does mean that we should seek to understand other Christians and work with them.

The net's efficiency depends on the soundness of the entire fiber and the skill with which it is woven together. Every part of God's kingdom should contribute to the other parts in order to make the net as large and strong as it possibly can be. We need each other, and we need to learn how to help each other further God's work in the world.

The net is not to blame because some bad fish get into it. Neither is the fishing a failure any more than the sowing of the seed was a failure because so much that was sown fell on stony soil or weed-encumbered ground. The Lord is continually sending out his fishermen, and they are constantly casting their nets into the sea. We shall never win everybody to Christ, but we need to keep on trying to reach as many as possible!

SUNDAY EVENING, AUGUST 25

Title: What Jesus Preached about His Death

Text: "For even the Son of man came not to be ministered unto, but to minister, and to give his life a ransom for many" **(Mark 10:45).**

Scripture Reading: Luke 24:25–27, 44–49

Introduction

Records of Jesus' death and related events take up from one-fourth to one-third of the space in the Gospels. This shows how important his death seemed to the writers. Paul gave much space to the death of Christ. What place did Jesus' own death hold in his mind?

I. In his early ministry Jesus did not emphasize his death as much as later.

A. *This was necessarily so.* An early emphasis would have confused the disciples. They must first come to know and experience his divine character.

B. *There is clear evidence that from the beginning of his ministry Jesus knew he was born to die.*

1. His baptism (Matt. 3:13–17). Baptism is a picture of death and resurrection. Jesus was dedicating himself to a ministry that will culminate in death and resurrection. The voice of the Father, saying, "This is my beloved Son, in whom I am well pleased" (Matt. 3:17), combined Psalm 2:7 and Isaiah 42:1 to designate Jesus as the beloved Son of God and the Servant of Jehovah. He is now "fulfilling all righteousness" (Matt. 3:15) by publicly declaring his purpose to die and rise again.

2. The temptations in the wilderness (see Matt. 4:1–11; Luke 4:1–13) seem to be clearly based on the assumption that Jesus has committed himself to the way of death in submitting to God's will. Satan proposed the way of military power, of miracle working, and of compromise.

3. In his early Judean ministry Jesus predicted his death and resurrection, but no one understood his sign at that time (see John 2:17–22).

4. In his famous interview with Nicodemus, Jesus said, "And as Moses lifted up the serpent in the wilderness, even so must the Son of man be lifted up: That whosoever believeth in him should not perish, but have eternal life" (John 3:14–15). Probably neither Nicodemus nor the disciples understood, but Jesus knew that he would be lifted up on the cross and that it would be effectual for the salvation of believers.

5. In the synagogue at Nazareth, Jesus identified himself as the Servant of Jehovah proclaimed by the prophet Isaiah. He read Isaiah 61:1–2 and said, "This day is this scripture fulfilled in your ears" (Luke 4:21). A person, upon the authority of Jesus himself, is justified in applying to Jesus all of the Servant of Jehovah passages including Isaiah 52:13–53:12, which reveals much about Jesus' concept of his death by crucifixion.

6. Two other early incidental references are found in Mark 2:18–20 and in Matthew 12:39–40, in which Jesus implied that he had come to die.

II. Jesus introduced a new emphasis at the Great Confession.

A. *At Caesarea Philippi, Simon Peter, undoubtedly speaking for all of the disciples, affirmed, "Thou art the Christ, the Son of the living God" (Matt. 16:16).* Now that the disciples knew by revelation that Jesus was the Messiah (although the subsequent record shows that they were far from understanding the nature of his messiahship), Jesus seemed almost eager to explain to them about his coming death. "From that time forth began Jesus to shew unto his disciples, how that he must go unto Jerusalem, and suffer many things of the elders, and chief priests and scribes, and be killed, and be raised again the third day" (Matt. 16:21). When we read in succession Mark 8:31; 9:31–32; and 10:32–45, we are impressed with Jesus' eagerness to instruct them. Very significant is Jesus' explanation, "For even the Son of man came not to be ministered unto, but to minister, and to give his life a ransom for many" (Mark 10:45). The ransom was the price paid to free a slave. Jesus paid the price to free us from the penalty of sin. He did for us what we could not do for ourselves. The disciples did not understand the nature of Christ's death until after the resurrection. The record of his prediction stands, however, that we need not misunderstand.

B. *During his later Judean ministry, Jesus spoke the parable of the Good Shepherd (John 10:1–21).* In this allegory Jesus affirms that he is the Good Shepherd. He knows his sheep and loves them. He voluntarily will give his life for the sheep. It is the Father's will that he do this. Death and resurrection are always united in Jesus' thought. His sheep from different folds (both Jews and Gentiles) will become one flock with one shepherd. "There are other sheep which belong to me that are not in this sheep pen. I must bring them, too; they will listen to my voice, and they will become one flock with one shepherd. The Father loves me because I am willing to give up my life, in order that I may receive it back again. No one takes my life away from me. I give it up of my own free will. I have the right to take it back. This is what my Father has commanded me to do" (John 10:16–18 TEV).

C. *The memorial supper.* (See Matt. 26:26–29; Mark 14:22–25; Luke 22:17–20; and 1 Cor. 11:23–26.) On the night before his crucifixion Jesus observed the Passover with his disciples in the upper room. The paschal meal commemorated the passing over of the children of Israel by the death angel. Jesus instituted a new Passover for perpetual observance of the passing over of our sins by the Lamb without blemish slain from the foundation of the world. The bread and the wine represent the body and blood of the Messiah, which were given for us sinners. Jesus' statement, "This is my blood of the new testament, which is shed for many for the remission of sins" (Matt. 26:28), affirms that his self-giving was essential to the forgiveness of sins. He does for us what we could not do for ourselves.

D. *In Gethsemane.* (See Matt. 26:36–46; Mark 14:32–42; Luke 22:39–46.) Jesus prayed earnestly, "Father, if thou be willing, remove this cup from me: nevertheless not my will, but thine, be done" (Luke 21:42). The cup was more than human death. The cup was filled with the penalty of the sins of all of us. Jesus' real prayer was not that the cup be taken away, but that the Father's will should be done. The author of Hebrews was correct when he wrote, "In his life on earth Jesus made his prayers and requests with loud cries and tears to God, who could save him from death. Because he was humble and devoted, God heard him" (Heb. 5:7 TEV).

E. *On Calvary's cross Jesus applied Psalm 22 to himself: "My God, my God, why hast thou forsaken me?" (Matt. 27:46).* The "why" is not so much "For what reason?" as "To what purpose?" Psalm 22 answers the question. The opening verses describe the crucifixion. In verse 21 the one crucified replies, "For thou hast heard me," and the remaining verses indicate that through him "all the ends of the world shall remember and turn unto the LORD and all the kindreds of the nations shall worship before thee" (Ps. 22:27).

III. In his postresurrection period Jesus taught about his death.

It is impossible to overemphasize the importance of Jesus' instruction to his disciples following his resurrection. In accord with his own predictions Jesus died and arose. The disciples could not understand how the Messiah could die. For example, witness the despair of Cleopas and his friend after Jesus' death. Hope had died. "But we trusted that it had been he which should have redeemed Israel: and beside all this, today is the third day since these things were done" (Luke 24:21). Hope was dead. They did not know their Bible. Jesus opened to them the teachings of the Scriptures about the

Messiah: "Ought not Christ to have suffered these things, and to enter into his glory? And beginning at Moses and all the prophets, he expounded unto them in all the scriptures the things concerning himself" (Luke 24:26–27). Later, to all of the disciples Jesus taught what God had been telling them through their Hebrew Bible: "These are the words which I spake unto you, while I was yet with you, that all things must be fulfilled, which were written in the law of Moses, and in the prophets, and in the psalms, concerning me. Then opened he their understanding, that they might understand the scriptures. And said unto them, Thus it is written, and thus it behooved Christ to suffer and to rise from the dead the third day: And that repentance and remission of sins should be preached in his name among all nations, beginning at Jerusalem. And ye are witnesses of these things. And, behold, I send the promise of my Father upon you: but tarry ye in the city of Jerusalem, until ye be endued with power from on high" (Luke 24:44–49). His death was in accordance with the Old Testament. Through death he has now come to glory. All authority is now his (Matt. 28:19). The gospel of repentance and remission of sin in his name is to be preached to all nations in the power of the Holy Spirit.

Conclusion

A. *Jesus went voluntarily to the cross.* He taught that his death was necessary for the forgiveness of sin.

B. *It was not simply that Jesus died, but that it was Jesus who died.* His deity and sinlessness are essential to his atonement.

C. *Every prophecy about salvation spoken by God in time past was fulfilled in Jesus.* He is the interpreter of the Scriptures about his death.

D. *In the cross are magnified and demonstrated God's hatred of sin and his love of the sinner.*

E. *All was in accord with God's will. Because God so loved the world, Jesus died on the cross.* His death did not cause God to love the world.

WEDNESDAY EVENING, AUGUST 28

Title: A First Worship Service

Text: "And Abel, he also brought of the firstlings of his flock and of the fat thereof. And the LORD had respect unto Abel and to his offering" (**Gen. 4:4**).

Scripture Reading: Genesis 4:1–6

Introduction

A young couple was excited as they prepared for worship on a particular Sunday. For four years their young son had been in preschool care during the church service and thus had never attended a service with his parents.

The time had arrived for the son to have his first visit in worship. Naturally, he was inquisitive about almost every element of the service.

Genesis is a book of beginnings. The fourth chapter has a record of man's first experience in worship. Abel knew how to worship. The acceptability of Abel's offering revolved around his attitude. Abel chose the "firstlings," which means the best.

Believers in today's world need to learn how to worship. Let us observe the attitudes that make worship acceptable.

I. A profound reverence for God.

A. *Abel acknowledged the transcendence of God.* Though primitive in his concept of God, Abel recognized the greatness of God. He knew about God's omnipotent power. He had a great respect for God. By giving an offering, Abel acknowledged that the Lord deserved his admiration.

B. *Worship can be enhanced by a profound reverence for the Lord.* Rudolph Otto, in his book *The Idea of the Holy,* indicated that the distinctive feature of worship in a human being is awe of the presence of God.

Check through the Bible, and you will discover that worship begins with reverence. "And one cried unto another, and said, Holy, holy, holy, is the LORD of hosts: the whole earth is full of his glory. And the posts of the door moved at the voice of him that cried, and the house was filled with smoke" (Isa. 6:3–4).

II. A confession of sin.

A. *Abel acknowledged his creatureliness.* Abel faced the fact that he was a frail creature of dust subject to the fallibilities and rebellions of life. Having this self-concept moved Abel to tell God the truth about himself. His offering to God could have been confession that he belonged to a fallen race. Abel was familiar with sin because of his parents' past. Sin was not a doctrine to him; it was a real experience.

B. *Worship involves a confession of sin.* Since sin is a problem, proper worship includes confession of sin. This means that we acknowledge our humanity. Confessing our humanity leads inevitably to the acknowledgment and confession of sins.

Check through the Bible and discover that after a person's profound vision of God, a painful view of self occurs. "Then said I, Woe is me! for I am undone; because I am a man of unclean lips, and I dwell in the midst of a people of unclean lips; for mine eyes have seen the King, the LORD of hosts" (Isa. 6:5).

III. A personal commitment to God.

A. *Abel's worship led to action.* Abel's worship did not involve just the use of words. It involved action. He brought a choice animal from his flock.

Abel was not content merely to adore God and to look within himself. He gave his best to God.

Abel's commitment cost him his life, but he continued to influence the lives of people. "By faith Abel offered unto God a more excellent sacrifice than Cain, by which he obtained witness that he was righteous, God testifying of his gifts: and by it he being dead yet speaketh" (Heb. 11:4).

B. *Worship involved personal commitment.* Worship falls short if it involves only emotional adoration of God and sorrow over sin. Authentic worship leads us to give of our possessions. It leads us to give our best in personal dedication before a watching world.

Conclusion

Have you evaluated your worship lately? Abel caught a glimpse of the great God and the inadequacy of himself. He gave his best in worship, demonstrating his personal commitment to God.

Once a man came to the church building just as the benediction was being pronounced. He asked the usher, "Is the service over?" "No," the usher replied, "the worship is over, but the service is just about to begin."

SEPTEMBER

■ Sunday Mornings

Complete the series "The Master Speaks to the Present through the Parables" on the first Sunday of the month. Then begin the series "The Joy of Being a Giver." The fun of receiving is so great that many people never fully experience the joy of being givers. Jesus taught that we are to be givers if we would find the true joy of living.

■ Sunday Evenings

Continue with the theme "Jesus Came Preaching," emphasizing some of the great truths that Jesus dealt with in his ministry to human needs.

■ Wednesday Evenings

Continue the series "Warnings from the Past."

SUNDAY MORNING, SEPTEMBER I

Title: We Need Both the Old and the New

Text: "Therefore...the kingdom of heaven is like unto a man that...bringeth forth out of his treasure things new and old" **(Matt. 13:52).**

Scripture Reading: Matthew 13:51–53

Hymns: "Faith of Our Fathers," Faber
"Serve the Lord with Gladness," McKinney
"Face to Face with Christ," Breck

Offertory Prayer: Lord, help us to remember that Jesus is not merely a person in a book. Nor is he merely someone who lived and died. Help us rather to know that he is with us even though we cannot see him and that through his gift of the Holy Spirit he can warn us in our times of temptation and help us in our times of difficulty. May we realize that he is present as we bring our tithes and offerings. Help us to give because we love our Savior, not merely because we know he is aware of how much we give. May we, because we love him dearly, love the people whom he loves, even the whole world, including those who have not yet come into a saving relationship with the Savior. Bless this offering that it might be used to tell people everywhere the "old, old story" that is ever new. We pray in Jesus' name. Amen.

Introduction

When Jesus finished the series of parables found in Matthew 13, he added one in summary. He inquired as to how much of what he had been saying was comprehended by his listeners. To his question as to whether or not his disciples understood all of these things, they immediately replied, "Yea, Lord" (Matt. 13:51). Whether or not they actually did, we do not know. In all probability they had caught something of his message, but there was much more to it than they realized. Jesus did not debate with them any more than he did with the rich young ruler who insisted that he had kept all the commandments from his youth (Mark 10:20). Rather, Jesus went on to make a point that he felt was significant.

I. The old is important.

Since truth is timeless, it is literally "as old as the hills." A part of the treasure God gives us is that of a great heritage. Jesus reached into the Old Testament for much of his teachings. Indeed, scarcely anything can be found coming from the mouth of Jesus that does not have its roots deep in the Jewish faith. Jesus insisted he did not come to destroy the law. He loved old things and built his teaching on truths that had been accepted for centuries.

Wise people listen to the voices of those who have lived a long time. Someone said that experience is the *best* teacher, but another answered, "Experience is the *only* teacher." Whether or not we learn anything from any source except experience may be debatable, but one thing is certain: We can learn much from the past! The true meaning of conservative is not a mossback, anti-progressive "killjoy" who refuses to accept anything new. Rather, a true conservative is one who wishes to "conserve" the good things of the past. All of us need that spirit. The kingdom of God is built on that which has been tested, tried, and proved.

II. But Jesus brought us something new.

Although our Master did not intend for those who came to him to forget all they knew, at the same time, he demanded that they see their previous knowledge in a new light and use it in a new service. When we do this, life becomes greater than it ever has been previously.

Many new things are happening every day. Christianity does not demand or even suggest that we try to halt the world's progress. Life will go on, new methods of doing things will be discovered, and new approaches in every field will make previous ones outdated. In the realm of the moral and spiritual, however, we will never improve on our Savior's message. Based on the Old Testament, but adding life and spirit to it, Jesus gives us a way of life that can cope with new conditions as they arise. When a person declares himself for Christ, he does not always give up things, but sometimes he rather uses them to the glory of God's kingdom. A man in business does not necessarily give up his business, unless it is an absolutely wicked one; rather, he runs it as a Christian should. In whatever field we are engaged, we can use the gifts and talents that make us successful in that field to further the work of our Lord.

Indeed, those countries that have accepted Christ and the light of the gospel have been those that have been most creative and innovative in discovering new things. Why? Because Jesus is truth, and truth always moves forward. One should not fear that the gospel cannot defend itself when investigated and examined. In fact, Jesus invited people to investigate his teachings when he said, "If any man will do his will, he shall know of the doctrine, whether it be of God, or whether I speak of myself" (John 7:17). When Pilate asked Jesus, "What is truth?" (John 18:38), the Savior might have replied, "Truth is that which gives a person inner security because he is willing to accept the realities of the past but also willing to receive new revelations, examine them, and give allegiance to them if they are worthy of acceptance."

> *Truth, crushed to earth, shall rise again;*
> *Th' eternal years of God are hers;*
> *But Error, wounded, writhes in pain,*
> *And dies among his worshipers.*

> —Author unknown

Jesus brought us a kingdom of truth because he himself was and is the Truth. This means more than the fact that he never told a falsehood. Of course, he didn't! When Jesus made this great claim about himself, however, he meant that he was the fullness of the Fatherhood come to earth in human form. People had been searching for centuries to understand what God was like. Jesus came to earth to show them the truth about God because he himself was and is God. He came to "make all things new" (Rev. 21:5).

III. The old must have a new birth.

The transition from the old life to the new is by means of a spiritual birth. Although many metaphors and figures of speech are used in the New Testament to describe the Christian life, one consistent figure describes the entrance upon the new life. Jesus calls it a "birth from above," and Paul used the same figure of speech when he said, "Therefore if any man be in Christ, he is a new creature" (2 Cor. 5:17). Paul combined both the old and the new when he said, "Old things are passed away; behold, all things are become new." This is the supreme truth of the gospel.

Paul's previous statement must, of course, be interpreted in light of other truths. The "old things" that are sinful are passed away in that they are forgiven, washed in the blood of the Savior. This is not inconsistent with saying that Jesus can use the "old things" in our life and build upon them. Not all old things are sinful. They may be inadequate and incomplete. If so, God can incorporate them into Jesus Christ and use them. If they are sinful, they must, of course, be eliminated. It should be emphasized again, however, that in Christ all things become new!

Conclusion

This parable was not meant so much to be a theological statement as it was to be a practical one. Jesus concluded his teachings in parables on this occasion with one that would combine and interpret all of the others. Wherever truth is found, Jesus is present. A wise follower of Jesus will give proper respect to the past, evaluate it in terms of its relationship to Jesus Christ, and do with it as the Spirit leads. A wise person will accept the truth in Jesus because he is the Truth. In him we can build our lives with assurance and find security in knowing that he is God and in him God's truth has come to earth in human form!

SUNDAY EVENING, SEPTEMBER I

Title: What Jesus Preached about His Church

Text: "I tell you, you are Peter, and on this rock I will build my church, and the powers of death shall not prevail against it" **(Matt. 16:18).**

Scripture Reading: Matthew 16:13–23; 18:15–20

Introduction

More than one hundred times in the Gospels Jesus is reported as using the terms *kingdom, kingdom of God,* or *kingdom of heaven.* On only two occasions is he reported as using the word *church,* namely, in Matthew 16:18 and 18:17. To conclude from this fact, however, that the church was of minor importance in Jesus' thinking, would be erroneous.

Jesus had promised that the Holy Spirit would guide the disciples into all truth (see John 16:12–14). The added light thrown on the nature and purpose of the church by Acts and the Epistles is doubtless a fulfillment of Jesus' promise. The purpose of this message, however, is confined to "What Jesus Preached about His Church."

I. The principles and teachings about the kingdom of God are valid for his church.

A. *What Jesus taught about salvation as the gift of God received on the basis of repentance and faith is an eternally valid principle.* He certainly would not establish a church where salvation could be obtained by some other means.

B. *Jesus taught that the kingdom of God is a democracy of equals.* No one is given preferred treatment. Greatness in his kingdom will be on the basis of faithful service (see Mark 10:36–45). Surely Jesus would not establish a church with autocratic principles.

C. *Jesus taught that a Christian had obligations to God and obligations to the state.* He said, "Render therefore to Caesar the things that are Caesar's; and to God the things that are God's" (Matt. 22:21 RSV). The implication is that when the civil authority and the religious representatives remain in their proper spheres, a person can be a good Christian and a good citizen without compromise or conflict. Surely our Lord would not want his church to dominate the state nor to be controlled by it.

D. *Jesus clearly taught that it is not his disciples' right nor responsibility to destroy heretics by force (see Matt. 13:24–30, 36–43).* Jesus intends to conquer, but his weapons are love and truth. He has not established his church to conquer by force.

E. *Jesus is Lord.* His lordship is undelegated. He would not and has not established a church to which he delegates authority to forgive sins or to grant or to withhold salvation.

F. *Everything that Jesus has taught in his parables, in the Sermon on the Mount, or elsewhere will be consistent with what he teaches about his church.* Every promise or command that applies to a disciple as an individual continues valid for that disciple as a church member. The church is to help Christians to do better cooperatively what they desire to do anyway because they are Christians.

II. Jesus teaches about his church in the Scriptures.

A. *It was important that the disciples come to believe on Jesus as Messiah and Lord (Matt. 16:13–23).* In answer to Jesus' direct question, "But who do you say that I am?" Simon Peter replied, "You are the Christ, the Son of the living God" (Matt. 16:15–16 RSV). Jesus was obviously pleased with Peter's reply. Peter was now acting like a rock—living up to the name Peter, or "Rock," which Jesus had given to him at their first meeting (see John 1:42). Peter was no more actually a rock than a few minutes later he was actually the devil when he tried to dissuade Jesus from going to the cross (Matt. 16:23). In the first instance he was acting like a rock; in the second he was acting like Satan. Jesus said, "And I say also unto thee, That thou art Peter, and upon this rock I will build my church; and the gates of hell shall not prevail against it" (Matt. 16:18).

The word translated *church* is a Greek word that means "called out," or "assembly" or "congregation." In secular Greek it was used for the calling out of the citizens of the city to transact business. In the Septuagint it was used for the congregation of Israel assembled before the tabernacle. Christ's church or assembly or congregation is composed of all who have been called out of sin to salvation.

Jesus had already begun to build his church on the foundation of men such as Peter, Andrew, James, John, Matthew, and the other apostles who believed in him. He will continue to build his church of believers. In a general sense the church of Christ is composed of all the redeemed, both those in paradise and those on earth. Not one saved person is missing. Not one unsaved is among them. This is the true church, indeed. Death has no power over Christ's church. Every member of it has eternal life. The "gates of hell" (the word is *hades* or the unseen world) cannot prevail. "The powers of death shall not prevail against it" (v. 18 RSV). Jesus is not promising the perpetuity of an institution, but the eternal life of his disciples.

B. *Jesus used the word "church" as a local congregation of believers (Matt. 18:15–18).* This is the usage usually found in the Scriptures. He is giving practical advice about how to deal with a brother who has sinned against you, a fellow church member. You are to take one or two other people with you. If that fails, you are to tell it to the church. "But if he neglect to hear the church, let him be unto thee as an heathen man and a publican" (Matt. 18:17). A heathen is to be prayed for and witnessed to but is not to be left on the church roll. The authority of the local congregation to withdraw membership from one who is manifestly not Christian implies the duty of the congregation to allow only those who profess Christ to become members.

Conclusion

The church has an eternal responsibility as the steward of the gospel. The word Jesus spoke to Peter in Matthew 16:19 he also spoke to the church in Matthew 18:18: "I will give unto thee the keys of the kingdom of heaven: and whatsoever thou shalt bind on earth shall be bound in heaven: and whatsoever thou shalt loose on earth shall be loosed in heaven" (Matt. 16:19). The steward carried the keys to the building. The keys to the kingdom of heaven are repentance and faith. The church (all believers) has been entrusted with a gospel of eternal consequences. What people do on earth has eternal results. The responsibility for the gospel is not confined to Peter and the apostles but is the responsibility of the whole church.

Jesus clearly teaches that every person must respond to the gospel for himself or herself. It would be a fatal error to push the figure of the keys to mean that the church can save apart from personal faith in Christ. Jesus saves. We are the trustees of salvation.

WEDNESDAY EVENING, SEPTEMBER 4

Title: The Rupture of a Relationship

Text: "Cain talked with Abel his brother: and it came to pass, when they were in the field, that Cain rose up against Abel his brother, and slew him. And the LORD said unto Cain, Where is Abel thy brother? And he said, I know not: Am I my brother's keeper?" (**Gen. 4:8–9**).

Scripture Reading: Genesis 4:1–16

Introduction

John Steinbeck's novel *East of Eden* resembles a modern interpretation of the ancient story of Cain and Abel. With the skills of a literary genius, Steinbeck searches into the cause and consequences of conflict between people who ought to be close to each other.

The story of Cain and Abel represents two people who had a ruptured relationship. Actually, they should have lived close to each other. They were brothers. According to the Genesis record, sin separated man from his fellow man. Sin is not just personal. It is interpersonal, marring basic human relationships. Looking at life causes us to see tragic conflicts between people who ought to be close to each other. Let us look at the life of Cain and discover some reasons why his relationship was ruptured with Abel, his brother.

I. Ruptured relationships result when worship is ignored.

A. *Cain's offering was rejected by the Lord.* Abel was a shepherd, and Cain was a farmer. In the course of their lives, each man brought an offering to God. Cain brought produce from the ground, and Abel brought a sheep. God accepted Abel's offering, but he refused Cain's offering.

Many reasons have been proposed as to why Cain's offering was rejected. Perhaps the reason for the acceptance of Abel's offering is in the word *firstlings* (Gen. 4:4). It comes from a Hebrew word that means "something carefully chosen." It meant that Abel selected the best of the animals. Cain merely brought an offering. Evidently he did not bring the "firstlings."

B. *The attitude of the worshiper is important.* The spirit of the offerer is more important than the offering. The prophets of the Old Testament taught that justice, kindness, and communion with God were more important than thousands of rams and rivers of oil. Not to have a teachable attitude when worshiping God could lead to ruptured relationships. How one worships God affects how one will relate to others.

II. Ruptured relationships result when divine counsel is rejected.

A. *Cain disobeyed God's counsel.* When God rejected Cain's offering, Cain, jealous because God had accepted Abel's offering, acted in bitter resentment toward God. Sin crouched like a wild beast ready to devour him. Cain had an opportunity to check his resentment and jealousy.

B. *To get along with people you need to listen to God.* One great tragedy of life is that people do not listen to the Lord's counsel. This failure to listen to God leads to numerous hostilities. People disregard God's Word and allow jealousy and hatred to go unchecked.

III. Ruptured relationships result when brotherly love is ignored.

A. *Cain rejected Abel as a brother.* Because Cain ignored God's counsel, he failed to treat Abel as a brother. God had intended that Cain and Abel live together in brotherly love. It was not God's will for Cain to have jealousy and resentment for his brother. It was certainly not God's will for Cain to murder his brother. God appealed to Cain immediately after Cain murdered Abel. "And the LORD said unto Cain, Where is Abel thy brother? And he said, I know not: Am I my brother's keeper?" (Gen. 4:9). Cain felt no responsibility for his brother.

B. *Interpersonal relationships are shattered when people deny their responsibility to other people.* What are your responsibilities to others? First, you are to have a supreme reverence for the life of another person. Second, you are to check any resentment and jealousy that begins against another person. If unchecked, it could lead to murder. Third, you are to acknowledge: "I am my brother's keeper." In other words, you will strive to seek the best interests of other human beings.

Conclusion

Do you want to get along with other people? God wants you to relate properly to others. Some valuable lessons can be learned from the mistakes of Cain's life. Look carefully at his mistakes and learn from them. If applied correctly, you will be able to have better relationships in life.

SUNDAY MORNING, SEPTEMBER 8

Title: Give the Gift of Forgiveness

Text: "Whenever you stand praying, forgive, if you have anything against any one; so that your Father also who is in heaven may forgive you your trespasses" **(Mark 11:25 RSV).**

Scripture Reading: Matthew 18:21–22

Hymns: "Saved, Saved!" Scholfield

"Christ Receiveth Sinful Men," Neumeister

"Though Your Sins Be as Scarlet," Crosby

Offertory Prayer: Loving Father, we have received your rich gifts into our hearts and lives. Thank you for the gift of forgiveness. Thank you for the gift of eternal life. Thank you for the opportunity to witness and serve. Thank you for the opportunity to work and earn a livelihood. Thank you, Father, for the capacity and the disposition that cause us to want to contribute today to the advancement of your kingdom's work. Accept our tithes and offerings and bless them to that end. We pray in Jesus' name. Amen.

Introduction

Much consideration is given to the giving of gifts during the month of December. Special gift catalogs are received through the mail. Newspaper ads portray lovely gifts for sale. Television and radio commercials inform people concerning beautiful and desirable gifts. Pressure is applied to encourage us to purchase gifts for those we love.

Perhaps the Christmas season came to be a time of gift giving because the birth of Christ reminds us of God's great gift to us. We also read in the nativity account of how the Magi came from the East bringing expensive and wonderful gifts and presenting them as tokens of reverence and worship to the Christ child (Matt. 2:11).

But we should not be givers only at Christmas. We should be givers all the time. Jesus taught his disciples on many different occasions to be givers. He said, "You received without pay, give without pay" (Matt. 10:8 RSV). Luke's gospel encourages us, "Give, and it will be given to you; good measure, pressed down, shaken together, running over, will be put into your lap. For the measure you give will be the measure you get back" (Luke 6:38 RSV). Jesus is also quoted as having declared, "It is more blessed to give than to receive" (Acts 20:35 RSV).

Some great gifts each of us need to give do not require that we be materially wealthy. Today let us consider giving the rich gift of forgiveness to others.

I. Forgiveness is a gift that everyone needs.

In thinking about a gift for others, some attention should be paid to the need of the recipient for the gift.

A. *All of us need the gift of forgiveness.*
   1. All of us are sinners.
   2. All of us are mistake makers.
   3. All of us bring some hurt into the lives of others.
   4. All of us need God's forgiveness. Our God forgives us.
B. *All of us need the forgiveness of those whom we have caused to suffer.*
   1. Do you need forgiveness from your parents?
   2. Do you need forgiveness from your children?
   3. Do you need forgiveness from your companion?
   4. Do you need forgiveness from friends?
   5. Do you need forgiveness from total strangers?
C. *We need to forgive ourselves. Sometimes that is difficult to do.*
   1. Not to forgive ourselves brings unnecessary suffering into our lives.
   2. Unwillingness to accept forgiveness from ourselves can produce deep depression that can lead to drug and alcohol abuse.

II. Forgiveness is a gift that everyone needs to give.

One of the greatest hindrances to spiritual growth is the neglect or the refusal to give the gift of forgiveness to those who have injured us. The moment you refuse to forgive, you stymie your spiritual growth and rob yourself of the joy that God has provided for the community of the forgiven.

A. *Do you need to forgive your parents?* Some children have been wounded by their parents. Ask God to help you give the gift of forgiveness to your parents if they have wounded you.

B. *Do you need to forgive your companion?* Ann Landers, a Jew, has repeatedly recommended the use of forgiveness as a method of dealing with injury and hurt. Often she is severely criticized because she recommends that a wife forgive her husband for inexcusable conduct, and Ann recommends to a husband that he be forgiving toward a wife who has been something less that wise. In recommending forgiveness, this Jewish woman is encouraging a Christian response to injury. Do you need to forgive your companion? Not to do so will sour your marriage and bring harm into your life.

C. *Do you need to forgive your children?* Children can be cruel and break their parents' hearts. Some parents have gone to the grave ahead of schedule because of the ingratitude and stupidity of their children. Many parents tremble with pain because of hurt that comes through their children. Give to your child the gift of forgiveness, not because it is deserved, but because it is needed. Your child needs your forgiveness. You need to be forgiving even more than your child needs your forgiveness.

D. *Do you need to forgive those who have injured someone near to you?* A mother-in-law once attended a prayer service and requested prayer on her own behalf. She said, "I have found it impossible to forgive my son-in-law for the hurt that he has inflicted upon my daughter and her children. I have lost the joy of my salvation because of my inability to forgive him. Please pray for me."

Many times we think that we would be willing to forgive when it is deserved. Forgiveness is never earned. Forgiveness is always a gift.

E. *Do you need to forgive yourself?* Some people suffer every day because of careless mistakes or stupid decisions they made in the past. Some inflict punishment on themselves repeatedly because of these past mistakes. When we confess and turn from the love of evil, God forgives us. God wants you to forgive yourself.

III. Forgiveness is a gift that we must give.

Forgiveness is a gift that, if you withhold it from the one who needs it, you will do so to your own harm.

Forgiveness and forgetfulness are not identical. It is nearly impossible to totally forget something. Thus, Jesus said that we must forgive seventy times seven times. Every time you hurt because of some injury that has been inflicted on you, you are to forgive again if you would obey Jesus' instructions.

A. *We must forgive if we would experience forgiveness (Matt. 6:14–15).* Forgiveness is not a price we pay for the Father's forgiveness; rather, it is a condition that we must meet in order to receive his forgiveness.

B. *We must forgive those who have injured us to avoid the acid of hate from collecting in our heart.* The most expensive luxury that you can afford is a pocket of hate in your mind and in your heart. It will destroy you.

C. *We must forgive if we would prevent the rupture of meaningful relationships.* This is true particularly in marriage. The spouse who never practices forgiveness toward husband or wife is in for a miserable marriage. There is no marriage of a perfect man to a perfect woman. All of us are mistake makers. All of us have a selfish streak. This requires a continuous attitude of forgiveness on the part of each one so as not to bring about destruction of the marriage relationship.

D. *We must give the gift of forgiveness if we would enjoy fellowship with God.* He is the great forgiver. By his grace we are part of the community of the forgiven. To enjoy intimate fellowship with the Father, we must be forgiving toward others.

Conclusion

Forgiveness is a gift that we can give to others because of God's gracious forgiveness of our sins. God forgives us freely, fully, and forever. He does this on the basis that Jesus Christ has died for our sins.

Forgiveness is a gift that we need to give, because it is required of us. If it were impossible for us to give forgiveness, then it would not be required of us.

Forgiveness is a gift that we need to give others, because it is absolutely essential for our own peace of mind and joy of heart.

Be a giver of forgiveness to others.

SUNDAY EVENING, SEPTEMBER 8

Title: What Jesus Preached about Sin

Text: "Forgive us our sins; for we also forgive every one that is indebted to us. And lead us not into temptation; but deliver us from evil" **(Luke 11:4).**

Scripture Reading: Matthew 6:7–15

Introduction

Jesus' teaching about sin must be seen in its true perspective against his concept of God as goodness and light. Jesus' goal is for all persons to become children of God in holy, happy fellowship.

Sin is any person's lack of conformity with God's holy will. John's definition, "For sin is the transgression of the law" (1 John 3:4), is accurate if law be correctly understood to be God's law, which is God's will. Jesus speaks of sins as trespasses. "For if ye forgive men their trespasses, your heavenly Father will also forgive you" (Matt. 6:14). Some sins are sins of commission. One stops where God has said, "No trespassing." Jesus bids us to pray, "Forgive us our debts, as we forgive our debtors" (Matt. 6:12). These are sins of omission committed by failing to fulfill one's obligation to do God's will.

The prodigal son confessed, "Father, I have sinned against heaven, and before thee" (Luke 15:18). What had he done? He had turned his back on his father's will for him. He rebelled against the restraints of home. The son sought freedom in following his own will rather than his father's will. The common word for sin that the prodigal used means to "miss the mark." The figure is of one shooting an arrow at a target and missing. The target is God's will. Missing it is sin.

I. Jesus always discusses sin in personal terms.

A. *Sin is done by persons.* Inanimate objects do not sin. A rock rolled down a mountain and killed a person on the highway below. We do not say that the rock sinned. Nor do nonhuman creatures sin. A squirrel came down the chimney to tangle with the resident dog. The resulting battle left the interior of the house in shambles. We do not say that the dog and the squirrel sinned.

   Sin is personal. It is not something one catches as a disease. Nor is it inherited.

B. *Sin is committed against persons and against God.* One may sin against another person or against oneself, but all sin is against God. One sins against others or oneself by failing to conform to God's will for one's relationships. Note again the confession of the prodigal son: "Father, I have sinned against heaven [that is, against God who is in heaven], and before thee" (Luke 15:18). The examples of Joseph (Gen. 39:9) and of David (Ps. 51:4) are instructive.

II. Why sin?

Why God allows persons to be tempted to do other than his holy will is a great mystery the Bible does not explain. The tempter appears in Genesis 3. Why did God allow him? Why didn't God kill him? Jesus does not explain, but neither does he explain away. He recognizes Satan as an enemy. In the parable of the tares he explains, "The enemy that sowed them is the devil" (Matt. 13:39). On the basis of Jesus' teaching, the answer may be along the line that God made humans with free wills and gave them choices so that they in turn would develop character. God desires sons and daughters, not slaves.

III. When we come to the age of accountability and become conscious of sin, we know that we have sinned.

Jesus assumes that all persons have sinned and need forgiveness. Concerning parents who love their children and give them good things, Jesus said, "If ye then, being evil..." (Luke 11:13). As compared to the holy God, even the best persons are sinful. "And forgive us our sins" (Luke 11:4) is a universal petition.

Jesus calls on every person to repent. "Except ye repent, ye shall all likewise perish" (Luke 13:3). He taught that repentance and remission of sins should be preached in his name among all nations (Luke 24:47).

Jesus taught Nicodemus that every person needs to be born from above. "Jesus answered and said unto him, Verily, verily, I say unto thee, Except a man be born again, he cannot see the kingdom of God" (John 3:3). Apart from God's salvation, persons are lost (see John 3:16; Luke 15:10, 24; 19:10; et al.). Paul writes in Romans 11:32, "God has bound all men over to disobedience so that he may have mercy on them all" (NIV). His conclusion accords with Jesus' teaching.

IV. Sin that issues in guilt presupposes freedom to do otherwise.

A. *To the extent that we do what we must do and cannot help ourselves, we are victims rather than sinners.* If the predicament in which we find ourselves "by nature" is "original sin" or "total depravity," we may say with Paul, "Where sin abounded, grace did much more abound" (Rom. 5:20).

B. *Guilt presupposes a knowledge of right and wrong adequate to form a basis of choice.* "But sin is not imputed when there is no law" (Rom. 5:13). While there is no specific statement, the whole tenor of Jesus' teaching leads us to conclude that he would not impute guilt to an infant, to one mentally impaired, or to one for some offense against a law of which he was ignorant. In civilian law ignorance of the law is no excuse. Jesus, we believe, will make allowance for ignorance—not willful ignorance, but lack of knowledge. Hear Jesus pray, "Father, forgive them; for they know not what they do" (Luke 23:34).

C. *When we realize that we have sinned and God convicts us of our sin, we have to repent.* We must change our mind from what we have been thinking to what God thinks. As a result, our actions will also change. To refuse to repent, and to go on thinking and acting contrary to what God thinks, is to incur guilt. As we add sin to sin, we add penalty to penalty.

V. Sin is a matter of heart purpose, of motive, of disposition.

A. *Only persons have motives.* "A good man out of the good treasure of the heart bringeth forth good things: and an evil man out of the evil treasure bringeth forth evil things" (Matt. 12:35). A good tree brings forth good fruit. A bad tree brings forth inedible fruit. The kind of tree determines the kind of fruit (see Matt. 7:15–20). Murder begins in anger (see Matt. 5:21–22); adultery begins in lust (see Matt. 5:27–30).

B. *The heart not right will manifest itself in sins.*
   1. Sins of commission. For example: censorious speech (see Matt. 7:1–5) or an unforgiving spirit (see Matt. 6:14–15).
   2. Sins of omission. For example: "Forgive us our debts" (Matt. 6:12) and "Verily I say unto you, Inasmuch as ye did it not to one of the least of these, ye did it not to me" (Matt. 25:45).

C. *The greatest sin is to reject Jesus Christ.* He is the full, clear revelation of the Father. Jesus said the Holy Spirit convicts "of sin, because they believe not on me" (John 16:9). When the light is full and clear, the rejection of Jesus closes the door on God's offer of salvation (see John 3:17–20, 36).

Conclusion

Only God can be the final judge, for he alone knows the motive, the light against which one has sinned, and the repentant or unrepentant state of a person's heart.

The Lord indicates that at the judgment he will have no more difficulty separating the saved from the lost than a shepherd has in separating sheep from goats. Those who do not know Jesus personally will be judged on the basis of their actions toward others (see Matt. 25:34–46).

In repentance from sin and faith in the Lord Jesus is salvation, life, wisdom, and joy. God rejoices to forgive, but the prodigal son must repent to be welcomed home and forgiven (see Luke 15:10, 20–24).

WEDNESDAY EVENING, SEPTEMBER 11

Title: The Best Exercise

Text: "Enoch walked with God: and he was not; for God took him" **(Gen. 5:24).**

Scripture Reading: Genesis 5:21–24

Introduction

Diet and exercise are important to people today. Look over the magazines at the grocery store checkout, and you will notice that a good number of them feature articles on diet and exercise. Such articles sell magazines, because people want to know the newest trends in exercise and the fastest ways to lose weight and tone up.

A man early in Bible times found the best exercise—walking with God. Genesis 5:24 says, "Enoch walked with God: and he was not; for God took him." The word translated "walk" is a Hebrew expression that means to live according to God's lifestyle. Let us examine the characteristics of walking with God.

I. Walking with God means to go in God's direction.

The Hebraism "walking with God" is used to describe God's lifestyle. For Enoch to walk with God meant that he had to go in the same direction as God. If you are going to walk with anyone, you must go in the same direction in which that person travels.

A. *God's way is clearly marked.* Enoch responded to God's revelation. Whatever God disclosed to him he accepted as the way he was to live.

Today one does not have to guess or to imagine which way God is walking. God's supreme revelation has been given in Jesus Christ. "He that saith he abideth in him ought himself also so to walk, even as he walked" (1 John 2:6).

B. *God's way is always the best way.* To read Genesis 5 is to be convinced that Enoch found the best type of life. The other personalities mentioned in the chapter lived meaningful but rather uneventful lives, but Enoch stood distinct by walking with God.

Sometimes walking with God is not the most comfortable or the easiest way to travel, because you have to walk in a direction in which others are not walking.

II. Walking with God means to proceed at God's pace.

For Enoch to walk with God, it meant that he had to proceed at the same pace that God moved. If you are going to walk with anyone, you must travel at the same pace that person travels.

A. *God's pace is a deliberate, determined one.* Enoch found meaning in walking with God, and so can you. God wants to lead you. If you want to live according to his lifestyle, you need to commit your life to him. He will then move you in a direction that will allow him to create godly character within you.

B. *God's pace varies on different occasions.* Enoch did not find walking with God one continuous, monotonous pace. He found that God varied his leadership. Sometimes God walked fast, at other times, slow. And sometimes God just waited. Walking with God means that you proceed at God's pace. You are not to attempt walking ahead of God; nor are you to lag behind. At times you will need to wait patiently and let God lead you.

III. Walking with God means to make progress.

When Enoch walked with God, he made noticeable signs of progress. You cannot walk without moving.

A. *Walking with God begins with a simple first step.* For Enoch to walk with God, he had to take a first step. That means he had to have faith initially in the Lord. One day he started the journey of living according to God's lifestyle. Likewise, beginning the Christian life starts with a simple step of faith. Parents take delight in the first step their child takes, because it marks a significant beginning for the child. The first step means that other steps will come. The angels in heaven rejoice when a person takes the first step in a walk with God.

B. *The walk with God continues with a series of successive steps after the first step.* The first step is not the final step. No, walking with God means a series of successive steps—it is a growing kind of experience.

IV. Walking with God means to share an intimacy.

Enoch walked with God. Whenever you walk with anyone, you share your thoughts with that person. Enoch shared his life with God, and God shared his life with Enoch.

A. *God shares life with human beings.* One of the most amazing facts of life is that God chooses to share life with sinful human beings. He lets us know of his love and concern for us. Because one walks with God, he or she gets to understand more about the nature and character of God.

B. *God allows human beings to share life with him.* Walking with God suggests an intimate friendship with him. As we walk with the Lord, we may share our hopes, dreams, and aspirations. Or we may share with him our frustrations, troubles, and disappointments.

V. Walking with God means to arrive at a destination.

The Bible speaks of Enoch's destination: "And he was not." This refers to Enoch's translation. "By faith Enoch was translated that he should not see death; and was not found, because God had translated him: for before his translation he had this testimony, that he pleased God" (Heb. 11:5). Because Enoch started walking with God, he arrived at his destination.

A. *God causes us to reach potential while we live.* Enoch did not find the ultimate meaning of life after his translation. No, every day as he walked with God, he discovered the meaning and significance of living God's type of life.

B. *God causes us to reach our final destination.* Beginning to walk with God leads to a pilgrimage that ends with ultimate fellowship in heaven with God.

Conclusion

Are you tired of wandering through life without purpose? You need to begin a profitable journey, a walk with God. Open your life to Jesus Christ, and you will be strengthened for successive steps and for a final home in glory.

SUNDAY MORNING, SEPTEMBER 15

Title: Give the Gift of Encouragement

Text: "I have derived much joy and comfort from your love, my brother, because the hearts of the saints have been refreshed through you" **(Philem. 7 RSV)**.

Scripture Reading: Philemon 1–7

Hymns: "Great Redeemer, We Adore Thee," Harris
"I Will Sing the Wondrous Story," Rowley
"All the Way My Savior Leads Me," Crosby

Offertory Prayer: Holy Father, thank you for being the giver of the best gifts that we have. Thank you most of all for your love and grace revealed in Christ. Thank you for the gift of your Holy Spirit who abides within us to be our guide, our teacher, and our helper. Thank you for your gifts to us through the church and for your blessings to us through the Bible. We come now to express our love for you through our tithes and offerings. Accept these and bless them to the end that others shall experience your grace and fulfill your plan for their lives. In Jesus' name we pray. Amen.

Introduction

God is the great giver. Every good gift and every perfect gift comes through him (James 1:17).

God so loved a needy and sinful world that he gave his Son, Jesus Christ, for us. Jesus came into the world as the servant of God and as a giver of the gifts of God.

Jesus taught his disciples to be unselfish servants who would define their purpose for being in terms of giving. To his apostles he said, "You received without pay, give without pay" (Matt. 10:8 RSV). Jesus believed that it was much more blessed to give than to receive.

Each of us has an acquisitive instinct. We receive great joy and satisfaction from acquiring things. This joy is exceeded, however, by the joy of giving. Nevertheless, many of us feel as Peter did in the presence of great need when he said, "I have no silver and gold, but I give you what I have" (Acts 3:6 RSV). Many gifts can be given that cannot be purchased with money.

Today let us think about giving the gift of encouragement. In our text Paul commended Philemon because Philemon was a great encourager of those about him. He was a beloved fellow worker, and his house was the meeting place for a group of believers (Philem. 2). He was the kind of man who provoked an attitude of gratitude in the heart of Paul when he prayed to the Father God (v. 4). Philemon was genuinely concerned for those about him. He had a great faith in God, a great faith in himself, and a great confidence in others that served to bless them and to lift them (vv. 5–6). Paul remembered Philemon with joy and comfort because of the many things he had done to bring refreshment to Paul's soul (v. 7). Philemon was a great giver, because he gave the gift of encouragement to others. You do not need silver and gold to be this kind of giver.

God has given many rich gifts to his church for the good of the body. Significantly, when Paul gives us a list of the gifts of God, exhortation or encouragement is among them (Rom. 12:8).

I. Give yourself the gift of encouragement.

Have you ever decided to give yourself a gift that you needed and that you would appreciate and that would do you good? Doing so is not selfish if the gift is encouragement. You can give yourself this gift in a number of ways.

A. *Accept yourself as a unique creation of God.* Your fingerprints are uniquely distinctive. Your voice is your very own. You are the only one of your kind, and God created you and made you as you are.

B. *Appreciate yourself as one for whom Jesus Christ died.* God loves you. Place yourself right in the middle of John 3:16. The world that God loved has your address on it. As you realize that God loved you enough to let Jesus die for you, you will see that you are precious to him. Accept the fact that God loves you and appreciate and respond to his love.

C. *Forgive yourself for past failures and imperfections.* God did not make you perfect. Although you may be flawed, God still loves you. He forgives fully, freely, and forever those who come to trust Jesus Christ as Savior. If God has forgiven you, then it follows that you should forgive yourself. You must quit despising yourself because of some imperfection or some past mistake. When God forgives, God forgets. If God forgives you, then you should forgive yourself.

D. *Dedicate yourself to the doing of the Father's good will on a day-by-day basis.* Go out of your way to be God's love and mercy to others. You will encourage yourself as you try to give your faith away and as you try to be God's blessing to others.

II. Give the gift of encouragement to those near and dear to you.

A. *Give encouragement to your companion.* There is not a husband or wife among us who does not need the encouragement of his or her companion.

   1. Husbands need the commendation of their wives. Each wife can be a great blessing to her husband if she appoints herself as a cheerleader to encourage him and to commend him for the good she sees in his life. Try to overlook his imperfections and deficiencies. Affirm that which is good in your husband if you would give him the gift of encouragement.

   2. Wives need appreciation. Dr. James Dobson wrote a book about what wives wished their husbands knew without asking. He declares that a wife's greatest need is a sense of good self-esteem and that this comes primarily through her husband. How long has it been since you have expressed appreciation to your wife for what she means to you? Do it with words. Do it with deeds. Do it with kindness and tenderness. Give the gift of encouragement to your wife.

B. *Children need encouragement more than they need criticism.* Perhaps the greatest sin that parents commit against their children other than the sin of neglect is the sin of being overly critical. The Bible strictly prohibits us from being overly corrective to the extent that we provoke our children to anger. How long has it been since you have given to your children—each of them—a good gift of encouragement? Encourage your children to use their gifts to reach their highest potential. Do not expect them to be perfect. Affirm them in the direction in which they need to go. Help them to become all that God has created them to be.

III. Give encouragement to outsiders.

By outsiders I am referring to those outside the immediate family circle. Everybody needs encouragement. Exclude no one; include everyone.

A. *You can give the gift of encouragement by words of admiration.* When you admire the craftsmanship of others, you can encourage them by speaking words of admiration.

B. *You can give the gift of encouragement by words of appreciation.* How long has it been since you have written a letter expressing appreciation for a service rendered? Have you expressed appreciation to those who serve in public office? Have you expressed appreciation to those who teach in the school system? Have you expressed appreciation to the police officers who help your community to be a safe place in which to live? How long has it been since you expressed appreciation to the firefighters who stay on duty in order to protect your property?

C. *You can give the gift of encouragement by words of recognition.* There are times when individuals perform above and beyond the call of duty. This takes place in your church, in your community, and in your nation. You can give those people the gift of encouragement simply by recognizing their unselfish giving of service to others.

Conclusion

You may not have a vast fortune out of which you can give expensive gifts to others. But all of us can give the gift of encouragement. Write a letter or make a phone call and give the gift of encouragement. Speak face to face to others and give them the gift of encouragement. Speak on the spur of the moment when the occasion is appropriate and give the gift of encouragement.

In these closing moments, let me encourage you to receive Jesus Christ into your heart if you have not yet trusted him as Savior and Lord. Let me encourage you to give yourself to a life of faith and faithfulness and spiritual growth in and through the church. Let me encourage you to sing the good news and tell others the story of God's goodness to you. Let me encourage you to give your best to God and to others.

SUNDAY EVENING, SEPTEMBER 15

Title: What Jesus Preached about Salvation

Text: "For God so loved the world, that he gave his only begotten Son, that whosoever believeth in him should not perish, but have everlasting life" **(John 3:16).**

Scripture Reading: John 1:11–13

Introduction

The most important consideration for every person is: Are you saved? Is your heart right with God? Are you justified? Do you know deep down in your heart that you are a child of God? Have you found the peace that passes understanding? Have you found the way to quiet an accusing conscience?

How good it is to get right with God! "Blessed is he whose transgression is forgiven, whose sin is covered. Blessed is the man unto whom the LORD imputeth not iniquity, and in whose spirit there is no guile" (Ps. 32:1–2).

I. God wants to save us not damn us.

Heathen people often think that God or the gods are angry and must be appeased. They bring offerings, offer sacrifices, and even at times give their infants in sacrifice.

But Jesus says, "God loves you" (see John 3:16–17).

A. *With courageous love God made you a person.* You have power to choose for God or for evil, which is a truth Jesus always acknowledges in his appeals for repentance and faith.

B. *God knew that you would use your freedom to sin against him.* So, before you were born, God did all that was necessary to offer you salvation. To all persons before Jesus came there was the promise of the Savior symbolized in the altar, the sacrifices, and the promises. "But when the fulness of time was come, God sent forth his son, made of a woman, made under the law, to redeem them that were under the law, that we might receive the adoption of sons" (Gal. 4:4–5). He was the "Lamb slain from the foundation of the world" (Rev. 13:8). Everyone who ever has or ever will be saved, will be saved by the atoning death of Jesus Christ. This Jesus affirms: "I am the way, the truth, and the life: no man cometh unto the Father, but by me" (John 14:6; cf. Matt. 26:26–28; Mark 10:45; John 3:16; Acts 4:12).

C. *If God wanted to damn you, all he would need to do would be to leave you alone.* Without salvation you are lost (see Luke 15:11–32; 19:10), you will perish (see John 3:16), you are under condemnation (see John 3:36).

D. *God does not let you alone.* He wants you to be saved.

　　1. "For the Son of man is come to seek and to save that which was lost" (Luke 19:10). The shepherd who found his lost sheep rejoiced. The father who welcomed his lost son home rejoiced. God wants to have that same kind of joy because of your salvation.

　　2. God convicts you of sin. The Holy Spirit convicts of sin, of righteousness, and of judgment—all with reference to Jesus (see John 16:8–11). The Lord Jesus knocks on the door of one's heart and invites to salvation (see Rev. 3:20). God uses his Word, his providence, and your conscience to convict you, which is evidence of his love.

II. Jesus offers the salvation you need.

A. *His salvation brings justification.* This is a new standing in God's sight. It is a right relationship with God. The sinner who has been under condemnation for his or her sins comes out from under condemnation to eternal life and will never enter condemnation again (John 5:24).

In Jesus' parable of the Pharisee and the publican, the Pharisee complimented himself before God. But having no sense of sin, he did not ask for forgiveness. The publican had such a deep sense of sin that he, "standing afar off, would not lift up so much as his eyes unto heaven, but smote upon his breast, saying, God be merciful to me a sinner" (Luke 18:13). Jesus added, "I tell you, this man went down to his house justified rather than the other" (Luke 18:14).

B. *His salvation brings forgiveness of sins.* Sin is a breach of personal relationships. Sin is *by* persons *against* persons. Forgiveness removes the barrier to fellowship. All sin is a personal affront to God. Sin may be against others or even against oneself, but every sin is against God. By definition, sin is anything that is contrary to God's will. One who has sinned ought first to get right with God and then seek forgiveness from any person against whom he or she has sinned.

Jesus and his hearers were all familiar with the rich teaching about forgiveness in their Scriptures. Here are some examples: "For thou hast cast all my sins behind thy back" (Isa. 38:17). "I have blotted out, as a thick cloud, thy transgressions, and, as a cloud, thy sins: return unto me; for I have redeemed thee" (Isa. 44:22). "For I will forgive their iniquity, and I will remember their sin no more" (Jer. 31:34). "And thou wilt cast all their sins into the depths of the sea" (Mic. 7:19). "As far as the east is from the west, so far hath he removed our transgressions from us" (Ps. 103:12).

C. *Forgiveness brings restored fellowship.* A woman in the house of Simon the Pharisee showed her gratitude for forgiveness by washing Jesus' feet with her tears and wiping them with her hair. Our Lord said to her, "Thy sins are forgiven. Thy faith hath saved thee; go in peace" (Luke 7:48, 50). When the prodigal son confessed his sin and asked for forgiveness, his father forgave him and took him back as a son rather than as a servant. He was now at home and content to be there. Saved people are adopted as children of God.

D. *Salvation brings new birth.* When is person is born again from above by the Holy Spirit, that person now loves what Christ loves and purposes to do what God would have him or her to do (see John 3:1–18; 2 Cor. 5:14–21).

E. *Salvation brings eternal life.*

   1. Salvation brings us life that is eternal in quality. Jesus said, "I am come that they might have life, and that they might have it more abundantly" (John 10:10).

2. Salvation brings us life that is eternal in duration. Jesus pledges the eternal security of the saved: "My sheep hear my voice, and I know them, and they follow me: And I give unto them eternal life; and they shall never perish, neither shall any man pluck them out of my hand. My Father, which gave them me, is greater than all; and no man is able to pluck them out of my Father's hand. I and my Father are one" (John 10:27–30).

Conclusion

How does one get right with God?

A. *Not:*
   1. By birth. There is no favored race (see Matt. 3:9).
   2. By education or the lack of it (see Matt. 11:25–30).
   3. By ceremony. Not circumcision, nor baptism, nor the Lord's Supper, nor church membership, nor any other religious ceremony can make one a Christian (see John 3:3; Eph. 2:8–10; Titus 3:5).

B. *But by repentance and faith.*
   1. Repentance and faith are really two sides of the same action. Repentance is coming to see sin as God sees it and turning from it. Faith is coming to see Jesus as God sees him and turning to him.
   2. This is an essential condition—that one repent and believe. If God wants to save you, and he does, he would not make any arbitrary condition. But in the very nature of the case a sinner must repent before God can save him or her (see Matt. 21:31–32; Luke 13:3; 24:27; John 3:16, 36; 5:24).

   If a father had a son old enough to know right from wrong, and this son was stealing, the father might say, "Son, I know you are stealing. I love you. If you will give it up, I'll forgive you; and if you cannot give back what you have stolen, I'll replace it." The son might reply, "Father, it is my business what I do. I am going to steal whenever I think I can get away with it." No matter how much the father loves his son and wants to forgive, he cannot do so until the son is willing to be forgiven. God loves you. Christ offers to pay for your sins. Forgiveness depends on your repentance.

WEDNESDAY EVENING, SEPTEMBER 18

Title: A Faithful Man

Text: "These are the generations of Noah: Noah was a just man and perfect in his generations, and Noah walked with God" **(Gen. 6:9).**

Scripture Reading: Genesis 6:8–10, 22; 7:5; 9:20–29

Introduction

A homeless dog of mixed breed trotted imploringly up to a sentry outside St. James Palace. The ground was covered with snow, and the dog was cold and hungry. The sentry picked him up, fed him, and named him Jack. Jack became greatly attached to the sentry whose regiments—the Scots Guard—adopted him as a mascot. Jack went through the Crimean War with his master, always at his side on the battlefield. When his master fell, mortally wounded, Jack stood faithfully by until both were removed from the battlefield.

Hearing of the splendid service record of the noble dog, Queen Victoria was deeply touched. She had a miniature Victoria Cross made, which she had placed on Jack's collar.

God also rewards his faithful people. Noah was a man who remained faithful to God during adverse circumstances. Let us learn some lessons on how to be faithful.

I. To be faithful, one must be loyal to God.

A. *Other claims clamor for loyalty.* The people in Noah's day lived apart from God. "God saw that the wickedness of man was great in the earth, and that every imagination of the thoughts of his heart was only evil continually" (Gen. 6:5). People decided to walk in a different direction. God was deeply grieved over the people's sins. Wherever God looked, he saw corruption, violence, and departure from God's ways. Noah could have walked in the direction of the world. Without a doubt the pull of the world was a strong factor.

B. *Faithful people must have a single-minded loyalty.* The conjunction "but" of Genesis 6:8 introduces Noah as a different kind of person. He decided to be faithful to God. He was righteous and blameless, and he walked with God. He dared to be faithful to God when the majority moved in the other direction.

II. To be faithful, one must obey God's Word.

A. *God gives instructions.* In Genesis 6:11–21 are recorded God's instructions, which must have seemed strange to Noah. God told Noah about the end of the earth. "God said unto Noah, The end of all flesh is come before me; for the earth is filled with violence through them; and, behold, I will destroy them with the earth" (v. 13). Then the Lord commanded Noah, "Make yourself an ark of cypress wood; make rooms in it and coat it with pitch inside and out" (v. 14 NIV). The following verses record God's specific instructions to Noah regarding the ark. Furthermore, the Lord told Noah to gather two of every species of animal for the ark.

Sometimes God's instructions seem strange to our ears. For example, he says to love instead of hate, turn the other cheek, go the second mile, and overcome evil with good.

B. *God expects obedience.* In spite of the unusual instructions, Noah obeyed: "Noah did everything just as God commanded him" (Gen. 6:22). Noah obeyed in spite of ridicule. Spectators must have laughed at the idea of a great flood and the crazy concept of building an ark. Being faithful amid ridicule is difficult. When Nehemiah sought to build the walls of Jerusalem, his opponents belittled the efforts (Neh. 4:1–4). Nehemiah remained faithful though, and the wall was finished.

III. To be faithful, one has to resist the world.

A. *The world has its attractions.* Noah was a faithful man. Some Old Testament scholars call him an extraordinary person. Even extraordinary people, however, are susceptible to becoming ordinary when they conform to the world. For a long time Noah lived above the temptations of his times, but in a moment of weakness he got drunk.

B. *The world must be resisted.* The story of Noah's sin teaches us that temptation can defeat us. For many years Noah resisted the power of evil, but in a weak moment he succumbed to the pull of the world.

Temptation often strikes immediately after a great victory. One constantly needs to be aware of the susceptibility of yielding to temptation.

Conclusion

Do you want to be recognized as a faithful person or an unfaithful person? Of course you want to be faithful. To be faithful you need to learn lessons from Noah. Be loyal to God, obey God's Word, and resist the world.

SUNDAY MORNING, SEPTEMBER 22

Title: Give the Gift of Your Personal Testimony

Text: "'Go home to your friends, and tell them how much the Lord has done for you, and how he has had mercy on you.' And he went away and began to proclaim in the Decapolis how much Jesus had done for him; and all men marveled" **(Mark 5:19–20 RSV)**.

Scripture Reading: John 4:27–30, 39–42

Hymns: "Come, Thou Almighty King," Anonymous
"I Love to Tell the Story," Hankey
"Oh, for a Thousand Tongues to Sing," Wesley

Offertory Prayer: Loving Father, we come today to thank you for the testimony of your children down through the ages concerning your kindness, greatness, goodness, and faithfulness. We come today to worship you in spirit and in truth. We come offering the love of our hearts and the praise of our lips. We come offering tithes and offerings that we might publish to the ends of the earth the good news of your love in Jesus Christ. Accept these gifts and bless them to that end. In Jesus' name we pray. Amen.

Introduction

On festive occasions we often go home to those whom we love bearing precious gifts to them. We give gifts in connection with birthdays, anniversaries, and weddings. At Christmas time we do more giving and receiving than at any other time of the year. But we should be busily engaged 365 days of the year in giving the great gifts that are within our power to give.

We have seen the necessity of giving the gift of encouragement and have considered the importance of giving the gift of forgiveness. Today let us recognize the valuable opportunity of giving to those about us the gift of our personal testimony.

It is interesting to note in our text that our Lord declined to grant the request of the man out of whom the demons had been driven. The man requested the privilege of accompanying Christ and his disciples. Instead, our Lord wanted him to go home and give to his family and friends the great gift of his personal testimony concerning what God had done in his life. Perhaps this man was greatly disappointed. We can be certain that he could not begin to believe how important the gift of his testimony would be. But our Lord knew that if this man would give his testimony, it would be the means of others coming to God so that they might receive liberation and healing too.

You and I have it in our power to give the rich gifts of forgiveness, encouragement, and our personal testimony concerning what God has done in our lives. To withhold these gifts is to impoverish others, and it will at the same time deprive us of great joy.

Jesus gave the Great Commission to his church in the form of a command that his disciples go out into the world and give the precious gift of personal testimony concerning what God had done in Jesus Christ and what he was doing in their lives (Acts 1:8).

When you give the gift of your personal testimony, you never deplete your supply. The more you give this gift to others, the more you have to give.

In a court of law a good witness functions when three things are true. First, a good witness must *know* something. Hearsay and speculation are not acceptable in a court hearing. Second, a good witness must *say* something. It is absolutely essential that a witness give a verbal testimony. To be silent and to withhold information is not only cruel but can be criminal. One can be held in contempt and put in jail for withholding needed verbal testimony. A good witness speaks. Third, a good witness must *be* something. A good witness must have a reputation that does not disqualify or void his verbal testimony in court. If one has a reputation for being untruthful, this can be held against him in a court of law and can discount the validity of his verbal testimony.

These three rules also apply in the matter of giving our Christian testimony. We must *know* something, *say* something, and *be* somebody. We must practice our personal Christianity to the extent that when we give a verbal testimony it will have weight. When Jesus said, "You shall be my witnesses," he was saying, "You must go and give the gift of your personal testimony." Paul declares to the Romans that faith comes by hearing.

I. The testimony of a satisfied customer is a gift that you can give.

Four men in the Midwest were riding together when they passed a new restaurant featuring Korean food. One of these men, an outstanding judge in his community, volunteered the information that he had become a customer at the new Korean restaurant and that the oriental food was superb. One of those who heard this testimony went to the restaurant for dinner and tested the food. He found it to be all that the judge said it was.

The judge *knew* something. He *said* something, and because he was a significant person, the restaurant obtained another customer.

A. *You can give your testimony regarding Jesus Christ as the Bread of Life who satisfies the deepest hunger of the heart.*

B. *You can give your testimony regarding Jesus Christ as the Water of Life who quenches the thirst of the heart.*

II. The testimony of one who has found peace with God through Christ is a gift that you can give.

A. *Everyone wants to be right with God.*

B. *Everyone needs the peace of being right with God.* If you have trusted Jesus Christ as Savior and experienced the peace that comes as the result, you can share this verbally with others. You can give your personal testimony regarding the joy of knowing that your sins are forgiven. You can give to others your personal testimony regarding the joy of having Christ as your companion along the road of life.

A college teacher shared his personal experience with a student who had a drinking problem. The teacher had gained victory over the same habit through faith in Jesus Christ, whom he had let become the Lord of his life. The student had faith in his teacher and decided to let Jesus Christ become his Lord. The teacher had thus given the student the great gift of a personal testimony.

Perhaps you could give the gift of your personal testimony concerning the benefits of regular church attendance or the gift of your personal testimony regarding the joy that comes as a result of being a tither. Some of you could give your personal testimony concerning the comfort that comes from God in the time of grief.

Conclusion

If you know something about God that is good, you have a gift to give. If you have a tongue that can speak, you have the opportunity to give a testimony that can enrich the lives of others.

If you are a significant person to someone and if that someone needs Jesus Christ, you have a gift to give.

A good witness is someone who knows something and says something; and because he or she is somebody, others can be greatly enriched by the gift of his or her personal testimony.

Today, you would be wise to respond to Jesus Christ affirmatively and let him become real to you.

SUNDAY EVENING, SEPTEMBER 22

Title: What Jesus Preached about His Kingdom

Text: "From that time Jesus began to preach, and to say, Repent: for the kingdom of heaven is at hand" **(Matt. 4:17).**

Scripture Reading: Psalm 103:15–22

Introduction

The synonymous terms *kingdom of God* and *kingdom of heaven* were often on Jesus' lips. He used them interchangeably in the parables as recorded in the Gospels. The ancient Jews were very careful about saying "God" lest by pronouncing the name they might profane it. Even today we hear some people pray, "May heaven grant," when of course they mean, "May God who is in heaven grant...." The gospel of the kingdom was the very heart of the Lord's preaching.

I. Meaning of the kingdom of God.

The term *kingdom of God* is hard to define, not because it is obscure, but because it means so much.

A. *The term sometimes refers to God's providential rule over the universe (Ps. 103:19; 1 Chron. 29:11).* Often Jesus said, "The kingdom of God is like..." and then he would tell a story to illustrate how God in his sovereign rule deals with humankind.

B. *More specifically the kingdom of God or the kingdom of heaven refers to God's reign through Christ in the hearts of persons.* Christ is the King.

    1. He was prophesied by Isaiah (see Isa. 9:6–7). He was proclaimed by the angel to Mary before his birth (see Luke 1:32–33) and to the shepherds (Luke 2:9–11).

    2. Jesus proclaimed himself in the triumphal entry into Jerusalem. Jesus deliberately fulfilled Zechariah 9:9, a passage the people

understood to refer to the messianic king, as Matthew explains: "All this was done, that it might be fulfilled which was spoken by the prophet, saying, Tell ye the daughter of Zion, Behold, thy King cometh unto thee, meek, and sitting upon an ass, and a colt the foal of an ass" (Matt. 21:4–5).

3. Jesus claimed himself as King before Pilate in John 18:33–38.

4. Jesus claimed himself as King following his resurrection: "All power is given unto me in heaven and in earth" (Matt. 28:18).

II. The kingdom of which Christ is King is a present reality, is coming, and will come.

A. *The kingdom is a present reality.*

1. People were being saved. John the Baptist preached, "Repent ye: for the kingdom of heaven is at hand" (Matt. 3:2). "Jesus came into Galilee, preaching the gospel of the kingdom of God, and saying, The time is fulfilled, and the kingdom of God is at hand: repent ye, and believe the gospel" (Mark 1:14–16). Jesus said, "The law and the prophets were until John: since that time the kingdom of God is preached, and every man presseth into it" (Luke 16:16).

2. The kingdom of God is inner and spiritual rather than geographical or political. It is the reign of God through Christ in the hearts of persons. Jesus said, "The kingdom of God cometh not with observation: Neither shall they say, Lo here! or, lo there! for, behold, the kingdom of God is within you" (Luke 17:20–21). Jesus explained to Nicodemus, "Verily, verily, I say unto thee, Except a man be born again, he cannot see the kingdom of God" (John 3:3). The entrance to the kingdom is by the new birth.

   Jesus described the citizen of the kingdom, or, as we now say, the Christian, in the Beatitudes in Matthew 5:1–12. He said, "For theirs is the kingdom of heaven" (Matt. 5:3, 10).

B. *The kingdom of God is coming.* It grows by the sowing of the gospel seed under the leadership and power of the Holy Spirit.

1. Jesus' parables show the vitality of the gospel. See, for example, the parable of the seed growing of itself (Mark 4:26–29). As the soil and the seed were made for each other, so are the soul and the Savior.

   The parable of the gospel feast (Luke 14:16–24) shows that God has prepared salvation well. The invitation is extended to all. Those who make excuses miss the feast, but God's house will be filled with guests.

   The parable of the wedding garment (Matt. 22:11–14) shows that one who comes must come on the King's terms. God provides the wedding garment of salvation by repentance and faith. One does not enter the kingdom on his or her own terms.

2. The kingdom will grow.

The parable of the leaven (Matt. 13:33) shows that the kingdom will grow by one person witnessing to another person, just as yeast leavens dough.

Jesus believed that the gospel would be preached to all nations (Matt. 28:18–20). The kingdom has come in so far as persons have accepted Jesus as King. It is coming as more and more persons enter the kingdom by salvation and obedience to Christ.

3. To be in the kingdom is more important than anything else. Jesus said, "Seek ye first the kingdom of God, and his righteousness" (Matt. 6:33).

In the parable of the treasure in the field (Matt. 13:44), the man who found the treasure recognized that it was worth more than everything else he owned. Jesus is to be valued above all else.

4. Greatness in the kingdom is on the basis of love, service, and faithfulness (see Mark 10:35–45). There are no favorites in Christ's kingdom.

C. *The kingdom of God will come.* The kingdom will be consummated when Jesus comes again at the end of the gospel age.

1. "When the Son of man shall come in his glory, and all the holy angels with him, then shall he sit upon the throne of his glory: And before him shall be gathered all nations: and he shall separate them one from another, as a shepherd divideth his sheep from the goats" (Matt. 25:31–32). All persons who have ever lived, as well as those living when Christ returns, will appear before him. He will assign them to an eternal state as easily as a Palestinian shepherd could separate sheep from goats.

2. Eternal states as well as rewards and punishments will be made manifest. "Then shall the King say unto them on his right hand, Come, ye blessed of my Father, inherit the kingdom prepared for you from the foundation of the world" (Matt. 25:34). The kingdom in this verse means the blessings of the kingdom, such as heaven, the marriage feast of the Lamb, the new Jerusalem, eternal life in the heavenly home—all of the blessings God has in store for the redeemed.

3. All else is temporal. Only the kingdom of God endures. The apostle Paul sums up the consummation as follows: "Then cometh the end, when he shall have delivered up the kingdom to God, even the Father; when he shall have put down all rule and authority and power. For he must reign, till he hath put all enemies under his feet" (1 Cor. 15:24–25).

Conclusion

Under God's rule in his kingdom, as responsible persons, we shall give account for our lives. Basically two questions will be asked at the judgment.

Are you in the kingdom of which Christ is the King? What have you done for the King and for others in his name? The answer to the first question determines destiny. The answer to the second determines rewards.

"Now unto the King eternal, immortal, invisible, the only wise God, be honour and glory for ever and ever. Amen" (1 Tim. 1:17).

WEDNESDAY EVENING, SEPTEMBER 25

Title: Blurred Vision

Text: "Lot lifted up his eyes, and beheld all the plain of Jordan, that it was well watered every where, before the LORD destroyed Sodom and Gomorrah, even as the garden of the LORD, like the land of Egypt, as thou comest unto Zoar" **(Gen. 13:10).**

Scripture Reading: Gen. 13:1–13; 19:15–38

Introduction

Millions of people worldwide have sight problems. Over 50 percent of all Americans over age thirty wear eyeglasses. Many sight problems exist—near-sightedness, far-sightedness, blurred vision, tunnel vision, and numerous other difficulties.

Lot is a character in the Bible with a sight problem that could be diagnosed as blurred vision. We read, "Lot lifted up his eyes, and beheld all the plain of Jordan, that it was well watered every where, before the LORD destroyed Sodom and Gomorrah, even as the garden of the LORD, like the land of Egypt, as thou comest unto Zoar" (Gen. 13:10). Abraham's and Lot's flocks grazed together until trouble emerged between their herdsmen. Abraham wisely chose to end the conflict by urging Lot to choose a separate land. Lot looked at the Jordan Valley near Sodom and saw the agricultural promises of the valley but failed to see the evil influences of the Sodomites. We too may suffer with blurred vision. We need the help of the Holy Spirit to discern God's will when we have decisions to make. Let's observe Lot's visual problems.

I. We need to look deeper than what we see on the surface.

A. *Lot could see only the materialistic attraction of the Jordan Valley.* Wealth took center stage in his life. He was not willing to consider other factors. Good spiritual vision requires a careful look and the Holy Spirit's interpretation. One needs to look carefully at the immediate and the ultimate results of a decision.

B. *Lot could see only himself.* His vision consisted of his selfish interests. He should have considered Abraham, who led him from Mesopotamia to Canaan. Our vision is impaired when we can see only ourselves.

II. We need to look at what we fail to see.

A. *Lot failed to see the sinfulness of Sodom.* Lot's vision problem was not so much in what he saw but more in what he failed to see. He failed to see the danger of the sinfulness in Sodom. "But the men of Sodom were wicked and sinners before the LORD exceedingly" (Gen. 13:13).

B. *Lot failed to see the downward pull of sin.* Sin has a downward pull. Lot chose a good place to raise sheep but a poor place for human life. Evil in Sodom gradually pulled him downward. Lot's downfall can be easily seen.

   1. He looked toward Sodom. "Lot lifted up his eyes, and beheld all the plain of Jordan, that it was well watered every where, before the LORD destroyed Sodom and Gomorrah, even as the garden of the LORD, like the land of Egypt, as thou comest unto Zoar" (Gen. 13:10).

   2. He pitched his tent toward Sodom. "Abram dwelled in the land of Canaan, and Lot dwelled in the cities of the plain, and pitched his tent toward Sodom" (Gen. 13:12).

   3. He dwelt in Sodom. "And they took Lot, Abram's brother's son, who dwelt in Sodom, and his goods, and departed" (Gen. 14:12).

III. We need to be careful not to lose our vision.

A. *Lot failed to have his values checked.* Lot's uncorrected worldly involvements led to spiritual blindness. He lacked the ability to focus on the things of God.

Periodically we need to check our values. Slipping into ungodly values comes gradually. We periodically ought to ask ourselves these questions: Do I really love the ways of God? Am I obeying the Word of God? Do I spend my money and time on the endurable elements?

Physical sight needs periodic checks so that sight problems can be corrected. Failure to have your eyes checked could lead to a loss of vision. Likewise, if one fails to check on one's spiritual value system, spiritual blindness could occur.

B. *Lot lost his spiritual vision.* Lot became blind to genuine happiness. Sinful pleasures do not afford ultimate pleasure. Also, Lot became blind to character. The culture of Sodom corrupted him, and he was willing to sacrifice the chastity of his own daughters. He said to the wicked men who came to his door wanting to have sex with his heavenly visitors, "Behold now, I have two daughters which have not known a man; let me, I pray you, bring them out unto you, and do ye to them as is good in your eyes: only unto these men do nothing; for therefore came they under the shadow of my roof" (Gen. 19:8).

Lot became blind to the truth of God's word. God warned him repeatedly of Sodom's destruction, but Lot lingered and had to be forced to leave. Secularism has that awful tendency of desensitizing people to God's word.

Furthermore, the culture of Sodom had blinded Lot to human decency. Lot's two daughters made him drunk, and they conceived children by their father. Lot had lost all sense of spiritual perception.

Conclusion

Now is the time for a spiritual vision checkup. Examine your life to see if your values are on the Lord and his ways.

SUNDAY MORNING, SEPTEMBER 29

Title: Give the Gift of Affirmation

Text: "He brought him to Jesus. Jesus looked at him, and said, 'So you are Simon the son of John? You shall be called Cephas' (which means Peter)" **(John 1:42 RSV).**

Scripture Reading: John 1:35–42

Hymns: "God, Our Father, We Adore Thee," Frazer
"It Is Well with My Soul," Spafford
"Rise Up, O Men of God," Merrill

Offertory Prayer: Holy heavenly Father, open our eyes that we might behold the wonders of your grace. Help us to see your love for us and your love for others. Help us to respond to your grace and power and help us to be the instruments that communicate your love to others. Accept these tithes and offerings and bless them to the end that suffering will be relieved and that needs will be met and that your name will be proclaimed to the ends of the earth. In Jesus' name. Amen.

Introduction

Two decades ago the Associated Press carried the news that a man named Scott McVay had been given the responsibility of dispensing $3.5 million from the estate of the late Geraldine Rockefeller Dodge. Mrs. Dodge, who died in 1973, bequeathed her subsidiary estate to a foundation for "charitable, scientific, literary or other educational purposes, or for the prevention of cruelty to animals or for the encouragement of art." As the executive director of the Dodge Foundation, McVay had the task of deciding who was to receive the money. His was a thrilling but fearful responsibility.

Jesus came into the world to give away something more than $3.5 million each year. He came bringing the rich gifts of God to the hearts and lives of all humankind. He gave the gift of forgiveness and the gift of a new life. He gave the gift of encouragement and the gift of truth. He also encourages his followers to be givers of great gifts.

If we wait until we can give great sums of money such as Scott McVay could give, we will never become the givers that our Lord would have us to be. Today let us consider the possibility of giving the gift of affirmation to others.

A young and very successful pastor would often say to individuals and to his congregation, "I affirm you," as he spoke concerning some decision or action that had been made. In this manner, he was encouraging them and strengthening them in the decision that had already been made.

Webster defines *affirm* as "to confirm or ratify; to assert as valid." The word *affirmation* is defined as being "confirmation of anything established; ratification."

Jesus majored on giving the gift of affirmation to people. John's gospel declares, "For God sent the son into the world, not to condemn the world, but that the world might be saved through him" (John 3:17 RSV). Jesus did not come into the world to be a critic; he came to be our Savior. To accomplish this task, he affirmed the worth of individuals in a manner that attracted them to him and caused them to listen to him. You and I can also give this priceless treasure to those about us.

I. Jesus gave the gift of affirmation to Peter (John 1:42).

Our Lord had the habit of seeing the good in others. He recognized the volatile or fluid nature of Peter's heart and visualized the fact that this man could become a great rock. He thus affirmed him at the very beginning of his acquaintance. This gift of affirmation helped Peter to develop into the man that he later became.

Do you know people who have great potential and who need the gift of affirmation? Your affirming them in the decisions they have made and in the potential they have could be God's good gift to them.

II. Jesus gave the Samaritan woman the gift of affirmation (John 4:7–28).

Our Lord crossed racial, gender, religious, and cultural barriers to minister to the Samaritan woman at the well. She had been terribly abused and had become a nobody.

Our Lord honored her by requesting a service of her. This was a compliment that brought shock and surprise to her (John 4:9). While our Lord asked questions that probed to the very heart of her being, he did not do so in order to depress her or to embarrass her. If we could hear the tone of his voice, we could understand why the woman was not frightened away. Jesus was eager for the poor woman to enjoy the privilege of drinking living water from the fountain of life. He had to affirm her as a person of worth before he could communicate to her the truth of his messiahship.

Do you know some spiritually destitute person who has experienced the heartbreak of disappointment after disappointment? Do you know someone who is living in the gutter who could benefit by a proper affirmation on your part? This woman was one for whom Jesus was going to die. God so loved the worst among us that he sent Jesus Christ to die on the cross for them. We must give to them the gift of affirmation if we would communicate with them effectively.

III. Jesus gave the gift of affirmation to Zacchaeus (Luke 19:1–10).

Among the Jewish people, the publicans were about the worst of the worst. They were considered as traitors and as the hirelings of the Roman army of occupation. It was they who purchased the right to collect taxes and profited at the misfortune of their own people. Consequently, they were excluded from the synagogues and from all acceptable social contact with Jewish people.

When Jesus visited Jericho on his way to Jerusalem, he took the initiative and affirmed Zacchaeus publicly. The people were shocked at Jesus' insisting that he must go home with Zacchaeus. Zacchaeus was shocked that Jesus would want to go to his home. We can be assured that Mrs. Zacchaeus was even more shocked when Zacchaeus and Jesus appeared for lunch.

Jesus did not criticize and accuse Zacchaeus of all kinds of crimes so as to cause him to feel negatively about himself. Instead, with wisdom and compassion, Jesus affirmed him in such a way that Zacchaeus made some radical changes in his lifestyle.

Do you know someone in the community who is held in disrepute by most of the religious people? Have you sought in any way to affirm this person in such a manner as to be God's love and mercy and grace to him? It may not be easy to give the gift of affirmation to this person, but such a gift could be worth more than a sizable sum of money.

Conclusion

We seemingly have a built-in tendency to be critical toward others. Some of us never give the gift of affirmation to others.

How long has it been since you affirmed the worth of your companion in a manner so as to convince him or her of your deep appreciation and your sincere admiration? How long has it been since you have given the gift of affirmation to your child? Have you been stingy with the gift of affirmation?

Life will take on new meaning and beauty for you when you look for the positive and the good in others. Develop the habit of giving the gift of affirmation. Help others to recognize that in the eyes of God they are of infinite, indescribable worth. Help them to accept and appreciate themselves. Help them to dedicate themselves to God and to others.

If you would discover the joy of giving, give the gift of affirmation.

SUNDAY EVENING, SEPTEMBER 29

Title: What Jesus Preached about Property

Text: "Remember the words of the Lord Jesus, how he said, It is more blessed to give than to receive" **(Acts 20:35)**.

Scripture Reading: Matthew 25:14–46

Introduction

Medieval theologians are reported to have discussed such abstruse questions as, for example, "How many angels can stand on the point of a needle?" Some modern preachers are said to answer questions the laity are not asking. The theme for this message is practical rather than academic. It deals with the problem of a Christian's acquisition and use of material things.

The basic relationship in life is one's relationship to God. The person who is right with God then asks: "What, Father, is your will with reference to my relations to others and to myself?" This response immediately involves one's relations to property. What did Jesus preach about property?

I. Jesus recognized the right of individuals to possess property.

A. *In his parables, Jesus assumed the right to buy, sell, and lease property, to collect rent, and so on.* Jesus did not have much property, but he had some. He sent his disciples to buy bread. He gave to the poor. He accepted hospitality from homes of means. His seamless robe was of sufficient value that the soldiers gambled for it.

B. *God is the property owner, and man is the trustee or steward.* All of the parables emphasize this truth but especially the parable of the talents. The master gave his goods to his servants to invest for him. He called them to account for the use of his money. The truth is clear: God has given to everyone life and property in trust. One is to use the entrustment in accord with the will of the owner.

II. It is a Christian's duty to increase his or her earnings by legitimate means.

A. *The parable of the talents makes clear that the servants were to invest their master's money with a view to making more money.* The master indicated to the man with one talent that it would have been better for him to put the money in the bank to draw interest than to have done nothing with it.

B. *Jesus never would approve dishonest means in the accumulation of wealth.*
   1. Jesus would not compromise with Satan to gain the whole world.
   2. The Mosaic law, which includes, "Thou shalt not kill," "Thou shalt not steal," "Thou shalt not bear false witness," and "Thou shalt not covet," is summed up in the great commandment, "Thou shalt love." A person is not to break the law to get gain.

3. Human rights are more important than property rights. "How much then is a man better than a sheep?" (Matt. 12:12). "For what does it profit a man, to gain the whole world and forfeit his life? For what can a man give in return for his life?" (Mark 7:36–37 RSV). One man of Gadara in his right mind was worth much more than all of a farmer's hogs (see Mark 5:1–20). Getting wealth must be done in such a manner that it does no injustice to God, to others, or to oneself. One cannot think of Jesus approving of making money from liquor, narcotics, prostitution, pornography, or any other business not approved by a good conscience. If one is in a business that God does not approve, let him or her get out and find a way to make an honest living. Many have done just that.

III. Large gifts to the church and charity do not justify dishonest acquirement or a wrong heart attitude.

A. *Doing alms in order to be seen of others does not receive commendation from our heavenly Father (see Matt. 6:1–4).*

B. *It is more important to be reconciled to one's fellowman than to offer a gift.* "Therefore if thou bring thy gift to the altar, and there rememberest that thy brother hath ought against thee; Leave there thy gift before the altar, and go thy way; first be reconciled to thy brother, and then come and offer thy gift" (Matt. 5:23–24).

C. *Jesus confirmed the scribe's appraisal that love to God, neighbor, and self "is more than the whole burnt offering and sacrifices" (Mark 12:33).*

D. *The giving of tithes and offerings does not in any wise excuse the neglect of "the weightier matters of the law, justice and mercy and faith" (Matt. 23:23 RSV).*

IV. The right use of possessions.

Money and property are a trust from God and are to be used in accordance with his will. Just as one should practice good stewardship in one's use of time, talents, and influence, so should we use good stewardship in the use of material things. Money and property are really an extension of oneself.

A. *Jesus would certainly expect us to care for the personal needs of ourselves and our families.* Jesus' model prayer contains the petition, "Give us this day our daily bread" (Matt. 6:11). His reply to Satan, "Man shall not live by bread alone, but by every word that proceedeth out of the mouth of God" (Matt. 4:4), assumes that bread is necessary to life.

B. *Jesus would have us pay taxes.* He said, "Render therefore unto Caesar the things which are Caesar's" (Matt. 22:21). He paid the civil tax as well as the temple tax.

C. *Jesus most certainly approves generous giving to the church.* An argument from silence is always precarious, but Jesus must surely have paid the tithes expected by the religious authorities. The scribes and Pharisees accused him of breaking the Sabbath laws and of not observing the distinction of clean and unclean, but there is no complaint about his failure to tithe. While Jesus stoutly contended that tithing could not substitute for justice, mercy, and faith, he indicated that people ought to tithe (see Matt. 23:23).

Jesus said, "Render therefore... unto God the things that are God's" (Matt. 22:21). He commended the liberality of the widow who cast her last two coins into the temple treasury (see Mark 12:41–44).

He commanded his disciples to witness to the uttermost parts of the earth. He expected the expenses of spreading the gospel to be borne by willing gifts from Christians.

Gifts for persons in need were a special concern of Jesus. The parable of the Good Samaritan has helped to build thousands of hospitals, orphanages, and homes for the aged and needy. The parable teaches that anyone anywhere who needs help is our neighbor (see Luke 10:30–37). When one feeds the hungry, clothes the naked, visits the sick and those in prison, he or she is really ministering to Jesus (see Matt. 25:31–46).

The church has no rival in the work of winning people to Christ. It is the finest agency for helping to meet the physical needs of people beyond that which government and private philanthropies can do.

Conclusion

The Christian accumulation and distribution of money and property bring many blessings.

A. Blessings to those who receive the gifts are obvious.

B. Even greater blessings come to Christian stewards. Paul recalls for us the words of the Lord Jesus, how he said, "It is more blessed to give than to receive" (Acts 20:35). It is good to receive. It is better to be able to give and to do it. Christian stewards have a good conscience. By supporting their home, government, and church generously, they will have more interest in them. "For where your treasure is, there will your heart be also" (Matt. 6:21). Christian stewards look forward to hearing the Lord's "Well done, good and faithful servant, thou hast been faithful over a few things, I will make thee ruler over many things; enter thou into the joy of thy lord" (Matt. 25:23). They look forward expectantly to heavenly rewards (see Matt. 6:18–20; 10:42; Luke 14:12–14; 16:1–12).

C. Serving God with mammon (money) is the only antidote to the terrible folly of serving mammon. "Ye cannot serve God and mammon" (Matt. 6:24). Note our Lord's warning against covetousness in Mark 10:17–27 and Luke 12:13–21.

D. Follow the example of Jesus. "For ye know the grace of our Lord Jesus Christ, that, though he was rich, yet for your sakes he became poor, that ye through his poverty might be rich" (2 Cor. 8:9).

Suggested preaching program for the month of

OCTOBER

■ Sunday Mornings

The books of the New Testament contain the written testimony of inspired writers concerning who Jesus was and what he was trying to accomplish in the hearts and lives of people. "The Main Emphasis of Inspired Writers" is the theme for a series of messages based on the first five books in the New Testament.

■ Sunday Evenings

Biographical messages are suggested illustrating the importance of "Facing the Stresses of Life with Faith." The great spiritual giants of the past were not immune from the problems that plague us in the present. They faced life with faith in a God who is at work to bring out good in everything that happens.

■ Wednesday Evenings

A devotional study of a book of the Bible, chapter by chapter and verse by verse, has the potential for bringing great blessings into the lives of those who participate. "Concerning Colossians" is the theme for a series of studies.

WEDNESDAY EVENING, OCTOBER 2

Title: The Foundation for Life

Text: "Grace be unto you, and peace, from God our Father and the Lord Jesus Christ. We give thinks to God and the Father of our Lord Jesus Christ, praying always for you, since we heard of your faith in Christ Jesus, and of the love which ye have to all in the saints, for the hope which is laid up for you in heaven, whereof ye heard before in the word of the truth of the gospel" (**Col. 1:2–5**).

Scripture Reading: Colossians 1:1–8

Introduction

Sir Edmund Grey wrote in 1914 that the lights were going out all over Europe and they might not come on again in his generation. It was a time when people were questioning the very foundation of life.

The letter to the Colossian church was also written in a time of turmoil. The whole first-century world was facing the turmoil of faith and the facts of life under Roman domination. There was also turmoil in the church. Teachers had infiltrated the Colossian church with doctrines that threatened their understanding of the original gospel message. Specifically, the church was threatened by the teaching know as Gnosticism. This was a philosophy based on the knowledge of "the knowing ones," who taught a dualism between flesh and spirit. They believed in a series of emanations between God and humankind of which Christ Jesus was only one emanation. They recognized that Jesus died on the cross, but they taught that his death alone was not sufficient for salvation. They taught that Jesus was not the supreme revelation of God. Thus, in his letter to the Colossians, Paul argued for both the supremacy and the sufficiency of Jesus Christ.

As we look at the foundation for life, we can recognize three irreducible elements of the Christian life: faith, hope, and love. Emil Brunner once said:

> Every Christian lives in three dimensions of time—the past, the present, and the future. He lives in the past, for he has a history without which he could not be a man. He lives in the present, for he is a responsible soul obligated to serve God in his own day and generation. He lives in the future, for he is an immortal soul. How can he live concurrently in these three dimensions? He lives in the past by faith, in the present by love, and in the future by hope. (Emil Brunner, *Faith, Hope, and Love* [Philadelphia: Westminster, 1956], 13)

These are the foundations for life. And these Paul enumerated in his opening remarks to the Colossian Christians.

I. Faith is a foundation for life.

A. *Faith centers in Christ.* The Christian life is centered in Christ and sustained by Christ. It is the means of putting the strength of the past into the present.

B. *Faith includes action.* Faith is not passive but active. It always involves acting in faith. The story has been told many times about Blondin, the tight-rope artist who stretched a wire across Niagara Falls. One day he walked the tightrope across Niagara Falls pushing a wheelbarrow before him. He announced that the next day he would push a man across the wire in the wheelbarrow. As the crowd gathered the next day to see him push the wheelbarrow with a man in it across Niagara Falls, many people said that he could not do it. One boy said that he could. When a man in the crowd questioned him, the boy said that he was sure Blondin could do it. Then the man invited the boy to come with him and get into the wheelbarrow. The man was Blondin, and he had not found anyone previously who believed in him enough to get into the wheelbarrow himself. Faith always acts.

II. Love is a foundation for life.

A. *Love finds its source in God, who loved us.*

B. *Love is manifested toward other Christians.*

III. Hope is a foundation for life.

A. *Hope comes through the gospel. It is through the gospel of Jesus Christ that we are introduced to a hope that sustains throughout life.*

B. *Hope points us toward a future with God.*

C. *Hope rests on the mercy of God.* A missionary in Canada traveled so widely that his visits to the settlements were often separated by long intervals of time. On one trip he visited an invalid boy in a settler's home. He taught the boy the text, "The LORD is my shepherd," by letting each finger represent a word and fitting his actions to his words. He said to him. "Remember always to hold on to the fourth finger—'the LORD is *my* shepherd.'" When he came back to that home two years later, the boy was not there. He had died in the dark of a winter night. His mother had found him in the morning with his hands outside the covers, his left hand clasped around the fourth finger of his right hand.

Conclusion

Faith, love, and hope stand firmly entrenched in our minds and our experience as the foundation of life. Knowing Christ as Savior, we can depend on these as a sure foundation upon which to build life even if the lights go out all around us.

SUNDAY MORNING, OCTOBER 6

Title: When Dreams Come True

Text: "Now all this was done, that it might be fulfilled which was spoken of the Lord by the prophet, saying, Behold, a virgin shall be with child, and shall bring forth a son, and they shall call his name Emmanuel, which being interpreted is, God with us" **(Matt. 1:22–23).**

Scripture Reading: Matthew 1:18–23

Hymns: "Fairest Lord Jesus," Anonymous
"Go, Tell It on the Mountain," Work
"Joy to the World," Watts

Offertory Prayer: Our heavenly Father, we love you because you first loved us and proved your love by the gift of your Son. In a world that is tempted to abandon hope, the coming of Jesus Christ restores hope. May we never lose the thrill of sharing the good news of Christ with others. In the coming of Christ, both into our world and into our hearts, may we ever be mindful that dreams really do come true. In our Lord's name we pray. Amen.

Introduction

During October and into the first week of November we will be taking a tour through the Gospels and the book of Acts. Our purpose is to stress the main emphasis of each of these books so that we may first grasp the continuity of the entire gospel account and, second, learn the central message of each book.

We shall devote one sermon to each of these five books. Today we begin with the Gospel of Matthew, whose central message is the messiahship of Christ and thus the basis for our sermon title, "When Dreams Come True." Dreams really do come true! The Gospel of Matthew is written to prove it. For ages Israel dreamed of that day when the Messiah would come, the kingdom would be built, and the future made secure.

At long last that dream did come true through the birth of Jesus Christ. To prove that Jesus is the Messiah, that Israel's dream did come true in fulfillment of all the prophecies of old, Matthew records no less than twenty miracles of our Lord. He is saying concerning the coming of Jesus the Messiah, "Dreams really do come true!"

I. When the Messiah comes (Matt. 1:22–23).

Matthew is saying, "Dreams really do come true—the Messiah has come, our hopes have been realized!"

A. *In fulfillment of Old Testament prophecy.* There are sixty references in Matthew's gospel to Jewish prophecies and forty quotations from the Old Testament. Throughout the twenty-eight chapters of the gospel, Christ's mission to the Jews is emphasized. Matthew is saying, "Christ is for real; he is the long-awaited Messiah. You can believe in him. Our dream has come true!" The word *fulfilled* is repeated thirteen times to indicate that Old Testament prophecies are fulfilled in Christ (Matt. 2:14–15, 23; 8:16–17; 13:34–35; 27:35).

B. *To meet humankind's basic need (Matt. 1:21).* Even before the birth of Christ the salvation of people was established as his prime mission. Many of the 1,068 verses in Matthew underscore this fact. Jesus, as Messiah, came not only in fulfillment of prophecy, but he did so for a purpose—"to save his people from their sins."

He could have come to save his people from:

1. Their poverty.
2. Their suppression by Rome.
3. Their ignorance.
4. Their despair.

But he did not. He came to meet basic human need. He came to forgive our sins, to make us new creatures, to be born in us, and to live through us.

O holy Child of Bethlehem,
Descend to us, we pray;
Cast out our sin and enter in—
Be born in us today!

The basic aim of the Gospel of Matthew is to show that God has moved in history to redeem a lost world. This salvation is not military, political, or social. It is spiritual. People cannot save themselves; a mighty act of God is required.

"He shall save his people from their sins." This salvation is a spiritual deliverance. The Jews thought in terms of military and political deliverance. The apocryphal writing of the Jews just before and during the lifetime of Jesus pictured the Messiah as a military conqueror. Under him, Israel would drive out the Romans and from Jerusalem would rule the world (Luke 24:21). Such a deliverance included only the Jews.

From the New Testament it is clear that "His people" involves all people. "God so loved the world (inhabited earth)…whosoever believeth…" (John 3:16). The Jews regarded themselves as God's people exclusively. But Paul is careful to point out that not all citizens of political Israel were God's people (Rom. 9:6–13). Furthermore, Peter says that those who were formerly not a people will be called the people of God (1 Peter 2:9–10). This new relationship is spiritual.

Again and again the word *save* echoes throughout Matthew's account. Early in his ministry, Jesus clearly defined the purpose of his coming: "For the Son of man is come to save that which is lost" (Matt. 18:11). He then goes on to illustrate this dominant purpose by the parable of the shepherd who sought one lost sheep until it was placed again in the fold with the other ninety-nine. Christ adds, "Even so it is not the will of your Father which is in heaven, that one of these little ones should perish" (Matt. 18:14).

Even the enemies of Christ recognize that he considered this to be his supreme calling, for they said, "He saved others; himself he cannot save" (Matt. 27:42). They failed to realize that in saving others he had to lose himself.

And dreams come true when you welcome the Messiah as your Savior, when you allow his mission to be accomplished in your life, when you permit him to meet your basic need. Your dream of forgiveness of sins, freedom from guilt, clearness of conscience, right standing with God, abundant life in the present, and eternal life in the hereafter will all come true when you embrace Christ as your Savior.

II. Dreams come true when a kingdom is built (Matt. 25:34).

Christ sees himself as King ruling over his own kingdom. When he shall return the second time in his glory, "Then shall the King say unto them on his right hand, Come, ye blessed of my Father, inherit the kingdom prepared for you" (Matt. 25:34).

The word *kingdom* appears fifty times in Matthew's gospel, and the term *kingdom of heaven* appears thirty times. Seven times Christ is referred to as "King." The good news of Matthew is that dreams of a kingdom do come true.

The kingdom of heaven is the spiritual reign of Jesus Christ in the hearts of those who accept him as Savior. It is a kingdom that shall have no end. It is a kingdom over which Christ shall reign forever and ever.

This kingdom is open to all. Jesus said, "The kingdom of heaven is like unto a certain king, which made a marriage for his son, And sent forth his servants to call them that were bidden to the wedding: and they would not come" (Matt. 22:2–3). Then the king said, "Go ye therefore into the highways, and as many as ye shall find, bid to the marriage. So those servants went out into the highways, and gathered together all as many as they found, both bad and good: and the wedding was furnished with guests" (Matt. 22:9–10).

You can enter it now. Matthew quotes John the Baptist as saying, "The kingdom of heaven is at hand" (Matt. 3:2). That is, it is near—it is open to you right now. When through faith in Christ you enter that kingdom, you will discover that dreams come true.

III. Dreams come true when the future is secured (Matt. 6:25–33).

The people of Jesus' generation lived in great insecurity—insecurity created by the occupational army of Rome, by the threat of drought and famine, by irrevocable financial losses, and by plagues and diseases. They dreamed of the day when needs would be met, fears would subside, and worries cease. So Matthew is careful to record these words of Christ. Christ's parting words to his disciples assured them that the future is secure. "All power is given unto me in heaven and in earth" (Matt. 28:18). You can't have much more security than that!

Conclusion

Are you resting in the keeping power of Christ? Have you committed your all to him? Have you embraced him as your Messiah?

If not, you can do so now. And when you do, you will discover that dreams really do come true. You will discover for yourself that the Messiah has come, his kingdom has been built, and your future is secure!

Then you too can sing:

> *I once was an outcast stranger on earth,*
> *A sinner by choice, and an alien by birth;*
> *But I've been adopted, my name's written down.*
> *An heir to a mansion, a robe, and a crown.*
> *I'm a child of the King, a child of the King:*
> *With Jesus my Saviour, I'm a child of the King.*

SUNDAY EVENING, OCTOBER 6

Title: The Man of Faith

Text: "Abraham believed in the LORD; and he counted it to him for right-eousness" **(Gen. 15:6).**

Scripture Reading: Genesis 15:1–11

Introduction

Years ago there was a popular television game show called *Password,* which was played with two contestants. One participant would say a word, and the partner would have to give a word closely associated with it. If you were to play *Password* with biblical characters, what would you say if someone would say, "Abraham"? More than likely your response would be "Faith," for that word is closely associated with Abraham.

Abraham was the father of the multitudes who would trust in the Lord. Abraham found purpose in life by means of his faith experience. Faith brought him new adventures and brought him through numerous hardships as well. Let us look into Abraham's life and discover the various aspects of faith.

I. Faith is an adventure.

A. *Abraham was instructed by God to leave Ur of the Chaldees.* "Now the Lord had said unto Abraham, get thee out of thy country, and from thy kindred, and from thy father's house, unto a land that I shew thee" (Gen. 12:1). God made some strong demands on Abraham. He wanted Abraham to leave his country, his kindred, and his father's house. Abraham left Ur to go to the land of Canaan. All along the way he lived in openness to God. Each experience became an adventure in faith.

B. *Trusting God is an adventure.* The Christian life may be compared to a pilgrimage. It is certainly not a life of monotonous living. It is an adventure, a step in the dark with the knowledge that God is there.

II. At times our faith wavers.

A. *Abraham did not always act in perfect accord with his faith.* While Abraham was in Egypt his faith wavered. He tricked the Egyptians by letting them think that Sarah was his sister, but the Egyptians discovered the false-hood. "Pharaoh called Abram, and said, What is this that thou hast done unto me? why didst thou not tell me that she was thy wife? Why saidst thou, She is my sister? so I might have taken her to me to wife: now therefore behold thy wife, take her, and go thy way" (Gen. 12:18–19).

B. *Walking by faith does not mean a perfect life.* Faith does not guarantee absolute perfection. At times we will waver, as the pilgrimage of faith is marked by ups and downs. The cure to wavering is to "get back in line" with God. Abraham repented often of his failure to walk by faith.

III.At various times our faith needs authentication.

A. *Abraham proved his faith by sacrificial living.* When Abraham was ninety-nine God appeared and repeated the former promise of a land and of descendants to occupy it. "God said, Sarah thy wife shall bear thee a son indeed; and thou shalt call his name Isaac: and I will establish my covenant with him for an everlasting covenant, and with his seed after him" (Gen. 17:19). When a son was born to Abraham and Sarah, they named him Isaac. The boy grew into a fine young man.

While Abraham and Sarah rejoiced over their young son, God made a strange command. He told Abraham to sacrifice Isaac. Abraham demonstrated the reality of his faith by obeying the command of God. Of course God stopped Abraham from sacrificing his son and provided a ram for the sacrifice.

B. *Proving our faith is a vital part of living.* God presents opportunities for people of faith to demonstrate its reality. Each day faith needs to be authenticated to a watching world.

James urged people to prove their faith. "Yea, a man may say, Thou hast faith, and I have works: shew me thy faith without thy works, and I will shew thee my faith by my works" (James 2:18).

IV. Faith is always adequate for life's crises.

A. *Abraham found God to be adequate for the crises of life.* All throughout Abraham's life, God had helped with his needs. God helped when he needed guidance, encouragement, assurance, and comfort. Without his relationship with God, Abraham would have had a tragic deficiency in his life.

B. *Faith in God helps us through the crises of life.* The person of faith has an edge, for he or she has a Savior to help with the crises of life. You need the Lord as you go through life. As you seek him, you will find that he is adequate.

Conclusion

Are you a person of faith? If you are not, you should be. Open your life to Jesus Christ.

WEDNESDAY EVENING, OCTOBER 9

Title: A Prayer for the Knowledge of God's Will

Text: "For this cause we also, since the day we heard it, do not cease to pray for you, and to desire that ye might be filled with the knowledge of his will in all wisdom and spiritual understanding" **(Col. 1:9).**

Scripture Reading: Colossians 1:9–14

Introduction

The will of God is a phrase that we use quite often. Its use ranges from a statement of resignation ("It was the will of God that this accident happened") to a statement of resolve ("It is the will of God that I enter the ministry").

For most of us it is much easier to talk about the will of God than it is to find the will of God. As we search for God's will in our lives and activities, we have to use the best of our spiritual faculties and perceptions as well as a great deal of prayer and much searching of the Scriptures.

It comes as no surprise, then, that Paul prays that the Colossian Christians should have a knowledge of God's will.

Using the familiar pattern of Paul's letters, the greeting is followed by a prayer, a prayer that these people might have a knowledge of God's will. That is a good prayer for us too.

I. Spiritual insight (Col. 1:19).

A. *Spiritual insight rests on an experiential knowledge of God.* Our knowledge of God cannot be from hearsay alone. We must have the knowledge of God that comes from an experience with God. Chad Walsh, in *Campus Gods on Trial* (Macmillan, 1964, pp. 107–8), suggested a six-month experiment in which a person could try to find God.

   1. Set aside fifteen minutes each day for reading the Bible.
   2. Set aside another fifteen minutes each day for prayer.
   3. Go to church each Sunday.
   4. Do your best day by day to live according to the teachings of Christ.

B. *Spiritual insight rests on an obedient following of God.* Jesus gave us an extremely helpful word at this point. "If any man will do his will, he shall know of the doctrine, whether it be of God, or whether I speak of myself" (John 7:17). A way to know the will of God is to obediently follow God.

C. *Spiritual insight rests on the full understanding of God.* Paul prayed that the Colossians might have both wisdom and spiritual understanding. Wisdom refers to the whole range of mental faculties. Intelligence or understanding is the special faculty of discriminating between the false and the true, of grasping the relationship in which things stand to each other. This comes through the inspiration of the Holy Spirit.

II. A worthy walk (Col. 1:10–11).

A. *A worthy walk will show results.* Paul prayed that the people would be fruitful in every good work. Results would show in their lives. Doctrine and ethics go together.

B. *A worthy walk will show growth.* The knowledge of God is not an end in itself, but the means to grow into the likeness of Christ.

C. *A worthy walk will show power (v. 11).* Paul used a play on words here: "Empowered with all power." This includes the graces of patience and longsuffering that are exhibited with joy. Paul and Silas in the Philippian jail knew joy in Christ while undergoing trials.

III. A thankful heart (Col. 1:12–14).

A. *Be thankful that God has qualified for us an inheritance (v. 12).* Roy Angell told in *The Price Tags of Life* (Broadman, 1959) about a wealthy man who had a son who was both willful and wild. The son stated most emphatically that he did not intend to go to college. His father pointed out to him the advantages of a college education and pleaded with him to go to college. Still he refused. So his father told him that he had opened a bank account in the boy's name for ten thousand dollars. The only stipulation was that the checks had to be made out to some university. God has already provided us with a great inheritance.

B. *Be thankful that God has rescued us from a power (v. 13).*

C. *Be thankful that God has transported us to a kingdom (v. 13).* The verb "translated" (v. 13) is used by classical writers for the removal of whole bodies of men, like colonists or military prisoners. When converted or born again, we have entered into the kingdom of light, the kingdom of God's own Son. How has this come about? It is by redemption through Christ, which redemption is the forgiveness of sin (v. 14).

Conclusion

We can know the will of God for our lives. We join in prayer with Paul that we can determine and follow God's will. This prayer for the knowledge of God's will centers in knowing God through faith in Jesus Christ.

SUNDAY MORNING, OCTOBER 13

Title: The Joy of Unselfish Service

Text: "He sat down, and called the twelve, and saith unto them, If any man desire to be first, the same shall be last of all, and servant of all" **(Mark 9:35).**

Scripture Reading: Mark 9:33–37

Hymns: "Make Me a Blessing," Wilson
"Serve the Lord with Gladness," Lee
"When We Walk with the Lord," Sammis

Offertory Prayer: Our Lord and our God, we honor and praise your name. As unworthy children we confess our sins to you. Thank you for life, for health, for family, for friends, and most of all for Christ our Savior. Remove from us greed and selfish ambition that cloud and cripple our witness. May we forget about being first and joyfully become servants of all. In the name of Christ we pray. Amen.

Introduction

Where the primary emphasis of the Gospel of Matthew is the "Messiahship of Christ," the primary emphasis of Mark is the "Servanthood of Christ." And how quickly Mark moves to his central theme! In eight brief verses he passes over thirty years of our Lord's life. In seven more verses Mark records the baptism and temptation experiences of Christ. By verse 16 Jesus is busy recruiting disciples.

Then Mark quickly moves to his first recorded act of Christ's unselfish service. Before Mark concludes his first chapter, he has reported four miracles and cast Christ in the role of an unselfish servant. Jesus is perfectly cast for this role. It requires no "acting" or "dramatics" on his part; he is simply being himself—a servant of all.

Seeing Christ through the eyes of Mark as servant of all, we discover the "Joy of Unselfish Service."

I. The joy of unselfish service is the joy of making life better for others (Mark 1:33–34).

After healing the man with the unclean spirit (Mark 1:23) and curing Peter's mother-in-law of her fever (v. 30), Christ continued to make life better for others. No doubt Peter's home was well known and scores of people knew of Peter's mother-in-law's illness. It was not hard to imagine the excitement throughout the city as the people, relieved of their daily duties because of the Sabbath, gave themselves to the discussion of what was taking place right in their own neighborhood. What a compliment is paid to our Lord that the people believed he had the power and the willingness to heal their diseases and to relieve their distresses. What hope and joy must have been theirs just to know that Christ had come to make life better for others!

Where Matthew is bent on proving the messiahship of Christ by quoting Old Testament prophecies fulfilled in Christ, Mark is quite content simply to record the wonderful works of Christ and allow them to testify of his deity. Only God through such unselfish service could make life better for others!

Nineteen miracles of Christ are recorded in this brief book, all of which demonstrate the joy Christ received from making life better for the people around him. In eight of these miracles he makes life better for others by healing. In five, by proving his power over nature. In four, he makes life better for others by casting out demons, and in two, by reversing the process of death.

A. *Jesus put people above programs (Mark 2:1–4, 11–12).* News of Christ's coming to Capernaum had spread like wildfire. Life in Palestine was very public. In the morning the door of the house was opened and any who wished could enter. When the word got out that Christ was in the house, in no time a crowd had filled the house. The doorway was jammed, and people even blocked the windows. They had come to see and hear Jesus. And so "he preached the word unto them" (2:2).

While Jesus was speaking, one solitary human need arose. A young man, too ill even to walk, was carried by four friends to see Jesus. Unable to press through the crowd, the ingenious four went up the outside stairway to the roof. They removed a portion of the roof and lowered their helpless friend into Jesus' presence. Immediately Jesus interrupted the "worship service," turned from the crowds, and focused his attention on this one needy man. In so doing, he was saying, "People are more important than programs. One lonely sinner is more important than a series of sermons."

Paul echoed the same conviction when he wrote, "Though I speak with the tongues of men and of angels and have not love, I am become as sounding brass, or a tinkling cymbal." And we prove our love for others, not through public proclamation, but through personal and unselfish service. Otherwise, teaching or preaching or any other avenue of service can be little more than a spiritual ego trip. The joy of unselfish service is the joy of making life better for others by putting people above programs.

B. *Jesus dealt with the man's most basic need (Mark 2:5–12).* To the surprise of all, Jesus said nothing about paralysis. Instead, he said, "Son, thy sins be forgiven thee" (v. 5). The word *son* was used to address a small child. Here Jesus used it as a tender address to this sick man. He did not reprimand him as a sinner, but spoke kindly to him as a sinner in need of his ministry. Jesus hated sin but loved sinners. Why did Jesus speak of sins rather than the man's physical condition? It is possible that his sins had caused his paralysis. So Jesus began at the proper place. He went to the heart of the matter. Though some people might not think so, the man's greater need was spiritual healing. If Christ had healed only this man's body and not his soul, in time he would die—then what? This man's most basic need in this life and in the life to come was met when Jesus said, "Son, thy sins be forgiven thee."

II. The joy of unselfish service is the joy of living before you die.

"For whosoever will lose his life for my sake and the gospel's, the same shall save it" (see Mark 8:35).

A very wise man once said, "Fear this: That you might die before you live." And you only really live when you lose yourself in unselfish service to others.

Some things are lost by being kept and saved by being used. A talent is like that. If used, it will develop into something much greater. If it is not used, it will be lost.

In the fourth century there was a monk in the East named Telemachus who made a visit to Rome. A Roman general, Stilicho, returned from a victory over the Goths. As a part of the celebration, gladiator games were held. No longer did Christians have to fight. Instead, those captured in war had to fight to the death. Telemachus leaped over the barrier, still in his hermit's robes, and positioned himself between the gladiators. The crowds threw stones at him. "Let the games go on," the commander of the games ordered. A gladiator's sword struck Telemachus, and he fell dead on the floor of the Coliseum. The crowd suddenly fell silent. The people were shocked that a holy man should have been killed in such a way. The games ended abruptly that day—never to be held again! By losing his life, Telemachus ended the games and saved countless lives. He lived more during those brief moments between the two gladiators than he had lived all his years in the desert. Telemachus experienced the joy of living before he died!

III. The joy of unselfish service is the joy of drawing attention to our heavenly Father (Mark 2:12).

"We have never seen anything like this before" (Mark 2:12 PHILLIPS).

Jesus did not heal this man or forgive his sins to draw attention to himself. Rather, the purpose of his unselfish service was to draw attention to his heavenly Father, on whose mission he had come to earth. And he was successful in attaining his purpose. The unbiased crowd, amazed at what Christ had done, gave glory to God.

In a time when it is so difficult to draw people's attention to our heavenly Father, there is no better way than the way of unselfish service. With so many people interested only in self, only in accumulating and keeping, it is a refreshing experience indeed for someone to see you busily involved in unselfish service. Like your Savior, you will stand out as an exception to the rule. An amazed world will see your good works and will glorify your Father who is in heaven. As was the experience of those early disciples who lost themselves in unselfish service, it will be said of you, "They took knowledge of them that they had been with Jesus." And if this be done, the mission of our unselfish service will be accomplished!

Conclusion

Have you discovered the joy of unselfish service? If not, this joy can be yours today. Our Lord promised, "Whosoever shall lose his life for my sake, the same shall find it."

When you lose your life in unselfish service, you will discover the joy of making life better for others, the joy of living before you die, and the joy of drawing attention to our heavenly Father.

SUNDAY EVENING, OCTOBER 13

Title: A Cure for the Blues

Text: "He himself went a day's journey into the wilderness, and came and sat down under a juniper tree: and he requested for himself that he might die; and said, It is enough; now, O LORD, take away my life; for I am not better than my fathers" **(1 Kings 19:4).**

Scripture Reading: 1 Kings 19:1–18

Introduction

Mood changes are a problem for many people. Sometimes we are in a good mood, and at other times we are in a bad mood. The low mood is often called "the blues," or "depression." A practicing psychologist in Tucson, Arizona, told me that 80 percent of the patients he counsels are in a mild or severe case of depression. A psychiatrist lecturing to a group of seminary students said that 12 percent of the population of America suffers from some form of depression. Without a doubt the low mood affects a lot of people.

Elijah suffered from an acute case of depression immediately after a high religious experience. The prophets of Baal had increased in number because Jezebel, the wife of Ahab, permitted the worship of Baal when she moved to Israel. Elijah challenged the prophets of Baal at Mount Carmel. The contest was an interesting and exciting one. The challenge was for the authentic God to consume the offering with fire. The prophets of Baal called to their god, but he could not answer, for he did not exist. Elijah called to the Lord, and he rained fire consuming the sacrifice.

Elijah came out a winner. But his happiness was marred by Jezebel's threat on his life. His high spirits were short-lived. He immediately got alone and developed a low spirit. "But he himself went a day's journey into the wilderness, and came and sat down under a juniper tree: and he requested for himself that he might die; and said, It is enough; now, O LORD, take away my life; for I am not better than my fathers" (1 Kings 19:4). In this mood the Lord ministered to him. From this ministry we may learn a cure for the blues.

I. The Lord wants us to get into good physical condition.

A. *Think about Elijah's condition.* The battle with the prophets of Baal had been a constant one. Elijah advocated firmly and continuously that Jehovah was the true and living God, and he alone was worthy of worship. Day upon day the constant zeal of Elijah's ministry had been to work for the Lord and to help prevent worship and service to the idol Baal. This task had consumed his time, energy, and thoughts. Being consumed constantly in the Lord's work had drained Elijah, leaving him mentally, physically, and spiritually exhausted. This condition caused him to turn inward in self-pity. His spirits were low.

The Lord needed to minister to him, and he did. As Elijah lingered in self-pity, the Lord ministered to his physical condition. "And as he lay and slept under a juniper tree, behold, then an angel touched him, and said unto him, Arise and eat. And he looked, and, behold there was a cake baked on the coals, and a cruse of water at his head. And he did eat and drink, and laid him down again" (1 Kings 19:5–6). The Lord recognized that Elijah's physical condition needed reviving and provided this as a form of therapy for Elijah's blues.

B. *Now think about your condition.* Sometimes moods of depression come to people because of physical or mental exhaustion. Doctors recommend to depressed counselees that they consider strongly an exercise program as well as proper diet and eating habits. Human beings are holistic, and physical conditions do affect our moods. Thus, we must heed God's therapy for our physical condition.

II. The Lord wants us to change our mental attitude.

A. *Observe Elijah's mood.* The prophet developed the bad habit of looking on the dark side of life. Elijah looked at the conditions caused by Jezebel, and he could see no bright prospect. Some of the Israelites had diverted their affection and loyalty from Jehovah to the idol worship of Baal. Listen to the despondent mood of Elijah: "I have been very jealous for the LORD God of hosts: for the children of Israel have forsaken thy covenant, thrown down thine altars, and slain thy prophets with the sword; and I, even I only, am left; and they seek my life, to take it away" (1 Kings 19:10).

What did God do for Elijah's negative attitude? The Lord helped him to take his mind off the bad situations and to turn his attention to the positive matters. The Lord boosted Elijah's image about himself. He complimented Elijah for being faithful in times past. He affirmed Elijah as a powerful leader. Furthermore, the Lord pointed to other faithful leaders. "Yet I have left me seven thousand in Israel, all the knees which have not bowed unto Baal, and every mouth which hath not kissed him" (1 Kings 19:18). With these resources Elijah could turn the people from paganism to the true God.

B. *Examine your attitude.* So many times the cause of our depression is not just our physical exhaustion, but our negative attitude—we develop a habit of focusing on the negative. Think about your thoughts toward the people you meet and the circumstances you encounter. Focusing on a negative issue can rob your positive attitude. And your attitude affects your moods. Study carefully the Lord's ministry to Elijah's attitude. With a positive mental attitude you may be able to overcome depression.

III. The Lord gives a meaningful task.

A. *Look what the Lord gave Elijah to do.* The Lord had helped Elijah with his physical condition and with his mental attitude. Now he gave him something to do. "What are you doing here, Elijah?" God asked. Of course Elijah had not been doing anything but sitting under a juniper tree feeling sorry for himself. "And the LORD said unto him, Go, return on thy way to the wilderness of Damascus: and when thou comest, anoint Hazael to be king over Syria: And Jehu the son of Nimshi shalt thou anoint to be king over Israel: and Elisha the son of Shaphat of Abel-meholah shalt thou anoint to be a prophet in thy room" (1 Kings 19:15–16). God gave Elijah some responsibilities.

B. *Listen to the Lord's call for service.* Living life without meaningful responsibilities does bring depression. Thus, depression often can be helped by getting involved in meaningful service for the Lord. Find out what service you can render for others.

Conclusion

Are you depressed? Get in touch with your mood. If your feelings are low, try God's therapy. Check on your physical condition. On the advice of a physician, get an exercise program started and begin proper eating habits. Check on your mental attitude. If you have been majoring on the negative, look for the positive. Then ask the Lord, "What would you have me to do?"

WEDNESDAY EVENING, OCTOBER 16

Title: The Absolute Supremacy of Jesus Christ

Text: "Who is the image of the invisible God, the firstborn of every creature: for by him were all things created, that are in heaven, and that are in earth, visible and invisible, whether they be thrones, or dominions, or principalities, or powers: all things were created by him, and for him: and he is before all things, and by him all things consist" **(Col. 1:15–17).**

Scripture Reading: Colossians 1:15–23

Introduction

We are interested in finding the best. *Time* magazine's "Man of the Year" is a recognition of the man who is considered to have contributed a great deal to the world in that year. Organizations also feature a man or woman of the year. The Heisman Trophy recognizes the college football player of the year. High school and college yearbooks usually have a section dealing with the best in many categories. All of these are attempts to find and identify the one who is the best, the one who has supremacy in his or her field.

Above all these stands the one who is absolutely supreme: Jesus Christ. Paul turned from prayer to the magnificent presentation of the preeminence of Christ. The Colossian heretics had degraded Christ. They had indicated that he was not unique, but just one among many manifestations of God.

They believed that all matter was evil, and therefore Jesus did not have a real manhood. In the face of this, Paul set out the absolute supremacy of Jesus Christ.

Christianity stands or falls on the fact of the person of Jesus Christ. Either he is what we have believed—that he is the unique Son of God—or else a gigantic hoax has been perpetrated. These verses that interrupt a prayer with a presentation bear out that Jesus is what we have believed him to be—the unique Son of God who has absolute supremacy.

I. The scope of the absolute supremacy of Jesus Christ is noted (Col. 1:15–19).

A. *The scope of the supremacy of Jesus Christ is seen in his relationship to deity (v. 15).* Jesus was called "the image of the invisible God." This is the idea of a representation of another. God is invisible, but Jesus is visible and is an exact likeness of God. Beyond that, the representation becomes a manifestation.

B. *The scope of the supremacy of Jesus Christ is seen in his relationship to the creation (vv. 16–17).* That he was the "firstborn of all creation" indicates honor rather than time. This can be said for three reasons that are outlined in the text.

1. Because he is creator. The sphere of creation was "in him." This shows that Jesus was the mediating agent of creation, "through him." And he is the goal of all creation.

2. Because he is before all things. Jesus is before all things both in time and rank. John's prologue (John 1:1) indicates that he was from the very beginning. And he is also before all things in rank. He is Number 1!

3. Because he holds all things together. Christ is the principle of cohesion by which all things are held together in our world.

C. *The scope of the supremacy of Jesus Christ is seen in his relationship to the church (v. 18).* Christ is the head of the church. The church is under the direction of Christ, serves the purpose of Christ, and exists to be used by Christ. In *The All Sufficient Christ,* William Barclay told of the man in India who came before a pastor and wanted to be a member of the church. The pastor knew that the man had no connection with a church and no instruction in the faith. So he asked him why he wanted to be a member of the church. The man replied that he had read the Gospel of Luke and, believing what he had read, had taken Jesus as his Lord and Master. But he thought that his salvation was just a matter between him and Christ until he discovered what the book of Acts had to say. Here there was a difference. Jesus had ascended to the Father, and the book of Acts was about what Peter and Paul and others in the early church said and did. So, the man said, he felt that he must become a member of the church that carries on the life of Christ.

II. The basis of the absolute supremacy of Jesus Christ is presented (Col. 1:19–23).

A. *It is based on who he is (v. 19).* All the fullness of God dwells in Christ. This complete revelation of God is made in the incarnation. *Fullness* is a technical term that means "sum total." All the divine attributes and powers dwelt in the Son.

B. *It is based on what he had done (vv. 20–23).* He has reconciled us to God.

   1. Scope of reconciliation: "all things."

   2. Means of reconciliation (v. 21): the death of Christ on the cross. All the powers that have produced humankind's hostilities to God—sin, death, law, rebellion—have been vanquished in the cross. Christ destroyed them all.

   3. Purpose of reconciliation (vv. 22–23): God intended for us to be set apart for him (holy), without blame, and irreproachable. How? By allowing his Holy Spirit to live within us. As we continue in the faith, remaining stable and steadfast to the one who has called us and saved us, we will bear the fruit of the Spirit.

Conclusion

Jesus Christ is absolutely supreme. There is none like him in all the universe. And through him we find God and his grace.

SUNDAY MORNING, OCTOBER 20

Title: A God Who Understands

Text: "Then drew near unto him all the publicans and sinners for to hear him. And the Pharisees and scribes murmured, saying, This man receiveth sinners, and eateth with them" **(Luke 15:1–2).**

Scripture Reading: Luke 15:1–2

Hymns: "I Love to Tell the Story," Hankey
          "Tell It to Jesus," Rankin
          "Just When I Need Him Most," Poole

Offertory Prayer: Our Father, we are grateful that you are a God who cares. Indeed, you cared enough to send your very best, even your Son. When we forget your care and succumb to the sins of self-pity or resentment, forgive us and remind us again how much you care. In response to your love and understanding, we offer our gifts today. May they be used to spread the good news of Christ to others who do not know a God who understands. In the name of Christ your Son, we pray. Amen.

Introduction

Luke, in emphasizing the humanity of Jesus in his gospel account, is saying, "We have a God who understands." Matthew stresses the messiahship of

Christ, Mark his servanthood, but Luke (a physician committed to alleviating human suffering) chooses to stress the humanity of Jesus. He is concerned that suffering humanity know we have a God who understands.

Luke's name appears only three times in the New Testament, and not one of these instances is in either book he wrote. Rather, references to Luke can be found in Colossians 4:14 where he is called the "beloved Physician," in Philemon 24 where he is called Paul's "fellow-worker," and in 2 Timothy 4:11 where he stands by Paul during the dark hours of Paul's approaching martyrdom. In all three passages, Luke's life bears evidence that he had come to know in Christ "a God who understands."

Regardless of who we are, where we live, or what we have done, Luke's message to us is that in Jesus Christ we have a God who understands. In an effort to see what Luke says about this subject in all twenty-four chapters of his book, I have reduced his statements to three.

I. God understands what it is to be human—for he was human.

"Thou shalt conceive in thy womb, and bring forth a son, and thou shalt call his name Jesus" (Luke 1:31). Apart from being conceived by the Holy Spirit, Christ's birth was as human as anyone else's. He was conceived in the womb of a woman, as any other, and the physical aspects of his birth were identical to any other human's birth. Jesus did not drop down from the sky as a full-grown Messiah. His was a natural birth, a natural growth, a natural development. O yes, he was divine, but he was very much human.

The title "Son of man" is used in Luke's account twenty-three times to stress the humanity of Jesus. It is Christ's favorite designation for himself. Whatever else this title may mean, it means that Christ is human—that he is one with humankind—that he understand us.

"The Son of man hath not where to lay his head" (9:58).
"The Son of man hath power upon earth" (5:24).
"The Son of man is come eating and drinking" (7:34).
"The Son of man is Lord also of the sabbath" (6:5).
"The Son of man shall be delivered into the hands of men" (9:44).
"The Son of man cometh at an hour when he think not" (12:40).

These, plus seventeen other such references to "the Son of man," assure us that ours is a God who understands what it is to be human—for he was human.

For many of us it seems strange that a person would question Jesus' humanity. Theoretically, very few have ever done so. The Docetics believed that the body of Jesus was not real. They held that Christ was only God appearing in human form. Many theologians have so emphasized the deity of Christ and assumed such a chasm between God and man that they have practically nullified the human life of Jesus. This is wrong. We should begin with the facts of the life of Jesus as recorded in the New Testament. Nobody who takes the New Testament seriously will ever question Jesus' humanity.

As a man, Jesus was subject to the law of growth and development. Luke tells us that he grew in wisdom and stature and in favor with God and men (Luke 2:52). This seems to describe normal human growth.

A. *His temptations were human.* When Jesus said to his disciples on the night he was betrayed, "Pray that ye enter not into temptation" (Luke 22:40), he knew what he was talking about! Jesus ministry was launched in the midst of a barrage of temptations (Luke 4:1–13), and his temptations never let up. They hounded him until his last breath on the cross.

Jesus' temptations and battles were real. His struggles with sin and evil were no sham battles. We sometimes make the mistake of thinking that there can be no temptation unless there is something base and ignoble in our lives to which temptation can appeal. But this was wrong. The temptation to satisfy Jesus' physical appetite was real! (Bread.) The temptation to turn from the Father's will for his life and gain the world through compromise was real! (Worship Satan.) The temptation to win the world through sensationalism was real! (Leap from temple.)

This is why we can go to Christ unashamed of our temptations. For Hebrews 4:15 (TLB) assures us that "this High Priest of ours understands our weaknesses, since he had the same temptations we do, though he never once gave way to them and sinned." Yet Jesus' understanding does not mean that he condones our giving in to temptation. Rather, it means that when we go to him in time of temptation, we don't need to explain what it is all about, for he understands what it is to be human and to be tempted—he was human too.

B. *His compassion was human (Luke 7:11–15).* There is no stronger word than "compassion" for pity and sympathy and feeling, and it is a word that is used again and again in the gospel story to describe Jesus. At that time this must have been a staggering thought. The Stoics held that the primary characteristic of God was apathy or the incapability of feeling, yet in Luke we were presented with the amazing conception of one who was the Son of God and yet was human enough to be moved with compassion.

C. *His disappointments were human.* Jesus was disappointed in his own home town (Nazareth). "No prophet is accepted in his own country" (Luke 4:24). He was disappointed in those whom he healed. "Were there not ten cleansed? but where are the nine?" (Luke 17:17). He was disappointed in one whom he had chosen. "Behold, the hand of him that betrayeth me is with me on the table" (Luke 22:21).

D. *His prayer life was human.* "And he withdrew himself into the wilderness and prayed" (Luke 5:16). "And being in an agony he prayed more earnestly: and his sweat was as it were great drops of blood falling down to the ground" (Luke 22:44). Jesus was not stage-playing. He prayed because he needed to pray! He had human temptations.

E. *His suffering was human.* When the cat-of-nine-tails lashed across Jesus' back, tearing flesh, it hurt just as it would hurt any other human's back. When the nails were driven into his hands, he felt pain as any other person would. When the spear was thrust into his side, and when he said, "I thirst," it was for real. He understands human suffering because he suffered. Luke is saying, "Come down from the ledge; don't leap. There is someone who understands, and his name is Jesus."

II. God understands the difficulty of forgiveness—for he forgave (Luke 7:41–48).

A. *Simon was having a difficult time forgiving the woman who cleansed Jesus' feet with her tears.* Her sin was known everywhere. How could Jesus possibly forgive her, he wondered. The woman was notoriously bad—a prostitute! No doubt she had heard Jesus speak. Around her neck she wore, like all Jewish women, a small vial of concentrated perfume. These vials were called alabasters, and they were very costly. She wanted to pour it on Jesus' feet, for it was all she had. But as she saw his compassion, tears formed and fell upon his feet. Barclay reminds us that for a Jewish woman to appear with her hair down was an act of the gravest immodesty. On her wedding day a girl bound her hair, and never would she appear with it unbound. The fact that this woman loosed her long hair in public showed that she had forgotten all others except Jesus.

The whole story reveals a contrast between two attitudes of mind and heart.

1. Simon was aware of no need and felt no love; therefore he offered no forgiveness.
2. Christ hated sin but loved the sinner. To him there was no problem in forgiving so repentant a sinner.

B. *Jesus also forgave those who were not repentant.* For those who nailed him to the cross and taunted him by saying, "He saved others; let him save himself, if he be the Christ," he prayed, "Father, forgive them; for they know not what they do" (Luke 23:34). This was not easy, but he did it anyway. He understands the difficulty of forgiveness—for he forgave.

When you, like Simon Peter, would ask, "Lord, how often shall my brother sin against me and I forgive him? till seven times?" remember the words of Christ, underscored again by his prayer on the cross, "I say not unto thee, Until seven times; but, until seventy times seven!"

He understands the difficulty of forgiveness—for he forgave.

III. God understands the need of assurance—for he was assured.

After Christ had incurred the wrath of the Pharisees for healing the man with the withered hand on the Sabbath, Luke records, "They were filled with madness; and communed one with another what they might do to Jesus. And it came to pass in those days, that he went out into a mountain to pray, and continued all night in prayer to God. And when it was day, he called unto him his disciples: and of them he chose twelve, whom also he named apostles" (Luke 6:11–13).

Christ understands what it means to need assurance. Undoubtedly shaken by the threats and schemes of his enemies, he needed assurance that only his Father could give him. And so he prayed. In fact, Luke says he prayed all night long.

The next day, assured by his Father that he would live to see his mission accomplished, Jesus chose his twelve apostles. Christ understands the need of assurance—for he was assured.

A. *He offers assurance in the present (Luke 12:22–23, 31–32).*
B. *He offers assurance for the future (Luke 21:26–28).*

Conclusion

The newspapers ran a story of one woman who had decided to end her life but changed her mind for one reason: someone understood!

In the words of the patrolman who called her back from the ledge, I say to you, "I don't know who you are, or where you live, or what you have done. But I do know there is someone who understands, and his name is Jesus."

SUNDAY EVENING, OCTOBER 20

Title: The Problem of Suffering

Text: "Then Job arose and rent his mantle, and shaved his head, and fell down upon the ground, and worshipped, and said, Naked came I out of my mother's womb, and naked shall I return thither: the LORD gave, and the LORD hath taken away; blessed be the name of the LORD" **(Job 1:20–21).**

Scripture Reading: Job 1:1–22

Introduction

In December 1958 a play opened on Broadway that had only two letters for a title—*J.B.* The play had several handicaps to overcome. First, the newspapers were on strike, and not a single notice was printed of its appearance. Second, it did not have any of the elements that seem to make a play successful—comedy, romance, music, dancing, and sex. Third, the play was written in verse and dealt with a biblical theme. Nonetheless, every performance of *J.B.* was sold out.

Why did people take such an interest in the play? The answer is simple. *J.B.* is short for Job, and Job is the book in the Bible that deals directly with the agonizing problems of human suffering. The story of Job hits people where they live; therefore, insights into the story of Job will interest people.

The story of Job is an ancient one. Some say Job lived during the age of the patriarchs. More than likely the book of Job was written during a time in Judah's national suffering. The story of Job gives us several insights for living in our own time.

I. Life brings many baffling questions.

A. *The story of Job is a baffling one.* Reading the circumstances of Job does raise questions. The Lord described Job: "There is none like him in the earth, a perfect and an upright man, one that feareth God, and eschewed evil" (Job 1:8). Job was blessed with a great family, seven sons and three daughters. He was further blessed with great wealth.

Job became a test study in motivation when Satan proposed that Job served the Lord because it brought great dividends, such as great wealth. God permitted these externals to be removed so Satan could see that Job served the Lord from a good motivation.

In quick succession, blows of adversity hit Job. An Arab tribe stole his cattle. A storm destroyed his sheep and goats. The Chaldeans carried off his camels. A hurricane killed all of his children. Then Job lost his health. In all of these losses Job never lost his faith in the Lord.

The story of Job baffles people. "Why did Job deserve those tragedies? Didn't it pay him to do good?"

B. *Numerous circumstances puzzle our minds.* Observing some of life's situations brings questions to our minds. Why does a child suffer from a brain defect? Why is a young wife and mother killed by a drunk driver? Why is a young physician beginning an exciting career in surgery stricken with leukemia? These and numerous other questions baffle our minds and prompt us to ask, "Why?" The circumstances of life bring baffling questions. Fortunately, the book of Job gives some insight.

II. The world's thinkers have inadequate answers.

A. *The friends of Job did not help him with his dilemma.* Three friends of Job—Eliphaz, Bildad, and Zophar—heard of Job's problems and came to visit him. They were shocked when they saw Job. They sat with him in silence for seven days and seven nights. Perhaps the silence provided their best comfort to Job.

When the friends finally spoke, they ceased to comfort Job. Rather, they proposed to have the answer to Job's suffering. They said Job suffered because of his sin. If he would admit and confess the sin in his life, his suffering would cease.

Later another friend, a young man named Elihu, came to visit Job. His proposal was simple: Job's suffering was given by God to refine his character like gold in the fire. Thus, none of Job's four friends provided adequate answers for his suffering.

B. *Life's problems do not have easy answers.* Not every circumstance of suffering can be attributed to sin. You remember Jesus' observations of the man born blind (see John 9). He would not explain the man's suffering in terms of his sin. Furthermore, God does not give trouble only for the purpose of developing character. God may use trouble to develop character, but not every case of suffering can be attributed to this purpose.

There are no easy answers to the baffling problems of life. Simple formulas will not fit some of life's circumstances. Yet the book of Job does not end in question; it ends with another insight.

III. The Lord has a word for us.

A. *The help for Job's suffering comes with a word from God.* "Then the LORD answered Job out of the whirlwind" (Job 38:1). God did not appear in order to take away Job's sufferings. Rather, he came to be with Job. To teach Job some lessons on knowledge, the Lord interrogated him, asking hard questions: Were you present at creation? Did you make the sea? Did you ever cause a sunrise? Can you explain rain? God knew that Job could not ignore these questions. Job needed to see the might of God and the inadequacies of human beings.

B. *The Lord speaks to us amid life's baffling circumstances.* What does the Lord say? Does he tell us the intellectual reasons for our suffering? No, he does not give us answers. Instead, the Lord gives us the adequacy of his presence. We must be willing for trust in the Lord to take over when we are confronted by situations we cannot understand.

Conclusion

One Christmas two brothers expected and received new bicycles. Christmas day came, and both started riding and enjoying their gifts. In a few hours both of them became ill. The older boy became so ill that he had to be hospitalized. Spending the Christmas holidays in a hospital and knowing there was a new bicycle at home did not make him happy.

He asked, "Daddy, why did I have to get sick on Christmas?" The answer was obvious and simple. "Son, a virus exists, and many people are getting sick this way." Those were the facts. But the boy was not satisfied with the facts, and learning the facts did not help him. However, the presence of his mother and father in the hospital room brought him comfort.

Now do you see? What a person needs amid life's baffling situations is not an intellectual answer, but the presence of the Lord. Why not let the Lord come into your life?

WEDNESDAY EVENING, OCTOBER 23

Title: An Open Secret

Text: "Whereof I am made a minister, according to the dispensation of God which is given to me for you, to fulfil the word of God; even the mystery which hath been hid from ages and from generations, but now is made manifest to his saints" **(Col. 1:25–26).**

Scripture Reading: Colossians 1:24–29

Introduction

The world of New Testament times was not a nonreligious world. In fact, it was saturated with religion. We could say that it was long on religion but short on revelation. For many people, the old religions of Greece and Rome had lost their luster, and Judaism had hardened into legalism and exclusivism. People were hungry and searching for a religion that would satisfy their lives and fill their souls.

One of the ways the ancients tried to find a satisfying religion was through the mystery religions. These religions gathered weird and wonderful legends of gods and goddesses. Usually the chief features of the legends were portrayed in symbolic rites that were largely kept secret and were supposed to be known only by those who had been initiated as full participants. These secret doctrines and rites were called the "mysteries" of the religion and were closely guarded.

Strangely enough, Paul used their very word, *mystery,* to describe what God has now made known to humankind. The fullness of God's revelation was not known until God became man in Jesus Christ. But now this revelation has been unveiled, now this mystery has been made known, now this secret has been let out. In English, *mystery* usually means something that is baffling and defies solution or understanding. But to the Greeks it meant something that once had been hidden but now had been revealed—a revealed secret.

The glorious message of God to us through Paul is that this secret has now been made known, and not to just a select few, but to all persons. It was an open secret. And what is that open secret? It is "Christ in you, the hope of glory" (Col. 1:27). All people can know Christ. Everyone can know the fullness of God's revelation.

I. The open secret shows us the significance of suffering (Col. 1:24).

A. *Suffering takes on significance when it is done for others.*
B. *Suffering takes on significance when joy can be found in the suffering.* Suffering does not have to embitter. Joy comes with the purpose of suffering. A sympathizer expressed sorrow that a soldier had lost a leg. The soldier replied that he did not *lose* a leg but that he *gave* it.
C. *Suffering makes fellowship with Christ possible.*

II. The open secret shows us the glory of the gospel (Col. 1:25–27).

A. *The glory of the gospel centers in the union of the believer with Christ.* That the believer is united with Christ by faith is a key concept in Paul's writings. It is seen in such phrases as "in Christ" or "in him." Paul assures us that Gentiles too can know the salvation that is in Christ.

B. *The glory of the gospel is that it produces hope in this life.* The world of Christ's time knew sin, but it did not know what to do with sin. Christ now brings hope and forgiveness to all who turn to him in repentance. He is the world's only hope.

A shepherd in the highlands of Scotland had become infirm and blind. He was so crippled with rheumatism that he could not stir from his seat by the fire. One day a visitor asked if the hours he spent like that were not weary. Then the visitor spoke of the blessedness of heaven. The old shepherd answered simply that he knew the blessedness well; he had been in heaven during the past ten years since he had known Christ.

C. *The glory of the gospel is that there is hope for the world to come.*

III. The open secret shows us the urge to universality (Col. 1:28–29).

A. *The gospel is universal in its application.* The gospel is for all people. God had always intended that his revelation would be universal. And now through Christ it has been brought about. Everyone can know salvation through Christ. The attempt to limit the gospel to a particular class, economic strata, or race is a denial of the universality of the gospel. It obscures it rather than makes it known.

B. *The gospel is universal in its appeal.* Paul worked hard to make the gospel appeal to all persons.

An evangelist described the doorway into the kingdom of God as being like an electric-eye door at a department store entrance—the door opens for anyone who approaches it. Any person who accepts Christ can gain entry.

Conclusion

We have an open secret. Christ has come into the world to give salvation to all who accept him. He indeed indwells everyone who believes. That is the hope of glory, the hope for anyone who comes to him in faith.

SUNDAY MORNING, OCTOBER 27

Title: Simply Divine!

Text: "These are written, that ye might believe that Jesus is the Christ, the Son of God; and that believing ye might have life through his name" **(John 20:31).**

Scripture Reading: John 1:1–3

Hymns: "All Hail the Power," Anonymous
"Come, Thou Almighty King," Perronet
"Jesus Is Lord of All," McClard

Offertory Prayer: Although we can never comprehend the glory of Christ's deity, we rejoice in you, O Father, that you have sent him to us. For the miracles he performed, for the lessons he taught us, and for the death he experienced for us, we are thankful.

May in this hour a spark of the divine be kindled in us. May that spark ignite the flames of love and compassion, and may Christ in us create a new zeal to share him with others through our lives and our gifts. In Christ's name. Amen.

Introduction

More than 92 percent of the Gospel of John is not found in the gospels of Matthew, Mark, or Luke. Out of his vast storehouse John chose to record incidents, "signs," and conversations that would convince the world that Jesus is "simply divine."

Consequently, John's gospel has no account of the birth of Christ, his baptism, nor his temptations. It tells nothing of the Last Supper, nothing of Gethsemane, and nothing of Christ's ascension. It records not one experience of Christ's healing of people possessed by demons. Perhaps most surprising of all, it contains none of the parables of our Lord. Although John's gospel says nothing about any of these events that hold so prominent a place in the other three gospels, it has everything to say about Christ's deity!

In fact, so concerned is John that we know Jesus is divine that the opening statement of his gospel is an assertion of Jesus' deity. "Before anything else existed, there was Christ, with God. He has always been alive and is himself God. He created everything there is" (John 1:1–3 TLB).

Philip Schaff called the Gospel of John "the most important literary production ever composed." F. C. Thompson called it "the deepest and most spiritual book in the Bible." William Barclay said it is "the most precious book in the New Testament." Kyle Yates referred to it as "the Holy of Holies of the entire Bible." And A. T. Robertson said it is "the greatest of all books produced by man."

The book presents the personal recollections of an old man who knew and loved and revered his Lord. It throbs with life and color. With dramatic power and attention to details, John produced a never-to-be-forgotten picture of Christ as "simply divine." The theme of the deity of Christ runs throughout the whole of this gospel.

I. Jesus' nature is divine (John 1:1–3).

"In the beginning"—takes us back to the book of Genesis, doesn't it? "In the beginning"—when was the beginning? Who knows. The geologists say one thing. Scientists in other areas say something else, and some theologians say something still different.

How old is the world? When was the beginning? Was it six thousand, six hundred thousand, six million, or six hundred million years ago? I don't know, and I don't think anybody else knows for sure.

A. *Notice that "in the beginning was the Word."* That refers to the Lord Jesus Christ, the living Word. In Revelation 19 he is spoken of as the "Word." Take note of three things.

1. Jesus is eternal. He didn't begin in time, and he wasn't the product of his own generation. "In the beginning was the Word" speaks of the *eternity* of Jesus. What John is saying is this: Christ is not one of the created things; Christ existed before creation. Christ is not part of the world that came into being in time; Christ is part of eternity and was with God before time and before the world began. This thought of John has a technical name in theology—the preexistence of Christ. What Jesus did was to open a window in time that we might see the eternal and unchanging love of God. He is telling us that God was and is and ever shall be always like Jesus; but people could never know and realize that until Jesus came.

2. "The Word was with God." The word *therewith* means "face to face," indicating fellowship. Thus, I use the word *affinity* to describe the relationship between God and Jesus. Christ and God have always had the most intimate fellowship. No one can tell us what God is like, what God's will is for us, what God's love and heart and mind are like, as Jesus can. John is saying that Jesus is so close to God that God has no secrets from Jesus. Thus, Jesus is the one person in all the universe who can reveal to us what God is like and how God feels toward us.

3. "The Word was God." Here we have the *identity* of Christ. Christ is of the very same essence and being as God. When John said the Word was God, he was saying that Jesus is the same as God in mind and heart. At the very beginning of his gospel, John makes clear that in Jesus alone there is perfectly revealed all that God always was and always will be, and all that God feels and desires for us.

So here are the three tremendous truths that we need to begin with: The *eternity* of Christ, the *affinity* of Christ, and the *identity* of Christ. He is God. He is "simply divine." It is his nature to be so.

B. *After twenty chapters of proclaiming the fact that Jesus is God, John very pointedly states the main purpose of his book.* "These things are written, that ye might believe that Jesus is the Christ, the Son of God; and that believing ye might have life through his name" (John 20:31).

Two friends from Civil War days sat talking on a train. Both men, one a general and the other a colonel, were professed atheists. Soon their conversation moved to the place of Jesus in religion.

"I think it's a shame that the historical Jesus has become so encrusted with supernatural superstition," one said. They continued refuting various gospel miracles as legends and myths. Finally, the general suggested, "Someone ought to write a novel about the real Jesus."

"That's a good idea," replied the colonel. "General, you should do it. You could portray Jesus as he really was: a wonder man but nothing more."

"I'll do it," the general said.

He began careful research on the life of Christ, intending to prove that Jesus was only a man and nothing more.

The book was finally written and published, and it sold over two million copies. A movie of the book has proved to be one of the most popular motion pictures of all time. The name of the book and movie: *Ben Hur.* The author: Gen. Lew Wallace. The colonel who challenged him to write the book was Col. Robert Ingersoll, America's "great agnostic."

While writing the book, General Wallace became a sincere believer in the divinity of Christ. He became a believer, not because of rational discovery, but because of a personal experience with a divine Lord who John said, "was with God and was God." The voice of Gen. Wallace joins the throngs of countless believers throughout the ages in saying, "Jesus is divine!"

II. Jesus' mission is divine (John 1:14).

"Christ became a human being and lived here on earth among us" (John 1:14 TLB).

A. *This Christ, with a divine nature, came on a divine mission!* His mission was authorized by no one less than God himself! In the fifth chapter of John, Christ states six times that he has been sent by God (John 5:23–24, 30, 36–38).

B. *John records eight miracles (not counting Christ's resurrection) to prove that Christ's mission is divine.* Six of the eight are found only in John's gospel.

1. Turning of water into wine (2:1–11).
2. Healing of the nobleman's son (4:46–54).
3. Healing of the man at the pool (5:1–9).
4. Healing of the man born blind (9:1–7).
5. Raising of Lazarus (11:1–46).
6. Miraculous supplying of fish (21:1–6).

C. *In John the miracles are more than expressions of compassion; they are demonstrations of the glory of Christ.* After the miracle at Cana of Galilee, John comments, "This beginning of miracles did Jesus in Cana of Galilee, and manifested forth his glory" (John 2:11). The raising of Lazarus happened "for the glory of God" (John 11:4).

Whatever Christ did, whatever he said, whatever good was done was for one reason: he was on a divine mission! And for that reason he "was made flesh and dwelt among us."

III. Jesus' accomplishments are divine (John 19:30).

"When Jesus therefore had received the vinegar, he said, It is finished" (John 19:30).

The Christian faith does not begin with a big *do* but with a big *done*. Of course, our American activist reason protests at this. If we do not get moving, how can we ever reach the goal? How can we ever achieve anything if we do not work for it? The fact is that if we seek to attain, we miss it all. "It is finished," said Jesus. Jesus has accomplished for us what only God could accomplish. We are invited from the very outset to enjoy what Christ has already accomplished for us.

What we need we can never accomplish. But the divine accomplishments of Christ meet our every need.

A. *Salvation is a divine accomplishment.* When Jesus said, "It is finished," he was saying that the payment for humanity's sins has been made. Salvation has been accomplished!

As Christ prayed to the Father, he said, "You have given your Son power over all flesh, that he should give eternal life to many as Thou hast given him. I have finished the work which thou gavest me to do" (see John 17:1–4). Salvation is not an unfinished project that Christ began on the cross but was unable to complete. It is not a partial accomplishment whose completion is dependent on our joining the church, being baptized, taking the Lord's Supper, and doing all kinds of marvelous works. "Not by works of righteousness which we have done, but according to his mercy he saved us" (Titus 3:5). This was a finished divine accomplishment; we never could have accomplished it ourselves.

B. *Security is a divine accomplishment.* "I give unto them eternal life; and they shall never perish, neither shall any man pluck them out of my hand. My Father, which gave them me, is greater than all, and no man is able to pluck them out of my Father's hand. I and my Father are one" (John 10:28–30).

After assuring believers of their security, Jesus tells them why he can do this. "I and my Father are one. I am divine, and thus both the salvation I offer and the security I promise are divine accomplishments!"

The resurrection (John 20) is the one most important event in the entire life of Christ. His resurrection is a stamp of divine validation on his death as payment in full for our salvation. It is a guarantee that we are secure in trusting one who could conquer even death. Christ's resurrection is the greatest single evidence that Jesus is divine. Only God himself could return from the dead!

"When he had said this, he breathed on them, and saith unto them, Receive ye the Holy Ghost" (John 20:22). The daily, hourly infilling of the Holy Spirit is ours for the claiming. Christ has provided it. It is a divine accomplishment. And yet we, like the early church, must be admonished again and again, "Be filled with the Spirit."

Conclusion

The divine accomplishments of Christ are a handle given us by God on which our faith can lay hold. We can be saved! We can have security! Every day we can experience spiritual empowering! All because Jesus Christ is "simply divine."

SUNDAY EVENING, OCTOBER 27

Title: Lessons Learned in the School of Life

Text: "The LORD said to me, "Go, show your love to your wife again, though she is loved by another and is an adulteress. Love her as the LORD loves the Israelites, though they turn to other gods and love the sacred raisin cakes" **(Hos. 3:1 NIV).**

Scripture Reading: Hosea 1:1–11; 3:1–5

Introduction

Several men discussed where they attended college. One conspicuously avoided telling where he attended, so another man in the crowd asked him, "Jim, where did you get your education?" Jim timidly replied, "I got my education in the school of life, and I majored in hard knocks."

In the Old Testament there is the story of a prophet who got his education in the school of life. He too majored in hard knocks. His name was Hosea. The prophet's marriage to a prostitute name Gomer marked the beginning of his education. "The beginning of the word of the LORD by Hosea. And the LORD said to Hosea, Go, take unto thee a wife of whoredoms and children of whoredoms: for the land hath committed great whoredom, departing from the LORD" (Hos. 1:2–3). The inevitable result was domestic tragedy. Three children were born in Hosea's home, but he had a suspicion that the last child did not belong to him.

Amid the domestic tragedy, Hosea applied his situation to the Lord's work with Israel. God had married Israel, and Israel was unfaithful to the Lord.

I. Hosea learned about the nature of sin.

A. *Sin is a selfish rebellion against God.*
   1. Gomer rebelled and went after her other lovers. Her action was deliberate. It was her action.
   2. Sin is a self-centered action on the part of a person. It is a deliberate attempt to be the master of your life.

B. *Sin is a grief-bringing action.*
   1. Gomer's action wounded her family. Hosea was hurt. Three children were hurt.
   2. Sin is a wounding matter. Rebellion against the Lord brings deep hurt to God, yourself, and others around you.

C. *Sin is a separation situation.*
   1. Gomer left Hosea, and he was left alone with the three children. Hosea learned about the tragic alienation that sin brings.
   2. Sin separates, or alienates, people from God.

II. Hosea learned about the nature of religion.

A. *Religion is not just an external matter.*
   1. Gomer fulfilled the external obligations of a wife. Hosea wanted a loving mother for his children and a devoted homemaker.
   2. Real religion consists of more than external observances. Listen to Micah: "Wherewith shall I come before the LORD, and bow myself before the high God? Shall I come before him with burnt offerings, with calves of a year old? Will the LORD be pleased with thousands of rams, or with ten thousands of rivers of oil? Shall I give my firstborn for my transgression, the fruit of my body for the sin of my soul? He hath shewed thee, O man, what is good; and what doth the LORD require of thee, but to do justly, and to love mercy, and to walk humbly with thy God?" (Mic. 6:6–8).

B. *Religion is a relationship with God.*
   1. Gomer did not have a relationship with Hosea. She had his children, cooked his meals, and cleaned his house, but her love was for others.
   2. Real religion is a personal relationship with God.

C. *Real religion results in a companionship.*
   1. Gomer was never an authentic companion of Hosea. She lived with him, but she did not relate to him.
   2. Real religion is a harmonious relationship with God. It means to walk and talk each day with the Lord.

III. Hosea learned about the nature of God.

A. *God does not give up on human beings.*
   1. Gomer left Hosea for other lovers. She went the way of the world, but Hosea did not give up on getting her back. He persisted until he found and reclaimed Gomer again.

2. God searches relentlessly for erring human beings. He seeks continuously to bring rebellious people back to himself.

B. *God has a loving attitude toward sinners.*

1. Gomer's rebellion gave Hosea an insight into how God felt toward Israel. He did not want to destroy the people. He still loved them.
2. God is not angry at the world. He is in love with the world. He wants a relationship.

C. *God restores erring human beings.*

1. Hosea learned about God's redemptive nature. After Hosea found Gomer, he bought her and took her home again.
2. God restores wandering human beings back into fellowship.

Conclusion

Hosea had a real problem—he had an unfaithful wife. A domestic tragedy occurred in his life, yet he was able to learn some valuable lessons from it. Have you learned these lessons? God wants to relate to you. God wants you to walk with him. Why don't you let him into your life?

WEDNESDAY EVENING, OCTOBER 30

Title: The Marks of Faithfulness

Text: "As ye have therefore received Christ Jesus the Lord, so walk ye in him: rooted and built up in him, and established in the faith, as ye have been taught, abounding therein with thanksgiving" **(Col. 2:6–7).**

Scripture Reading: Colossians 2:1–7

Introduction

J. B. Gambrell, a great Texas hero of pioneer days, referred to a dog's territory, which was limited to the area around his master's wagon. Since the wagons rode high off the ground, the dog could run along underneath the wagon as it traveled. Gambrell said, "I would never have a dog that ran under someone else's wagon." That was his rather homey way of saying that faithfulness is a necessity.

We all understand Gambrell's point. When we list characteristics desirable in a person, we usually mention faithfulness.

One of the desires Paul had for the Colossian Christians was faithfulness. Paul had just drawn with bold strokes a sweeping panorama of the cosmic significance of Christ and the world mission of Christianity (Col. 1). Now with personal abandon, Paul, himself a part of this mission, applied his concern to the Colossians. He said, "What great conflict I have for you" (Col. 2:1). *Conflict* is a word from the athletic games meaning "struggle, agony." But this was not some general, vague concern. It was specific. It was aimed at some specific problem and some specific person. Paul was concerned with the issues but more so with the persons involved. We see this in his prayer for faithfulness in the church. In his prayer we can see some marks of faithfulness.

I.The strengthening of others is a mark of faithfulness.

A. *The church must be a source of ceaseless encouragement.* Paul prayed "that their hearts might be comforted" (Col. 2:2). The word *comfort* can mean to encourage, exhort, give comfort to. Charles Trentham once observed that it is not comfort in the sense of solace for which Paul yearned. Nor was it encouragement in the sense of cheering words or flattering phrases. Rather, it was the encouragement that comes from divine reinforcement.

B. *The encouragement must be to heroic action.* There was once a Greek regiment in ancient times that had lost heart, lost courage, and was utterly dejected. The general sent a leader to talk to that regiment. As he spoke, courage was reborn, and a body of dispirited men became a body of men fit again for heroic action.

This is Paul's prayer. The mark of faithfulness in Christians is to strengthen one another so that the church is filled with courage to deal heroically in any situation.

II.The bond of love is a mark of faithfulness.

Paul also prayed that the church might be "knit together in love." The bond of love must be a distinguishing mark of the church that follows Christ. The Christ whose whole life was a life of love forms a bond of love for his followers that knits them together.

The story has been told many times and in many forms, but it bears repeating when we consider that the church that loves Christ must also love the people of Christ. A young girl loved her father, but she had difficulty getting along with her brother. When her father came home from work one evening she ran to him, threw her arms around his neck, and hugged him. At the same time she stuck out her tongue at her brother. The father told her that she could not love her father and at the same time stick out her tongue at her brother.

III.The discipline of life is a mark of faithfulness.

A. *Discipline means order in life.* The "order" and "steadfastness" mentioned in Colossians 2:5 are military terms. They give the picture of a well-disciplined army standing firmly rank upon rank in a formation that could hardly be broken.

The church that is faithful to Christ must have discipline. It does not move without purpose. It does not function randomly. Instead, it functions in discipline and order so that work can be accomplished and the gospel can be proclaimed.

B. *Discipline means ministry through life.* Discipline includes attendance, worship, and ministry in the name of Christ.

IV. The growth of faith is a mark of faithfulness.

A. *The growth of faith is toward maturity.* The Christian church must be a maturing family as indicated in verses 6–7. There is much mental, emotional, and spiritual immaturity because we have deserted the only soil in which we can grow. Elton Trueblood spoke of a "cut flower civilization" in which we were cut flowers in a vase. They are beautiful and brilliant, but they can never grow and prosper because they have no roots.

B. *The growth of faith comes "in the faith."*

C. *The result of the growth of faith is thanksgiving.*

Conclusion

The marks of faithfulness are displayed in Paul's prayer. As we seek to be faithful to God, we must develop these characteristics in life.

Suggested preaching program for the month of

NOVEMBER

■ **Sunday Mornings**

Complete the series "The Main Emphasis of Inspired Writers" with a message from the book of Acts. Then begin a series on stewardship entitled "What Giving Does for You." The Bible teaches the concept of stewardship, in which we are responsible to God for all that we are and have. To truly be responsible, we must not only graciously receive, but we must generously give.

■ **Sunday Evenings**

The book of Acts is a record of the evangelistic and missionary activity of the early church. We still need to proclaim the message that calls people to conversion and faith. "Great Conversions from the Book of Acts" is the theme.

■ **Wednesday Evenings**

Continue the devotional studies based on Paul's letter to the Colossians.

SUNDAY MORNING, NOVEMBER 3

Title: The Church Triumphant

Text: "Ye shall receive power, after that the Holy Ghost is come upon you: and ye shall be witnesses unto me both in Jerusalem, and in all Judaea, and in Samaria, and unto the uttermost part of the earth" **(Acts 1:8).**

Scripture Reading: Acts 1:1–8

Hymns: "The Church's One Foundation," Stone
"Onward Christian Soldiers," Baring-Gould
"O Church of God, Triumphant," Harlow

Offertory Prayer: God the Father, God the Son, God the Holy Spirit, we love and honor you. You have continually reached down to us. We thank you that in your wisdom you have chosen to make of your family the church triumphant. For the glowing record of its growth in Acts, we thank you. May we today continue to be the church triumphant until that day when your Son shall come to claim it. In his name we pray. Amen.

Introduction

The book of Acts records the thrilling story of the growth and victories of the church triumphant. From a handful of 120 members in chapter 1, the infant church grew to 3,000 in chapter 2. By chapter 4 the church exploded to more than 5,000!

In the face of persecution and martyrdom, the church in Acts continued to march on like a mighty army. The church's archenemy, Saul of Tarsus, was conquered by the grace of God and became its greatest advocate. On three missionary journeys this convert to the Christian faith established churches from one end of the Roman Empire to the other. For fifteen years, it seems that wherever Paul placed his foot, a New Testament church sprang up—Antioch, Ephesus, Philippi, Iconium, Lystra, Derbe, and even Rome.

"The church triumphant" is the theme that echoes throughout the twenty-eight chapters of Acts. This is the theme the church today needs to hear that it might be challenged to become the church triumphant in our time.

I. The purpose of the church triumphant.

Christ knew that for the church to become the church triumphant its marching orders must be clear, its purpose spelled out in such a manner so that no one could misunderstand. And so he says, "Ye shall receive power, after that the Holy Ghost is come upon you: and ye shall be witnesses unto me both in Jerusalem, and in all Judaea, and in Samaria, and unto the uttermost part of the earth" (Acts 1:8). The marching orders are clear! The purpose of the church is without question: "Ye shall be witnesses!"

A. *The secret of witnessing.* "Ye shall receive power, after that the Holy Ghost is come upon you" (Acts 1:8). Power is never obtained when pursued for itself. Power always goes with a commission. It came to the disciples at Pentecost; it comes to anyone whenever he or she squarely faces an undertaking. Churches often pray, "O Lord, give us power," and forget that an essential part of the answer is in their own hands. That answer is to tackle something definite for which they need power.

B. *The subject of witnessing.* "Ye shall be witnesses unto me" (Acts 1:8). Throughout Acts, the person of Christ is central. Christ is the heart of the good news for a non-Christian world. Each person must encounter the living Christ.

Paul said, "I am determined not to know any thing among you, save Jesus Christ, and him crucified" (1 Cor. 2:2).

C. *The sphere of witnessing.* "In Jerusalem, and in all Judaea, and in Samaria, and unto the uttermost part of the earth" (Acts 1:8).

II. The persecution of the church triumphant (Acts 12:1–3).

A. *Persecution from outside the church.* "Now about that time Herod the king stretched forth his hands to vex certain of the church" (Acts 12:1). There is nothing novel about this statement. The Herods of the world have always hated the church of our Lord Jesus Christ. That ungodly monster who was the grandfather of this Herod had sought to destroy the infant Jesus. And now his "worthy descendant" sought to destroy the infant church.

Thus, right from the very beginning the church learned to cope with opposition and antagonists. The church learned not to fear greatly, no matter how strong the mighty Herod looked on his throne and how little and insignificant the church seemed to be! But because the Christians learned that there was a power on their side, fighting in them and through them, they knew they could conquer the mighty Herods!

But notice the rest of this story in Acts 12:23–24.

B. *Persecution from hypercritical Christians.* Certain earnest souls have apparently become convinced that the church is so encrusted with evil and so entangled with the world that it faces perilous times and is doomed to failure. They have ceased to hope; they have ceased to work; and it seems that they have ceased to pray that the church of Jesus Christ will become the church triumphant. They have been so deceived that they believe there is nothing left to do but get outside the church and throw rocks at it. They feel that they must find some other institution, or start an institution of their own, to carry on the work of God. But separating Christianity from the church is an impossibility. Such a concept never existed in the minds of the early Christians, for "the Lord added to the church daily such as should be [were being] saved" (Acts 2:47).

III. The perplexities of the church triumphant.

As so often happens, when the church was growing and the future was full of promise, problems arose from within its own fellowship. "In those days, when the number of the disciples was multiplied, there arose a murmuring of the Grecians against the Hebrews, because their widows were neglected in the daily ministration" (Acts 6:1).

This was only the beginning of the perplexities of the early church. On the first missionary journey, Mark deserted the party and returned home. Before the second missionary journey, Paul and Barnabas had a falling out over Mark. Luke records, "The contention was so sharp between them, that they departed asunder one from the other: and so Barnabas took Mark, and sailed unto Cyprus" (Acts 15:39).

Two things usually create all the problems a church ever experiences. They are: (1) programs and (2) people. A church with no program and no people would have no perplexities!

A. *The perplexity because of its program.* Imagine being a member of that little church back there that launched the revival on the Day of Pentecost. Suppose somebody had made a motion like this in the business meeting: "I move that on Pentecost Day we launch a campaign to introduce the gospel of Christ to Jerusalem and that our goal be three thousand converts in one day; I further move that following this we send out a missionary force that will affect the whole world."

I can hear myself getting up and saying, "Now, now, brethren, I have a lot of faith, but there is no need in being presumptuous about this thing. I believe in the promise of God, and I think that in time we should give due consideration to carrying out Christ's great commission. But there is not any need for our being foolish enough to think that we can do a wild impossible thing like that. Taking the gospel to the entire world—that's ridiculous." And I could have given a lot of reasons why we couldn't do it—more reasons than you can give today. That church didn't have a ghost of a chance. Its whole program was wrong!

B. *The perplexity because of its people.* They had twelve charter members, all Galileans, obscure men, except one. Apparently only one had any standing in his hometown. He was called "The Man of Kerioth." Maybe the Chamber of Commerce had elected him the "man of the year." But since he was such an outstanding man, they elected him treasurer, and you know that scoundrel turned out to be a thief! The treasurer of the first church that ever existed turned out to be a thief! Now, with members like that, you can't do much, can you? One-twelfth of their membership— thieves and betrayers of the Lord! We have a better average than that, don't we?

Now the purpose of looking at the first-century church in comparison with Christ's church today is this: I want to remind you that God has always had to do his work through weak and imperfect men and women. No hardships we have today are as great as those of that early church, yet they invaded their entire world with the gospel. Before a generation had passed away, not a city of any importance in the Roman Empire had not been invaded by Christians and did not have its own church.

How did they do it? How can we do it? With such persecution and perplexities, how can the church experience victory and truly become the church triumphant? Let's see how victory came to the early church, for victory comes to the church today in exactly the same way.

IV. The power of the church triumphant (Acts 4:2).

After Peter and John had "preached through Jesus the resurrection from the dead" (Acts 4:21), Luke reports that "many of them which heard the word believed; and the number of the men was about five thousand" (Acts 4:4). This resulted in Peter and John being arrested and asked by the Sanhedrin, "By what power...have ye done this?" (Acts 4:7).

The question is still asked of the church triumphant today. What is the power of the church triumphant?

A. *The power of prayer.* Luke tells that for ten days and nights before launching their crusade on Pentecost, the church prayed. That made the difference!

They prayed ten days and nights, preached thirty minutes, and had three thousand saved. We do it differently today. We preach ten days and nights, pray thirty minutes, and have three saved. We must place the emphasis where the early church placed it to experience the victories they experienced.

B. *The power of personal involvement.* When they launched the campaign, doubting Thomas, swearing Simon Peter, bad-tempered James and John, in spite of their weaknesses, were all there. Isn't that wonderful? The power of personal involvement is still required today.

C. *The power of unity.* "They were all with one accord" (Acts 2:1). That doesn't mean the members of the early church always agreed, but they did always love one another. They were united in Jesus Christ. Pagans would say, "Behold how those Christians love one another!"

D. *The power of joyous optimism.* The early church knew that in spite of their small numbers, in spite of their lack of money, in spite of all their personal limitations, they were going to win. And so they went out in joy even in the midst of persecution. And that's the spirit in which we must win the victory today if we are going to continue to be the church triumphant! Jesus said, "Be of good cheer, for I have overcome the world!"

Conclusion

> *Like a might army moves the church of God;*
> *Brothers, we are treading where the saints have trod;*
> *We are not divided; all one body we,*
> *One in hope and doctrine, one in charity.*

SUNDAY EVENING, NOVEMBER 3

Title: Conversion As a Result of Receiving the Word

Text: "Then they that gladly received his word were baptized: and the same day there were added unto them about three thousand souls" **(Acts 2:41).**

Scripture Reading: Acts 2:37–47

Introduction

You will notice that the title of this message refers to the receiving of the Word. The text tells what happens when the Word is received. The Word that was received was the message preached by Simon Peter and is recorded in Acts 2:14–36. The description of what happened as a result of receiving the Word is found in Acts 2:37–47. These results will be considered under two headings.

I. The immediate results (Acts 2:37–41).

A. *Conviction and inquiry.* "They were pricked in their heart, and said…what shall we do?" (v. 37).

343

1. This conviction was twofold. First, Peter's listeners were convicted of the lordship of Christ. They saw him as the Messiah who was crucified and risen from the grave. This conviction of the lordship of Christ led to the second conviction, namely, the conviction of personal sin.
2. The cry, "What shall we do?" is a necessary question for any lost person to ask in order to be converted. It is a natural result of conviction.

B. *Instruction and exhortation (Acts 2:38–40).*

1. Peter instructed his hearers to repent and be baptized (v. 38). Repentance is the basic and primary requirement for conversion. There is no conversion apart from repentance. Baptism is the second requirement. It follows conversion as an outward sign by which individuals who believe the gospel make their faith publicly known.
2. Peter exhorted his hearers to save themselves from an untoward generation (v. 40). Verse 40 must be coupled with verse 38. To be saved, as described in this verse, is a commitment to clean living. Their sins had been the cause of the crucifixion of the Lord Jesus. Now that conversion had taken place, they were exhorted to live lives commensurate with the conversion.

C. *Obedience and church growth (v. 41).* "They that gladly received his word were baptized." They believed the message of salvation. Since the early church knew nothing about believers who were not baptized, naturally they were baptized. Then they were added to the church.

II.The continuous results (Acts 2:42–47).

A. *The four activities in verse 42 are ordinances of fellowship.*

1. "They continued stedfastly in the apostles' doctrine," the teaching of the apostles. The principle of authority is presented here. This authority is the death and resurrection of Jesus as proclaimed by the apostles. They were qualified teachers.
2. "They continued stedfastly in the apostles'...fellowship." Fellowship is the communion of the saints based on a common life of sharing. It is fellowship with God and with one another, a spiritual partnership.
3. "They continued stedfastly...in breaking of bread." Eating is a sign of fellowship. It forms a bond. Bread is the divine source of support and growth.
4. They continued stedfastly...in prayers." They prayed individually and as a church, thus including both private and public prayers.

B. *The five attitudes mentioned in verses 43–47 are the effects produced by such a company of believers.*

1. "Fear came upon every soul" (v. 43). This fear is holy reverence. All the people felt a sense of awe.
2. "Wonders and signs were done by the apostles" (v. 43). Signs and wonders were spiritual forces that affected others.

3. "All that believed were together, and had all things common" (v. 44). Their sharing was a voluntary act following the example and teaching of the Lord Jesus.

4. "They, continuing daily with one accord in the temple, and breaking bread from house to house, did eat their meat with gladness and singleness of heart" (v. 46). Gladness is a natural joy of the conversion experience and Christian fellowship. Being of one mind and heart is also a product of these experiences.

5. "The Lord added to the church daily such as should be saved" (v. 47). Perhaps a clearer rendering of this verse would be, "And the Lord added to their number day by day those who were being saved." Only those who were saved were added to the church—not the unsaved.

Conclusion

The most dynamic experience of a human life is conversion to Christianity. I am making an urgent appeal to every lost person here to be saved today. You are saved in the same way as people described in this passage of Scripture. You are saved by repenting of your sins and believing on the Lord Jesus Christ. After you have repented and believed, you are exhorted to make this public by being baptized and joining the church. Do it today.

WEDNESDAY EVENING, NOVEMBER 6

Title: The Well of Wisdom

Text: "In [Christ] dwelleth all the fulness of the Godhead bodily. And ye are complete in him which is the head of all principality and power" (**Col. 2:9–10**).

Scripture Reading: Colossians 2:8–15

Introduction

We are confused. We had thought there were absolute standards of right and wrong. Now we hear that there is a new morality, that all matters are relative. We had thought that God was the ground of all our existence. Now we hear that God is dead.

Why has such confusion come about? It is because we have listened to the philosophies of fallible humans. We need some well of wisdom from which we can draw that will help us to get life back in focus. We need to know someone who can point us to truth and help us to order our lives. This one is Christ. He is our well of wisdom.

I. Christ is our well of wisdom because of what he is (Col. 2:8–9).

A. *Christ is fully human.* Those who knew Christ personally knew him first as a man. When they heard him teach, saw him heal, and followed him, they followed a man. The Samaritan woman at the well, who ran into her city telling about Christ, cried out, "Come see a man who..." (John 4:29). Here was a man who brought people uniquely to God.

B. *Jesus Christ is fully divine.* In verse 9 Paul assured us that in Jesus Christ all the fullness of the godhead dwelt bodily. This meant that Jesus was fully God. He was not a representative of God nor a representation of God. He was God in human form.

The early Christians struggled for several centuries with this concept of how Jesus could be fully human and fully divine at the same time. Finally, in the Council of Chalcedon in A.D. 451 the orthodox formulation was reached: Jesus Christ was fully human and fully divine.

A scientist studying ants marveled at their intelligence as he observed them under a microscope. He was disappointed, however, at a weakness in their ability to reason. Upon seeing their limited intelligence, the professor became exasperated and exclaimed that he wished he could become an ant and tell them what to do. Then he realized that if he became an ant he would be limited to an ant's intelligence. He would have to become an ant yet remain a man. Then there flashed through his mind a phrase he had heard in his study of theology: "Truly God, truly man," and he had some understanding of what it meant for God to come to earth in human flesh.

II. Christ is our well of wisdom because of what he shows (Col. 2:10–12).

A. *He shows us fullness of life.* We come to fullness of life only as we come to Christ in faith. He becomes, then, the one who is the head for us. He becomes our authority in what we should think and how we should act.

B. *He shows us symbols of life in himself.* For the Jew, circumcision was the physical mark that indicated a person was a part of the covenant community. Christians have the symbol of baptism, which identifies an individual with Christ and the church.

C. *He shows us the power of life in himself.* Jesus was raised from the dead by the power of God. The Christian is "raised to walk in newness of life" through baptism. The power of life—resurrected life for Christ and new life for the believer—is shown in Jesus Christ.

III. Christ is our well of wisdom because of what he did (Col. 2:13–15).

A. *Christ has given us life through forgiveness of our sins.* Whereas we could only be described as spiritually dead through trespasses and sin, Christ has given us life. This new life comes by the forgiveness of sin through faith in Christ.

B. *Christ has given us freedom through the cross.* In picturesque language, Paul described how our sin stood as a debt against us. The time to pay the note had arrived, but we could not pay it. So Christ took that note of our sin, our rebellion, and our legalistic attempts to be right with God and nailed them to his cross. By his death on the cross, Christ gave us freedom.

C. *Christ has given us triumph over the powers.* All that would defeat the Christian has been defeated in Christ on the cross. The principalities and powers that would destroy the believer have been destroyed by the Savior.

To show how completely they have been destroyed, Paul used the word *triumph.* A triumphal entry, or great parade, into the city of Rome was given a Roman general who had won a great victory. His soldiers in their battle array would march through the city in splendor. The chariots would roll and the charioteers would be welcomed as heroes. The triumphant general would be given the acclaim of a god as he was driven through the streets in his glory. Behind him would come the trophies of war: slaves who had once been leaders, defeated warriors, treasures from the city, the wealth of the defeated people.

Thus completely did Christ give victory over the powers that would seek to defeat the Christian.

Conclusion

Christ is indeed the well of wisdom. Because of who he is, what he shows, and what he has done, we can learn from him how to live.

SUNDAY MORNING, NOVEMBER 10

Title: Living for Treasures or Trash

Text: "Do not store up riches for yourselves here on earth, where moths and rust destroy, and robbers break in and steal. Instead, store up riches for yourselves in heaven, where moths and rust cannot destroy, and robbers cannot break in and steal. For your heart will always be where your riches are" (**Matt. 6:19–21** TEV).

Scripture Reading: 1 Corinthians 3:10–15

Hymns: "Praise the Lord, the King of Glory," Reno
"I Gave My Life for Thee," Havergal
"Something for Thee," Phelps

Offertory Prayer: Heavenly Father, we come today to bow down before you in worship. We recognize you not only as the source of our life, but as the sustainer of our lives. We thank you for the blessings that make physical life possible, but we also thank you for nourishing our spiritual lives. We come today to thank you for the privilege of working and earning an income. From our earnings we come to bring tithes to express our gratitude, and at the same time, our concern for others. Bless these gifts to the end that we shall all worship you in spirit and in truth and practice love toward one another. In Christ's name. Amen.

Introduction

Have you ever been to an estate auction following a death when personal items were put up for sale? This can be a sad and sobering experience. Someone has said, "One person's junk is another person's treasure." While this may be true, one cannot help but observe that there is always a lot of trash that remains when the average person passes away. This should cause each of us to raise the question, "Am I living for trash? Will the values I live for have eternal significance?"

Today let us ask ourselves, "Am I living for true treasures or am I living for trash?"

I. Christ Jesus came to save us earthlings for a heavenly life.

A. *God, the Creator, has given us bodies that are perfectly adapted to our earthly habitat (1 Cor. 15:35–41).* In this great classic passage dealing with the hope of resurrection from the dead, Paul illustrates the power and wisdom of God. God gave us an earthly body that is perfectly adapted to an earthly habitat.

 To depict the wisdom and power of God regarding our earthly life, Paul used illustrations from botany, zoology, and astronomy. The plants of the field have a body perfectly adapted for the fruit that is to be produced. Man, animals, birds, and fish have bodies adapted for their natural habitats. In the realm of astronomy, each star is different and is perfectly appropriate for its orbit and its place in the universe.

B. *The wisdom and the power of God will provide for believers a body perfectly adapted for the heavenly home (1 Cor. 15:42–44).* Paul declares, "So is it with the resurrection of the dead." The Father God's wisdom and power will make available to us spiritual bodies that are perfectly adapted for a heavenly habitat.

C. *The Father God has given us the Holy Spirit to help us live with the values of eternity (2 Cor. 5).* By giving us the Holy Spirit, the Father God is giving us a present guarantee that we will experience resurrection and that we will live eternal in the heavens, in the house not made with hands.

II. Christ teaches us to live and work with heaven always before us.

A. *The words of our text are not a gimmick for receiving an offering.*

B. *In these words our Lord is seeking to enrich us rather than to impoverish us.* God is no pauper. Nor is he a thief. He is not a beggar who sits on the sidewalk begging alms from us. Our gifts do not enrich him.

C. *God is interested in our highest possible good in the present as well as in the future.* When we live with the issues and values of eternity, we are going to be richer both in the present and in the future.

III. Christ wants us to be rich with the riches that do not perish.

Christ our Lord is giving us some excellent financial advice and spiritual counsel. His concern is not for the gifts that we might give; rather, he is concerned about the location of our heart, "Where your treasures are there your heart will be also."

A. *It is possible for you to live all of your life for treasures that will turn out to be nothing but trash.* Trash is that which is worn-out, broken, or worthless.

  We cannot take earthly treasures with us into eternity. Thus, they hold no permanent value for us.

  Note to pastor: If you wish to use some visible illustrations, do so at this point. Secure a trash container of some sort, possibly a plastic bag or a waste can. Use toys or other objects, such as a toy house, automobile, furniture, or boat. Include some coins and, if possible, a diamond ring. These should be placed in the container one by one as you deal with the following thoughts.

  1. A house is possibly our very best investment, but in the final analysis, a house will have no value for us.
  2. In much of the world an automobile is considered a necessity. We will not be able to take our automobiles with us through the strainer that people call death.
  3. In our homes we need furniture, but the day will come when furniture will have no more value than trash.
  4. Some people enjoy the luxury of a boat, but we can't take a boat to heaven with us.
  5. You cannot take even one silver coin with you to heaven. It is like other trash.
  6. A diamond ring is a beautiful and highly valued thing, but not even our most highly prized treasures on earth can pass through death into our heavenly home. They will be considered as having no more value than trash.

B. *It is possible to live for treasures that will last forever.*

  1. You can take your soul through death to heaven. Your greatest possession is your own personal welfare.
  2. You can take your personal spiritual growth with you into heaven. You do not have to remain in spiritual infancy. With the help of the Holy Spirit and by nurturing yourself on the Word of God, you can grow and take that growth to heaven with you.
  3. You can take your memory with you to heaven. In Luke 16 we read of the memory of the unsaved man who found himself in torment. If people can remember in hell, by all means we can remember when we get to heaven. Today's experiences are tomorrow's memories.
  4. You can take those whom you have won to Christ with you into heaven. These will be your richest treasures and your most prized valuables once you enter into eternity.
  5. You can take to heaven the service that you have rendered to God and to others.
  6. You can take to heaven the believers you discipled.

Conclusion

What are you living for? Are you living for earthly treasures that someday will have no more value than mere trash? Will you go off and leave your treasures behind?

Ours is the choice of living for true treasures that have eternal significance or for values that will eventually be considered as worthless. What will it profit a person if he gains the whole world and loses his own soul?

The highest wisdom that any person can use is the wisdom of accepting Jesus Christ as Lord, Savior, leader, guide, and teacher.

Jesus challenges us to live for the true treasures that will be valuable throughout all eternity.

SUNDAY EVENING, NOVEMBER 10

Title: The Conversion of the Ethiopian Eunuch

Text: "I believe that Jesus Christ is the Son of God" **(Acts 8:37).**

Scripture Reading: Acts 8:26–40

Introduction

We all need to have firmly established in our minds that God loves us. God wants the best for everyone's life, and thus constantly works to see that each person has an abundant life. This life comes through a conversion experience. The conversion of the Ethiopian eunuch gives us three factors in such an experience.

I. Conversion is a divine transaction.

A. *The Spirit of God is seen at work (Acts 8:26, 29).* Supernatural messengers manifested the divine presence and worked on both Philip's and the eunuch's side of the encounter.

 1. An angel of the Lord gave direction to Philip. He told him where to go and what to do.

 2. The Holy Spirit prepared the heart of the Ethiopian eunuch. God saw to it that Philip and the eunuch came to the same place at the same time for a divine encounter.

B. *The influence of the divine work of God is seen (vv. 28, 32–33).* God used the reading of the Word from the prophet Isaiah to bring conviction to the Ethiopian eunuch. The Word of God is sharper than a two-edged sword and pierces asunder the soul and the spirit (Heb. 4:12). However, if the Word is to have this effect, it must be read, preached, and obeyed.

C. *The work of the Son of God is seen in conversion (v. 35).* Philip "preached unto him Jesus." Jesus was the one about whom the Scripture spoke. He still

350

is. He suffered and died for sinners and will save anyone who responds as the Ethiopian eunuch.

II. The human instrument is used in bringing about conversion.

A. *The human instrument was Philip.* Found here are some marks of a person whom God can use.

1. One mark is divine leadership. Under God's leadership, Philip left a burning revival to go down to a desert place. Apart from divine leadership, this would not have made sense, but in doing so, Philip ministered to a man lost in sin (vv. 29, 35).

2. Another mark is the use of the inspired Word of God in answering the questions of a hungry soul. Philip also exemplified this mark superbly.

B. *The statements made about Philip can be made about current human instruments.* These are pastors, the church, the Bible, and laypeople.

III. Conversion requires the human response.

A. *The Ethiopian eunuch was a seeker of truth.* He had gone to Jerusalem to worship (v. 27). Those who attended a place of worship are in their Jerusalem and can identify with the eunuch. He also read the Bible (v. 28). There is no substitute for personal reading of the inspired Word. Further, the eunuch was eager to hear what Philip had to say. These are essential ingredients to the conversion of any person.

B. *The Ethiopian eunuch was obedient to the message he heard.* The truth, "I believe that Jesus Christ is the Son of God" (v. 37), is the truth to be obeyed. It was the practice of the early church and is still the proper procedure to follow. Upon acceptance of Jesus as Savior, the eunuch was baptized. These are examples that every lost person should follow. The only way to be saved is to accept Jesus. To publicly confess this, follow him in water baptism as did the Ethiopian.

C. *The Ethiopian eunuch went away a happy man (v. 39).* No joy compares to that which comes from a genuine conversion experience. Many souls are searching, as did the Ethiopian eunuch, and the result of their discovery is joy. Salvation brings joy to the one who is converted and also to the one who bears the witness. Those who have already been converted also rejoice in the conversion of another.

Conclusion

God, in his providence, led a preacher to a desert road. God, in his providence, led a seeker to that same road and led him to a specific passage of Scripture. God gave that preacher the wisdom to interpret that passage and lead that man to accept Jesus and be converted. Listen and be saved.

WEDNESDAY EVENING, NOVEMBER 13

Title: From Shadow to Reality

Text: "These are only a shadow of what is to come; but the substance belongs to Christ" **(Col. 2:17 RSV).**

Scripture Reading: Colossians 2:16–23

Introduction

Many today want the good life, but they want it apart from a relationship with Jesus Christ. Karl H. A. Rest writes concerning this attitude:

> Ethics without religion has little power to endure. The French Revolution began by striking the idealistic notes of liberty, equality, and fraternity; but it was no deeper than its own idealism. Its power for good was soon exhausted, and it broke loose in uncontrolled violence. When man has nothing more to rely upon than his own spirit, his goodness turns sour. He needs divine support. He lives most meaningfully when he responds to the gracious overtures of God. (Quoted in Charles L. Wallis, ed., *Speaker's Illustrations for Special Days* [New York and Nashville: Abingdon Press, 1956], 131–32)

People want the results of religion without the discipline and commitment.

Paul cautioned the Colossian Christians against having this attitude. He had just demonstrated how Christ had set them free by his death on the cross from all the things that would enslave and destroy them. But people were coming along behind Paul teaching the people that there were certain matters of Jewish practice they had to keep, certain observances they had to maintain, certain ways of looking at life and religion they had to adopt. Paul replied that these things were only shadows; the real thing was Christ. We too are often tempted to take the shadow and pass up the reality. But we are to go from the shadow to the reality—to Christ.

I. We can go from shadow to reality in the matter of observances.

A. *Ceremonials can become substitutes.* The Colossians were observing religious rituals. Such ceremonies can become substitutes for the real thing. Rather than meeting Christ in faith, some substitute ritual for reality.

One summer three college students went to Oklahoma to sell Bibles. While there, these young men accepted Christ. This was unusual, because they were already church members. But they had never met Christ in faith. The ritual had substituted for the reality.

B. *Ceremonials can lead to spiritual pride.* Spiritual pride was one of the problems at the Colossian church. Those who were calling for the ceremonials and the accompanying philosophies thought themselves better than others. In fact, the very name of the party—Gnostics—means "the knowing ones." They thought themselves the ones in the know; all others were in the dark.

II. We can go from shadow to reality in the matter of freedom.

A. *Christian freedom is found in Christ.* Paul declared in Galatians, "For freedom Christ has set us free" (Gal. 5:1 RSV). Freedom comes in Christ.

B. *Christian freedom lives in love.* Freedom in Christ does not mean license; rather, it is freedom lived in love. Love gives a lot more limits than law, yet these are the self-imposed limits of love, not the externally imposed limits set by ritual and requirements. It was Augustine who said that Christians should love God and do what they like. If they love God, they will like the things of God.

    H. G. Wells wrote that he was newly married when the sweets and the perils of success were opening up for him. He said that it was good for him that behind the folding doors of 12 Mornington Road there slept one so pure and so clean that he could not bear to stand before her in a squalid, drunken, unshaven, or base condition.

III. We can go from shadow to reality in the matter of restrictions.

A. *Restrictions do not originate in Christ.* Colossians 2:20 indicates that in Christ believers have died to the world's control of their lives. If they have died to externally imposed controls on life, why should they continue to live under them?

B. *Restrictions do not lead to devotion to Christ.* When religion is negative it is because it is based on keeping the regulations, not on devotion and dedication to Christ. Just keeping the restrictions may be an exercise in duty, not an exhibition of love to the Lord who gives life.

C. *Restrictions do not lead to victory in life.* The person who lives under those restrictions may appear to have a regulated and disciplined life, but the regulation is coming from rules; it is not the victory of faith. It does not overcome temptation; it does not win over the pull of the world. Verse 23 makes it plain that the indulgence of the flesh is restrained by faith in Christ and dependence on his power. Merely keeping the rules is inadequate. God treats us as real people who have to make decisions and live with victory in the cauldron of the daily world. The ability to do this comes only through faith in Jesus Christ.

Conclusion

    We can go from shadow to reality when we pass from a mere keeping of the regulations to living by faith in Christ. Why be satisfied with the shadow when there is a reality that frees and gives a new life? The good and moral and ethical life comes with Christ.

SUNDAY MORNING, NOVEMBER 17

Title: What Giving Does for You

Text: "Not that I seek the gift; but I seek the fruit that increases to your credit" **(Phil. 4:17 RSV)**.

Scripture Reading: Philippians 4:14–20

Hymns: "Because He Lives," Gaither
         "Savior, Like a Shepherd Lead Us," Bradbury
         "Take My Life, and Let It Be," Yarbrough

Offertory Prayer: Heavenly Father, thank you for being such a generous giver to us. Thank you for giving us a true understanding of your nature and purpose and plan for our lives in the life of Jesus Christ. Thank you for the gift of your Holy Spirit who dwells within us to lead us to maturity and to effectiveness in service. Thank you, Father, for granting us the privilege of cooperating with you in helping others to know about your love and your salvation. We bring our gifts today that we might cooperate with you. Accept these gifts and bless them to your name's honor and glory. In Jesus' name. Amen.

Introduction

Paul's epistle to the Philippians has been called the epistle of joy. He writes from a prison cell to express his gratitude for their fellowship and partnership with him in the gospel ministry. They had sent a gift to meet his pressing needs, and this had made it possible for him to concentrate on sharing the good news of God's love even as a prisoner. His bondage had served to advance the gospel in a difficult place (Phil. 1:12–14).

Paul disavowed any desire to receive a gift as such. He was thinking more in terms of the benefit that giving brought into the hearts and lives of the givers—"I seek the fruit which increases to your credit" (Phil. 4:17 RSV).

Satan won a great victory when he injected the idea that God was trying to impoverish us by teaching us to be givers. The greatest need is not the need of the church for our gifts. The greatest need is our personal need to be givers.

Have you stopped to think about the benefits of being a generous giver to the point of giving above your tithe?

I. Giving generously gives us the privilege of entering into partnership with God's servants around the world (Phil. 4:15; 3 John 8).

By means of our gifts we have the privilege of going to many different places and ministering in the name of Jesus Christ. We can perform surgery in Christian hospitals. We can preach the gospel in foreign lands. We can care for orphans and for the aged. We can participate in the life of the pastor as he or she visits and ministers on behalf of the local congregation.

II. Giving generously places us in a position to receive the blessings promised to the tither (Mal. 3:10–12).

God does not promise riches to those who faithfully tithe and give generously. He does promise to bless them financially and to help them meet the needs of their families. There is no way that you can read these words from Malachi and come to any other conclusion.

A. *He may help us by making us immune to high-pressured advertising.*
B. *He may help us to resist impulsive buying.*
C. *He may help us to find better bargains.*
D. *He will help us to be better managers.*
E. *Many testify to the fact that God has blessed them with additional income.*

The greatest blessing that comes to the generous giver is in the joy that results when God's blessings come into his or her heart and life.

III. Giving generously makes it possible for us to have treasure in heaven (Matt. 6:19–21).

A savings and loan company had a huge clock on the corner of their building with a caption that said, "Time to Save." Those who make regular deposits in a savings account accumulate a significant sum over the years. These are earthly treasures.

The person who gives generously to God's work throughout the years is accumulating spiritual treasures that will not tarnish in heaven's bank. These gifts are used in such a manner as to bless the lives of those who will some day go to heaven. In this manner we transfer the coin of earth into the coin of heaven.

IV. Generous giving increases our capacity to receive both the blessings of God and the favor of others (Luke 6:38).

A person's "pocketbook protection instinct" causes him or her to miss the great truths in this tremendous statement from Jesus. The first word is a command that should also be considered as an invitation. It simply says, "Give." It doesn't say what or how much. Jesus is talking about a total way of life. The rest of the verse is the promise. It tells us how God will bless us and how other people will also bring benefits to us. "The measure you give will be the measure you get back."

This great principle is true in the business world, in family life, and in every other area of life. The more you give, the more you will increase your capacity to receive.

V. Generous giving increases our feelings of security with God (2 Cor. 9:6–10).

The principles of good farming apply in the realm of the spirit as well as in the realm of agriculture. Those who are stingy with their seed will reap a small harvest. Those who sow an adequate amount of seed have the hope of an abundant harvest. Those who give generously can expect the blessings of a gracious God to be upon the work of their heads, their hearts, and their hands. God is the great giver, and Scripture tells us that God loves those who imitate him. The Great Giver will not let those who imitate him suffer want and poverty. He will increase both the harvest of the field and the harvest of the Spirit as the givers see themselves as channels through which his blessings can flow to others.

Conclusion

Jesus taught that "it is more blessed to give than to receive" (Acts 20:35). Jesus discovered this truth in actual experience. Jesus was saying that there is more excitement and joy and happiness in a life of giving than there is in a life of acquiring and keeping.

Each of us would be exceedingly wise to try giving ourselves away. Let us first of all give ourselves to God. Let us give ourselves, our time, our talents, our energy, our words of affirmation and encouragement to those nearest and dearest to us. Let us determine to be contributors to the well-being of those about us rather than just being consumers of that which others produce.

The benefits of being a giver are far greater than the benefits received by those who think of life only in terms of it being a goblet to be filled. Paul encourages us to give as did the Philippians that we might be partners with God in his work of seeking to save the lost.

SUNDAY EVENING, NOVEMBER 17

Title: The Conversion of Saul of Tarsus

Text: "What wilt thou have me to do?" (**Acts 9:6**).

Scripture Reading: Acts 9:1–9

Introduction

The conversion of sinners is always a marvel. The person whose conversion experience is presented in this passage was one of the most unlikely prospects for Christianity ever known to humankind. He was not only an unlikely prospect, but he also had one of the most dynamic conversion experiences in the annals of history. And it turned out to be one of the most far-reaching conversions in the history of Christendom. His names was Saul. This experience will be presented in three steps on the road to conversion.

I. A human soul pushing in its own wrong course (Acts 9:1–2, 5).

This is a picture of sin in the life of any unbeliever.

A. *Examine the life of Saul for some lessons today.* He doubted that Jesus was the Messiah, and his doubt drove him hard to stomp out the spread of the gospel. He was determined, by persecuting Christians, to drown all question of the possibility of Jesus' being the Messiah. His determination to persecute the Christians made bad matters worse.

B. *Examine the present human race and you will find a similar course of action.* Twenty-first–century people are guilty of pushing in the wrong direction, as can be seen in their self-indulgence. This is especially manifested in the use of drugs and alcohol, in the practices of illicit sex, and in the increasing emphasis on materialism. Human beings of this era are going in the wrong direction, as seen in confirmed unbelief in and rejection of Christ. The state of indecision and procrastination on the part of many are pulling them in the wrong direction.

II. The divine arrest of that soul (vv. 3–5).

A. *There are two ways to consider the confrontation of Saul's soul.*
   1. One way is the influence of previous experiences. Saul had seen Stephen stoned to death and had heard him praying for those who were casting the stones. Saul was unable to forget what he saw and heard. This inevitably made a profound impression on him. A man with Saul's religious training had to be haunted by his conscience as he walked 140 miles down the road toward Damascus.
   2. Another way is the somewhat suddenness of the arrest, or confrontation. The hand of God struck powerfully on the human heart.

B. *The two ways that Saul's soul was arrested also work today.*
   1. The Lord works at times suddenly, but more often gradually. He works slowly through the lives of Christian people, such as Sunday school teachers, ministers, neighbors, and friends.
   2. The Lord works at times in extraordinary ways, but usually in the ordinary. Occasionally someone will have a vision or some unusual or remarkable experience that will confront him or her. But more often, the words of a Christian witness given in either a personal way or in a public address are the means by which a person is saved.

III. The submission of the soul to the divine will (v. 6).

A. *Here a change is seen in Saul.* Up until this submission, Saul had been doing what he liked, what he thought best, and what his will dictated. After the submission, he was told what to do.

B. *Four lessons on conversion can be found in Saul's experience.*
   1. He was baptized (9:18). Baptism is to follow conversion.
   2. He entered into fellowship with God's people (9:19). All converted people ought to become identified with a local congregation of believers.

3. He began witnessing (9:20). A true mark of a conversion experience is to share the Good News with others. It is the duty and privilege of all believers to tell others about the saving power of the Lord Jesus.

4. He prepared for a life of ministry. In order to be a servant of God, Saul had to change his lifestyle. Everything was new and strange to him. Therefore, he had to spend some time in preparation. So it is with each follower of Christ. The task is overwhelming, but the Lord enables each one. Believers must enroll in Bible study, participate in prayer meetings, and engage in worship in order to prepare for a life of ministry.

Conclusion

We have taken a look at the conversion experience of one of the greatest Christians of all times. Any of us who becomes a Christian must have a similar experience. Do you know Christ as your Savior?

WEDNESDAY EVENING, NOVEMBER 20

Title: New Life with Christ

Text: "If ye then be risen with Christ, seek those things which are above, where Christ sitteth on the right hand of God" **(Col. 3:1).**

Scripture Reading: Colossians 3:1–4

Introduction

One of the classic sermons of all time is "The Expulsive Power of a New Affection" preached by the Scots preacher Thomas Chalmers. It seems that one day Chalmers was riding with a man in a carriage on a country road. The man suddenly began to lash the horse unmercifully. When Chalmers asked him why he had done that, the man replied that he had seen something in the road that would frighten the horse. By lashing the horse, he diverted its attention long enough to get by the object. Chalmers went back home to write a classic sermon that tells us how to get by the frightening and demoralizing objects of life—it is by the expulsive power of a new affection, love for Christ.

This is what Paul had in mind in this passage of Scripture. In the preceding section he had reminded us that we do not have to be subject to a long list of rules, regulations, and restrictions devised by men. He concluded the matter by saying, "They are of no value in checking the indulgence of the flesh" (Col. 2:23 RSV).

If we cannot check or control the indulgence of the flesh by observing certain regulations, how can we control it? He answered that question with the beginning phrase of 3:1: "If ye then be risen with Christ, seek those things which are above." We have a new life in Christ since we are risen with Christ. We can divert our attention from the things of the world that would pull us away from Christ by setting our minds on the things that are above, the things of heavenly and eternal value.

Paul, then, was not satisfied with the negative statement. He added the positive. This is what we have with new life in Christ.

I. New life in Christ gives us a new view (Col. 3:1–2).

A. *The Christian lives with a view of the eternal.* Paul advised us to set our minds on the things that are above, to look up to eternal things. The Greek word for man means literally "the upward looker." Man was made to look up.

New life in Christ causes us to look up to the eternal. A visitor to a great art gallery saw one of the maintenance crew hard at work polishing the floor. He spoke to the cleaning woman and said that there were some wonderful pictures in that gallery. She replied, "I'm sure there are, if a body had time to look up." New life in Christ causes us to look up.

B. *The Christian lives in tension between the two worlds.* The Christian always lives in tension between the upward world of the eternal hope in Christ and the present world of reality. While living here we look toward the beyond. But that does not divorce us from reality and working for God's glory now. A sign in front of a church asked, "What on earth are you doing for heaven's sake?" That expresses the tension.

II. New life in Christ gives us a new value (Col. 3:3).

A. *Living for Christ.*
B. *A life hid in Christ.*
C. *A life hid in Christ on display to the world.* The Christian has union with Christ by faith in him. Because of this the Christian's life is hid in Christ, but it is also lived out in the world. So while the life is hid in Christ—Christ gives it life and meaning—its display to the world shows the new value.

III. New life with Christ gives us a new verdict (Col. 3:4).

A. *The verdict is victory.*
B. *The verdict of victory is seen in the resurrection of Christ.*
C. *Through new life Christians share in the resurrection of Christ.* What had once been considered defeat is now known to be victory. And it is not just a victory for Christ; it is also a victory for the Christian who shares that resurrection.

The news of Wellington's defeat of Napoleon reached the south coast of England by way of a sailing vessel. Then the message was wig-wagged in semaphore code overland to London. Atop Winchester Cathedral the semaphore began to spell out the eagerly awaited message: "W-e-l-l-i-n-g-t-o-n-d-e-f-e-a-t-e-d," and then a dense fog settled oppressively over the land. The semaphore could no longer be seen, and the heartbreaking news of the incomplete message went on to London: Wellington defeated.

But after a while the fog lifted. The signaling semaphore on top of the cathedral became visible, spelling out the complete message of the battle: "W-e-l-l-i-n-g-t-o-n-d-e-f-e-a-t-e-d-t-h-e-e-n-e-m-y!" The message was all the more glorious because of the preceding gloom. The word began to spread throughout London and lifted the spirits of the people. We have a new verdict: Christ defeated death. And we can join in that victory.

Conclusion

We have new life in Christ, a life that is completely different from our old way of life. It comes to us through faith as we are risen with Christ, who defeated death and sin.

SUNDAY MORNING, NOVEMBER 24

Title: Thanks Be unto God

Text: "At midnight I will rise to give thanks unto thee because of thy righteous judgments" **(Ps. 119:62).**

Scripture Reading: Luke 17:11–19; Psalm 100:1–5

Hymns: "Count Your Blessings," Oatman
"We Gather Together," Anonymous
"Come, Ye Thankful People, Come," Alford

Offertory Prayer: Our Father, we count our blessings and we name them one by one. And, dear Lord, we do more than count our blessings—we come to give our thanks to you for them. You are so good to us. You have blessed us beyond measure. We can truthfully say that every good and perfect gift comes from above, from your bountiful hands. Help us to love you more each day. In Jesus' name. Amen.

Introduction

Thanksgiving is an American holiday and a biblical principle. The psalmist said, "At midnight I will rise to give thanks unto thee" (Ps. 119:62). The heathen philosopher Cicero said, "A thankful heart is not only the greatest virtue, but the parent of all the other virtues." Plutarch said, "The worship most acceptable to God comes from a thankful and cheerful heart." Izaak Walton said, "God has two dwellings: one in heaven, and the other in meek and thankful hearts." Samuel Johnson said, "Gratitude is the fruit of great cultivation; you do not find it among gross people."

Thanks be unto God for the many blessings. Let me mention a few for you.

I. Thanks be unto God for our country.

The first Thanksgiving Day in America was held December 13, 1621. Governor William Bradford of the Massachusetts Plymouth Colony declared a Thanksgiving Day, one of feasting and prayer. For many years thereafter, no Thanksgiving Day was observed. Mrs. Sarah Hale worked for thirty years to get a national Thanksgiving Day. On October 3, 1863, President Abraham Lincoln issued the first Thanksgiving Day proclamation, setting apart the last Thursday in November. For seventy-five years Thanksgiving was celebrated on the fourth Thursday of November. In 1939 Franklin D. Roosevelt changed it to the third Thursday. Congress ruled after 1941 that Thanksgiving Day would be the fourth Thursday in November.

America is a great and grand country. Let us take our stand as good citizens. Let us pray that America's greatest days are yet to come.

II. Thanks be unto God for our city, our place of abode.

Dr. J. Harold Smith, in addressing a religious convention in Arkansas a few years ago, said that a Christian was:

A. *A person who understands his city.*

B. *A person who undergirds his city.* He stands for a program of righteousness. He is upright. He believes and supports what is right.

C. *A person who under God tries to win his city to Christ.* The great cities of America are in trouble—financial trouble, crime trouble, labor trouble, race trouble—all kinds of trouble. Our cities need Christ more than anything else. Let us seek to point our people to the Savior, the Lord Jesus Christ. He is our greatest need.

III. Let us give thanks for those who have blessed our lives.

A. *Our parents: our mothers and fathers.*

B. *Our children.* Tom Paine said, "The first five years of my life I became an infidel."

No wonder Lord Byron was a scoundrel. His mother said to him when she saw him one day limping across the floor with his unsound foot: "Get out of my way, you lame brat!" What chance is there for a boy with a mother like that?

C. *Our teachers.* We have been blessed with great teachers in the church. They are good men and women who love the Lord, his cause, and his people.

D. *Our pastors and religious leaders.*

E. *Our special friends and relatives.* Let us give thanks to those who have encouraged us and helped us in so many ways.

IV. Let us give thanks for the Christian home.

The home is the primary institution. It is a citadel of civilization.

A. *The socializing agency of society.* The home is the community into which a child is born. In the home, first impressions are made and first acquaintances are formed. In the home, a child learns to live with people.

B. *The fundamental educational agency of society.* Someone said, "The greatest university in the world is a mother reading to her children."

C. *The primary religious institution of society.* In the home, a child first hears the name of God and offers his or her first prayer. By careful observation at home a child learns what it is to have and serve Christ.

D. *The greatest evangelizing agency (Prov. 22:6).*

V. Let us give thanks for the church.

A. *Let us give thanks for the founder of the church—Jesus Christ (Matt. 16:13–20).*

B. *Let us give thanks for the message of the church.*
   1. A message of conversion (Matt. 28:19–20).
   2. A message of comfort (Matt. 11:28–30).
   3. A message of challenge (Rom. 12:1–2).

C. *Let us give thanks for the influence of the church.* The church lifts up the fallen, gives strength to the weak, gives hope to the hopeless, gives help to the helpless, and gives freedom to the enslaved. The church abides. No loss can come to those who invest their lives in the service of Christ and his church.

VI. Let us give thanks for Christ our Lord and Savior.

A. *Christ offers forgiveness (Eph. 1:7).*

B. *Christ offers redemption (Eph. 1:7).*

C. *Christ offers an eternal home (John 14:1–6; 2 Cor. 5:1).*

D. *Christ offers power for daily living (Phil. 1:13; 4:19).*

Conclusion

We are truly a blessed people. Let us express our gratitude. Let us give thanks!

SUNDAY EVENING, NOVEMBER 24

Title: The Conversion of the Philippian Jailer

Text: "Sirs, what must I do to be saved? And they said, Believe on the Lord Jesus Christ, and thou shalt be saved, and thy house" **(Acts 16:30–31).**

Scripture Reading: Acts 16:19–32

Introduction

"The Conversion of the Philippian Jailer" is the title of this evening's message. The purpose of using this message is to encourage all who are unsaved to be saved now. In discussing this subject, five specific incidents involved in the jailer's conversion will be used to assist each unsaved person to a conversion experience.

I. A great earthquake was used to get attention (Acts 16:26).

A. *God accomplished a great deal through such an event.* Prison doors were opened, stocks loosened, hearts smitten, and consciences pricked. The jailer was awakened physically and spiritually. This was a necessity before he could be saved. The Scripture passage indicates that this awakening was an outward answer to prayer and worship. In those days as now, heaven and earth were moved by holy people praying and singing.

B. *God still accomplishes his purpose in getting the attention of the lost.* How does he go about doing so now? What methods does he use? What are his earthquakes today?

Sometimes the Lord uses physical crises in the life of the lost to get their attention. On the other hand, he may use a simple confrontation of a spiritual truth. He may use a word softly spoken by a Sunday school teacher, friend, neighbor, or pastor.

II. The jailer's predicament produced an agitation of the soul (vv. 27–28).

A. *The jailer was awakened to anguish and despair.* He thought his prisoners had escaped. Their escape would not only bring disgrace to him in discharging the responsibility of keeping the prisoners, but because of his failure, his life would be in jeopardy. In all probability, the rulers would have had him put to death. It is easy to read the anguish and despair in the life of this man as one reads the pages of God's Word. Those physical threats opened a larger concern—namely, his spiritual condition.

B. *The anguish of the jailer is a picture of the same in all lost people when they are awakened to their terrible plight.* Some lost people are conscious of their condition. They know disaster lies ahead, and they need to settle matters with God immediately. Other lost people are not conscious of being lost but know something is lacking in their lives. They need an awakening.

III. The agitation of the soul led to a soul-searching question.

"What must I do to be saved?" (v. 30).

A. *The Christian witness had caused an experience in him that raised the question.* Paul and Silas may have spoken to the jailer about their Lord when they were put into prison. At least the jailer would have heard them singing and praying.

Here a progression of events can be discovered. First, the jailer was afraid. This fear provoked desire, and the desire prompted willingness.

B. *The question raised by the Philippian jailer is a must for every lost person who is to be saved.* It must be asked either openly and verbally or inwardly. The delay in asking this all-important question can be extremely dangerous. Each lost person needs to ask this question for himself or herself right now.

IV. The soul-searching question brought forth a dynamic answer.

"Believe on the Lord Jesus Christ and thou shalt be saved" (v. 31).

A. *This answer involves two specifics.*
1. To believe is to receive and trust. There is no conversion apart from these two essentials.
2. The object of the faith was the Lord Jesus Christ.
B. *It is only through Christ that a person can have a conversion experience and be saved.* The principle of trusting the Lord Jesus Christ for salvation still remains true.

V. The question that was asked and the answer that was given resulted in conversion (v. 33).

A. *This is implied but not specifically pointed out.* The Bible does tell what happened. The man's heart was transformed. Instead of ruthlessly thrusting Paul and Silas back into prison, he became a man of compassion. He washed their stripes, took them to his home, fed them, and listened to what they had to say.
B. *This conversion experience is what some people need today.* This is the moment to ask, "What must I do to be saved?" Each lost person whose heart has been pricked needs to trust the Lord Jesus as Savior and openly respond to God's invitation.

Conclusion

In this message five incidents have been used to review a wonderful conversion experience. These are lessons I hope the Holy Spirit will use to bring you to the Lord Jesus right now. I am asking you who are lost to trust him as Savior and come forward during the invitation.

WEDNESDAY EVENING, NOVEMBER 27

Title: Thanksliving

Text: "As ye have therefore received Christ Jesus the Lord, so walk ye in him: rooted and built up in him, and stablished in the faith, as ye have been taught, abounding therein with thanksgiving" **(Col. 2:6–7).**

Scripture Reading: Colossians 2:6–7

Introduction

T. B. Maston taught Christian ethics at Southwestern Baptist Theological Seminary, Fort Worth, Texas, for forty-one years. After receiving a Doctor of Religious Education degree from Southwestern Seminary, he also earned a Doctor of Philosophy degree from Yale University. While at Yale he had a serious illness. In fact, he said that he came as near to death as one could come and still live. At one point in his illness he dreamed that he was on a fence. To fall on one side was death; to fall on the other side was life. He lived. But he also said that he lived the rest of his life with a sense of gratitude and obligation.

This expresses the Christian approach to "thanksliving" on this Wednesday evening prior to Thanksgiving. Because we have found grace and forgiveness in Jesus Christ, all of life is lived as an expression of thanks and gratitude to God.

This is seen in the principle Paul stated in Colossians 2:6. "As ye have therefore received Christ Jesus the Lord, so walk ye in him." Thanksliving results in thanksgiving. Thanksgiving shows thanksliving. We should live in thanks to God.

I. Thanksliving rests on a firm foundation of faith.

A. *The foundation of faith is expressed by four metaphors.*
1. A metaphor from daily life: walk. The word *walk* has to do with the manner of life. Christians live as pilgrims in this world. They walk with God.
2. A metaphor from agriculture: rooted.
   The Christian is rooted in Christ. A plant will not grow unless properly rooted in good soil. Through faith we are rooted in Christ.
3. A metaphor from construction: built up.
4. A metaphor from the legal sources: stablished.
B. *The foundation of faith is essential for life.* All things must have a good foundation. A building will not stand unless it has a good foundation. Some footings go as far down into the ground as the building goes up in the air.
C. *The foundation of faith rests on Christ.* Jesus Christ is the only adequate foundation for life. The common element in the four metaphors of faith that Paul used is Jesus Christ. They are all based on Jesus Christ. The Christian walks in Christ, is rooted in Christ, is built up by Christ, and is stablished in Christ. Christ is the only adequate foundation for life.

II. Thanksliving exists in a fine functioning of faith.

A. *When faith functions through thanksliving, it will seek to reproduce the spirit of Christ.* We could name people who have dedicated their lives in service to humankind, who have shown Christ's spirit of care, concern, and sacrifice.
B. *When faith functions through thanksliving it will show mercy, kindness, and grace to others as Christ did.* As Christians try to reproduce the spirit of Christ, they will also seek to live out the characteristics of Christ. The things that Christ did in the world will become their goals.

Joe Martin of Massachusetts had a long and varied career in politics. He held a political position until he was in his eighties. He was a Republican floor leader in the House of Representatives and twice Speaker of the House. He wrote a book entitled *My First Fifty Years in Politics* and closed the book by saying that after years of living with the coldest realities he still believed that one reaps what one sows, and that to sow kindness is the best of all investments.

C. *When faith functions through thanksliving, we can have victory over self.* We have victory in Jesus Christ, which allows us to live with victory in life.

Roger Ward was a race car driver. He won many races, including the Indianapolis 500. He had come out of World War II and learned racing the hard way on the small-time circuits. He would drive two or three times a week, risking his life with every lap on poor tracks and abused machinery. After one crash he could not drive for five months. He found escape from his tension in alcohol. After meeting a girl he loved he asked her to marry him. For four years she said no but finally agreed. He tried hard to make her happy and to lay off the booze. At her suggestion he began to attend church and to tithe. Soon he found it easier to turn down a drink. One New Year's Eve a drink was handed to him and he poured it over a porch railing, saying, "That is that." Later, when he won the Indianapolis 500, a reporter asked him if that race were not his greatest victory. Ward said that it was not. His greatest victory was to know that he had conquered himself. We can do that only through Christ.

Conclusion

Thanksliving is a way of life. It does not come just once a year. It comes throughout life by living in gratitude to God.

Suggested preaching program for the month of

DECEMBER

■ Sunday Mornings

Complete the stewardship series "What Giving Does for You" on the first Sunday of the month. Then use the theme "Isaiah's Messianic Prophecy," with messages based on Isaiah 12 as a series for Advent.

■ Sunday Evenings

"Christmas Celebration," a series of four candlelight services, is suggested using five different candles. The candle of hope emphasizes the prophecy of the Messiah's coming. The candle of peace represents the peace the Messiah brings. The candle of joy emphasizes the true joy that comes through Christ. The candle of love signifies the angelic announcement concerning the coming of the Christ. The fifth candle, lighted on the final Sunday of the series, symbolizes Christ as the Light of the World.

An advent wreath should be used for the five candles. The four candles in the wreath should be purple, with the center candle being white, or red if a white one cannot be secured.

The lighting of the designated candle on each Sunday evening can be very dramatic. Choose an elementary-age child to come down the aisle during the first hymn. Provide the child with a candle lighter, and as the candle is lit, explain the symbolism of this particular candle and how it supplements and illustrates the message plan for the hour.

■ Wednesday Evenings

Complete the series of devotional studies based on Paul's letter to the Colossians using the theme "Concerning Colossians."

SUNDAY MORNING, DECEMBER 1

Title: The Stewardship of Life

Text: "Moreover it is required in stewards, that a man be found faithful" (1 Cor. 4:2).

Scripture Reading: 1 Corinthians 6:19–20; 4:2

Hymns: "Take My Life, and Let It Be," Havergal
"Something for Thee," Phelps
"Our Best," Kirk

Offertory Prayer: Our Father, we come to you today because you made us, you redeemed us, and we acknowledge that every good and perfect gift comes from your bountiful hands. Make us good stewards of what you have given us. By your grace we have been bought with a price, and therefore we desire to glorify you. Receive from our hands and hearts these gifts. Bless them and use them for your glory. We pray in Christ's name. Amen.

Introduction

We are humbled when we realize that God has made us stewards of our lives and that we are responsible to him. Paul reminds us that we are not our own but have been bought with a price (1 Cor. 6:20).

Life is God-given. Life is a charge from God. Each of our lives has marvelous potential. Let us be good stewards and glorify God. Let us make the most of what God has given to us.

Now let us look at some of the principles involved in the stewardship of life.

I. We belong to God.

Underlying the stewardship of life is the fundamental truth set forth by Paul: "Ye are not your own; for ye are bought with a price" (2 Cor. 6:19–20).

A. *We belong to God because he created us.* "So God created man in his own image, in the image of God created he him; male and female created he them" (Gen. 1:27). "And the LORD God formed man of the dust of the ground, and breathed into his nostrils the breath of life; and man became a living soul" (Gen. 2:7).

B. *We belong to God because he has saved us.* "For by grace are ye saved through faith; and that not of yourselves: it is the gift of God: not of works, lest any man should boast" (Eph. 2:8–9). "For the wages of sin is death; but the gift of God is eternal life through Jesus Christ our Lord" (Rom. 6:23). God has saved us, given us eternal life. We belong to him.

C. *We belong to God because of his providential care for us.* Every resource we have is the gift of God. Paul said to Timothy, "For we brought nothing into this world, and it is certain we can carry nothing out" (1 Tim. 6:7). The psalmist said, "The earth is the LORD's, and the fulness thereof; the world, and they that dwell therein" (Ps. 24:1). Every good and perfect gift comes from his bountiful hands. God provides for us. He cares for us and meets our every need.

II. We are to place God first in our lives.

"But seek ye first the kingdom of God, and his righteousness; and all these things shall be added unto you" (Matt. 6:33). Jesus said, "He that loveth father or mother more than me is not worthy of me: and he that loveth son or daughter more than me is not worthy of me" (Matt. 10:37). The priority of God's claims is a biblical truth and is found throughout the Bible. God desires first place in our lives. To give him less than first place would be ungrateful of us.

Jesus Christ is first among the persons of the Bible. The Lord's day is first among the days of the week. The Bible is first among books. First among institutions is the church Christ loved and gave himself for. First among dollars is the tithe. First among all the calls that come to us is the Lord's call.

III. We are fellow laborers with the Lord.

Stewardship is a partnership. The rare privilege of partnership with God is set forth in many places in the Bible. "For we are labourers together with God" (1 Cor. 3:9). Paul said to the Corinthians, "I have planted, Apollos watered; but God gave the increase" (1 Cor. 3:6). In 2 Corinthians 6:1 we read, "We then, [are] workers together with him."

Since we are laborers together with God, we receive our orders from him (Matt. 28:18–20). Simon Peter said, "We ought to obey God rather than men" (Acts 5:29).

All honest work is honorable. "Whatsoever thy hand findeth to do, do it with thy might" (Eccl. 9:10). Working with the Lord is the greatest of all privileges.

IV. We are responsible to the Lord.

Paul said to the Romans, "So then, every one of us shall give account of himself to God" (Rom. 14:12). Too many Christians apparently take it for granted that being saved is all that is involved in the Christian life. Being saved is of primary importance, but the use of our talent, time, tithe, energies, and all else we possess is important too. We are not only to use what the Lord has given to us, but we are accountable for all that the Lord has given us to use for him.

Conclusion

Let us be good stewards of all of life, for God gave it to us. He sustains life. He supplies our needs. Therefore, let us honor him with all that we are and with all that we have.

SUNDAY EVENING, DECEMBER 1

Title: The Candle of Hope

Text: "For to us a child is born, to us a son is given, and the government will be upon his shoulders. And he will be called Wonderful Counselor, Mighty God, Everlasting Father, Prince of Peace" **(Isa. 9:6 NIV).**

Scripture Reading: Isaiah 9:2–7

Introduction

What short words we use to express our deepest emotions! We speak of love, joy, hope, and peace. Yet these words carry so much human feeling that they are almost inadequate to convey what we want to say.

These are the very words that are used during the Advent season of the Christian calendar. Advent is that period of four weeks just prior to Christmas. It is used in Christian churches to tell of events leading up to the birth of Jesus.

The four candles of the Advent wreath represent hope, peace, joy, and salvation or love. The hope candle is used to teach about the prophecy of the Lord's first coming. The peace candle teaches about how Christ is the Prince of Peace. The joy candle is for the joy the shepherds expressed because their prayers for the messianic age had been answered. The candle of salvation is an expression of God's love for humankind. The center candle is the Christ candle, and it is lit when all others have been lighted.

We will be following this outline each Sunday night during our celebration of Advent. Tonight we are lighting the candle of hope—the prophecy of the coming Messiah.

The Old Testament is filled with many prophecies about the Messiah. Our text tonight is only one of those. It illustrates the hope that Israel had for a Leader who magnified the best in us by his own good nature.

I. Our hope is centered in a wonderful Counselor.

A. *Isaiah lived in a time of national turmoil.* Assyria had already threatened Judah. Israel, the northern kingdom, was gone—crushed by Assyria. Yet Isaiah had a vision of hope. He prophesied, "The people walking in darkness have seen a great light; of those living in the land of the shadow of death a light has dawned" (Isa. 9:2 NIV). Isaiah's vision of hope is so vivid that it appears to him as though the great event has already occurred.

B. *A child is to be born, except that the prophet speaks as though he has been born.* By faith Isaiah saw him—a king unlike any other earthly king. He saw a son who was the gift of God. This child is a son of David (v. 7).

C. *He is given the title of Counselor, but he is no ordinary sage.* The adjective "Wonderful" indicates the marvelous wisdom he has and the mighty deeds he can accomplish. He is extraordinary. His wisdom and knowledge exceed that of any of David's descendants. All of the treasures of wisdom and knowledge are found in him.

II. Our hope is centered in a mighty God.

A. *This title of the newborn Son explains why he is such a wonderful Counselor.* It is because he is the Almighty God. Some people argue that there is no way Isaiah could have comprehended the divine incarnation at Bethlehem. This view omits the fact that not only is this prophecy from Isaiah, but it is a revelation from God.

B. *Isaiah believed this child to be born of the Spirit of God.* How much Isaiah understood, we have no way of knowing. Yet it is clear that the ancient prophet could see this child as being the Mighty One of God. He is invincible. No earthly king could ever be thought to be invincible.

C. *This Son of David would accomplish what others could not do.* He would capture the hearts of humankind by the thousands and win their loyalty and love. He would have a kingdom based on unusual power.

Today—on this side of Bethlehem—we can readily see how powerful Jesus is. Yet his might is not found in armies and machines of war, but in the overwhelming love he has for humankind. No other force on earth is more powerful than God's love.

III. Our hope is centered in an everlasting Father.

A. *The Bible clearly states that there will be no end to the Messiah's kingdom.* So many of David's sons had come to the throne only to see their accomplishments die at the same time they did. There was nothing lasting about their rule. If they accomplished good, their sons or grandsons might turn it around and begin to do evil.

Isaiah speaks of an "eternal" side to this Messiah. His kingdom is everlasting.

B. *The word "Father" refers to a unique quality of kingship.* He sees his followers as children, not as subjects. This Messiah considers the people of his realm as sons and daughters. He is like a "Father." He disciplines his children for their good. He provides for their needs out of his special relationship with them. He answers requests out of love. He is the Everlasting Father.

IV. Our hope is centered in a Prince of Peace.

A. *War, conflict, death, privation have always been the hallmark of kings who set out to rule the world.* Their rules cost the subjects in taxes and blood. Hardship and sacrifice were required.

Here the prophet points to the new Messiah as being an emissary of Peace. We must not be misled to believe that Jesus—the true object of Isaiah's prophecy—does not cause hardship and sacrifice. Christians face a hostile world. Living for Jesus may indeed cause difficulty and even the loss of physical life.

B. *Isaiah knows that the Messiah will not establish his kingdom by means of war.* Instead, the Messiah establishes peace. He seeks peace and teaches his children to seek peace. The end of conflict does not always mean that enemies are now friends. The cause of the conflict needs to be removed. This cause is sin. This child, the Messiah, will come to conquer sin, which is the real cause of hatred, jealousy, and bickering.

C. *Also, the enmity between God and humans is removed.* Sin keeps God and humans apart. Jesus is the Prince of Peace who restores fellowship between God and humans. The peace that this child provides has no end. In Isaiah 9:7 the prophet says, "Of the increase of his government and peace there will be no end" (NIV).

Conclusion

Certainly Jesus Christ is the fulfillment of Isaiah's prophecy. No ordinary descendant of David qualifies. Jesus left heaven and became the God-man who embodied all the qualities mentioned here. He and he alone is the Wonderful Counselor, the Mighty God, the Everlasting Father, and the Prince of Peace.

But some people did not believe in Jesus when he first came. He did not meet their standards. Although he met the scriptural standard, Jesus was not the kind of king most of the Jews wanted. Thus, they rejected him.

And people are still rejecting Jesus today. What will you do? Will you reject the "Hope of the World"? Or will you accept him as the long hoped for Messiah?

WEDNESDAY EVENING, DECEMBER 4

Title: The Garments of the Ungodly

Text: "Mortify therefore your members which are upon the earth; fornication, uncleanness, inordinate affection, evil concupiscence, and covetousness, which is idolatry: for which things' sake the wrath of God cometh on the children of disobedience: in the which ye also walked some time, when ye lived in them" **(Col. 3:5–7).**

Scripture Reading: Colossians 3:5–11

Introduction

The early church had an interesting custom for baptism. Whenever a person came out of the water after having been baptized, he or she would be given a new, clean, shining white robe. This robe was symbolic of the new life that person now had with Christ. New life in Christ demanded a new garment, a garment to match the demands of that life—clean, bright, shining. We still carry out the symbolism in a sense in using white robes as baptismal garments. This points up the truth that when you become a Christian there are certain garments, certain ways of life, that you can no longer wear.

Paul used strong words to show what Christians must do to these inferior and false ways of life. In Colossians 3:5 he used the word *mortify,* put to death. Then in verse 8 he used the words *put off.* This word in the Greek was used for taking off clothes, removing garments. There are, then, certain garments of the ungodly that Christians must take off.

As the apostle Paul so often did in his writings, he tied ethical demands to theological truths. These clear-cut demands are tied directly to our relationship with Christ—that Christians are raised with Christ, that we will set our minds on heavenly things, that we will share in the glory of Christ. Since this is true, Christians must "put to death therefore what is earthly in you"

372

(Col. 3:5 RSV). Then, after the popular fashion of his time, Paul gave two lists, each of five vices that Christians must put to death. These are the garments of the ungodly that must be removed from our lives.

I. Certain desires are garments of the ungodly (Col. 3:5–7).

A. *The compilation of the sins of the flesh.* Notice that this list includes the things that we often call the gross sins of the flesh. The list in the Revised Standard Version includes:

1. Immorality.
2. Impurity.
3. Passion (lust).
4. Evil desire.
5. Covetousness.

B. *The comprehensiveness of the sins of the flesh.* Covetousness is included in this list of sins of the flesh. This is the desire to have more, a ruthless self-seeking. This is a sin that ranges from the desire for more money to the desire for prestige. The Scripture here indicates that this desire is idolatry. How could that be? The essence of idolatry is the desire to get. People set up idols in order to get more from their particular god.

C. *The conclusion of the sins of the flesh.* The result of these five sins is an invitation to God's wrath, God's continual opposition to sin. It allows for no permissiveness. It allows for no relativism. These five sins must be removed from the life of a Christian.

II. Certain dispositions are garments of the ungodly (Col. 3:8–10).

A. *The compilation of the sins of the spirit.*

1. Anger.
2. Wrath.
3. Malice.
4. Blasphemy (slander).
5. Filthy communication.

In *Shields of Brass,* C. Roy Angell (Broadman, 1965) told of visiting a friend who owned a large cotton factory. During his visit, Angell told his friend that he was sorry for the heartache and embarrassment that the friend had experienced due to the imprisonment of his brother. The man replied that he hung his head in shame every time he thought of what his brother had done. In a moment of anger the brother had hit a man so hard that when he fell and struck his head on the pavement, he died. Then the friend said that sometimes he became angry with preachers who spent so much time preaching against liquor and gambling but so little time preaching against the wreckers of life like anger, envy, and jealousy. Those are the things, said the man, that put his brother behind bars.

B. *Commands for Christian speech.* If these matters of speech are turned into positive commands rather than negative prohibitions, then there are three laws for Christian speech. Christian speech must be:
1. Kind
2. Pure
3. True

C. *The conclusion from the sins of the spirit.* The apostle indicated that if a person continued to cling to those things as a pattern of life, there was no evidence that his or her nature had been changed by Christ.

III. Certain distinctions are garments of the ungodly (Col. 3:11).

A. *We must remove the artificial, arbitrary barriers that divide us.*
B. *How can we do this?* A number of phrases in the passage help us: "put on the new man" (v. 10), "renewed...after the image of him that created him" (v. 10), and "Christ is all, and in all" (v. 11).

Conclusion

These are the garments of the ungodly. Surely through God's help we will do all that we can to remove them, remembering that it will have to be through Christ's strength, power, and new life.

SUNDAY MORNING, DECEMBER 8

Title: What If There Were No Christmas?

Text: "Make known his deeds among the nations, proclaim that his name is exalted. Sing praises to the LORD, for he has done gloriously; let this be known in all the earth" **(Isa. 12:4–5).**

Scripture Reading: Isaiah 12:1–6

Hymns: "Angels from the Realms of Glory," Montgomery
"Joy to the World! The Lord Is Come," Watts
"One Day," Chapman

Offertory Prayer: Holy Father, as we approach the Christmas season, which reminds us repeatedly of the greatness of your love for us, help us to recognize how fortunate we are because of your supreme gift to us. Help us to give you the genuine adoration of our hearts. Help us, our Father, to let you be in sovereign control over our will. Help us day by day to imitate the example set before us by the Savior. Today we come offering to you the praise of our lips, the love of our hearts, and the gifts from our hands. Accept them and bless them we pray. In Jesus' name. Amen.

Introduction

We are Christians because someone was a missionary. We are Christians because someone communicated to us the wonderful deeds of God revealed in the life, death, and living presence of Jesus Christ. We can rejoice over the fact that those who went before us did not treat the gospel as a private treasure to be guarded.

We are the recipients of the blessings of our faith because of the missionary activity of others. The shepherds went forth from the stable with a story to tell. The wise men came bringing their best gifts and returned to their land by another way, communicating the good news of what they had discovered. The apostles gave themselves without reservation to sharing the good news. The early disciples went everywhere spreading the gospel. Our spiritual fathers were communicators of the good news the angels sang about and the shepherds told about.

What if there were no Christmas?

I. Christmas means different things to different people.

To some Christmas means Santa Claus. To others it means a Christmas tree and presents. To some Christmas is a time for visiting relatives and eating delicious food. To some Christmas is a time for communication between friends; cards and letters are exchanged.

To some Christmas is a time for escape from the realities of life through the use of alcohol or drugs. Although some memories bless and cheer, others bring us pain or sorrow.

More alcoholic beverages are purchased and consumed during the Christmas season than any other time of the year. The consumption of alcohol and drugs reveals that there is much pain abroad in the land, and people are in need of some kind of anesthesia.

II. Christmas really means communication from God to the earth.

God communicated through the angels and through his Son. He continues to communicate his love to the world through the church.

At least 1.5 billion people on the face of the earth have not heard enough of the good news of Christ to be able to make a responsible decision of faith in him. For these there is no real Christmas. These people do not know what we know about God's love nor feel what we feel as a result of Jesus' coming. They do not have the hope that we have because of Jesus' coming.

Think about the messages that come to us through Christmas cards. If there were no Christmas, we would not receive any Christmas cards. These cards bring messages emphasizing love, peace, joy, hope, and giving.

Doris Faulhaber writes about the results of Christmas in her poem "Love Came Down on Christmas Day."

> *LOVE came down on Christmas Day,*
> *So many years ago,*
> *And brought the greatest happiness*
> *The world would ever know....*

PEACE came down on Christmas Day
  To fill the hearts of men
With all the sweet tranquillity
  Each Christmas brings again....

JOY came down on Christmas Day
  As angels came to earth
  Heralding the miracle
  Of our Messiah's birth....

What lovely gifts to all of us,
  These three—so rich and rare—
And every year at Christmas time
  We see them everywhere!

Conclusion

Let us join our hearts in a prayer of gratitude and thanksgiving to God because of the meaning of Christmas. Let us respond to the love that came down on Christmas Day by loving God supremely and loving our brothers and sisters steadfastly. Let us rejoice in the peace that came down on Christmas Day by living in harmonious relationships with others. Let us allow the joy that came down on Christmas Day to fill our hearts as we meditate on the rich gifts of God's grace to us.

To really respond to Christmas, you need to let Christ live in your heart and life. If you have not already invited him to come in, today would be a good day.

SUNDAY EVENING, DECEMBER 8

Title: The Candle of Peace

Text: "Then what was said through the prophet Jeremiah was fulfilled: 'A voice is heard in Ramah, weeping and great mourning, Rachel weeping for her children and refusing to be comforted, because they are no more'" **(Matt. 2:17–18 NIV).**

Scripture Reading: Matthew 2:1–18

Introduction

In our minds the pain of suffering, injustice, and stark cruelty should never be associated with Christmas. The very thought of Christmas and enmity being companions is repulsive. Sentimental thinking believes that at Christmas humankind should lay aside differences and all should be at peace. Harmony and goodwill should be the order of the season.

The stark truth is that such is not the case and never has been. Jesus was born in the midst of cruelty, death, and suffering. The tyrant Herod epitomized all the evil of humankind for all generations. The cry heard in Ramah is the same cry that echoes in our own world.

Henry Wadsworth Longfellow's carol "I Heard the Bells on Christmas Day" points to the human condition:

> *And in despair I bowed my head,*
> *"There is no peace on earth," I said.*
> *"For hate is strong, and mocks the song*
> *Of peace on earth, goodwill to men."*

The Prince of Peace is a paradox in the world of anger, hatred, and malice. Christianity seems to float on a vast sea of mischief and mayhem.

Yet the life and work of this baby has been the cornerstone of Western civilization. He has influenced even nonbelievers and provided immense improvements in the human condition. This helpless Baby of Bethlehem has brought everlasting peace to innumerable segments of humankind. Tonight we light the candle of peace to honor the Prince of Peace.

I. Peace that calms in the face of terror.

A. *The land into which Jesus was born was ruled by the infamous Herod the Great.* He was a despot who ruled by terror rather than by concern for his subjects. Life was cheap during his reign. In a fit of anger he murdered his favorite wife, Mariamne, and killed his two sons. It was this act that caused Augustus Caesar to say, "It is better to be Herod's hog than his son."

Herod's warped nature can be seen in the request he made at his death. At the age of seventy he went to his winter palace in Jericho and prepared to die. He had a number of distinguished citizens arrested on trumped-up charges. He ordered that at the moment of his death, they should all be killed. He said he knew that no one would mourn his death, and he was determined that tears would flow at the time of his death.

B. *The Gift that was sent on that first Christmas demonstrated God's fondness for contrasts.* One would expect a more audacious entrance into human history by God. Instead, God entered through a stable, barely five miles from the capitol of Herod.

We still look for God to do the spectacular. We want him to open heaven and astound our enemies. We want him to dazzle the evil tyrants in our lives with his awesomeness and magnificent power. Instead, God persists in contrasts.

C. *He offers calm in the middle of chaos.* He contrasts the sword and terror of Herod with the peace and tranquillity of the manger.

The lesson for us here is that God works quietly to bring a lasting peace to humankind. This is not accomplished by bluster and spectacular political events. Our lives are filled with turmoil, but Christ works calmly with deliberate assurance that brings a peace that passes human understanding. Herod is gone, and all the Herods of our day will also pass into the pages of history. But the Baby of Bethlehem lives today and will live forever. In that fact alone is a sweet peace that calms the soul of every believer.

II. Peace that saves in the face of death.

A. *The slaughter of the innocent children of Bethlehem was but one more proof of Herod's treachery.* When the Magi did not return with the location of the newborn King, Herod reacted as he always did—with callous cruelty. To protect his throne, he ordered the death of all the boys in Bethlehem who were two years old or younger.

Death filled the city of David, and sin is always the author of death. The mothers who lived to protect their children were ruthlessly cast aside. Evil seemed to prevail.

B. *Yet God had made provision for the one who was to overcome death.* It seems like little comfort that Jesus was spared when so many others had to die. But the answer to that paradox is found in the governing hand of God in history. Those Jewish mothers would only have to experience a temporary sorrow. Far greater would be their grief if there was no salvation for anyone.

God was working out his eternal plan of salvation. God wanted to provide peace that wipes away tears, suffering, anguish, and death. Death for man, woman, or child is made easier to face because God preserved the life of Jesus.

C. *Death is the last enemy of humankind.* It is Satan's most vicious weapon. With death the Prince of Darkness hopes to swallow up all of humanity. As God defeated Herod at Bethlehem, so he can defeat death in our lifetime. As God provided for the escape of Jesus into Egypt, so he can provide for our escape now.

Conclusion

Our world is afflicted with human cruelty. The abuse of power by Herod did not cease with his death. Humanity has continued to inflict injustice on the weaker elements of civilization.

The world seeks peace that would put an end to strife and conflict. Yet Jesus said that there would always be wars and rumors of wars. Such upheaval and turmoil will never come to an end in this life.

Nevertheless, God has not abandoned us. In the middle of human misery he still slips quietly into our lives to reassure us that hate will not prevail. He calms our fears—our fear of life and our fear of death.

By putting our faith in Jesus we receive the peace of God. We can know that whatever happens, God will save us.

Do you believe in Jesus? Would you like to receive a peace that only he can provide? You can by accepting him into your life.

WEDNESDAY EVENING, DECEMBER 11

Title: The Clothing of a Christian

Text: "Therefore, as God's chosen people, holy and dearly loved, clothe yourselves with compassion, kindness, humility, gentleness and patience. Bear with each other and forgive whatever grievances you may have against one another. Forgive as the Lord forgave you" **(Col. 3:12–13 NIV).**

Scripture Reading: Colossians 3:12–15

Introduction

The apostle Paul was concerned about the Christian's clothing. In the verses just preceding this passage, he discussed what we called the garments of the ungodly. There are certain desires, dispositions, and distinctions that we must strip off our lives. Once we remove these things, however, what are we to put on? Paul gave some positive suggestions. Colossians 3:12 says to "clothe yourselves." Following are things that could be classified as the clothing of a Christian. These are things that we are to put on. Note that they are not things we just naturally add to our lives. They can come only to God's chosen people, holy and dearly loved."

I. Some desirable personal qualities make up the Christian's clothing (Col. 3:12).

A. *Notice the qualities.*
1. Compassion.
2. Kindness.
3. Humility.
4. Meekness.
5. Patience.

B. *Notice the relationship.* These qualities all have to do with personal relationships. These are the things that help people to relate well to one another and to get along together.

II. The practice of forgiveness makes up the Christian's clothing (Col. 3:13).

A. *The incentive for forgiveness.* The incentive for forgiveness is the forgiveness that we have experienced through Jesus Christ. Having been forgiven, we are to be forgiving.

B. *The inclusiveness of forgiveness.* "Bear with each other and forgive whatever grievances you may have against one another. Forgive as the Lord forgave you."

In his book *Love Is Eternal*, Irving Stone told of a fictional interview between Mary Todd Lincoln and Parker, the president's guard. She asked him why he had not kept the assassin out. The guard replied that he bitterly regretted it, but he had grown careless and had gotten interested in the play. He did not think that anyone would kill so good a man in a public place. Mrs. Lincoln said that the guard had no business being careless. Then in torment she covered her face with her hands and said it was not he that she could not forgive; it was the assassin. Then Tad Lincoln spoke up. He said that if his pa had lived, he would have forgiven the man who shot him. Pa forgave everybody.

III. The perfection of love makes up the Christian's clothing (Col. 3:14).

A. *Love is the binding power that holds the Christian body together.*

B. *Love is the greatest of all Christian virtues.*

IV. The peace of God makes up the Christian's clothing (Col. 3:15).

A. *The peace of God rules in the heart. Interestingly enough, the word translated "rule" is a word from the athletic arena, umpire.* The peace of God settles the disputes and divisions of the heart and soul.

B. *The peace of God brings unity and thankfulness.* On a house near Durham, England, there is a Latin inscription indicating that the house was built "in the year 1697 of the peace of the gospel and in the first year of the peace of Ryswick." The peace of Ryswick is almost forgotten now, but it was considered the most vital and permanent treaty at the time. When it was made, trade was revived, the army was disbanded, and a happier time was inaugurated. The treaty later proved to be an idle basis for peace. The peace of the gospel still abides.

Conclusion

These garments can be put on only as we let the word of God dwell in us. The garments of the Christian are only for the Christian.

SUNDAY MORNING, DECEMBER 15

Title: God Is My Salvation

Text: "Behold, God is my salvation; I will trust, and will not be afraid; for the LORD GOD is my strength and my song, and he has become my salvation" (**Isa. 12:2 RSV**).

Scripture Reading: Isaiah 12:1–6

Hymns: "Come, Thou Almighty King," Anonymous

            "Rejoice, Ye Pure in Heart," Plumptre

            "There's a Song in the Air," Holland

Offertory Prayer: Holy heavenly Father, today we bring to you the gold, frankincense, and myrrh of our tithes and offerings and present them to him who was born to be our King. We pray your blessings upon these contributions to the end that more and more people around the world might hear the good news that came on that first Christmas when angels sang about the birth of Christ. We thank you for the privilege of knowing him as Savior, as giver of life, as teacher, and as leader. Accept our gifts today in Jesus' name. Amen.

Introduction

The text declares that "God is my salvation." The Christmas season should focus our attention on the great salvation that is offered through Jesus Christ. Many of us can rejoice exceedingly over the fact that through Jesus Christ, "God has become my salvation."

The angel spoke to Joseph and said, "She shall bring forth a son, and thou shalt call his name Jesus: for he shall save his people from their sins" (Matt. 1:21). The angels hung out over the battlements of heaven to sing, "For unto you is born this day in the city of David a Saviour, which is Christ the Lord" (Luke 2:11).

Jesus Christ was born to be our Savior. He died on a cross to save us from the penalty of sin and from the separation from God that sin brings. Jesus Christ arose from the dead triumphant and victorious to be our Savior. This Christmas season will be greatly reduced in meaning if you cannot say with the prophet, "God is my salvation."

I. God is the God of salvation.

A. *Our nation needs God's salvation.* We need salvation from:
1. Ignorance.
2. Fear.
3. Anger and hate.
4. Rashness and harshness.
5. Greed.
6. Arrogance and pride.
7. Wickedness and ungodliness.
8. Selfishness and hard-heartedness.

B. *Our families need salvation.* We not only need Jesus Christ as the Savior from the penalty of sin, but we need him as our Savior from the power and practice of sin.

   Jesus Christ, who was born in Bethlehem and who conquered death and the grave, lives today to help you experience God's full salvation in family living.

II. The prophet declared, "Behold, God is my salvation."

Because God was his salvation, he was able to declare, "I will trust, and will not be afraid."

A. *We can trust and not be afraid of the past.* God is the gracious God who forgives our sin fully and freely and forever.

B. *We can trust and not be afraid of the present.* The song writer said, "Because he lives, I can face tomorrow." Jesus Christ is alive, and in the Holy Spirit he dwells within us as close as the very breath that we breathe. He wants to fill our hearts with the love of God. He wants to guide us with the wisdom of God. He wants to help us control ourselves by means of the Spirit of God.

C. *We can trust and not be afraid of the future.* As we approach the end of the year, there is always speculation about the future. None of us can know what the future holds, but in Jesus Christ we know him who holds the future.

Christ has conquered death and the grave. He has promised us the life that endures beyond the curtain that people call death. We can count on him for his presence with us. The psalmist said, "Surely goodness and mercy shall follow me all the days of my life, and I will dwell in the house of the LORD forever" (Ps. 23:6).

III. God is my salvation.

A. *As my Savior, God is the source of my strength.* A pastor visited a woman in the hospital who had just undergone major surgery following an automobile accident in which her husband had been killed and she had been seriously injured. On the day following her husband's unexpected death, she said, "God is my strength." Paul told this to the Philippians when he said, "I can do all things through Christ which strengtheneth me" (4:13). By that triumphant testimony, the apostle was saying that with the help of God he could face any obstacle or difficulty with confidence and hope.

B. *"God is my song."* The angels sang to announce the birth of the Savior. Our Lord and his disciples were able to sing a hymn of praise while in the upper room before departing to Gethsemane's gloom. Christianity is the religion that puts a song in the heart. This is one of the major themes of the Christmas season. God is the God who gives us a song in our hearts.

Conclusion

Isaiah could say, "God has become my salvation." There had been a time when God was not the prophet's salvation, but Isaiah had come to a point of faith and commitment when God's salvation became real to him.

Some say, "Education is my salvation." Some say, "Marriage is my salvation." Some say, "My family is my salvation." Some say, "My money is my salvation." Some say, "My government is my salvation." Let God be God in your life. He offers salvation from the past, the present, and the future.

If you will truly let God become your salvation as he has revealed himself in Jesus Christ, you will be able to join with the prophet who said, "I will trust, and will not be afraid."

SUNDAY EVENING, DECEMBER 15

Title: The Candle of Joy

Text: "She will give birth to a son, and you are to give him the name Jesus, because he will save his people from their sins" **(Matt. 1:21 NIV).**

Scripture Reading: Matthew 1:18–25

Introduction

No other word so completely captures the Christmas spirit as the word *joy*. It describes so many of the feelings of Christmas. Joy is when children see their presents, when relatives arrive at the homestead, when Christmas pageants feature the angelic qualities of children, when grandmother announces that dinner is served, and when the choir sings the annual Christmas cantata.

Undergirding all these activities is the quiet confidence that God has indeed invaded our lives. Not only did he enter the human race at that first Christmas, but he also has entered our own piece of history. The birth of Jesus provided the rebirth of our soul.

Yet, for some at Christmas, joy is absent. It is but a hollow day instead of a holiday. The "good tidings of great joy" is not real for them. Missing from their lives is the pleasant assurance that life has meaning. They are lost in the artificial whirlwind of Christmas. The decorating, baking, gift buying, and other activities of Christmas are but one more hassle in their already gloomy lives.

But it is at that point that the symbolism of the Advent wreath has the most to say. We light the candle of joy, because we believe people can indeed be freed from the dullness of life. The birth of Jesus provides the joy of abundant living.

I. The joy of the name Jesus.

A. *Joseph was a troubled man.* The news Mary had given him had brought many responses, but none of them could be described as "joy." He was deeply disturbed. He loved Mary and was betrothed to marry her. Betrothal was more binding than a simple engagement; it required divorce action to terminate it.

But Joseph was not a callous man. The Scriptures describe him as a righteous man who did not wish to make a public scandal of Mary. He had come to the decision that he could no longer be associated with Mary. His agony must have been overwhelming.

While Joseph was still considering what he should do, God sent an angel to explain Mary's condition. Joseph must have received the announcement with much joy. What a relief it had to be to know that

Mary was still the honorable and godly person he had always known her to be!

B. *In addition, the angel told Joseph to name the child "Jesus."* For us, names are usually little more than a means of identification. But for the Jews, names were descriptions of character or designated some human event.

The name Jesus is from the same root as the name Joshua. It means "Jehovah is salvation." The angelic announcement of a name added to Joseph's joy. This child "shall save his people from their sins" (Matt. 1:21). Every time anyone called his name, they would be reminded that "Jehovah is salvation." Just as Joshua led Israel to conquer the land, so Jesus would lead God's people to conquer sin. And just as there were still pockets of resistance when Joshua died, so at the death of Jesus all sinfulness was not eradicated.

C. *But Jesus did save us from our sins and from the penalty of our sins.* This was the fulfillment of prophecy. The psalmist had said, "He himself will redeem Israel from all their sins" (Ps. 130:8 NIV).

In Matthew 1:21 there is reference both to the person and work of Jesus. His personhood is found in his name, for he is the Savior of the world. His work is found in the descriptive phrase that he will save his people.

Life only has meaning in our salvation; that is, our failures, mistakes, and sins will not be held against us forever. The gloom of having to carry your failures forever is removed in Jesus.

II. The joy of the name Emmanuel.

A. *Matthew continues the birth narrative by adding an editorial comment that all of this happened to fulfill the prophecy of Isaiah 7:14.* In Matthew 1:22–23 he refers to a second name for Jesus. The name is Emmanuel, which means "God with us." Through the incarnation God has become a man. This is perhaps the greatest of all miracles.

There is much debate concerning the virgin birth of Jesus. Skeptics, for one reason or another, doubt the validity of the scriptural narrative. Suffice it to say that those of us who accept the miraculous nature of the Bible also accept this miracle.

But the greatest miracle at Christmas was not the virgin birth. As great as that miracle may be, it pales in importance to the spiritual fact that God had taken on the human form of a baby.

B. *God is suddenly no longer out there somewhere in space or hidden in another dimension.* He is here now, living among us. But how? How can this be? The mystery of Christ's birth is mind-boggling.

Parting the waters of the Red Sea or raining down fire on Mount Carmel seem so insignificant to this miracle. To believe that the God of creation, the Ruler of the universe, the all-powerful, all-knowing God of heaven has taken on the form of a baby is staggering. Yet this is exactly what we are called upon to believe.

C. *The gospel writer indicates that at last God is here in a way he has never been before.* "God is with us." Some believe that Isaiah only intended to convey the idea that "God is on our side." That is open to debate, but Matthew's interpretation of the Isaiah passage is crystal clear. God is not just on our side; he is with us and is living among us.

The Gospel of John says, "The word became flesh and dwelt among us" (John 1:14 RSV). God no longer needs a tabernacle or temple to symbolize his presence among us. The good news of the gospel is that Emmanuel is here.

Thus, this name also adds to our joy. God is among us as he never was before the incarnation. Walking in his presence without a priest or some "holy" man to intercede for us is now our joy.

Conclusion

Humankind continually seeks happiness. "The pursuit of happiness" is embedded in the preamble to our Constitution. Many achieve a human satisfaction that provides a temporary lift for their spirits. But joy that is permanent and eternal is found in the Christmas event.

God has come to live among us and to save us from our sins. This is the spirit of Christmas. This joy is easily found by faith. Thus, faith is the key to a joyful Christmas.

Do you have the joy of Christ in your life? Are you willing to accept Christ and celebrate Christmas all year long? You can by putting your faith in the one whose name is Jesus—"Jehovah is salvation."

WEDNESDAY EVENING, DECEMBER 18

Title: When God's Word Dwells in You

Text: "Let the word of Christ dwell in you richly in all wisdom; teaching and admonishing one another in psalms and hymns and spiritual songs, singing with grace in your hearts to the Lord. And whatsoever ye do in word or deed, do all in the name of the Lord Jesus, giving thanks to God and the Father by him" **(Col. 3:16–17).**

Scripture Reading: Colossians 3:16–17

Introduction

The editor of a well-known London newspaper sent a letter of inquiry to one hundred important men asking them one question: "Suppose you were sent to prison for three years and could take only three books with you.

385

Which three would you choose? Please state them in order of their importance." Out of those replies, ninety-eight put the Bible first on their lists.

The Bible is an all-time best-seller. The readers of the Bible have discovered that it is not just a book of the month—it is the book of life, eternal, unchanging, ever dependable.

There is no reason, then, for surprise that the apostle Paul told the Colossian Christians to "let the word of Christ dwell in you richly." The word of Christ could refer to Christ as the living Word. For as the prologue to John's gospel points out, Christ is the eternally living Word. But Paul could also have been referring to the written Word of God. The words of Christ were being collected and circulated by that time. Paul's own words were gathered into the Bible, where they became the Word of God.

Colossians 3 focuses on Christian life. Already we have given attention to some things that should be removed from, as well as things that must be added to, the Christian life. Undergirding it all is the fact that the Word of God should fill the Christian's life. What happens when God's Word dwells in you?

I. When God's Word dwells in you, it enriches you.

A. *It becomes a part of life.*

B. *It gives richness to life.* An atheist stood in one of England's great mill complexes, haranguing the mill workers about the inaccuracies of the Bible and the myths and fables in the Word of God. An old, uneducated mill hand interrupted him by saying that until recently he had been a vile sinner. He was a curse to himself, a curse to his family, and a curse to all who knew him. Then he heard the blessed story of Jesus and opened his heart to Jesus as his Savior. After that he was a happy man and a blessing to his family. He was a new man and lived a new life. Then he asked that if the Bible were false, what had happened to his soul, what had happened to his heart, what had brought him out of the depths of the mire and set him up before the Lord with his feet on a rock? The atheist had no answer.

II. When God's Word dwells in you, it educates you.

A. *It brings all wisdom.*

B. *It is to be taught.*

   1. God's Word can be taught as a means of instruction in living. Two teenagers grew up in Dallas. Both were rough and troublesome. The faithful Sunday school teacher of one of the boys contacted him every week for a year. But the other teacher felt that he did not need that type of boy in his class. The first boy was saved and is now the director of evangelism for a state convention of Southern Baptists. The other boy assassinated President John F. Kennedy.

2. God's Word can be taught through music. Some of our favorite theology is taught through the music we sing. The book of Psalms is a treasure of music and poetry that tells of God's dealings with persons and of persons' experience with God.

C. *It admonishes us to proper belief and action.*

D. *It brings grace and truth into life.*

III. When God's Word dwells in you, it encourages you.

A. *All things that Christians do are to be done in Christ's name, by his authority.*

1. This includes the things we say.
2. This includes the things we do.

B. *All things that Christians do are to be done in gratitude.*

Conclusion

When God's Word dwells in you, it makes you a new kind of person. The Word of God cannot dwell in the same life where deceitfulness, sin, and rebellion dwell.

SUNDAY MORNING, DECEMBER 22

Title: Christmas Gifts and Christmas Giving

Text: "They fell down and worshiped him. Then, opening their treasures, they offered him gifts, gold and frankincense and myrrh" **(Matt. 2:11).**

Scripture Reading: Matthew 2:1–12

Hymns: "Angels from the Realms of Glory," Smart
"The First Noel," Old English Carol
"O Little Town of Bethlehem," Redner

Offertory Prayer: Holy Father, in this Christmas season we are reminded of the greatness of your generosity to us. We thank you for songs of the angels announcing the birth of the Christ. We thank you for the shepherds who went to behold the newborn king. We thank you for the wise men who sought him and worshiped him. We come thanking you for the many gifts that have come to us through the Christ. Today we come bringing the love and gratitude of our hearts to you. We give you the best that we have because you have given your best to us. Accept our tithes and offerings as indications of our desire to give ourselves to your service. In Jesus' name we pray. Amen.

Introduction

The spirit of Christmas is the spirit of giving. We read that the wise men brought gifts and presented them to the newborn King of Israel. They brought gifts of gold, frankincense, and myrrh. Gold is the king of metals and is an appropriate gift for one born to be the King of men. This new King was to rule, not by force, but by love. His throne was to be a cross.

They brought a gift of frankincense, which is a gift appropriate for a priest. The Christ was to be the high priest who would open up the way to God for sinners. He was to build the bridge by which we could come into the presence of God and by which God in love would enter our lives.

The wise men also brought a gift of myrrh, a spice that was used to anoint the bodies of the dead. Even at the beginning of Christ's life there was an indication of a cross at the end of the way. Jesus Christ was to be the true King, the perfect priest, the supreme Savior.

The wise men are not the ones who started the practice of giving gifts at Christmas. It is appropriate for us to take note of their gifts for the King, but let us not forget the great gifts the King gives to us.

I. Gifts through the King.

The Christ of Christmas was born to be the King of our hearts. For the kingdom of God, he was born and lived a sinless life on earth. For the kingdom of God, he prayed and preached and wrought miracles and taught his disciples. For the kingdom, he suffered the darkness of Gethsemane and endured the awful agony of the cross. For the kingdom, he arose from the dead and lives to make intercession for those who come to God through him.

Jesus Christ is the one whom God has appointed to be our King.

A. *He offers us the gift of forgiveness.* Our part is to repent and turn from a life of evil and self-destructiveness.
B. *He offers us the gift of eternal life.* He gives us eternal life out of the generosity of the Father God (Rom. 6:23).
C. *He offers us adoption into the family of God (John 1:12).*
D. *He offers us guidance through the difficulties and perplexities of life (John 8:12).*
E. *He assures us of fruitfulness and significance if we will abide in him (John 15:5–9).*
F. *He wills that we be with him forever (John 17:24).*
G. *He has given us the Holy Spirit to be our guide.* The Holy Spirit will be our teacher and helper throughout all of the journey of our earthly life (Luke 11:13; John 14:16–18).

These precious gifts of God that come to us through his Son are perfect, precious, permanent, and personal.

II. Gifts for the King.

The wise men brought rich gifts and presented them to the Christ child while he was still a baby. They could not possibly know the joys of his salvation as we know them today. If they brought the best that they had, it follows that we should bring even greater gifts to this one whom God has appointed to be our King.

A. *Let us give Jesus Christ the throne of our hearts.* Satan wants to be enthroned in our hearts and be the sovereign of our lives. Perhaps Satan's greatest rival for this position is our own selfish selves. We have an ungodly desire to put ourselves above all persons and things. Instead of giving self the throne rights of our lives (which means giving them to Satan), let us give them to Jesus Christ.

 1. He deserves to be King because of who he is.
 2. He deserves to be King because of what he has done for us.
 3. He deserves to be King in our lives because of what he will do in us and through us.

B. *Present your body as a gift to God in gratitude for his great mercies to you (Rom. 12:1).* Paul taught the believers at Corinth that their bodies were the temple of the Holy Spirit (1 Cor. 3:16). He further declared that their bodies belonged to God because they had been purchased by God in the act of redemption (1 Cor. 6:19–20). In reality Paul was encouraging them to let God so abide within their bodies that others would be reminded of his gracious presence in them.

C. *Bring the gift of thanksgiving and give God the praises of your heart.* Through the psalmist God declares, "He who brings thanksgiving as his sacrifice honors me" (Ps. 50:23 RSV). To remain silent when we can give praises to God for his goodness is to rob God and at the same time to deprive others of the blessings this testimony could bring. To give a joyful testimony about God's goodness before nonbelievers is to encourage them to trust God with their lives. This is the greatest favor that we can give to an individual, and it is the greatest joy that we can bring to the Father God.

Conclusion

The spirit of Christmas is the spirit of giving. God initiated this spirit by giving his Son to be our Savior. To become our Savior, Jesus became our substitute. He bore our sin by dying on a cross, and God raised him from the dead to show his great love for us.

Because God loved us first, we should love him. Because God gave his best, we should give our best back to him. True worship is bringing the best we have to God, who has already given his best to us.

Why does God love a cheerful giver? It is because God is a generous giver. God loves in a special way those who have responded to his love and become the channel through which his love reaches others.

The spirit of Christmas is the spirit of giving. Let us become givers of ourselves to God, to our family, and to others.

SUNDAY EVENING, DECEMBER 22

Title: The Candle of Love

Text: "[Joseph] went there to register with Mary, who was pledged to be married to him and was expecting a child" **(Luke 2:5 NIV).**

Scripture Reading: Luke 2:1–7

Introduction

We take so much of God's nature for granted. We readily believe that he not only loves us, but he also loves the world. God loves his people, and furthermore, he loves his enemies.

The fact that God loves the whole world is a New Testament concept. Nowhere in the Old Testament does it say that God loved the whole world. It is implied but never stated.

This revolutionary idea sprang into theology full blown in the life of Jesus. God dramatically showed his love for Jews and Gentiles by becoming a man. He both personified that idea and demonstrated it.

Thus, the candle of love we light tonight is the last of the four candles of the Advent wreath. It shines brightly with the candles of hope, peace, and joy. We also light the center candle, representing Christ. Let us look now at our text and see the qualities of this candle called "love."

I. The promise of love.

A. *The census required by Caesar Augustus was a familiar event in the Roman Empire.* A census was taken every fourteen years. Each family was required to return to its tribal headquarters, so Joseph took Mary with him to Bethlehem—a journey of about eighty miles.

Travelers of Joseph's day knew nothing of our modern system of hotels and motels. Accommodations were primitive. Thus, Mary and Joseph were not shocked or angry when the innkeeper suggested a place in the stable.

The fact that there was no room for them in the inn was symbolic of Jesus' life. People's hearts were overcrowded throughout his earthly ministry, and that condition still exists today. He is continually put out in the barn, because there is no room for him in the main house.

B. *Our text says that Mary "was expecting a child" (Luke 2:5).* Mary had received this promise of God with both incredulousness and faith. When the angel told her she would bear a son, she responded, "How will this be, since I am a virgin?" (Luke 1:34 NIV). Her question did not indicate rejection of the idea but rather that it was a mystery to her. When the angel explained how the promise of God would be accomplished, she responded in faith, "I am the Lord's servant. May it be to me as you have said" (Luke 1:38 NIV).

Mary's obedience represented devoted love. It was obvious to her that she had been given a very great honor. She adopted the attitude of "whatever God says, I will accept." If only all of God's servants would have this attitude.

C. *Joseph also responded to God's promise with love.* God was promising to restore the kingdom of Joseph's forefather David. It was as obvious to Joseph as it was to Mary that God cared for him deeply.

Although Mary and Joseph did not understand all that was involved in God's law, they readily accepted their part in the drama of Christmas. They were determined to be worthy of the trust that God had placed in them.

God still places such trust in humankind today. We too must determine to be worthy of God's promises of love.

II. The power of love.

A. *Love is certainly the most powerful of all human emotions.* It compels people to do illogical things. Love will make a man rush into a burning building to save his family. Love will make a soldier sacrifice his life on a battlefield for his country. Love will cause parents to undergo many hard sacrifices for their children. None of these actions makes sense to a person who does not know how to love deeply.

But all of this is only "human love."

B. *Godly love is deeper and stronger than human love.* Joseph loved Mary, and Mary loved Joseph, and they both loved God. But God's love for Mary and Joseph was the same love he has for the whole world.

God's love is so strong that all of human history is centered around this one event. Before the foundation of earth, God had already determined to bring Christ into the world to save us from our sins. The first Christmas was predestined before Adam and Eve. The star, the Magi, the shepherds, the inn, and the manger were all in God's mind as he dealt with Abraham, Moses, David, and Isaiah. And all of this was the result of God's powerful love. It was the power of God's love that compelled him to take on human flesh and die on a cross. Again, to the nonbeliever, such love seems like nonsense. But therein lies the unexplainable power of love.

III. The pinnacle of love.

A. *In Luke 2:6–7 the Christmas story reaches its pinnacle.* "While they were there, the time came for the baby to be born, and she gave birth to her first-born, a son" (NIV). The focal point of God's love is now centered in one person, Jesus. History has never been at a higher point. Never before has heaven witnessed so great a demonstration of the majesty of God's love than was accomplished at Bethlehem.

This zenith of love brought music to heaven. The excitement of God's activity was becoming more understandable to both angels and humankind.

The night was split by heaven's rejoicing. Angels appeared to shepherds and announced the advent of the Good Shepherd. An unnatural and unexplainable star appeared to kings in the East and led them to the King of Kings. God had become fully man and yet was still fully God, and love was the reason.

B. *Love knows its pinnacle of expression when a gift is given to symbolize the depth of one's love.* At Christmas we give gifts to many people. Sometimes we give a gift to a fellow employee, but it seldom compares to the gift we give to a family member. The cost of the gift and the thought behind the gift are often directly related to the depth of our love.

The Gift of God at Christmas was such a gift. The depth of his love is seen in the birth of Jesus. God sacrificed more than we can ever know to provide this Gift for us. He, who was never dependent on anyone or anything, became a baby who was dependent on two individuals for his food, clothing, shelter, training, and health. Such sacrificial love is beyond human comprehension.

Conclusion

God asks for our love in return. He calls on us to sacrifice our plans and desires for him, to return a measure of his love to him. God knows we can never match his love, and he is not unreasonable in his demand. But he does ask us to give him our lives, our talents, our possessions, and our time.

The true child of God will willingly respond to God's love. He outgives us as he outloves us. Our calling is not to match his love; it is to respond with love. Do you love God? How do you show that? By answering these questions, you will show how deep your love for God really is.

WEDNESDAY EVENING, DECEMBER 25

Title: Principles for Personal Relations

Text: "Whatsoever ye do, do it heartily, as to the Lord, and not unto men; knowing that of the Lord ye shall receive the reward of the inheritance: for ye serve the Lord Christ" **(Col. 3:23–24).**

Scripture Reading: Colossians 3:18–4:1

Introduction

One of our greatest problems is the problem of personal relations—getting along with other people. We live in relationships with others and not as isolated individuals. The terms we use to describe people are usually terms taken from social relations. We say a person is kind or harsh, warm or cold, honest or corrupt, sweet or sour. All of these terms indicate how people behave or react to other people.

Does Christianity have anything to do with our personal relationships? Indeed, it does. The gospel of Christ has a practical application in the lives of believers. Sometimes people make a distinction between theology or belief and social concern or activity. This is a false distinction. What we believe is going to determine how we act.

Paul had already expressed this in general principles in the earlier verses of Colossians 3. He had shown us some things we should strip from our lives and some things we ought to add to them. This passage applies these principles to specific needs. And this application is made at the point of one of our greatest needs—domestic relationships. The real question of Christianity is not, "What does Christianity make a person within the church?" but "What does Christianity make a person in the home, in the office, at the school, at the factory, on the lake, in the woods?"

This is exactly what Paul was doing here: showing the relationship of Christian living to some very practical areas of our lives.

I. A principle of personal relationships shows mutual obligations (Col. 3:18–19).

A. *Marriage is a partnership in which each spouse has obligations to the other.*

B. *The wife shows submissiveness in love, not as a duty.* Women had no standing in the ancient world, Jewish or Gentile. The husband had all of the privileges, and the wife had all of the duties. Submissiveness mentioned here is not that which makes a doormat or a nonperson out of another. It is, instead, the willingness to submit oneself and one's desires to another for mutual benefit. In a parallel passage in Ephesians 5:21–6:9 the principle of submission is stated—"Submitting yourselves to one another in the fear of God"—then applied in the relationships between husband and wife, parents and children, masters and slaves. The general principle is that all Christians submit themselves to one another in love. The relationship between husband and wife is only one area in which that principle is applied.

C. *The husband shows lovingkindness, not harshness.* The husband has an obligation too. He is to treat his wife with love as Christ treats his bride, the church.

A couple who had been happily married sixty years gave as their prescription for happiness in marriage their version of the Golden Rule: "Do unto one another as you would a month before marriage."

II. A principle of personal relationships shows reciprocal responsibility (Col. 3:22–4:1).

A. *Workers are to work well.* This is the longest section, probably because many slaves were in the church. Onesimus, the runaway slave who had been converted, was carrying the letter. While Paul did not openly attack slavery, he introduced new concepts for the slave–master relationship. This passage lays a foundation for a Christian doctrine of work.

B. *Masters are to treat workers well.*

C. *A reminder: We all serve a Master in heaven.*

Conclusion

In matters of personal relationships we are reminded that all of our relationships are "in the Lord." Since this is true, each of us has responsibilities and obligations that must be carried out as we live together and serve together "in the Lord."

SUNDAY MORNING, DECEMBER 29

Title: Drawing Water from the Wells of Salvation

Text: "With joy you will draw water from the wells of salvation" **(Isa. 12:3 RSV).**

Scripture Reading: Isaiah 12:1–6

Hymns: "Angels We Have Heard on High," Old French Carol
"It Came upon a Midnight Clear," Sears
"As with Gladness Men of Old," Dix

Offertory Prayer: Gracious and loving Father, during this time of the year we are reminded over and over of the generosity of your gift to us in Jesus Christ. Today we bow with the wise men of old and bring to him the gifts of our love, our praise, and our treasure. Accept our tithes and offerings and bless them for the use of proclaiming the good news of Christ to the ends of the earth. In his name we pray. Amen.

Introduction

Christmas is a time for rejoicing, the time of the year when we are reminded over and over that our God is the great God who offers salvation to all people everywhere through faith in Jesus Christ.

Isaiah 12 is a messianic psalm in which the prophet is rejoicing in the salvation that God makes available to his people.

I. "With joy."

During this Christmas season let us join with the prophet and respond to God's grace with great joy. Let us join the psalmist who said, "Make a joyful noise to the LORD, all the lands! Serve the LORD with gladness! Come into his presence with singing! Enter his gates with thanksgiving and his courts with praise! Give thanks to him, bless his name!" (Ps. 100:1–2, 4 RSV).

A. *When the Christ was born, his birth was announced by an angelic choir.* We hear an angel proclaiming to the shepherds, "Be not afraid; for behold, I

394

bring you good news of a great joy which will come to all the people; for to you is born this day in the city of David a Savior, who is Christ the Lord" (Luke 2:10–11 RSV).

B. *Jesus came to produce joy in the hearts of those who would trust and obey him.* We hear him saying, "These things I have spoken unto you, that my joy may be in you, and that your joy may be full" (John 15:11 RSV). In his great high-priestly prayer, we hear him speaking to the Father regarding the joy that he desired for his disciples: "But now I am coming to thee; and these things I speak in the world, that they may have my joy fulfilled in themselves" (John 17:13 RSV).

II. The wells of salvation.

God's wonderful provisions through Jesus Christ are described as being comparable to wells of living water in a hot, dry country where water was scarce. This metaphor is used repeatedly in the Old Testament. God provided the people with fresh water as they traveled through the desert under the leadership of Moses. Jeremiah had grieved because the people of his nation had forsaken God, the fountain of living waters, and had hewn out for themselves broken cisterns that could hold no water (Jer. 2:13). Jesus described the gift of the Holy Spirit in terms of a fountain of living water that would be within the heart of the believer (John 7:38–39).

A. *God is no cistern.* A cistern is a tank used for the collection and storage of rain water. In some instances it is a bottle-shaped tank hewn out of solid rock. In other instances it is dug out of the ground, and then the walls are coated with a type of rock or cement. It is used to store water for times of drought.
   1. Cisterns are constructed by human effort.
   2. Cisterns are limited in both quantity and capacity.
   3. Cisterns are subject to leakage and destruction. God is no cistern.

B. *God's great salvation is described as a flowing stream, as an artesian well.*
   1. The water of life is always fresh.
   2. The water of life is always abundant in supply.
   3. The water of life is always free.
   4. The water of life is always health-giving.

III. "With joy you will draw water."

When it comes to the matter of salvation, each of us must draw our own water. We must recognize and respond to the resources God makes available.

We must not permit ourselves to be impoverished at this point. We must not seek for our joy or security in the wrong way or in the wrong place. Love, joy, peace, hope are to be found only as we draw water from the wells of salvation. To neglect the wells of salvation is to rob ourselves of joy, peace, and hope, as well as the privilege of being a helper to others.

A. *Draw water from the well of forgiveness (1 John 1:9).*
B. *Draw water from the well of your new relationship with God.* A poet rejoiced in her new relationship with God and composed a beautiful poem in which she sings:

> *I'm a child of the King, a child of the King:*
> *With Jesus my Saviour, I'm a child of the King.*
> *My Father is rich in houses and lands,*
> *He holdeth the wealth of the world in His hands!*
> *Of rubies and diamonds, of silver and gold,*
> *His coffers are full, He has riches untold.*
>
> —Harriet E. Buell

Fanny Crosby responded to this great truth and wrote:

> *I am Thine, O Lord,*
> *I have heard Thy voice,*
> *And it told Thy love to me;*
> *But I long to rise in the arms of faith,*
> *And be closer drawn to Thee.*

God is no tyrannical taskmaster. God is our loving Father.

C. *Draw water from the well of family relationships.* You can rejoice in your brothers and sisters in Jesus Christ. You may have only one or two "blood" brothers or sisters, but in Jesus Christ all believers are your brothers and sisters. We can all rejoice in the privilege of being a part of the family of God.
D. *Draw water from the well of the indwelling Spirit.* Jesus spoke of the gift of the Holy Spirit as being a river of living water that wells up from within the heart of the believer (John 7:37–39). The Holy Spirit has come to be our companion, our helper, our teacher, our guide, our source of spiritual energy. Let us draw water from this well of salvation.
E. *Draw water from the well of assurance that you have a house not made with hands, eternal in the heavens (John 14:2–3; 2 Cor. 5:1–5).*
F. *Draw water from the well of the promise of the Savior's personal presence (Acts 28:20).*

Conclusion

With joy we are to draw water from the wells of salvation. The word *wells* is plural. The words of our text should bring us great personal encouragement. They should assure us that Christ will be present in our every time of need. The challenge of our text is very personal in application. You must sleep your own sleep. You must eat your own food. You must do your own rejoicing in the Lord, and all of us must draw our own water from the wells of salvation.

To neglect brings poverty; to postpone is unwise. Let the Christ of Christmas come into your heart and bring you the living water of life that you might draw water from the wells of salvation throughout all of your days.

SUNDAY EVENING, DECEMBER 29

Title: Why Is Jesus Coming Again?

Text: "I go to prepare a place for you. And if I go and prepare a place for you, I will come again, and receive you unto myself; that where I am, there ye may be also" **(John 14:2–3).**

Scripture Reading: John 14:1–6

Introduction

The story of Christmas is incomplete without the second coming of Christ. Christianity had a historical incarnation, and it will have a historical consummation. Salvation, the purpose of Christ's first coming, would be incomplete without Christ's coming again. The second coming of Christ is the glorious event that will bring to fruition all the benefits and blessings of salvation.

Why is Christ coming again? Let us seek some answers to this great question.

I. Jesus is coming again to claim his own.

Jesus said, "I go to prepare a place for you. And if I go and prepare a place for you, I will come again, and receive you unto myself: that where I am, there ye may be also" (John 14:2–3). Christ returned to heaven from the earth to prepare a place for his people. He will gather his people to him.

A. *He will resurrect the righteous dead at his coming.* "And the dead in Christ shall rise first" (1 Thess. 4:16).
B. *He will translate the righteous ones who are living at the time of his coming.* "Then we who are alive and remain shall be caught up together with them in the clouds, to meet the Lord in the air: and so shall we ever be with the Lord" (1 Thess. 4:17).

II. Jesus is coming again to judge.

The Bible makes it clear that Christ is coming to judge. His coming will be glory for the believer but disaster for the unsaved person. "And to you who are troubled rest with us, when the Lord Jesus shall be revealed from heaven and with his mighty angels, in flaming fire taking vengeance on them that know not God, and that obey not the gospel of our Lord Jesus Christ; who shall be punished with everlasting destruction from the presence of the Lord, and from the glory of his power" (2 Thess. 1:7–9). One of the last things Jesus says in Revelation is, "Behold, I come quickly; and my reward is with me, to give every man according as his work shall be" (Rev. 22:12).

When our Lord comes again, everyone will have to give an account of his or her life.

III. Jesus is coming again to reward the righteous.

At the second coming of Christ, the righteous will be rewarded for their faithfulness. He will send his angels out to gather the elect. The redeemed will be suited in white robes for eternity, and crowns will be placed on their worthy brows. The redeemed will enter Christ's kingdom, where nothing can ever molest or make afraid or cause unhappiness. When the Chief Shepherd appears, his people will receive crowns of glory that do not fade (1 Peter 5:4).

IV. Jesus is coming again to reject unbelievers.

The second coming of Christ will be tragic for unbelievers who reject Christ as Lord and Savior. It will be a devastating time for those who are not redeemed, for Jesus will say: "Depart from me, ye cursed, into everlasting fire, prepared for the devil and his angels.... And these shall go away into everlasting punishment: but the righteous into life eternal" (Matt. 25:41, 46). Those who have refused his mercy, turned away from his truth, trampled on his law, neglected his church, persecuted his people, and despised his grace will meet their eternal fate at Christ's coming again.

V. Jesus is coming to make cosmic changes in the earth.

Bible passages that speak of cosmic changes at Christ's coming are found in several places, for example, Romans 8:19–23 and Revelation 21:1.

Peter asked, "Seeing then that all these things shall be dissolved, what manner of persons ought ye to be in all holy conversation and godliness, looking for and hasting unto the coming of the day of God, wherein the heavens being on fire shall be dissolved, and the elements shall melt with fervent heat? Nevertheless, we, according to his promise, look for new heavens and a new earth, wherein dwelleth righteousness" (2 Peter 3:11–13).

The earth was cursed after Adam and Even sinned in the Garden of Eden. The harmony and the beauty will be restored. The second Adam will completely undo the works of the first Adam, and there will be a new heaven and a new earth.

VI. Jesus is coming again to usher in the eternal kingdom of God.

At the second coming of Christ the work of redemption will be finished. He will then give the kingdom back to the Father. "Then cometh the end, when he shall have delivered up the kingdom to God, even the Father: when he shall have put down all rule and all authority and power" (1 Cor. 15:24).

VII. Jesus is coming again to manifest his glory.

Paul said:

> I give thee charge in the sight of God, who quickeneth all things, and before Christ Jesus, who before Pontius Pilate witnessed a good confession: That thou keep his commandment without spot, unrebukeable until the appearing of our Lord Jesus Christ; which in his times he shall shew, who is the blessed and only Potentate, the King of kings, and Lord of lords; who only hath immortality, dwelling in the light which no man can approach unto; whom no man hath seen, nor can see: to whom be honour and power everlasting. Amen. (1 Tim. 6:13–16)

Christ has been glorified with the glory he had with the Father "before the world was" (John 17:5). Christ also has been glorified in his death (John 12:23; 13:31).

Peter declared to the Jews that in the resurrection of Christ "the God of Abraham, and of Isaac, and of Jacob, the God of our fathers, hath glorified his son Jesus" (Acts 3:13; cf. 1 Peter 1:21). Christ now has a glorified body (Phil. 3:21). He is glorified by the Holy Spirit (John 16:14); and he is glorified in his redeemed (John 17:10), in the suffering of his own (1 Peter 4:14), and in the gospel (2 Cor. 8:19). The very gospel now preached is the "gospel of the glory of Christ" (2 Cor. 4:4) and the "gospel of the glory of the blessed God" (1 Tim. 1:11).

VIII. Jesus is coming again to reign forever and ever.

Jesus is coming as King of Kings and Lord of Lords, to reign forever and ever. Hear John the apostle: "I saw heaven opened, and behold a white horse; and he that sat upon him was called Faithful and True, and in righteousness he doth judge and make war.... And he hath on his vesture and on his thigh a name written, KING OF KINGS, AND LORD OF LORDS" (Rev. 19:11, 16).

The kingdom over which our Lord will reign is an everlasting kingdom. Gabriel said to Jesus' mother, Mary, "And he shall reign over the house of Jacob for ever; and of his kingdom there shall be no end" (Luke 1:33).

Daniel the prophet said, "In the days of these kings shall the God of heaven set up a kingdom, which shall never be destroyed: and the kingdom shall not be left to other people, but it shall break in pieces and consume all these kingdoms, and it shall stand for ever" (Dan. 2:44).

Conclusion

The first coming of Christ brought hope. His coming again is the blessed hope. As we contemplate his coming again, our hearts cry out with the apostle John, "Come, Lord Jesus" (Rev. 22:20).

MESSAGES ON THE LORD'S SUPPER

Title: Thanks Be unto God

Text: "Thanks be to God for his inexpressible gift!" **(2 Cor. 9:15 RSV)**.

Scripture Reading: 1 Corinthians 11:23–26

Introduction

It is rather astonishing and perhaps difficult for us to understand how our Lord could have an attitude of gratitude on the night before he was to endure the pain of crucifixion.

We read that, following the Passover Supper, he instituted the Lord's Supper. Before breaking the bread, he offered a prayer of thanks. After sharing the bread and before offering the cup, he again offered thanks. It is significant that on occasions such as this he could have an attitude of gratitude that expressed itself in thanksgiving.

Perhaps Jesus was thanking God for the privilege of being able to reveal the height and depth and length and breadth of God's love for a needy world. No one had ever seen the height and depth and length and breadth of God's love until Jesus Christ came (John 1:18). The ultimate revelation of God's love would be revealed by Jesus' substitutionary death on the cross.

Perhaps Jesus was thanking God for the personal privilege of being the Savior of all humankind. There was no other person good enough to bear the price of sin. Our Lord was very near the successful accomplishment of the task for which he had come into the world. By dying on the cross, he would become the Savior of the world.

Perhaps Jesus was thanking God for the pure joy of being a great giver (Heb. 12:2). Jesus taught that there was more to be obtained in a life of giving than was to be found in a life of getting (Acts 20:35). Jesus not only taught this great truth; he experienced it. He was giving his all to God for the good of others.

Paul overflows with gratitude in the words of our text when he says, "Thanks be to God for his inexpressible gift!"

I. God's gift to us is indescribable in the love that thought it.

No one can adequately describe God's love for a needy race. Christ's death on the cross was not God's hastily conceived plan to be used in an emergency. There was a cross in God's heart long before there was ever a cross on Calvary's hill. Our great salvation was a thought in God's heart from before the foundation of the world.

II. God's gift to us is indescribable in the love that brought it.

Jesus Christ came into the world to be the love of God for us. He took upon himself the garments of our humanity. As a human being he experienced hunger and weariness and found himself in need of nourishment and sleep. He could bleed like we bleed. He could hurt like we hurt.

Jesus' love for God was so great and his love for us was so true that he was willing to go to the cross to register that love. There is no way for a human being to adequately describe the love that brought salvation to us.

Conclusion

Let us be thankful as we partake of these elements of the Lord's Supper. As we partake of the bread, let us thank God for our Savior's humanity. As we partake of the cup, let us thank God for his substitutionary and sacrificial death on the cross for us. Let us recognize that apart from his sacrificial death, we would have no hope for the forgiveness of our sins.

Let us join with the apostle Paul in thanking and praising God for his goodness to us.

Title: An Affirmation of Divine Love

Text: "Do this in remembrance of me" **(1 Cor. 11:24 RSV).**

Scripture Reading: 1 John 3:1–3

Introduction

Many people in today's world experience the pain of feeling rejected. Often this is an invisible burden that is borne without others being aware of it.

A man in his upper thirties who was having personal problems went to see his pastor. The man was suffering intensely from the pain of feeling rejected. His mother had wanted a daughter rather than a son. She had made the mistake of revealing this to him, and from time to time she reminded him that she wished that he had been a daughter rather than a son. The constant reminder of her rejection of him as a son devastated his sense of self-esteem and caused him to feel negative about himself and about his mother. The end result was a case of severe depression that affected his health, his marriage, his total well-being. He died at age forty from a heart attack. It is impossible to know how much his feeling of rejection contributed to his early death.

Many students experience a feeling of rejection because of their inability to excel in the classroom. They feel rejected by their peers, by their teachers, and by their parents. Great numbers of people labor each day at their jobs with a feeling of rejection because they have not been able to enter the occupation of their first choice.

I. We may feel rejected when we dwell on our past failures.

We must avoid putting ourselves down because we have failed to achieve our highest potential.

II. We may feel rejected when we compare ourselves with others.

We need to be on guard lest we compare ourselves unfavorably with others who have achieved greater success and who have experienced greater happiness. This is an exercise in self-destructiveness. We should accept our gifts and appreciate and affirm ourselves as we are.

III. Our spiritual enemy tries to depress us.

Satan is our enemy, and he is our accuser. Jesus described him as a liar. Part of his strategy is to remind us of our failures and mistakes, of our weaknesses and inadequacies. Satan wants us to believe that God has rejected us. He wants to persuade us that others would reject us even before we begin doing what we should do.

Do you suffer from the pain of being rejected? Do you feel lonely and isolated and unloved? If so, you should be reminded that Jesus experienced rejection. "He was in the world, and the world was made through him yet the world knew him not. He came to his own home, and his own people received him not" (John 1:10–11 RSV).

Jesus was rejected by the people of his hometown. They were unwilling to accept correction and direction from one who had grown up in Nazareth (see Luke 4:16–30).

Jesus knows how to reveal and affirm God's love and acceptance of us. Perhaps this was one of his primary motives in instituting the Lord's Supper.

Conclusion

The observance of the Passover feast was an annual event that reminded the Jewish people of God's loving redemptive purpose and of his power to deliver them from the tyranny of Egypt. At the conclusion of the final Passover meal that Jesus ate with his apostles, he instituted the Lord's Supper. He took the bread and the wine and gave it a new meaning, a new significance, and a new purpose. He did this in order that there might be a recurring reminder, a continuing affirmation of God's love for sinners.

Jesus instituted the Lord's Supper to do something more than to establish a memorial monument to himself. Paul quotes him as saying, "Do this, as often as you drink it, in remembrance of me" (1 Cor. 11:25 RSV). The fact that we are to remember his death on our behalf is the strongest possible reaffirmation of God's divine love for unworthy sinners who have put their faith in Jesus Christ.

As you partake of the elements of this memorial supper, let them strongly affirm God's acceptance and affection for you revealed supremely in the death of Jesus Christ for your sins.

Title: The Memorial Supper of Our Lord

Text: "When he had given thanks, he broke it, and said, 'This is my body which is for you. Do this in remembrance of me'" **(1 Cor. 11:24 RSV).**

Scripture Reading: Matthew 26:26–28

Introduction

On the night before our Lord was betrayed into the hands of the Romans, he observed the Passover feast with his disciples.

Preceding the observance of the Passover feast, our Lord assumed the role of a servant Messiah and washed the feet of his disciples. In this manner he demonstrated that they were to identify themselves as the servants of God and the servants of people rather than to see themselves in positions of prominence.

I. A memorial to God's great redemption.

God the Father wanted the nation of Israel to remember their great deliverance from the tyranny and the slavery of Egypt. To accomplish this task, a memorial day was established for the people to remember what God had done for them (Exod. 12:14–17).

The observance of the Passover feast was intended to remind the Jewish people of God's benevolent purpose for them. As they observed this feast, they were to see it as an affirmation of divine love. It was also intended to encourage them to trust him for the future.

Moses encouraged the people to remember this day with gratitude (Exod. 13:3, 9). The book of Deuteronomy encourages the people to remember this great event once they have occupied the Promised Land (Deut. 16:1–6).

II. The memorial supper of our Lord (1 Cor. 11:23–26).

At the conclusion of our Lord's final observance of the Passover, he took some of the elements from the table and instituted a new memorial that we know as the Lord's Supper, or as Communion or the Eucharist.

Our Lord wanted us to be reminded often of the greatness of God's love for us. We may have negative traits that need to be eliminated. We may think demeaning thoughts about ourselves. We may measure ourselves unfavorably with others. We often criticize ourselves for past mistakes. We find it difficult to accept God's forgiveness. Many torment themselves unnecessarily by being unwilling to forgive themselves.

The recurring observance of the Lord's Supper as a memorial to Jesus' death should be a great affirmation of our personal worth and God's divine concern.

Conclusion

Let us allow this observance of the Lord's Supper to speak powerfully concerning our personal worth in God's sight. Let us accept ourselves as those whom God loves. Let us appreciate ourselves properly. Let us dedicate ourselves afresh to the will of our living, loving Lord as we partake of these elements that remind us of the giving of his life for us on the cross.

MESSAGES FOR CHILDREN AND YOUNG PEOPLE

Title: Be on Guard against Your Enemy

Text: "Be sober, be watchful. Your adversary the devil prowls around like a roaring lion, seeking some one to devour" **(1 Peter 5:8 RSV).**

Scripture Reading: 1 Peter 5:6–9

Introduction

Do you recognize that you have an enemy who is out to destroy you? To be unaware of his presence is to leave yourself wide open to his successful attack on you.

The enemy to whom I am referring is none other than the devil. Young people need to be aware of what the Bible teaches concerning the forces of evil in the world today. The Scriptures teach us that the devil really exists. Jesus had continuous opposition and conflict with the devil. Peter speaks repeatedly regarding the work of the devil. The apostle Paul issues numerous warnings about the character and strategies of the evil one. John, the apostle of love, calls our attention to the devil's work. Peter speaks of the devil as a roaring lion seeking someone to devour. He spoke out of personal experience, because there had been times when he had experienced defeat as a result of the activities of his enemy and your enemy.

I. The devil is a deceiver.

The devil is always camouflaged. He never reveals his nature, his character, or even his presence.

II. The devil is a discourager.

The devil uses even our friends at times to discourage us. He wants us to have negative thoughts about ourselves in order to discourage us. He points out the obstacles rather than the opportunities.

III. The devil is a divider.

The devil is seeking to divide families and to separate parents from children and children from parents. The devil will seek to do all that he can to alienate you from those who love you the most. He will deceive you and discourage you in order to divide you from the possibility of your achieving your highest and your best.

IV. The devil is a destroyer.

He destroyed the peace of the Garden of Eden. He is seeking to destroy your home, your school, your church, and he is seeking to destroy you. The devil seeks to defame those who are worthy of your respect and appreciation. We could describe the devil as one who diverts us from the high road and the good road.

Conclusion

While you may not have anyone looking for you with a gun or a club, each of us has an enemy that wants to destroy us. To be aware of this is to be forewarned as well as forearmed.

The only way that we can be sure of victory over our enemy, the devil, is by staying as close to our God as we can. James recommends that we recognize and submit to God's authority over every area of our life. He further suggests that we resist the devil with all of our being (James 4:7). As we draw near to God, God will draw near to us, and we will have victory over this one who is seeking to destroy not only us but others. Jesus overcame Satan by giving his supreme loyalty to God and by being thoroughly nourished on God's Word (Matt. 4:1–11).

Title: How to Study the Bible

Text: "His delight is in the law of the Lord, and on his law he meditates day and night" **(Ps. 1:2 rsv)**.

Scripture Reading: Psalm 1:1–3

Introduction

Psalm 1 presents two portraits. The first three verses describe the happy man of faith. The last three verses describe the unsuccessful man who has no faith in God and who lives a life of wickedness.

In this inspired portrait of a happy man, there is an explanation for his success. He makes some great choices. He gives the sacred Scriptures a prominent place in his life day by day. He takes delight in the teachings of God's Word and meditates on them both day and night.

How do you relate to the Bible? I hope that you recognize it as the inspired, authoritative record of God's self-revelation and of human response to him under the leadership of the Holy Spirit.

You need to do something more than just hold the sacred Scriptures in reverence. You need to study God's Word day by day and nourish your spiritual growth (1 Peter 2:1–2). No one can do your eating for you. No one can do your sleeping for you. No one can do your learning for you. No one can do your worshiping for you. No one can do your Bible study for you. Some things you must do for yourself. Bible study is one of those things.

Let us look at some of the ways that you can profitably study the Word of God and do it day by day.

I. Study to find promises to claim.

The Bible contains many promises from God to his people. By faith and with an attitude of obedience, you can claim those promises as your very own.

II. Study to find commands to obey.

God loves us and has absolutely no desire to deprive us of anything that is good. We need to believe in his benevolent purpose for us as we face the commandments of his holy Word.

Some commandments prohibit certain types of activity, but God is not trying to deprive us with prohibitions. Behind every prohibition there is the divine desire to help us avoid harming ourselves and others.

Some commandments call for affirmative action. Responding to these will bring joy into our lives and good into the lives of others.

III. Study to find examples to follow.

Some biblical characters can serve as ideals for us. We can follow their examples and reap good results. The Bible also contains accounts of some who failed. These examples should serve as red lights along the road of life to encourage us to stop the conduct that we might be engaging in.

IV. Study to find sins to avoid.

Sin not only hurts the heart of our Father God, but sin brings hurt into our lives and the lives of others.

As we study God's Word and discover there the end result of sinful behavior, we can recognize sins that we need to avoid.

V. Study to find solutions to your problems.

The daily study of God's Word can be considered as the listening side of the prayer experience. When we pray we should not only talk to God, but we should let him talk to us.

Conclusion

The psalmist said, "I have laid up thy word in my heart, that I might not sin against thee" (Ps. 119:11 RSV). We can only deposit God's Word in our heart by studying it. We should study it for the good of our spiritual life as regularly as we eat food for the good of our physical life.

May God bless each of you as you let the Word of God have a greater place in your life.

Title: Learning How to Pray

Text: "Pray then like this: Our Father who art in heaven" **(Matt. 6:9 RSV)**.

Scripture Reading: Matthew 6:9–13

Introduction

Can you remember the first prayer that you learned to pray? Some of us were taught a prayer that went like this: "Now I lay me down to sleep, I pray thee, Lord, my soul to keep. If I should die before I wake, I pray thee, Lord, my soul to take. Amen."

Although that may not be the best prayer for a child to learn, many parents were sincere and eager to be helpful and taught us to pray that prayer or something similar. The Bible teaches us that prayer is a privilege. It is also something to be learned. Jesus is the best teacher we can possibly have when it comes to learning how to pray.

Jesus spent much time in prayer. On one occasion when he finished praying, one of his disciples said to him, "Lord, teach us to pray, as John taught his disciples" (Luke 11:1). In the prayer that is often called the Lord's Prayer Jesus gave instructions to his disciples for how to pray effectively.

I. Jesus gave some examples of how not to pray.

A. *We are not to pray like the hypocrites (Matt. 6:5–6).* Hypocrites are those who pretend to be something they are not. Jesus is here prohibiting people from praying in public merely to be seen and heard by others in order that they might be considered very religious.

B. *We are not to pray like the heathen (Matt. 6:7–8).* The pagans had the concept that they were to wear down the reluctance of their deity by persistence. Jesus taught that our Father God is more eager to give than we are to receive.

II. Jesus gave some positive teachings about prayer.

"Pray then like this."

A. *Our prayer is to be directed to our heavenly Father.* We are to say, "Our Father." We do not come to God in prayer as strangers or as beggars or as criminals. We come as his dear children if we have trusted Jesus Christ as Savior.

Our Father God knows us better and loves us more than our earthly father does. Our Father God is eager to give us good gifts that we are capable of using in a trustworthy manner.

Our Father God may give us a negative reply if our prayer is selfish or if we would be incapable of handling the situation should he grant our request. Sometimes God's best answer for us is negative. Sometimes his answer is "Not yet."

B. *The disciples' prayer contains three elements.* As we look at Jesus' instructions for prayer, we will notice that there should be three major concerns in our prayer. They have been described as three looks—the "uplook," the "inlook," and the "outlook."

1. First, we should look up to God. He is our heavenly Father. We should hallow his name. We are to be concerned about the coming of his kingdom in our lives more than we are to be concerned about the coming of our own kingdom.

2. We should also look inward. In this model prayer we are to pray for our daily bread and for the forgiveness of our sins, and we are to pray for personal deliverance from evil. We are not only to have a good relationship with God, but we are to have a good relationship with ourselves.

3. And our prayers should reveal a concern for things outside ourselves. All of the pronouns in this model prayer are plural. While God may give to us personal attention as if we were his only child, we must remember always that we are just one of his children. He is "our" Father. We are to pray for "our daily bread." We are to ask for the forgiveness of "our debts."

Conclusion

In this model prayer, there are three vital elements: communion, petition, and intercession. First, we must establish communion with our Father. We are then encouraged to bring our petitions. We must also remember to pray for others. Let us listen closely to what Jesus said about prayer in order that we might pray effectively.

Title: Gifts You Can Give to Your Parents

Text: "Peter said, 'I have no silver and gold, but I give you what I have'" (**Acts 3:6** RSV).

Scripture Reading: Acts 3:1–10

Introduction

Most young people can identify easily with Peter's statement, "I have no silver and gold." Young people do not have an opportunity to earn a great amount of money, though some do have the opportunity for part-time work as they pursue their education.

When it comes to the giving of gifts at Christmas time or on birthdays, young people find it necessary either to use a part of their allowance, which is the gift of a parent, or money that they have earned through part-time work.

Are there some gifts that you can give that are more valuable than what you can purchase with silver and gold? Let's consider some gifts that are possible for every young person to bestow upon his or her parents.

I.You may give the gift of reverence to your parents.

"'Honor your father and mother' (this is the first commandment with a promise), 'that it may be well with you and that you may live long on the earth'" (Eph. 6:2–3 RSV). Parents should be worthy of honor. But even at times when you may be disappointed in them, it is the will of God for you to give proper respect to those who are the source of your life and who provided for you in your days of helplessness.

II.You may give the gift of obedience to your parents.

"Children, obey your parents in the Lord, for this is right" (Eph. 6:1 RSV). God has appointed parents to be not only the providers, but also the instructors of their children. The home is the basic unit in our society, before state, school, or church.

God holds parents responsible for instructing their children in the ways that are good and right. God holds children responsible for being obedient to their parents.

From our text it is implied that the only instance in which you would be free to disobey your parents would be in a situation in which they were asking you to do that which is contrary to the will of God and out of character with Jesus Christ.

Behind almost all requests that come from parents is a desire for the well-being of their children. Sometimes it may be difficult for you to believe this or to understand it. There are times when the prohibitions that parents give voice to may be misunderstood and not appreciated. Your parents may not be any more intelligent than you, but they have at least lived longer. Most parents desire what is highest and best for their children. As a general rule, you will experience more happiness and a better life if you give to your parents the gift of obedience.

III.You may give the gift of thanksgiving to your parents.

How long has it been since you have said from your heart, "Thank you, Mom," or "Thank you, Dad"?

An attitude of gratitude is not instinctive. It is an attitude that must be acquired. While all good and perfect gifts come from the Father God, many of these come through your parents.

You can bring joy to your parents' hearts by remembering to be grateful to them for their efforts and their energy and for everything that comes from them to you.

IV.You may give the gift of joy to your parents.

Joy is an inward state of being that is deeper and richer and higher than happiness. Happiness is the result of something that happens. Joy is an inward state of being because of something more than just an incidental happening. By being a respectful, obedient, grateful child, you can give to your parents the gift of joy.

Remember who you are and what you are and refrain from forms of conduct that will bring harm into your life and hurt into the hearts of your parents.

Dedicate yourself to being a good student. Work at your studies knowing that you will someday have to work to earn a living. Do not be content with a passing grade. Do your best to beat your best in the past.

Conclusion

What will you give to your parents when their birthdays roll around? You could perhaps go to a telephone and call your mother or your father and say something like this: "Mom (or Dad), I want to thank you for being my parent. I want to thank you for all that you have done to help me get to where I am."

Let us thank God for his blessings to us through our parents.

It is more blessed to give than to receive. You can't give what you don't have. Silver and gold you may not have, but you can give the gifts that have been mentioned, plus others. I challenge you to use your own creativity to think up some good gifts that you can give to your parents.

FUNERAL MEDITATIONS

Title: He Continues to Speak

Text: "By faith Abel offered to God a more acceptable sacrifice than Cain's. Through this he received approval as righteous, God himself giving approval to his gifts; he died, but through his faith he still speaks" **(Heb. 11:4 NRSV).**

Scripture Reading: Genesis 4:1–7

Introduction

The writer of the book of Hebrews assembles in chapter 11 a long list of the heroes of the faith. These giants from the past are described as a great cloud of witnesses who not only watch us, but who cheer us on as we run the race of life (Heb. 12:1–2).

In our text the spotlight is placed on Abel and his generous and appropriate sacrificial gift to God. The writer of Hebrews declares that by means of Abel's faith and faithfulness expressed in giving, though he is no longer present with us, "he is still speaking."

Long after our tongue is silent in death and long after our visible appearance is no longer possible, we continue to speak to the living. This possibility can be frightening if we leave a negative and destructive message. It can be exciting and challenging if we continue to speak as a servant of God and a helper to others. Abel, though he is dead, continues to speak to us.

I. Abel speaks of the necessity of faith.

"By faith Abel offered to God a more acceptable sacrifice." This character from the very dawn of human history speaks to us of the importance and value of believing in God. The psalmist says that only the fool declares that there is no God (Ps. 14:1). One can believe that God exists, but this belief does not necessarily have a vital effect on one's life (see James 2:19–23). Abel had a faith in God that enabled him to involve himself with God and for God.

II. Abel can speak to us of the importance of worship.

Although Abel's act of worship contributed to his untimely death, the fact that he worshiped God speaks to us of our need to open ourselves up to God and to give ourselves to him.

Worship is something more than just attending a Bible class or being present for a worship service. Genuine worship is the response of our innermost being to God's revelation of himself in Jesus Christ. To genuinely worship is to let God's Holy Spirit do his work within us and upon us and through us.

III. Abel speaks to us concerning the grace of generosity.

Abel gave a gift to God that was acceptable to God. He gave what he had. He gave the best that he had. He would recommend to us that we generously give of ourselves, our time, our energies, and our words of appreciation and encouragement. The only thing we can take with us when it comes our time to depart from the walk of life are those things we have given to God for the good of others.

IV. Abel speaks to us of the importance of being prepared for death.

Abel died an early death. Life at its longest is brief. The time for our departure is almost always unexpected.

In a world that emphasizes the value of being prepared in every area of life, we need to recognize the value of being prepared for the experience of death.

Conclusion

We should have our finances in order before death. Many people secure insurance to provide resources for their families as they contemplate this inevitable experience. Likewise, we should have our legal papers in order before death. Many persons could greatly aid their families by giving careful thought to the making of a will.

But the highest wisdom we can demonstrate is to have our spiritual lives in order before death by trusting Jesus Christ as Savior. Only Jesus Christ can save us from the penalty of sin, which is spiritual death. Sin separates us from God, and Jesus Christ died on the cross for our sins that he might return us to God (1 Peter 3:18).

Let each of us live each day that we have left in such a way as to speak for God and for those things that are good. Thus, we will be speaking for God, not only while we are living, but in the days when we are no longer among the living.

Title: Happy Are the Dead

Text: "Moreover, I heard a voice from heaven, saying, 'Write this: "Happy are the dead who die in the faith of Christ! Henceforth," says the Spirit, "they may rest from their labours; for they take with them the record of their deeds." '" **(Rev. 14:13 NEB).**

Scripture Reading: Revelation 14:1–13

Introduction

The words of our text come from John the Revelator, who reports hearing a voice from heaven describing the state of the saints who have departed from us. The voice declares, "Happy are the dead who die in the faith of Christ."

Many of us associate sadness with the death of those we love. Grief is the sense of emotional loss we have when someone is taken from our midst. Especially for Christians when another Christian dies, grief is an expression of a sense of personal loss that may border on selfishness.

I. We can be happy for this believer.

Today we experience joy in the assurance that the one who has gone from our midst was a believer in Jesus Christ. This makes all of the difference in the world for the one whom we love and for us also.

II. We can be happy because of the love of this one.

We experienced love from this one who has gone to be with the Lord. The family experienced love. The church experienced love. Friends experienced love. We feel impoverished because this great channel of love has gone from our midst.

III. We can be happy for this one who prayed much.

We were remembered in the prayers of our loved one. We received the gifts of God because of the prayers offered by this one. If it is possible to offer prayers after you get to heaven, we can be sure that this one who prayed so much in life will continue to remember us in the future.

IV. We can be happy for this one who was a giver.

God is the great giver, and he teaches us to be givers. This one whom we loved so much learned from God and from Christ that the highest joy of living comes as a result of giving. Each of us has been enriched by the gifts of God through this one.

Conclusion

We can now rejoice for the one who has gone from our midst, because the Scriptures tell us, "Happy are the dead who die in the faith of Christ." The Scriptures also tell us, "They rest from their labours and their works do follow them." Our loved one has gone to be with the Father and with his/her family. One day, through Jesus Christ, you and I will also move through the curtain that people call death and enter into the house not made with hands eternal in the heavens.

Let us thank God that we can be happy in death and beyond death. Let us be grateful today in the presence of the death of this one who meant so much to us.

Title: Overcoming Our Fear of Death

Text: "Since therefore the children share in flesh and blood, he himself likewise partook of the same nature, that through death he might destroy him who has the power of death, that is, the devil, and deliver all those who through fear of death were subject to lifelong bondage" **(Heb. 2:14–15 RSV)**.

Scripture Reading: Revelation 1:17–18

Introduction

The fear of death is no simple response with simple causes. But the Scriptures tell us that Jesus Christ came into this world to deliver humankind from the fear of death. He did this by means of his personal victory over the devil, death, and the grave.

Many different factors enter into the fear of death. Our age and state of physical health affect us. Our family and religious background affect our fear of death. Our personal degree of emotional or psychological maturity has a large influence on our attitude toward death.

Someone has stated that the fear of death falls into three different categories.

I. Some fear death because of what happens after death.

A. *Some have fear that is associated with the fate of the body.* They do not like to think of caskets, cemeteries, graves, or mausoleums.

B. *Some fear death because they have a great fear of punishment that will come after death.* The Bible teaches in many places that those who have lived a wicked, ungodly life will be punished for such after this life is over. The evil will be judged on the basis of their deeds (Rev. 20:11–15). This is enough to make any person tremble.

II. Some fear death primarily because of the process of dying.

Many Christians have no fear of death as such, but they have great fear of the experience that leads to the moment of death.

413

A. *It is normal for all of us to fear pain.*
B. *It is normal to have a great dread for the indignity associated with the process of dying.*
C. *It is normal for many to fear the possibility of becoming a burden.* No one likes to be a physical, emotional, or financial burden on someone else.

III. Many fear death because it means the loss of life as we know it here.

A. *Death comes in to assert its mastery over our life.* No one likes to lose control.
B. *Death often comes earlier than we anticipated.* It deprives us of a sense of completeness and fulfillment.
C. *Many fear death because it means separation from those who are near and dear to us.*

IV. Jesus came to help us be delivered from the fear of death.

A. *Jesus wants to deliver us from the fear of what happens after death.* He is able to do this by virtue of his having died for our sins on the cross. He has paid the wages of our sins. He has made it possible for us to be accepted by a holy and just God. He has granted to us the gift of eternal life, which comes in the moment of conversion and as we become a member of the family of God through faith.
B. *Jesus wants to help us overcome the fear of the process of dying.* Death has never been a pleasant subject for thought or a pleasant experience for people to contemplate. We can be exceedingly grateful for living in a time in which medical science is able to provide much release from pain.

    We can face the indignity of the process of dying if we will strengthen ourselves in the faith that someday this old house in which we dwell will be replaced with a house not made with hands eternal in the heavens. God has given us the gift of the Holy Spirit as a guarantee that death is not the end and that the grave is not the goal of this life (2 Cor. 5:5). We are assured that our resurrection body will be a body perfectly adapted for living with God in his eternal home (1 Cor. 15:38–44).
C. *Jesus wants to help us overcome the fear of losing control of our lives by giving us the assurance of his control.* There are many times when we have to trust others with our care and custody. In fact, we do this every time we ride in a vehicle that someone else is driving. Jesus has entered death and conquered it and has come forth with authority over the abode of the dead (Rev. 1:17–18). He strengthened his apostles with the promise, "Because I live, you will live also" (John 14:19 RSV).

Conclusion

To overcome the fear of death, we need to trust Jesus, the one who conquered death. To overcome the fear of death, we need to believe his precious promises regarding victory over death. To conquer the fear of death, we need to live to the maximum for God and others each day. Then when the day comes for us to die, God will give us grace to die by.

WEDDINGS

Title: Conducting a Premarital Conference

A pastor should assume when a couple comes for a wedding ceremony that they look upon it as having spiritual significance. Christian marriage is more than just a legal contract. It is the beginning of a divine institution. Because of this, the pastor should plan for the service to be a religious ceremony.

With marriage and the family experiencing the stresses and strains that threaten it so much, pastors need to do everything they can to help couples not only avoid divorce but avoid the unhappiness that leads to divorce. Premarital conferences in which the essentials for success are discussed can be an effort in that direction. The only way to prevent some divorces is to prevent some marriages. If pastors take the opportunity far enough in advance to discuss with couples the basic essentials for happiness, it is possible that some marriages and, consequently, some divorces will not occur.

In premarital conferences, the minister can get acquainted with the couple and establish a relationship that makes it comfortable for them to return for counsel at a later time if they face difficulties adjusting to each other.

Pastors should stress to couples that success in marriage is determined as success is determined in any other enterprise. Success in marriage is never automatic or accidental. It is always the result of devotion and dedication to each other that expresses itself in hard work.

I make it a point to discuss with couples the nature of love. I warn them that if romantic love is the only factor bringing them together, they are in great danger of experiencing failure in marriage. I have found it helpful to discuss with them the nature of love using the three Greek words *eros, philia,* and *agape*. I define *eros* as romantic love or "me" love. This type of love is the chemical reaction of the male to the female and the female to the male. It is part of God's good gift to humankind. It is instinctual and must be controlled by our higher nature. I define *philia* love as "respect" love expressed in friendship and mutual appreciation. I define *agape* love as sacrificial, self-giving love, or "help" love. For a marriage to succeed, there needs to be a happy combination of these three types of love, for a good marriage is based on sexual love, social love, and sacrificial love.

After filling out the "Premarital Conference Information Sheet," I then give to both the prospective bride and groom a copy of "Subjects for Discussion in a Premarital Conference." I assure them that the purpose of our conference is to help them avoid divorce and at the same time to enrich the quality of their love and life as husband and wife. This conference may take an hour to two, or we may have two or three conferences if they come to me well in advance of the wedding date.

You may want to adjust these forms to your own liking. I have found them to be helpful.

Subjects for Discussion in a Premarital Conference

I. Many are involved in your marriage.

A. Parents.
B. Church.
C. Community.
D. The state.
E. You personally.
F. Unborn children.
G. The plan and purpose of God.

II. Christian marriage—a bond of honor based on five basic principles.

A. Monogamy—one man and one woman.
B. Permanency—until death alone parts you.
C. Mutuality—the highest good for both of you.
D. Fidelity—faithfulness to each other in all things.
E. Love—a persistent unbreakable spirit of goodwill.

III. Rules that help insure success in marriage.

Success is never an accident. It is always the result of concentrated efforts.

A. Maintain your personal attractiveness.
B. Eliminate needless irritations and sources of antagonism.
C. Do not cherish feelings of resentment. Practice forgiveness.
D. Develop mutual interests in which both can joyfully participate.
E. Be loyal in all things.
F. Let neither try to dominate the other.
G. Remember the importance of the little courtesies of life.

IV. Practical matters.

A. Maintain the best of health.
B. Keep out of heavy debt by living within your income.
C. Discuss your desires and plans for children.
D. Seek personal growth and development.
E. Participate in restful recreation.

V. The new relationship.

A. The possibility of in-law problems.
B. Plans for the operation of a home.
C. The problem of physical adjustment.

VI. Spiritual matters.

A. Always be Christian.
B. Maintain a family altar.
C. Make an investment in God's kingdom.
D. Settle on a church home.
E. Let God help you grow and serve.

Premarital Conference Information Sheet

Date of conference: _____ Date of wedding: _____

Groom: Birthplace: _____ Age: _____
Residence: _____
Occupation: _____
Phone: (home) _____ (work) _____
Religious affiliation: _____

Bride: Birthplace: _____ Age: _____
Residence: _____
Occupation: _____
Phone: (home) _____ (work) _____
Religious affiliation: _____

Details of wedding: _____
_____
_____
_____

Place of wedding: _____ Date: _____ Hour: _____
Place of rehearsal: _____ Date: _____ Hour: _____
Witness: _____ (Relationship) _____
Witness: _____ (Relationship) _____
Number of bride's attendants: _____ Number of groomsmen: _____
Number of ushers: _____ Others in wedding party: _____
Assisting minister, if any: _____ Organist: _____
Singers: _____
Double- or single-ring ceremony: _____
What men are wearing: _____
What minister should wear: _____
What rooms of church are needed: _____
Any extra janitorial service required: _____
Florist: _____ Caterer: _____

Request of change in wording of ceremony or other variations: _____
_____
_____

Address of couple after marriage: _____
Who will know couple's address in case of a move?
_____ (Relationship) _____

Remarks: _____
_____
_____
_____
_____

Title: Marriage Ceremony

Holy and happy is the sacred hour when two devoted hearts are bound by the enchanting ties of matrimony. Marriage is an institution of divine appointment and is commended as honorable among all people. Marriage is God's first institution for the welfare of the race. In the quiet bowers of Eden, before the forbidden tree had yielded its fateful fruit or the tempter had touched the world, God saw that it was not good for the man to be alone. He made a helpmate suitable for him and established the rite of marriage while heavenly hosts witnessed the wonderful scene in reverence.

The contract of marriage was sanctioned and honored by the presence and power of Jesus at the marriage in Cana of Galilee and marked the beginning of his wondrous works. It is declared by the apostle Paul to be honorable among all people. So it is ordained that a man shall leave his father and mother and cleave unto his wife, and they twain shall be one flesh, united in hopes and aims and sentiments until death alone shall part them.

If ye, then, _____ (Groom), and _____ (Bride), after careful consideration, and in the fear of God, have deliberately chosen each other as partners in this holy estate, and know of no just cause why you should not be so united, in token thereof you will please join your right hands.

Groom's vow

_____, wilt thou have this woman to be thy wedded wife, to live together after God's ordinance in the holy estate of matrimony? Wilt thou love her, comfort her, honor and keep her in sickness and in health, and forsaking all others, keep thee only unto her so long as ye both shall live?

Answer: I will.

Bride's vow

_____, wilt thou have this man to be thy wedded husband, to live together after God's ordinance in the holy estate of matrimony? Wilt thou love him, honor him, and keep him in sickness and in health, and, forsaking all others, keep thee only unto him so long as ye both shall live?

Answer: I will.

Vows to each other

"I, _____ (Groom), take thee _____ (Bride), to be my wedded wife, to have and to hold from this day forward, in prosperity or adversity, in sickness or in health, in advances or reverses, to love and to cherish till death do us part, according to God's holy ordinance, and thereto I plight thee my troth."

"I, _____ (Bride), take thee _____ (Groom), to be my wedded husband, to have and to hold from this day forward, in prosperity or adversity, in sickness or in health, in advances or reverses, to love and to cherish till death do us part, according to God's holy ordinance, and thereto I plight thee my troth."

Then are ye each given to the other for richer or poorer, for better or worse, in sickness and in health, till death alone shall part you.

From time immemorial the ring has been used to seal important covenants. The golden circlet, most prized of jewels, has come to its loftiest prestige in the symbolic significance which it vouches at the marriage altar. Its untarnishable material is of the purest gold. Even so may your love for each other be pure. May it grow brighter and brighter as time goes by. The ring is a circle, thus having no end. Even so may there be no end to the happiness and success that come to you as you unite your lives together.

Do you, _____ (Groom), give this ring to your wedded wife as a token of your love for her?

Answer: I do.

Will you, _____ (Bride), receive this ring as a token of your wedded husband's love for you, and will you wear it as a token of your love for him?

Answer: I will.

Do you, _____ (Bride), give this ring to your wedded husband as a token of your love for him?

Answer: I do.

Will you, _____ (Groom), receive this ring as a token of your wedded wife's love for you, and will you wear it as a token of your love for her?

Answer: I will.

Having pledged your faith in and love to each other in the sight of God and these assembled witnesses, and having sealed your solemn marital vows by giving and receiving the rings, acting in the authority vested in me as a minister of the gospel by this state, and looking to heaven for divine sanction, I pronounce you husband and wife.

Therefore, what God hath joined together, let not man put asunder.

Prayer.

Title: The Responsibilities and the Rewards of Marriage

On this high and holy occasion, when two devoted hearts are bound together by the enchanting ties of Christian matrimony, we should rejoice in the glad consciousness that this is a part of God's good plan for humankind. Marriage is more than just a human arrangement. Christian marriage should be something infinitely more than a legal contract between two individuals, for marriage is a divine institution that was born in the heart of God and designed to produce the highest possible human happiness.

Since marriage is a divine institution, we should look to the Scriptures for guidance and help if we would achieve the highest possible success in this most important of human relationships. One of the most beautiful passages dealing with the mutual responsibilities of husbands and wives is found in Paul's epistle to the Ephesians.

(The minister should now read Ephesians 5:21–33).

I would call your attention to the fact that in the first verse of this passage both the husband and the wife are encouraged to recognize the absolute lordship of Christ in the marriage relationship. Marriage should not be entered into lightly or without inward assurance that the union of your two lives into one is according to the will of the Savior. This verse implies that God is to have first place, and that we are responsible to him for the manner in which we relate ourselves to our companion in marriage.

This passage of Scripture compares the relationship of the husband and the wife to the mystical relationship that exists between Christ and his church. The passage emphasizes the mutual responsibilities within the marriage relationship rather than the rights and privileges of the relationship.

This passage contains a commandment to the husband to love his wife in a twofold manner. First of all, the husband is commanded to love his wife "even as Christ also loved the church, and gave himself for it" (Eph. 5:25). This is sacrificial love that places the welfare of the wife before his own private welfare. The second command to the husband is that he is to love his wife as he loves his own body (Eph. 5:28). By a combination of sacrificial love and self-love the husband is to devote himself to the welfare and best interests of his wife.

This passage contains two commandments also to the wife. Verse 22 encourages the wife to recognize her husband as the head of the household, and verse 33 exhorts the wife to "see that she reverence her husband." Nothing is said about the wife loving her husband, though it is implied. Genuine and abiding love is based on respect. We can safely assume that it is the purpose of God that the husband should so conduct himself as to merit the reverence and respect of his wife, and that the wife will so conduct herself that the husband will find it easy to love her even as Christ loved the church.

The vows

(At this point the minister may use the vows of his own choice.)

The rings

From time immemorial the ring has been used on important occasions. In ages gone by, the official seal of the empire was often worn as a signet on the hand of the reigning monarch and was used to authenticate documents of state. But the golden circlet, the most prized of jewels, has reached its loftiest prestige in the symbolic significance it vouches at the marriage altar.

Holding the ring(s) up before the bride and groom, the minister may say: The wedding ring(s) is (are) an object of great beauty. This is true because the ring is made of a precious metal that will not tarnish with the passing of time. I would remind you as we look at this ring that at one time it was but crude ore in the depths of the earth. Someone discovered it, mined it, and refined it.

Master craftsmanship was brought to bear upon it, and the result is this beautiful ring. Today you bring to your marriage the raw materials of character, unselfishness, love, truthfulness, honesty, kindness, and courtesy. Combine these materials together with master craftsmanship and continued effort and you will discover that even as there is no end to the ring, there will be no end to the happiness and to the joy that you can experience together as husband and wife. Give to your Lord first place in your thoughts and in your affections. Give to your companion a place second only to your Lord. Place your own private, personal welfare on a lower rung of the ladder and you will discover that as the ring does not tarnish, so your relationship as husband and wife will be more beautiful and more precious with the passing of each year.

As a permanent reminder of the vows that you have made and entered into on this holy occasion, you will now give and receive these rings as a solemn seal to be known by all.

(The minister shall then present the rings with the suggestion that they be placed upon the finger.)

In a moment of high and holy dedication you have solemnized your marriage vows. Acting in the authority vested in me as a minister of the gospel by this state, I take great joy in pronouncing you husband and wife. What God therefore has joined together, do not let anything put asunder.

(The minister should then offer a prayer of benediction.)

Addressing the groom, the minister may say: You may now claim your bride with a kiss.

SENTENCE SERMONETTES

Trusting in God:

Pray hardest when it is hardest to pray.

No problem is too big for God's power, and no person is too small for God's love.

Faith is the daring of the soul to go farther than it can see.

If God sends us on stony paths, he provides strong shoes.

God always gives the best to those who leave the choice up to him.

Faith opens the door to the heart of God.

Peace is seeing a sunset and knowing who to thank.

Prayer is a need crying out to God.

The church is the apple of God's eye here on earth.

Every day is a victory if you put it in the hands of the Lord.

An apple a day keeps the doctor away; a chapter a day prevents truth decay.

Faith cannot grow in an atmosphere of doubt.

The reservoir of God never runs dry.

God always gives enough strength for the next step.

Has your soul lost its appetite?

God is greater than any problem you have.

The Lord's blessing is our greatest wealth.

If we pause to think, we will have cause to thank.

We are called to be full-time Christians. God has no part-time jobs.

God's mercies are fresh with each new day.

When you get all wrinkled up with care and worry, it is a good time to get a faith lift.

God never asks about our ability or our inability, but about our availability.

The Bible is like a compass—it always points the believer in the right direction.

Every sunrise is a message from God, and every sunset his signature.

The boy who gave Jesus his loaves and fishes did not have to go without his lunch.

God's lamp of love never burns out! It has a lifetime guarantee.

Getting along with others:

No joy is complete unless it is shared.

Nothing is so strong as gentleness, and nothing is so gentle as strength.

The moment you become proud of your humility, you have lost it.

Friends are flowers in the garden of life.

A smile is the light in your face that tells everyone your heart is at home.

Is your marriage a duel or a duet?

Happy people are helpful people.

All people smile in the same language.
Faults are thick when love is thin.
Be cheerful! Of all things you wear, your expression is the most important.
One snowflake isn't much by itself, but it takes a bulldozer to move them
    when they cooperate.
A person of words and not of deeds is like a garden full of weeds.
Shoulders were made to wear burdens, not to carry chips.

Developing character:

A person is not old until regrets take the place of dreams.
Worry never robs tomorrow of its sorrow; it only robs today of its strength.
It takes both rain and sunshine to make a rainbow.
Do you see opportunities in every difficulty or difficulties in every
    opportunity?
No man ever injured his eyesight by looking on the bright side of things.
A pessimist is a person who is seasick during the entire voyage of life.
A journey of a thousand miles begins with a single step.
The impossible is often the untried.
Courage is not the absence of fear; it is the mastery of it.
When you get to where you are going, where will you be?
Goals unset are goals unmet.

INDEX OF SCRIPTURE TEXTS

SUBJECT INDEX

This We Believe

Pastor's Edition

John N. Akers, John H. Armstrong, and John D. Woodbridge
General Editors

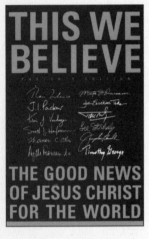

As you lead your church this third millennium, now more than ever you need to define what true faith is. In a world that resists truth and pays the price in escalating evil, Jesus says we're the salt of the earth—people of truth advancing the Gospel of peace. But how well does your congregation understand that Gospel?

A panel of prominent church leaders and scholars has drafted a clear, definitive statement of the essentials of the Gospel for the 21st century titled "The Gospel of Jesus Christ: An Evangelical Celebration." Hundreds of leaders from across the denominational landscape have endorsed it, and the list of names, already impressive, continues to grow. This remarkable show of unity powerfully affirms the core beliefs about our salvation that evangelicals hold in common. In the face of our differences, these are what bind us together as the church of Jesus Christ and make the Gospel the Good News of Great Joy.

This pastor's edition contains everything you need guide your congregation to study the essence of the Gospel and help your people live it anew:

- 12 illuminating sermon outlines on the meaning of the Gospel
- Interactive worship resources and suggestions
- Small-group discussion material suitable for Bible studies, Sunday school classes, and new member classes
- An invitation to each one in your congregation to own a copy of *This We Believe* for his or her personal library

Hardcover   ISBN: 0-310-23663-0
Softcover   ISBN: 0-310-23990-7

www.ThisWeBelieve.com

ZONDERVAN™

GRAND RAPIDS, MICHIGAN 49530
www.zondervan.com

The Usher's Manual
Leslie Parrott, Sr.

From the perspective of a veteran pastor and communicator, Dr. Leslie Parrott describes the function of the usher and provides practical guidelines on how this vital role in the church may be carried out with grace and efficiency. Not only does he apply scriptural principles, but he relies completely upon Scripture in his development of the various qualifications and duties of the usher.

In this practical, how-to-do-it book, Dr. Parrott explains:

- The Ministry of Ushering: what makes a good usher; why ushers are important
- The Function of an Usher
- The Authority and Responsibility of an Usher
- The Usher as a Greeter

Every church can have an effective usher corps—and this group will be even more effective if based on *The Usher's Manual.*

Softcover   ISBN: 0-310-30651-5

The Greeter's Manual
A Guide for Warm-Hearted Churches
Leslie Parrott, Sr.

Dr. Leslie Parrott, a veteran pastor and communicator, describes the function of the greeter and provides practical guidelines on how this vital role in the church may be carried out with grace and efficiently. Not only does he apply scriptural principles, but he relies completely upon Scripture in his development of the various qualifications and duties of the greeter.

In this practical, how-to-do it book, Dr. Parrott explains:

- The Ministry of Greeting: what makes a good greeter; why greeters are important
- The Function and Responsibility of a Greeter
- Developing a User-friendly Foyer
- The Parking Lot Ministry

Every church can have an effective ministry—and this group will be even more effective if based on *The Greeter's Manual.*

Softcover   ISBN: 0-310-37481-2

Time-Saving Ideas for...
Your Church Sign
1001 Attention-Getting Sayings

Verlyn D. Verbrugge

Your Church Sign offers sound pointers on sig-
nage. You'll find tips on impactful sign place-
ment, captions, themes, and how to write
effective messages. And you'll get more than
one thousand ready-made, eye-catching sayings. Some are humorous, some are encouraging, some are wise, some are convicting. All are
designed to turn a scant second of drive-by time into active spiritual
awareness.

Arranged by theme, *Your Church Sign* offers captions on:

Marriage and the Family	Seasonal Themes	Evangelism
Prayer	Christian Living	The Bible
Going to Church	God in Charge	Speech
... and more		

Turn to this practical, easy-to-use book for fast ideas and proven advice
for helping your church sign make a difference in people's lives.

Softcover   ISBN: 0-310-22802-6

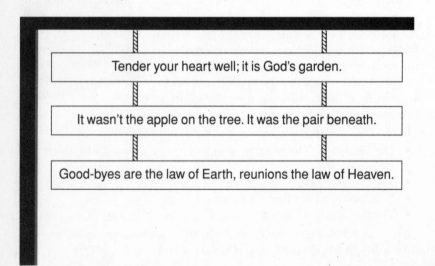

Tender your heart well; it is God's garden.

It wasn't the apple on the tree. It was the pair beneath.

Good-byes are the law of Earth, reunions the law of Heaven.

Dynamic Communicators Workshop

Prepare with Focus,
Deliver with Clarity,
Speak with Power

"For youth workers, pastors, business leaders—for anyone who speaks to groups, and wants to do it more effectively."　　　—Ken Davis

Filmed live at Ken Davis's popular Dynamic Communicator's Workshop, this four-tape video series (over 5 hours of quality instruction) includes the core curriculum that has helped thousands of youth workers transform their speaking.

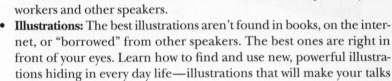

Lessons include:

- **The SCORRE method of preparation:** Learn to prepare your talk with crystal-clear focus. This foundational technique has been taught, tested, and refined over the last 15 years. It has revolutionized the effectiveness of thousands of pastors, youth workers and other speakers.
- **Illustrations:** The best illustrations aren't found in books, on the internet, or "borrowed" from other speakers. The best ones are right in front of your eyes. Learn how to find and use new, powerful illustrations hiding in every day life—illustrations that will make your talks unforgettable.
- **Body talk:** Your eyes, face, and body says as much as or more than your words. Learn how to use an expressive face, meaningful gestures, and powerful eye contact to enhance your communication.
- **Putting it all together:** Learn how to create openings that grab and hold the attention of your listeners. Learn how to use unforgettable closings that motivate students to action. Learn powerful time management techniques that will forever replace last-minute cramming.

The four videotapes in this series, combined with the interactive participant's guide, will help you to:

- Prepare your youth talks with focus
- Deliver your youth talks with clarity, and
- Speak with power

Curriculum Kit (4 videos: 5 hours, 55 minutes)　　　ISBN: 0-310-23726-2

ZONDERVAN™

GRAND RAPIDS, MICHIGAN 49530
www.zondervan.com

Effective Men's Ministry

The Indispensable Toolkit for Your Church

Phil Downer, Editor

From the National Coalition of Men's Ministries / Foreword by Patrick Morley, Author of *The Man in the Mirror*

Collective wisdom and experience in how to begin and continue effective ministry with men

The National Coalition of Men's Ministries is a partnership of over 75 ministries from over 30 denominations that represent more than half the churches in North America. Members of the coalition—experienced national leaders and pastors—have written this hands-on resource guide to assist local churches and denominations as they seek to both initiate and implement healthy ministries for men.

This is a comprehensive and practical ministry resource with 26 chapters that show how to plan, organize, and lead an effective ministry with men. Chapters include worksheets, charts, and checklists that can be photocopied.

Topics include:

- The goal of men's ministry
- The pastor's role
- Recruiting and training your staff
- Evangelizing men
- Discipling men
- Intercultural understanding
- Training programs
- Real men's retreats
- Brothers and reconciliation
- What drives men's ministries

Softcover   ISBN: 0-310-23636-3

ZONDERVAN™

GRAND RAPIDS, MICHIGAN 49530

www.zondervan.com

Discover the most effective tools available for your teaching ministry

ZONDERVAN | **groupware**

Zondervan*Groupware* consists of curriculum packages developed with the assistance of experts and based on education research. Each resource simplifies the leader's role by giving them an easy to use Leader's Guide and bringing in experts and examples on brief video segments. Individual Participant's Guides complete everything you need to help your church members experience dynamic personal spiritual growth in a group setting of any size.

Zondervan*Groupware* delivers personal spiritual growth through:

- **Compelling biblical content**
- **Minimal preparation time** for both leader and participant
- **Proven learning techniques** using Individual Participant's Guides and a variety of media
- **Meaningful interaction** in groups of any size, in any setting
- **Emphasis on life application**

Church leaders depend on Zondervan*Groupware* for the best and most accessible teaching material that emphasizes interaction and discussion within group learning situations. Whether a Sunday school class, midweek gathering, Bible study, or other small-group setting, Zondervan*Groupware* offers video segments as catalysts to teaching, discussing, understanding, and applying biblical truth. Zondervan*Groupware* provides everything you need to effectively incite personal spiritual growth through interpersonal relationships.

Visit www.BibleStudyGuides.com for a complete list of Zondervan*Groupware* products.

Boundaries in Dating	ISBN: 0-310-23873-0
Halftime	ISBN: 0-310-23275-9
What's So Amazing About Grace?	ISBN: 0-310-23323-2
Becoming a Contagious Christian Youth Edition	ISBN: 0-310-23769-6
Saving Your Marriage Before It Starts	ISBN: 0-310-20451-8

Teaching Like Jesus
A Practical Guide to Christian Education in Your Church
La Verne Tolbert

As a teacher, you long to help others do more than understand the Bible. You want them to experience its relevance and power for their lives. *Teaching like Jesus* is the answer! This commonsense guide offers examples of Jesus' teaching style from the Gospels, then shows how you can make these principles work for you—regardless of what age group or ethnic background you're dealing with.

Using a proven, four-step plan, *Teaching Like Jesus* gives you action steps, summaries, and other practical resources that will make your classroom a lively place to learn and apply the lessons so vitally important for transforming lives and nurturing disciples. You'll learn to think in terms of "see, hear, and do" in your lesson plans. And you'll find sample plans for age groups and cultures ranging from African-American preschoolers to Chinese married couples.

Softcover   ISBN: 0-310-22347-4

ZONDERVAN™

GRAND RAPIDS, MICHIGAN 49530
www.zondervan.com

Surprising Insights from the Unchurched and Proven Ways to Reach Them

41% Attend Church Regularly— The Rest Are Unchurched

Thom S. Rainer, Dean of the Billy Graham School of Missions, Evangelism and Church Growth

A first-of-its-kind study of church growth that investigates what works in reaching the unchurched

This comprehensive research project conducted by the Billy Graham School of Missions, Evangelism and Church Growth has yielded some surprising answers that defy conventional wisdom. It explodes some of the myths about evangelism—such as how to name your church, the need to "dumb-down" teaching and preaching, and the need to be seeker-friendly.

The information the researchers gained from interviewing the formerly unchurched and the leaders who reached them will enable church leaders to address more than the surface symptoms and help them develop new paradigms for reaching and retaining the lost. It will help churches avoid past mistakes that were often based on misleading assumptions. The book not only reports the results of the study, but also illustrates them with numerous charts and graphs, and personal stories of a cross-section of formerly unchurched people.

Features include:

- Numerous stories from interviews with the formerly unchurched
- Conclusions based on national surveys and interviews
- Many charts and graphs to help visualize the survey findings
- An unchurched-reaching readiness inventory

Hardcover   ISBN: 0-310-23648-7

ZONDERVAN™

GRAND RAPIDS, MICHIGAN 49530

www.zondervan.com

The Equipping Church
Serving Together to Transform Lives
Sue Mallory

The Leadership Network has recognized that the lay mobilization movement is shifting:

- from workbook discipleship to real-life, on-the-street discipleship
- from the church growth emphasis on collecting people to emphasizing dispersing people to ministries that match their lifelong callings
- from spiritual gift programs to creating church-wide systems and proactively building internal cultures of empowerment

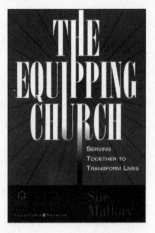

Based on five years of work and training, this book explains what an equipping church is, how an equipping church functions, why this is a biblical model, and what is involved in making this transition. It addresses the felt need of pastors who know they should mobilize laypeople but need to learn about examples of churches who are actually doing that successfully.

It moves from preparations (what you need to know), to foundations (what you need to change), to construction (what you need to do). It clarifies the difference between a church's system (what we do) and a church's culture (who we are). The foundational biblical text behind the book is Ephesians 4:11–13.

Hardcover   ISBN: 0-310-24067-0

ZONDERVAN™

GRAND RAPIDS, MICHIGAN 49530
www.zondervan.com

LEADERSHIP ❈ NETWORK

The Equipping Church Guide
Your Comprehensive Resource
Sue Mallory and Brad Smith

This guide starts with the biblical mandate to leaders from Ephesians 4:11–15, emerging not out of a theory of how this should be done from a journalistic effort, but to describe the best actual models of hundreds of churches who are actually doing healthy equipping ministry. It translates what was found in these healthy and innovative models into transferable principles, examples, questions, and exercises to help other church leaders build an equipping ministry tailored to meet the needs and calling of their own church.

This is a hands-on ministry resource manual to help churches develop leaders and systems for lay mobilization. The approach is open-ended so that a variety of types and sizes of churches can use it. Charts and worksheets are included. The material has been tested through several years of use in churches that have received the privately distributed notebook format. Now updated and extensively revised, this volume serves as a practical companion to *The Equipping Church*, which provides the philosophy and challenging vision for lay mobilization.

Section One: Build an Equipping Ministry and Culture
Section Two: Build an Equipping Ministry System

Softcover   ISBN: 0-310-23957-5

ZONDERVAN™
GRAND RAPIDS, MICHIGAN 49530
www.zondervan.com

LEADERSHIP ❋ NETWORK

Building a Contagious Church
Revolutionizing the Way We View and Do Evangelism
Mark Mittelberg with contributions from Bill Hybels

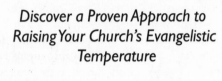

Discover a Proven Approach to Raising Your Church's Evangelistic Temperature

Evangelism. It's one of the highest values in the church. So why do so few churches put real time, money, and effort into it? Maybe it's because we don't understand the evangelistic potential of the church well enough to get excited about it.

Building a Contagious Church will change that.

This provocative book dispels outdated preconceptions and reveals evangelism as it really can be, radiant with the color and potential of the body of Christ and pulsing with the power of God. What's more, it walks you through a 6-Stage Process for taking your church beyond mere talk to infectious energy, action, and lasting commitment. Think it can't happen? Get ready for the surprise of your life! You and your church are about to become contagious!

The book includes:

- **A Contagious Plan**—Define the what, why, and how of your church's outreach to people in the neighborhoods all around you.
- **A Contagious Change Process**—Follow a 6-Stage Process that will help you raise the evangelistic temperature of your church, starting with the hearts of the leaders.
- **Contagious Diversity**—Learn to maximize outreach to all kinds of non-Christians by developing ministries and events around the six different evangelism styles.
- **Contagious Ministry**—Find out how to unleash the kind of genuine, empowered ministry in your church that will impact your community—and your world.

Hardcover   ISBN: 0-310-22149-8

GRAND RAPIDS, MICHIGAN 49530
www.zondervan.com

WILLOW CREEK RESOURCES

Becoming a Contagious Christian

Mark Mittelberg and Bill Hybels

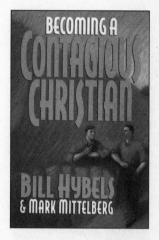

In *Becoming a Contagious Christian* Mittelberg and Hybels offer a practical plan of action illustrated with powerful, real-life stories for touching the lives of friends, family members, and others. Their emphasis is clear: be yourself in Christ, find a style that works for you.

Hybels and Mittelberg use simple, straightforward language and diverse biblical characters such as Paul, Dorcas, and the Samaritan woman to encourage us with the good news that God knew what he was doing when he made each of us. As a result, all of us can impact our world for Christ. It is an approach the authors have seen work again and again at Willow Creek Community Church. They articulate the important principles that have helped the believers at Willow Creek become a church of "contagious Christians," a church known around the world for its outstanding and effective outreach to the unchurched.

Becoming a Contagious Christian may well be one of the most important contributions to relational evangelism in decades. It presents a blueprint for starting a spiritual epidemic of hope and enthusiasm for spreading the Gospel of Christ.

Hardcover	ISBN: 0-310-48500-2
Softcover	ISBN: 0-310-21008-9
Audio Pages	ISBN: 0-310-48508-8

Groupware ISBN:0-310-50109-1
(60-min VHS video, Participant's Guide, Leader's Guide, Overhead Masters)

Participant's Guide	ISBN: 0-310-50101-6
Leader's Guide	ISBN: 0-310-50081-8
Video	ISBN: 0-310-20169-1
Overhead Masters	ISBN: 0-310-50091-5

GRAND RAPIDS, MICHIGAN 49530

www.zondervan.com

WILLOW CREEK RESOURCES

The Church of Irresistible Influence

Robert Lewis with Rob Wilkins

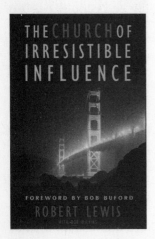

Foreword by Bob Buford

Today, instead of turning the world upside-down, the church has largely turned it off. When people think of church at all, a sobering majority view it as big on ideals but short on reality. We have a choice. We can maintain our trajectory and descend into irrelevance. Or we can reclaim our incomparable birthright—the irresistible influence of a church vitally connected with God, each other, and the world around us.

The Church of Irresistible Influence is about church transformation, about a vision worth living for and changing for because it pulses with the very heartbeat of God. If you are a pastor or church leader, prepare to be inspired, challenged, and equipped with practical insights for making your church a strong, well-traveled link between heaven and earth in your community.

Using bridges as a metaphor for irresistible influence—or i2, as he calls it—Robert Lewis shares the experiences and lessons of Fellowship Bible Church to show you:

- What it will take to reconnect your church with your community
- The how-tos of "incarnational bridge building"
- True stories of i2 in action
- How to expand the i2 effort through new partnerships and adventures
- Requirements of the church in the 21st century

Passionate, thought-provoking, and personal, this book will plant the want-to and pave the way for your church—no matter your size or location—to become a church of irresistible influence in your God-ordained corner of the world.

Hardcover   ISBN: 0-310-24149-9

GRAND RAPIDS, MICHIGAN 49530

www.zondervan.com

The Connecting Church
Beyond Small Groups to Authentic Community
Randy Frazee

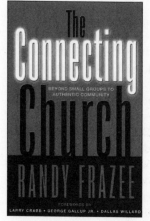

Forewords by Larry Crabb, George Gallup Jr., and Dallas Willard

The development of meaningful relationships, where every member carries a significant sense of belonging, is central to what it means to be the church. So why do many Christians feel disappointed and disillusioned with their efforts to experience authentic community? Despite the best efforts of pastors, small-group leaders, and faithful laypersons, church too often is a place of loneliness rather than connection.

Church can be so much better. So intimate and alive. *The Connecting Church* tells you how. The answer may seem radical today, but it was a central component of life in the early church. First-century Christians knew what it meant to live in vital community with one another, relating with a depth and commitment that made "the body of Christ" a perfect metaphor for the church. What would it take to reclaim that kind of love, joy, support, and dynamic spiritual growth? Read this book and find out.

Hardcover   ISBN: 0-310-23308-9

ZONDERVAN™

GRAND RAPIDS, MICHIGAN 49530
www.zondervan.com

WILLOW CREEK RESOURCES

The Purpose-Driven® Church
Growth Without Compromising Your Message and Mission

Rick Warren

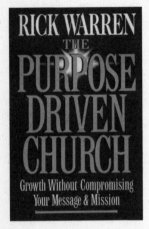

Every church is driven by something. Tradition, finances, programs, personalities, events, seekers, and even buildings can each be the controlling force in a church. But Rick Warren believes that in order for a church to be healthy it must become a purpose-driven church, built around the five New Testament purposes given to the church by Jesus. "The issue is church health, not church growth!" declares Warren. "If your church is healthy, growth will occur naturally. Healthy, consistent growth is the result of balancing the five biblical purposes of the church."

In this award-winning book, you'll learn the secret behind the fastest-growing Baptist church in American history. Saddleback Church grew from one family to over 10,000 in worship attendance in just fifteen years, while planting twenty-six other churches . . . and without owning a building. Founding pastor Rick Warren shares a proven five-part strategy that will enable your church to grow . . . warmer through fellowship, deeper through discipleship, stronger through worship, broader through ministry, and larger through evangelism.

The Purpose-Driven Church shifts the focus away from church building programs to a people-building process. Warren says, "If you will concentrate on building people, God will build the church."

Hardcover	ISBN: 0-310-20106-3
Audio	ISBN: 0-310-20518-2
Unabridged Audio Pages®	ISBN: 0-310-22901-4

ZONDERVAN™

GRAND RAPIDS, MICHIGAN 49530
www.zondervan.com

Transitioning
Leading Your Church Through Change
Dan Southerland

If you've been thinking about leading your traditional church toward becoming a purpose-driven church, *Transitioning* gives you the wisdom and guidance you need. Drawing from a wealth of experience, Pastor Dan Southerland takes you through the eight-step process of discovering and implementing God's unique mission for your congregation. With thought, prayer, planning, and patience, you and your church can discover the rich rewards of being purpose driven.

> "One of the most exciting and encouraging examples of transitioning from being program driven to purpose driven."
>
> —From the foreword by Rick Warren,
> Author of *The Purpose-Driven® Church*

Hardcover   ISBN: 0-310-23344-5

ZONDERVAN™

GRAND RAPIDS, MICHIGAN 49530

w w w . z o n d e r v a n . c o m

SoulTsunami

Sink or Swim in New Millennium Culture
10 life rings for you and your church

Leonard Sweet

SoulTsunami is a fascinating look at the implications of our changing world for the church in the 21st century. With uncanny wisdom and trademark wit, Leonard Sweet explores ten key "futuribles" (precision guesses that fall short of predictions), expanding on and relating topics ranging from the reentry of theism and spiritual longing in contemporary society, to the impact of modern technology, to the global renaissance, to models for the church to reach people caught in the cultural maelstrom. Here are eye-opening perspectives on the church from within and from without—from its surrounding society.

Lively, well-written, and provocative, *SoulTsunami* is a clarion call for Christians to remove their tunnel-vision glasses and take a good look at the swelling postmodern flood. It is also a voice of encouragement, affirming the church in its role as God's lifeboat. And it is a passionate, prophetic guide, pointing the way to reach a world swept out to sea.

Softcover   ISBN: 0-310-24312-2
Unabridged Audio Pages®   ISBN: 0-310-22712-7

ZONDERVAN™

GRAND RAPIDS, MICHIGAN 49530

www.zondervan.com

The Church on the Other Side

Doing Ministry in the Postmodern Matrix

Revised and Expanded Edition of *Reinventing Your Church*

Brian D. McLaren

If you are a sincere church leader or a committed church member, you're probably tired of easy steps, easy answers, and facile formulas for church health, growth, and renewal. You know it's not that easy. In *The Church on the Other Side*, you'll find something different: honest, clear, and creative thinking about our churches, along with a passionate challenge to thoughtful action and profound, liberating change.

In understandable language, with an energetic and engaging writing style and drawing from daily, down-to-earth pastoral experience, Brian McLaren offers 13 strategies for navigating the modern/postmodern transition. You'll learn the critical distinctions between renewed, restored, and reinvented churches. You'll discover the importance of redefining your mission, of finding fresh ways to conceive of and communicate the Gospel, and of entering the postmodern world by understanding it, engaging it, and debugging your faith from modern "viruses."

Even if you've read this book's first edition, *Reinventing Your Church*, you'll find enough new and revised material here to warrant a second purchase. And if you're encountering these concepts for the first time, you'll find wise guidance to help you and your church begin the journey toward the other side of the postmodern divide. You'll learn to think differently, see church, life, and these revolutionary times in a new way, and act with courage, hope, and an adventurous spirit.

Hardcover   ISBN: 0-310-23707-6

ZONDERVAN™

GRAND RAPIDS, MICHIGAN 49530

w w w . z o n d e r v a n . c o m

Escape from Church, Inc.
The Return of the Pastor-Shepherd
E. Glenn Wagner

This book was born out of a passion for the church—and for you, one of its pastors. If you struggle with burnout and disillusionment, if something within you keeps insisting, "This isn't what it's supposed to be about!" then Pastor Glenn Wagner offers a model for pastoring that can radically reshape how you relate to your congregation.

Wagner guides you into new vision, new values, and a new way of pastoring that begins not with doing, but with seeing and being. "I believe the one problem underlying all the others is that we have moved both pastors and churches from a community model to a corporation model," says Wagner. "If we go back to the very beginning, back to the Lord's bedrock idea for his people, what do we find? We find shepherds and sheep."

Escape from Church, Inc. offers hope to the weary and water to the thirsty. Find out for yourself, in both biblical and practical terms, how the model of the shepherd is best suited to growing a healthy, effective church—and discover deep satisfaction and joy in your role as pastor.

Hardcover   ISBN: 0-310-22888-3

ZONDERVAN™

GRAND RAPIDS, MICHIGAN 49530

www.zondervan.com

Jesus the Pastor

Leading Others in the Character and Power of Christ

John W. Frye

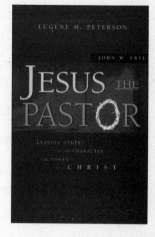

Get ready to lead your flock in the character and power of Christ.

For decades Paul has been the model for today's pastors, but senior pastor John Frye says we must instead look to Jesus. "While we may lift Christ up as Savior, as we bow down to him as Lord, as we marvel at his offices of Prophet, Priest, and King, as we walk with him as Friend, we seem to ignore him as the supreme Senior Pastor."

"There's no way to be a Christian pastor that's not single-minded in following Jesus. John Frye recovers that focus for us and proves out to be a good companion in just such following."

—Eugene H. Petersen

Hardcover   ISBN: 0-310-22995-2

www.JesusThePastor.com

GRAND RAPIDS, MICHIGAN 49530

www.zondervan.com

Help for the Small-Church Pastor
Unlocking the Potential of Your Congregation
Steve Bierly

Churches of fewer than 150 members remain the rule rather than the exception in American Christianity. However, seminaries don't equip students in every way that's necessary to lead smaller congregations effectively—despite the fact that most seminary graduates will become small-church pastors.

Help for the Small-Church Pastor offers pastors of small churches the guidance and encouragement they need. In this common-sense book, Steve Bierly draws from his many years in ministry to show what makes smaller congregations tick.

Softcover   ISBN: 0-310-49951-8

How to Thrive as a Small-Church Pastor
A Guide to Spiritual and Emotional Well-Being
Steve R. Bierly

Steve Bierly knows firsthand the needs and concerns of small-church pastors. He also knows how to meet the needs, handle the concerns, and thrive as a pastor with a congregation of 150 or less.

Drawing on his many years of small-church experience, Bierly helps pastors reframe their perspective of God, ministry, relationships, their own needs, and more. He offers seasoned, fatherly counsel—assurance to small-church pastors that they're not alone; a fresh outlook on the successes of their ministries; and an upbeat, practical approach to spiritual, emotional, and physical well being.

Filled with good humor, here is help for small-church pastors to face the rigors of their vocation realistically and reclaim their first love of ministry.

Softcover   ISBN: 0-310-21655-9

ZONDERVAN™

GRAND RAPIDS, MICHIGAN 49530
www.zondervan.com